MEDIEVAL
CANON LAW
AND THE
CRUSADER

The crusader receives the cross (Besançon, Bibl. Municipale,
MS. 138, fol. 157)

MEDIEVAL CANON LAW

AND THE

CRUSADER

by James A. Brundage

The University of Wisconsin Press
MADISON, MILWAUKEE, AND LONDON, 1969

PUBLISHED BY
THE UNIVERSITY OF WISCONSIN PRESS
BOX 1379, MADISON, WISCONSIN 53701
THE UNIVERSITY OF WISCONSIN PRESS, LTD.
27–29 WHITFIELD STREET, LONDON, W.I.

PRINTED IN THE UNITED STATES OF AMERICA BY
KINGSPORT PRESS, INC., KINGSPORT, TENNESSEE

STANDARD BOOK NUMBER 299–05480–2
LIBRARY OF CONGRESS CATALOG CARD NUMBER 74–84952

To Bridgie

CONTENTS

ACKNOWLEDGMENTS

The origins of this book go back to 1959, when I first began to inquire into some aspects of the institutional history of the crusades. I quickly discovered that I had blundered into a *selva oscura, chè la diritta via era smarrita,* and I can only hope that after ten years of wandering through it I may have trampled down enough of the underbrush so that those who come after me will find the path somewhat easier to make out than it was when I first chanced down it.

In the course of my lengthy *peregrinatio* I have incurred, as pilgrims always seem to do, a great number of personal obligations which it is both proper and pleasant to acknowledge here. I am grateful, first of all, to the John Simon Guggenheim Memorial Foundation for a fellowship which enabled me to spend 1963–64 at Cambridge and to investigate the resources of a number of libraries and record depositories, both in England and on the Continent. In addition, further grants from the Research Committee of the Graduate School of the University of Wisconsin have provided other periods of time for research, as well as travel funds and facilities for my work.

A great many libraries and librarians have hospitably furnished me with access to their collections and with a variety of special services, sometimes far beyond the call of duty. I am, of course, indebted to the staff of the University of Wisconsin's libraries at Madison and Milwaukee for almost continuous service over the whole of the time I have been engaged in this work. In addition, I should also like to thank the following: His Eminence, Richard Cardinal Cushing, and the staff of the Creagh Research Library, Brighton, Massachusetts; the staff of the Harvard University Libraries, especially at Widener, Houghton, and the Law Library; the late Dr. Eugene P. Willging and the staff of the Mullen Library of the Catholic University of America; the Pierpont Morgan Library; the New York Public Library; the Marquette University Library; the University of Minnesota Library; the Library of the Seminary of St. Mary of the Lake; the staff of the Manuscript Students' Room of the British Museum; and, at the University of Cambridge: the Cambridge

University Library, especially Mr. K. W. Robinson and Mr. H. L. Pink; the Master and Fellows of Corpus Christi College; Mr. Philip Grierson and the Master and Fellows of Gonville and Caius College; Mr. E. J. Kenney and the Master and Fellows of Peterhouse; Mr. A. G. Lee and the Master and Fellows of St. John's College; Dr. C. R. Dodwell and the Master and Fellows of Trinity College; Dr. J. Lyons and the Master and Fellows of Christ's College; Mr. M. J. D. Hodgart and the Master and Fellows of Pembroke College; the Master and Fellows of Sidney Sussex College. Thanks are due also to Miss Phyllis M. Giles of the Fitzwilliam Museum, Cambridge; Dr. R. W. Hunt and the staff of the Bodleian Library, Oxford; Mr. E. G. W. Bill and the staff of the Lambeth Palace Library; the Dean and Chapter of Lincoln Cathedral; the Dean and Chapter of Durham Cathedral; Mme. Jacqueline Rambaud-Buhot and the staff of the Cabinet des Manuscrits in the Bibliothèque Nationale, Paris; the staff of the Handschriften Abteilung of the Bayerische Staatsbibliothek and of the Deutsches Institut für Erforschung des Mittelalters, Munich; Dr. Josef Hoffinger and Dr. Hans Wieser of the Universitätsbibliothek, Father H. Zeller of the Jesuiten-Kolleg, and the staff of the Kirchenrechts Seminar of the Innsbruck Theological Faculty, Innsbruck; and Father Alfons Raes, S.J., and the staff of the Biblioteca Apostolica Vaticana.

Many friends and colleagues have generously furnished me with specific items of information, suggestions, and advice. I should particularly like to thank Professor Christopher R. Cheney of Corpus Christi College and Professor Walter Ullmann of Trinity College, Cambridge; Professor Hans Eberhard Mayer of the University of Kiel; Professor Gerhard B. Ladner of the University of California at Los Angeles; the Reverend Professor Charles P. Loughran, S.J.; and Professor John C. Moore of Hofstra University.

In addition, numerous other friends and colleagues have provided help and encouragement in various ways, among them Sir Steven Runciman; Professor David Daube of All Souls College, Oxford; Father Franz Braunshofer, S.J., of the Canisiunum at Innsbruck; Professor Kenneth M. Setton of the Institute for Advanced Study at Princeton; the late Professor Robert L. Reynolds of the University of Wisconsin; Mrs. J. C. Burkill, Professor and Mrs. G. R. Elton, Mr. H. S. Bennett, and Dr. R. C. Smail of Cambridge; Professor Richard Vaughan, now of the University of Hull; His Excellency Archbishop Iginio Cardinale; Professor Edgar N. Johnson, now of the University of Massachusetts; Professor Pardon E. Tillinghast, Middlebury College; Father Robert Stenger, O.P., of the school of Religion at the University of Iowa; Dr. Larry Desmond, St. Paul's College, Winnipeg; and Professor Joshua Prawer of the Hebrew University, Jerusalem.

Professors Peter Herde, Richard Kay, and Gaines Post have done me the great favor of reading through this book in manuscript form and suggesting corrections, emendations, and clarifications at many points. Professor Stephan Kuttner checked and suggested emendations in my readings of a number of manuscripts and also supplied me with other helpful information and comments. For their help and assistance I am most grateful. The errors which may remain are, naturally, my own.

I should also thank my student assistants who have contributed in various ways to the making of this book, particularly John Nesbitt, Kenneth Pennington, Robert Berberich, and Terrance Sanders. The History Department secretaries and typists of the University of Wisconsin—Milwaukee have had the onerous labor of typing both the final version of this book and also various preliminary and ancillary studies connected with it. I should like to thank especially Mrs. Shirley Darling, Mrs. Mary Schoultz, Mrs. Alice Schaus, Mrs. Donna Greischar, and Miss Cecily Bates.

By convention last, but in reality first, among those to whom I owe acknowledgment and thanks here must come my wife and children. They, too, have lived with my investigations, my travels, and the long hours of writing which have gone into the making of this book over the past ten years. It owes much to their patience and forbearance.

J. A. B.

Milwaukee, Wisconsin
May, 1969

INTRODUCTION

The enthusiasm of the first crusade is a natural and simple event, while hope was fresh, danger untried, and enterprise congenial to the spirit of the times. But the obstinate perseverance of Europe may indeed excite our pity and admiration; that no instruction should have been drawn from constant and adverse experience; that the same confidence should have repeatedly grown from the same failures; that six succeeding generations should have rushed headlong down the same precipice that was open before them; and that men of every condition should have staked their public and private fortunes on the desperate adventure of possessing or re-covering a tombstone two thousand miles from their country.

Edward Gibbon, *The De-cline and Fall of the Roman Empire*, ch. 59

One cannot study the history of the crusades for long without facing up to some crucial and perplexing questions: Why did men go on crusade? What motives impelled so many thousands of men over so many hundreds of years to undertake these dangerous, arduous, expensive, expeditions in the first place? Further, what kept them, once they had begun, from turning back en masse when they came face to face with the hazards and obstacles in their way? And if they did turn back, what happened to them then?

One naturally wonders, too, just how the whole intricate mechanism of the crusade worked. How did a man become a crusader? Having become one, what obligations did he assume and how might he discharge them? How were the obligations enforced and what were the rewards which the crusader might enjoy for his pains?

These are questions which this book attempts to explore and, in part, to answer. It is clear that the motives of the crusaders were marvellously mixed and that there is no wholly satisfactory answer or set of answers to the fundamental question: Why did men participate in the crusades? The great variety of motives involved was sometimes perceived by the crusaders themselves and by their contemporaries. The anonymous annalist of Würzburg, for example, writing about the second crusade, observed that:

> The intentions of the various men were different. Some, indeed, lusted after novelties and went in order to learn about new lands. Others there were who were driven by poverty, who were in hard straits at home; these men went to fight, not only against the enemies of Christ's cross, but even against the friends of the Christian name, wherever opportunity appeared, in order to relieve their poverty. There were others who were oppressed by debts to other men or who sought to escape the service due to their lords, or who were even awaiting the punishment merited by their shameful deeds. . . . A few could, with difficulty, be found who had not bowed their knees to Baal, who were directed by a holy and wholesome purpose, and who were kindled by love of the divine majesty to fight earnestly and even to shed their blood for the holy of holies.[1]

1. *Annales Herbipolenses*, s.a. 1147 (*MGH*, SS, 16:3; trans. in *CDS*, pp. 121–22). Pope Urban II, when he proclaimed the first crusade in 1095 at Clermont, was obviously aware that his project must appeal to a variety of men in a variety of ways if it were to succeed; witness his emphasis upon both the worldly and the spiritual benefits which crusaders might earn by participating in the expedition. For an analysis of the themes treated by the pope in his sermon at Clermont see Dana C. Munro, "The Speech of Pope Urban II at Clermont, 1095," *AHR*, 11(1906), 231–42; the two most trustworthy reports of his exhortation are by Fulcher of Chartres, *Historia Hierosolymitana* (*1095–1127*) 1.3.2–8 (ed. Heinrich Hagenmeyer, pp. 132–38), and Robert the Monk, *Historia Hierosolimitana* 1.1–3 (*RHC, Occ*, 3:727–30; trans. in *CDS*, pp. 17–21). Among modern historians of the crusades, none has made this point more piquantly than Thomas Fuller in *The Historie of the Holy Warre*, 1.12, p. 18: "It is not to be expected that all should be fish which is caught in a dragnet, neither that all should be good and religious people who were adventurers in an action of so large a capacity as this warre was. We must in charitie allow, that many of them were truly zealous and went with pious intents. . . . But besides these well-meaning people, there went also rabble-rout, rather for companie than conscience. Debtors took this voyage on them as an acquittance from their debts, to the defrauding of their creditors: Servants counted the conditions of their service cancelled by it, going away against their masters will: Theeves and murderers took upon them the crosse to escape the gallows. Adulterers did penance in their armour. . . . And . . . not onely green striplings, unripe for warre, but also decayed men to whom age had given a writ of ease, became souldiers; and those who at home should have waited on their own graves, went farre to visit Christs sepulchre. And which was more, women (as if they would make the tale of the Amazons truth) went with weapons in mens clothes; a behaviour at the best immodest, and modesty being the case of chastity, it is to be feared that where the case is broken, the jewel is lost."

Various as men's motives may have been in these expeditions, however, there was one set of attractions which was built into the very structure of the crusade and which was doubtless a potent factor in persuading large numbers of men to enroll themselves in its ranks. This was the complex bundle of privileges which were granted to crusaders from the beginning of the movement and which were gradually amplified and expanded in the course of time.

The historical background out of which the system of crusader status and these privileges developed is briefly discussed, but this book is fundamentally a study of the crusades as a canonistic institution. It attempts to show how this institution was created and subsequently modified by ecclesiastical authorities, how it was analyzed and described by the canonistic commentators, and also, to a limited degree, how it actually operated in practice. The study is based on the examination of four types of sources. First, there is the canon law itself, principally as it is embodied in the texts of the *Corpus iuris canonici,* together with a few of the canonistic collections before Gratian—chiefly the eleventh-century collections of Burchard of Worms and Ivo of Chartres—and the legislative enactments embodied in the decrees and canons of the councils, in papal letters, and in some of the decretal collections outside the *Corpus.* Second, I have used the glosses, commentaries, apparatuses, and summae of the major decretists and decretalists, insofar as these have been available to me. Third, I have used the contemporary narrative accounts of the crusade expeditions themselves to shed some light on the extent to which the provisions embodied in the law and described by the canonistic commentators were reflected in actual practice. Finally, I have made limited use of some administrative records and non-canonistic sources—records of the English royal administration, episcopal registers, liturgical books, formularies, and the like—to glean some further information about the working of the crusade as an institution.

The character of some of these sources, particularly the second group, accounts for one of the peculiarities which the reader may notice in this book. Because many of the important canonistic commentaries and glosses are available only in early printed editions or are not available in print at all, I have deliberately kept my documentation very full and have often loaded the notes with a heavy ballast of long quotations from the sources. It seemed proper to quote *in extenso* from the sources at many points where the relevant source material was difficult of access and might be found in only a few libraries in this country or in none at all. This practice, I hope, will make it possible for the reader to form some independent judgment of my summaries and characterizations of what the sources say. In general, too, I have translated source quotations in the body of the text into English, but I have normally appended in the notes the original language of the quotation, since any translation involves an interpretation and judgment of the meaning of the translated passage. One further anomaly should perhaps be explained: in a work which has been pursued over so lengthy a period of time as this one has, there has inevitably been some variation in the texts and editions of various works which were available at different times. Hence the reader will sometimes discover that the same work is referred to in more than one edition or in more than one manuscript. In order to conserve space, complete bibliographical descriptions of the works cited in this book have been given only in the Bibliography, not in the notes. Further, I have not attempted to furnish an exhaustive bibliography of all the works consulted in the course of this study, for this would have swollen the bibliographical section to disproportionate size.

In transcribing portions from the manuscript works cited in this book, I have generally followed the idiosyncrasies of the manuscripts I have used, with only minor alterations in the interest of normalizing the transcribed texts. Minor orthographical errors have been silently corrected, but common medieval spellings have been retained (e.g., *michi* for *mihi, set* for *sed, honus* for *onus,* etc.) where they occur. Where the scribes were obviously in error, emended readings have been given in pointed brackets (⟨⟩) and the original reading, where significant, has been supplied, together with editorial comments, in square brackets ([ ]). Punctuation of transcribed texts has been altered to conform to modern practice. Citations within the transcribed texts from canonistic and other authorities have been supplied in square brackets. Transcribed texts have been presented with an eye on, though not in complete conformity with, the system of the Institute of Medieval Canon Law (*Traditio,* 15 [1959], 452–64). A list of manuscripts cited will be found in a separate index.

In part this book retraces ground already touched upon by two earlier writers, Emile Bridrey[2] and Michel Villey,[3] to both of whom I am indebted on many counts. The present study differs from the earlier

2. *La Condition juridique des croisés et le privilège de croix: étude d'histoire du droit français.*

3. Especially in *La Croisade: essai sur la formation d'une théorie juridique,* and "L'Idée de la croisade chez les juristes du moyen âge," *Relazioni del X Congresso Internazionale di Scienze Storice,* 3:565–94.

works of Bridrey and Villey, however, in scope and emphasis. I have centered my work on the themes of holy war and pilgrimage, which seem to me the crucial concepts underlying the growth and development of crusade institutions. Basic to the whole subject is the mechanism of the vow, since it is upon the theory of votive obligations that both the obligations and the privileges of crusaders are largely founded. I have also focused particular attention upon the acquisition of crusader status and the discharge of obligations, as these are fundamental procedural matters which have hitherto been given only slight attention. I have given rather more attention, too, to the evidence furnished by the early crusades for the growth of the canonistic institutions of the crusade than has been done by my predecessors,[4] since it seems important to try to reconstruct, as far as the sources will allow, the growth and development of the system, rather than just to concentrate on the features of its maturity. In consequence of this emphasis, I have drawn upon a somewhat different range of sources than were used by my predecessors. On the other hand, I have not attempted to treat in great detail the status of the crusader before the French secular courts, a matter which is fully treated by Bridrey, nor have I re-examined all of the theoretical positions of the canonists, which Villey has treated.

The crusades were unquestionably a major episode in Western man's experience and have left a unique impress upon his subsequent history. Accordingly, these expeditions have for generations been a major focus of historical interest and the literature devoted to their history is enormous.[5] Despite this, however, their institutional and ideological history remains largely uncharted. There is, for example, no adequate treatment, or anything approaching one, of the theology of the crusades. Nor are there any very significant studies of the processes and techniques of crusade recruitment, or the organization and regulation of crusade armies, or of the law of war in the crusades. Although Professor John LaMonte concluded a generation ago that the history of the crusades had in many of its aspects been overworked by historians, his strictures certainly do not apply to the institutional or ideological history of the crusading movement.[6]

4. Cf. the criticism of Bridrey's neglect of the earlier evidence by A. Gottlob, *Kreuzablass und Almosenablass: Eine Studie über die Frühzeit des Ablasswesens,* pp. 140–41.

5. The best guide to this literature, Mayer's *Bibliographie zur Geschichte der Kreuzzüge,* lists more than 5,000 entries.

6. John L. LaMonte, "Some Problems in Crusading Historiography," *Speculum,* 15(1940), 57–75.

Knowledge of the crusade institutions that are the subject of this study is basic to an understanding of the place of the crusades in medieval European life. Only by examining how these institutions were established and how they worked (or were supposed to work) in practice can we begin to realize what the crusades meant to those who participated in them, and to learn how it was that the crusades succeeded as they did in drawing so many thousands of men into the medieval expansion movement. This movement was their most enduring result.

ABBREVIATIONS

I. *Decretum Gratiani*

D. 1 c. 1	Distinctio 1, canon 1
C. 1 q. 1 c. 1	Causa 1, quaestio 1, canon 1
De pen.	Causa 33, quaestio 3
De cons	Tractatus de consecratione
d. a. c.	Dictum Gratiani ante canon . . .
d. p. c.	Dictum Grantiani post canon . . .

II. *Decretal Collections*

Comp. I 1.1.1	*Compilatio prima,* Liber 1, titulus 1, canon 1
X 1.1.1	*Decretales Gregorii IX,* Liber 1, titulus 1, canon 1
VI 1.1.1	*Liber sextus,* Liber 1, titulus 1, canon 1

III. *Corpus iuris civilis*

Cod. 1.1.1	*Codex Justinianus,* Liber 1, titulus 1, lex 1
Dig. 1.1.1	*Digestum,* Liber 1, titulus 1, fragmentum 1
Inst.	*Institutiones Justiniani*
Nov.	*Novellae*
Auth.	*Authenticum*

IV. *Other References*

AASS	*Acta sanctorum quotquot toto orbe coluntur* . . . , 68 vols. (Antwerp, etc. [imprint varies], 1643——)
CDS	J. A. Brundage, *The Crusades: A Documentary Survey* (Milwaukee: Marquette University Press, 1962)
COD	*Conciliorum oecumenicorum decreta,* ed. Giuseppe Alberigo et al., 2d ed. (Freiburg i/Br.: Herder, 1962)
DDC	*Dictionnaire de droit canonique,* ed. R. Naz, 7 vols. (Paris: Letouzey & Ané, 1935–65)
JL	*Regesta pontificum romanorum* . . . , ed. Philipp Jaffé, rev. ed. S. Löwenfeld et al. Leipzig: Veit, 1885–88
Mansi, *Concilia*	*Sacrorum conciliorum nova et amplissima collectio,* ed. G. D. Mansi, 61 vols. (Paris, etc. [imprint varies], 1899–1927)
MGH	*Monumenta Germaniae Historica* (Hanover, etc. [imprint varies], 1826——)

SS	*Scriptores*
SSRG, n. s.	*Scriptores rerum germanicarum, nova series*
LL	*Leges in quarto*
Cap.	*Capitularia*
Conc.	*Concilia*
Const.	*Constitutiones*
Ep.	*Epistolae*
Ep. sel.	*Epistolae selectae*
PG	*Patrologia cursus completus* . . . *series Graeco-Latina,* ed. J.-P. Migne, 161 vols. (Paris: J.-P. Migne, 1857–66)
PL	*Patrologia cursus completus* . . . *series Latina,* ed. J.-P. Migne, 221 vols. (Paris: J.-P. Migne, 1844–64)
Po	A. Potthast, *Regesta pontificum romanorum inde ab anno post Christum natum MCXCVIII ad annum MCCCIV,* 2 vols. (Berlin: Rudolph Decker, 1874–75; r. p. Graz: Akademische Druck- und Verlagsanstalt, 1957)
RHC, Occ	*Recueil des historiens des croisades, Historiens Occidentaux,* 5 vols. in 6 (Paris: Académie des Inscriptions et Belles Lettres, 1841–1906)
RHDF	*Revue historique de droit français et étranger*
ZRG, KA	*Zeitschrift der Savigny-Stiftung für Rechtsgeschichte, kanonistische Abteilung*

MEDIEVAL
CANON LAW
AND THE
CRUSADER

CHAPTER I

The Pilgrimage Tradition
and the Holy War
Before the First Crusade

*So familiar, and as it were so natural to man, is the practice of
violence, that our indulgence allows the slightest provocation, the
most disputable right, as a sufficient ground of national hostility.
But the name and nature of a* holy war *demands a more rigorous
scrutiny; nor can we hastily believe that the servants of the Prince
of peace would unsheathe the sword of destruction unless the mo-
tive were pure, the quarrel legitimate, and the necessity inevitable.*

Edward Gibbon, *The Decline
and Fall of the Roman Em-
pire,* ch. 58

Qui multum peregrinantur, raro sanctificantur.

Imitatio Christi 1.1.23.4.

The Pilgrimage Tradition

The history of crusade institutions is largely grounded in the history of
the pilgrimage tradition in the period before 1095. Indeed, the crusade
itself was a pilgrimage, though a pilgrimage of a special kind. A brief
examination of the pre-crusade pilgrimage tradition, therefore, and especially of the juridical status of pilgrims, is a necessary preliminary to any
investigation of the status of crusaders.

THE IDEA OF PILGRIMAGE. The terms *peregrinus* and *peregrinatio*
are used in the Vulgate Old Testament primarily with the meaning of

3

"stranger," "alien," or "traveller," but without the later connotation of a traveller who journeys to a sacred place expressly for religious purposes.[1] The Old Testament makes it clear that the Israelites had obligations toward peregrini. They must do them no harm, for the children of Israel had themselves been peregrini and should know the hardships they suffer.[2] Further, they had a positive obligation to assist peregrini by loving them, by giving them food and clothing, and by doing justice to them.[3]

A similar idea of the peregrinus as a stranger or a wanderer, without any specific religious connotations, appears in the Latin authors of the ancient world, but there the Old Testament emphasis on the obligation to protect and assist peregrini is notably lacking. Instead, the classical authors repeatedly emphasize the stranger's lack of rights: he is by definition a person who lacks the protection of Roman law and has no political rights whatever.[4] True, he did enjoy the protection of the *jus gentium* and of a few rare provisions in the civil law of Rome which had been expressly extended to peregrini. He also had the right to seek remedies for his complaints in the court of the *praetor peregrinus*. Still, even at its best, the status of the peregrinus as compared with that of the *civis romanus* was scarcely an enviable one.

In the New Testament, although the term "pilgrim" (ξένος, peregrinus)

1. Thus in Gen. 17.8, Abraham is referred to as a "peregrinus" in the promised land and in 1 Par. 29.15, David speaks of himself and his people as "peregrini," i.e., strangers or wanderers. For similar usages, see Gen. 23.4, 28.4, 47.4, 47.9; Tob. 10.4; Job 19.15, 31.32, 38.13; Ps. 68.9, 118.54. (Names and divisions of Biblical books throughout follow the style of the Vulgate.) The religious pilgrimage in Judaism is mainly a development of the diaspora; see Bernhard Kötting, *Peregrinatio religiosa: Wallfahrten in der Antike und das Pilgerwesen in der alten Kirche*, pp. 57–69; also Salo W. Baron, *A Social and Religious History of the Jews*, 2d ed., 9 vols. (Philadelphia: Jewish Publication Society of America, 1952–60), 1:213–14.

2. Exod. 23.9; cf. Deut. 10.19.

3. Lev. 19.10, 23.22; Deut. 10.18–19, 14.21. An interesting story of Rabbi Elazar ben Shammua illustrating the rabbinical observance of these precepts may be found in the *Ecclesiastes Rabbah* to Eccles. 11.1, trans. in C. G. Montefiore and H. Lowe, *A Rabbinic Anthology*, pp. 432–33.

4. On Greco-Roman religious pilgrims, see Kötting, *Peregrinatio religiosa*, pp. 12–57. For examples, see the characteristic references to peregrini in Cicero, *De officiis* 1.34, *In Verrem* 2.4.35.77, *Tusculan Disputations* 5.37.107. On the legal status of peregrini under Roman rule, see W. W. Buckland, *A Text-book of Roman Law from Augustus to Justinian*, pp. 96–98; Paul F. Girard, *Manuel élémentaire de droit romain*, ed. Félix Senn, pp. 123–26; and Max Kaser, *Das römische Privatrecht*, 1:28–29, 243; 2:82–83. For a brief consideration of the early history of the term "peregrinatio" and the classical concept of "peregrini," see Jean Leclercq, "Mönchtum und Peregrinatio im Frühmittelalter," *Römische Quartalschrift*, 55(1960), 213–16.

continues to be used in the earlier sense of a "stranger" or "wanderer,"[5] the word is invested with a more deeply religious connotation. Jesus himself is described as homeless in this world, one who has no place to lay his head.[6] St. Paul exhorted his Corinthian congregation to conduct themselves in this life as pilgrims travelling to God.[7] Christians, he said in another place, should comport themselves as pilgrims and strangers on the earth.[8] Again, the author of 1 Peter, addressing himself to the Christian communities of Asia Minor, advised them as pilgrims and strangers to avoid the lusts of the flesh, which war against the soul. Thus, in the earliest Christian writings, the idea of pilgrimage (ξενιτεία, peregrinatio) emerges for the first time as a central religious ideal. The condition of the despised peregrinus is held up as a model for Christians to emulate. As peregrini they should beware of this world, which is not their homeland, while journeying toward the heavenly kingdom, which is their true fatherland.[9]

The New Testament idea of Christian life as "estrangement" from the world[10] and as a peregrinatio was taken up and amplified by the fathers of the early Church. The fullest development of the theme occurs in the writings of St. Augustine (354–430). The City of God in this world, he explains at the outset of his most famous work, "sojourns as a stranger in the midst of the ungodly"[11] and he consistently describes its earthly career in terms of pilgrimage. It is "the pilgrim city of King Christ," a "stranger in the world."[12] The citizen of the heavenly city is a pilgrim, too, a "stranger in this world, the citizen of the city of God, predestinated by grace, elected by grace, by grace a stranger below, and by grace a citizen above. . . . For the city of the saints is above, although here below it begets citizens, in whom it sojourns till the time of its reign arrives, when it shall gather together all in the day of the resurrection. . . ."[13] Man's

---

5. Thus, Matt. 27.7; Luke 24.18; Heb. 13.9; 1 Pet. 4.12; 3 John 5–8.
6. Matt. 8.20; Luke 9.58.
7. 2 Cor. 5.6–8.
8. Heb. 11.13.
9. 1 Pet. 2.11. Cf. Phil. 3.20; Heb. 13.14.
10. On the theme of "estrangement" see Kötting, *Peregrinatio religiosa*, pp. 302–7, and Gerhard B. Ladner, "Greatness in Medieval History," *Catholic Historical Review*, 50(1964), 5, 7–8.
11. *De civitate Dei* 1. praef. (ed. B. Dombart and A. Kalb, 1:1): "in hoc temporum cursu, cum inter impios peregrinatur ex fide uiuens." (The translation quoted throughout is that of Marcus Dodds.)
12. Ibid., 1.35 (ed. Dombart and Kalb, 1:33).
13. Ibid., 15.1 (ed. Dombart and Kalb, 2:454): ". . . isto peregrinus in saeculo et

journey through this life is, for Augustine, "this pilgrimage by faith," a trek in quest of the Christian's true homeland in heaven.[14]

The theological idea of the whole of Christian life as a pilgrimage and a corresponding endorsement of actual pilgrimages as a worthy form of asceticism underlay the beginning of Christian pilgrimage travel.[15] Certainly pious Christians very early began to visit the principal scenes of Christ's earthly career—travel which, naturally, focused on Jerusalem, the chief Jewish and Christian holy city. As early as the second century there may have been some pilgrimage traffic to Jerusalem and in the third century we find definite reference to such pilgrimages by two Christian bishops, Fermilian and Alexander, as well as some more doubtful instances of other journeys which may have had the character of religious pilgrimages.[16] By the turn of the fifth century St. Jerome (ca.347-419) had settled at Bethlehem, where he was accompanied by a group of high-minded Roman ladies. Two of them, in turn, wrote an enthusiastic letter to a friend, Marcella, urging her to make the Jerusalem pilgrimage and

---

pertinens ad ciuitatem Dei, gratia praedestinatus gratia electus, gratia peregrinus deorsum gratia ciuis sursum. . . . Superna est enim sanctorum ciuitas, quamuis hic pariat ciues, in quibus peregrinatur, donec regni eius tempus adueniat, cum congregatura est omnes in suis corporibus resurgentes. . . ."

14. Ibid., 15.6 (ed. Dombart and Kalb, 2:458): ". . . propter quod dicitur proficientibus bonis et ex fide in hac peregrinatione uiuentibus: Inuicem onera uestra portate et sic adimplebitis legem Christi (Gal. 6.2). . . ." See also Ladner, "Greatness in Medieval History," pp. 7-8, and his *Idea of Reform*, pp. 241-42; in addition, see Hans von Campenhausen, *Die asketische Heimatslosigkeit im altkirchlichen und frühmittelalterlichen Mönchtum.*

15. See Jean Leclercq, "Mönchtum und Peregrinatio," pp. 215-16.

16. St. Jerome, *De viris illustribus* 54 (*PL*, 23:665); Eusebius, *Historia ecclesiastica* 6.11.2 (ed. and trans. by Kirsop Lake et al., 2:36). On pre-crusade pilgrimages in general, and the Jerusalem pilgrimage in particular, see Sir Steven Runciman, "The Pilgrimages to Palestine before 1095," in *A History of the Crusades,* ed. Kenneth M. Setton et al., 1:68-78; Kötting, *Peregrinatio religiosa,* pp. 83-111; and the studies listed in Hans E. Mayer, *Bibliographie,* 1751-84, 1793-97. An abundance of guidebooks for intending pilgrims, furnishing details of distance between cities, housing accommodations, and notable sites, testifies to the popularity of the Jerusalem pilgrimage. The principal pre-crusade guidebooks are edited by P. Geyer in *Itinera Hierosolymitana saeculi III-VIII,* and by T. Tobler and A. Molinier, *Itinera Hierosolymitana et descriptiones terrae sanctae bellis sacris anteriora.* (For English translations of many accounts and guidebooks, see the *Publications of the Palestine Pilgrims' Text Society.*) "Pèlerinages aux lieux saints," an article by H. Leclercq in the *Dictionnaire d'archéologie chrétienne et de liturgie,* 14:65-176, contains comprehensive lists of pilgrimages and other journeys to the Holy Land between the first and the ninth centuries. A less complete list is in Ludovic Lalanne, "Des pèlerinages en terre sainte avant les croisades," *Bibliothèque de l'Ecole des Chartes,* 8(1845-46), 1-31.

describing the wonders she might glimpse if she did so.[17] The attitude of Jerome himself toward the Jerusalem pilgrimage seems to have been more equivocal. Although he encouraged his friend Desiderius to make the pilgrimage,[18] he rather disparaged the idea when writing to Paulinus of Nola. A man is no worse, he declared, for not having seen Jerusalem; although Jerome lived in the Holy Land himself, he professed not to think himself a better man on that account for, he added, *Non Jerosolymis fuisse, sed Jerosolymis bene vixisse laudandum est,*[19] a sentiment destined to be enshrined in Gratian's *Decretum,* where it became a focal point for canonistic commentators on pilgrimage themes.[20] There is evidence to suggest that large numbers of pilgrims continued to make the journey to the Holy Land during the fifth and sixth centuries,[21] but that the seventh century saw both a diminution in the number and a change in the character of pilgrimages.

PENITENTIAL PILGRIMAGES. Whereas the pilgrimages of the early Christian centuries had been almost purely devotional in character, from the seventh century onwards they were increasingly prescribed as a part of the penance enjoined upon confessed sinners. This change was apparently a result of the growing influence of the Irish church, both in Britain and upon the Continent. From at least as early as the time of St. Columban

17. St. Jerome, *Epist.* 46 (*PL,* 22:483–92).

18. Ibid., 47 (*PL,* 22:492–93). St. Jerome pleaded his own desire to see Desiderius once again and added: "Certe si consortia nostra displicuerint, adorasse ubi steterunt pedes Domini, pars fidei est; et quasi recentia nativitatis et crucis ac passionis vidisse vestigia."

19. Ibid., 58.2,4 (*PL,* 22:580, 582). St. Augustine, on at least one occasion, prescribed a pilgrimage (to the tomb of St. Felix of Nola, however, not to Jerusalem) as an act of devotion for a friend who consulted him. St. Augustine, *Epist.* 78 (*PL,* 33:268–69).

20. C. 12 q. 2 c. 71. The text of the *Decretum Gratiani* and the rest of the *Corpus iuris canonici* is cited throughout from the 1879 edition by E. Friedberg. The *glossa ordinaria* to the *Corpus* will be cited from the Venice, 1605, edition in 4 vols.

21. Leclercq, "Les Pèlerinages aux lieux saints," cols. 112–46, lists 129 references to fifth-century pilgrimages and 127 references for the sixth century. Lalanne, "Des pèlerinages," p. 24, notes the implications of Justinian's *Nov.* 40 as to the large numbers of pilgrims in Jerusalem (The *Corpus iuris civilis* will be cited throughout from the edition by P. Krueger et al., while the *glossa ordinaria* will be cited from the edition of Lyons, 1584, in 5 vols.). Both Theodoret and Palladius refer to fifth-century pilgrims who made the journey to Palestine from as far away as the British Isles: *Councils and Ecclesiastical Documents Relating to Great Britain and Ireland,* ed. A. W. Haddan and W. Stubbs, 1:4.

(fl. ca.600), Irish penitential discipline often required that the person guilty of particularly serious sins expiate his guilt by a lengthy—sometimes permanent—pilgrimage overseas[22]—a penalty very possibly derived from the ancient Celtic practice of prescribing exile as a punishment for major crimes.[23] By the early eighth century the use of pilgrimages as penitential exercises was reflected in Continental penitentials, at the same time as the Irish pilgrimage tradition itself began to undergo rather drastic modification.[24]

Although the authors of the early penitential handbooks did not normally specify the shrines which penitents were expected to visit while expiating their guilt, Jerusalem held a natural attraction for sinners sent on pilgrimage, both because of its manifold associations with the life of Christ and the major scenes of Biblical and early church history and also because of the very length and difficulty of the journey required to reach it. "The system had a practical value," Sir Steven Runciman has noted, "for it removed criminals from the community for several months; and if they survived the arduous journey they returned spiritually refreshed."[25]

22. Thus the *Penitentiale S. Columbani* B. 2 prescribed a seven-year pilgrimage for an adulterous cleric (*The Irish Penitentials,* ed. Ludwig Bieler, p. 98; trans. John T. McNeill and Helena M. Gamer, *Medieval Handbooks of Penance,* p. 252). Likewise pilgrimages were prescribed for incest and malicious murder in the *Penitentiale Cummeani*(ca.650) 2.7 and 4.6 (ed. Bieler, pp. 114, 118–20; trans. McNeill and Gamer, pp. 103, 107). Other prescriptions of penitential pilgrimages may be found in the *Collectio canonum Hibernensis*(ca.700–25) 29.7 and 44.8 (trans. McNeill and Gamer, pp. 141–42); *The Old Irish Penitential*(ca.800) 3.6 and 10 (ed. Bieler, p. 267; trans. McNeill and Gamer, p. 161); the three Irish canons of ca.1000 in Cambridge, Corpus Christi College, MS 265 (ed. Bieler, p. 182; trans. McNeill and Gamer, pp. 425–26); the *Sinodus Luci Victorie* can. 6 (ed. Bieler, p. 68); and the *Penitentiale quod dicitur Bigotianum* 4.3.4 (ed. Bieler, p. 228). On the penitential literature in general, see J. Lahache, "Pénitentiels," *DDC,* 6:1337–43, and Cyrille Vogel, "Le Pèlerinage pénitentiel," *Revue des sciences religieuses de l'Université de Strasbourg,* 38(1964), 113–53.

23. McNeill and Gamer, *Medieval Handbooks of Penance,* p. 34.

24. Thus pilgrimage is prescribed as a penance for incest in two early eighth-century penitentials of the "Roman" type; see the *Penitentiale Vallicellanum* 1.9 and the *Penitentiale Casinense* 24 in H. J. Schmitz, *Die Bussbücher und die Bussdisciplin der Kirche,* pp. 274, 404. Lalanne, "Des pèlerinages," p. 12, indicates that the earliest instance in Gaul of the canonical imposition of a pilgrimage to the Holy Land as a penance occurs in the late seventh century. Kathleen Hughes, "The Changing Theory and Practice of Irish Pilgrimage," *Journal of Ecclesiastical History,* 11(1960), 143–51, concludes that, as a result of the Viking invasions and of changes in ecclesiastical discipline, Irish pilgrimages from the eighth century on were generally confined to Ireland itself in actual practice, although the earlier tradition of pilgrimages overseas continued to be reflected in Irish literature.

25. "The Pilgrimages to Palestine," in *Crusades,* ed. Setton, 1:73.

JERUSALEM PILGRIMAGES FROM THE SEVENTH TO THE ELEVENTH
CENTURIES. In any event, pilgrims, both devotional and penitential,
continued to visit Palestine, although in small numbers, between the
beginning of the seventh and the end of the ninth centuries.[26] During the
tenth and eleventh centuries, both the numbers and the size of the
pilgrimage bands making the Jerusalem journey greatly increased, at least
in part because of the encouragement given by the monks of the congregation of Cluny through exhortation and through the building of hostels
along the major pilgrim routes.[27] One group in 1054 is said to have
numbered 3,000 persons and the largest of them all, the great German
pilgrimage a decade later, may have included as many as 7,000 persons in
its ranks.[28]

The popularity of pilgrimages in this period, however, was not universally approved. A number of eminent churchmen, although acknowledg-
ing the spiritual benefits to be derived from them, were troubled by the
abuses and temptations they discerned in pilgrim journeys. A conciliar
enactment of the Carolingian period, which was incorporated into both
the *Decretum* of Burchard of Worms (ca.965–1025) and the *Decretum* of
Ivo of Chartres (ca.1040–1116) denounced pilgrimage abuses. Priests,
deacons, and other clerics, the canon declared, deserted their flocks, yet
counted their ministry performed if they visited the pilgrimage sites,
while there were laymen who seemed to think that they might sin with
impunity because they had prayed at the sacred shrines. Moreover, the
canon disapproved of the poor who undertook these journeys in order to
give greater scope to their begging. Others, too, are said to have been so
senseless as to believe that they would be purged of their sins merely by
visiting the holy places. Charlemagne ordered all of these abuses to be put
down, we are told.[29] Criticism in the eleventh century seems to have been

26. We know of only 22 pilgrimages to the Holy Land during the seventh century, and even fewer during the eighth (see Lalanne, "Des pèlerinages," pp. 25–26
and Leclercq, "Les Pèlerinages aux lieux saints"). The dwindling numbers of
recorded pilgrimages in the eighth to the tenth centuries presumably reflect in part
the efforts of Carolingian church reformers to restrict or abolish penitential pilgrimages altogether. On this see C. Vogel, "Le Pèlerinage pénitentiel," pp. 137–38.

27. Runciman, "Pilgrimages to Palestine," in *Crusades*, ed. Setton, 1:74.

28. The principal source of information about this pilgrimage is the *Annales
Altahenses maiores*, s.a. 1065 (*MGH, SS*, 20:815–17; translation in *CDS*, pp. 3–7).
There is an excellent study of this pilgrimage by Einar Joranson, "The Great Ger-
man Pilgrimage of 1064–1065," in *The Crusades and Other Historical Essays*, ed.
L. J. Paetow, pp. 3–43.

29. Burchard of Worms, *Decreta* 20.51 (*PL*, 140:995); Ivo, *Decretum* 15:65 (*PL*,
141:877).

directed especially at monks who undertook pilgrimages without licence or permission of their superiors, for this violated the monastic promises of stability and obedience as well as the general ecclesiastical law.[30]

PILGRIMAGE AND CRUSADE. The crusades were, as has often been observed, an outgrowth, at least in part, of the eleventh-century pilgrimage tradition.[31] They represent a wedding of the tradition of pilgrimage with that of holy war, which had also for long played an important role in the life of the Latin church, and which will be discussed later in this chapter. So close-knit are the ideas of crusade and pilgrimage, that Latin writers down to the end of the twelfth century invariably refer both to pilgrims in the non-crusade sense and also to crusaders by the same word, peregrinus. This usage frequently makes it impossible to determine without some help from the context whether the person described in a given passage is a crusader or whether he is a simple pilgrim journeying to the Holy Land for purely devotional purposes. Likewise the crusades themselves are commonly referred to in the Latin sources as peregrinationes, and it is only after a century of crusading endeavor that specific terms (passagium, passagium generale, expeditio crucis) come into use to designate crusading expeditions.

The implications of this are quite plain: the crusader was considered a species of pilgrim and, at least in the twelfth century, his legal status was not conceived of as different in any essential way from that of the pilgrim, although he did enjoy some special privileges above and beyond those of other pilgrims.

Since the status of the crusader was an outgrowth of the status of the pilgrim and since the special privileges of the crusader were, in effect,

30. Thus St. Anselm (1033/34–1109), writing about the end of the century, cautioned a monk against undertaking the Jerusalem pilgrimage on these two scores and also added that the proposed journey would violate a recent papal injunction (Epist. 130 [PL, 150:165]). Monks had long been prohibited by ecclesiastical law from undertaking pilgrimages or other journeys without permission of their abbots. Most frequently cited in this connection is can. 27 of the Council of Agde (506), which was incorporated in the Pseudo-Isidorian collection (Decretales Pseudo-Isidorianae et capitula Angilramni, ed. Paul Hinschius, p. 334). This canon also appears in Ivo, Decretum 3.157 (PL, 161:234–35) and later in the Decretum of Gratian, C. 20 q. 4 c. 3.

31. Thus Runciman, "Pilgrimages to Palestine," in Crusades, ed. Setton, 1:78; Carl Erdmann, Die Entstehung des Kreuzzugsgedankens, pp. 306–7; Louis Bréhier, L'Eglise et l'Orient au moyen-âge: les croisades, pp. 50–54.

simply added to the bundle of privileges which all pilgrims possessed at law, it is necessary to try to define what the pilgrim's status involved at the time of the first crusade.

PILGRIM STATUS. The class of persons who might be referred to as peregrini in the middle ages was large and ill-defined; and medieval lawgivers and commentators alike made little attempt to limit it very sharply. Fundamentally, the term "peregrinus" might be used to describe anyone who for whatever reason was outside the diocese in which he was born or in which he was permanently domiciled. For purposes of discussion, we may translate "peregrinus," when it is used in this larger sense, simply as "traveller." This wide definition was, of course, rooted in Roman law and indeed persists in the canon law down to the present day.[32] Within the large, amorphous class of travellers, the religious pilgrims, that is persons who were travelling to or from a sacred shrine for predominantly pious reasons, formed a distinct group within which we may in turn distinguish two subgroups: (1) those who were travelling voluntarily and (2) the penitential pilgrims, who were travelling to a sacred shrine at the command of a confessor or other spiritual advisor in expiation of the guilt which they had incurred by their sins.[33]

Pilgrims in the restricted sense were probably set aside relatively early from travellers in general by pilgrim insignia that identified them and marked their status. The most important of these were the purse and staff, whose use eventually became normal symbols for religious pilgrims. Just how early this happened has not yet been definitely settled; in any event it is certain that the use of these insignia was common and was officially

---

32. Basic to the Roman and later canonistic use of the term "peregrinus" is the idea of domicile, i.e., a permanent place of residence. A peregrinus is a person possessed of a domicile, but who at a given moment is not physically resident there, even though he intends to return to his domicile; *Dig.* 50.1.20; 50.16.203; 50.16.239.2; *Cod.* 10.40.2, 7. For the modern canonistic terminology, which distinguishes between an *incola* (a person who is at the moment in his place of domicile), an *advena* (a person who is in a quasi-domicile, i.e. a place where he resides and where he intends to remain for the greater part of the year), a peregrinus, and a *vagus* (one who has no domicile or quasi-domicile), see *CIC,* can. 91–92. See also John L. Hammill, *The Obligations of the Traveler according to Canon 14;* John M. Costello, *Domicile and Quasi-Domicile;* R. Naz, "Domicile," *DDC,* 4:1372–83.

33. Raymond Oursel, *Les Pèlerins du moyen âge,* p. 9, attempts a definition along similar lines; also Luis Vázquez de Parga et al., *Las peregrinaciones a Santiago de Compostela,* 1:9.

recognized before the first crusade. At least one eleventh-century English pontifical, MS. Cotton Vitellius E.XII of the British Museum, contains a rite for formally bestowing these insignia upon pilgrims, thus marking them out from other travellers by an official liturgical rite.[34]

The whole class of travellers of every description was also included in the even larger class of *miserabiles personae,* to whom the Church in the pre-crusade period extended protection and assistance.[35] As far as pilgrims were concerned, this ecclesiastical protection took two basic forms, personal protection and hospitality.

PERSONAL PROTECTION OF PILGRIMS. The eleventh-century Church sought, as part of the larger peace movement of the period, to use its power to forbid attacks upon pilgrims and travellers of all kinds.[36] Although precursors can be identified, the peace movement is usually counted as beginning in France toward the end of the tenth century. From the Synod of Charroux (ca.989) onwards,[37] successive local church councils enacted canons which demanded the cessation of warfare during certain periods of the year and also the exemption of particular social groups, including pilgrims and travellers, from attack. Violations of the peace legislation were to be punished by ecclesiastical censures, including excommunication. Even before the peace movement took shape, sporadic

34. On these ceremonies, see my "Cruce signari: The Rite for Taking the Cross in England," *Traditio,* 22(1966), 289–310; also Francis Garrisson, "A propos des pèlerins et de leur condition juridique," *Etudes d'histoire du droit canonique dédiées à Gabriel Le Bras,* 2:1168–77; Adolph Franz, *Die kirchlichen Benediktionen im Mittelalter,* 2:271–89; Georg Schreiber, *Wallfahrt und Volkstum in Geschichte und Leben,* pp. 1–15; Vázquez de Parga et al., *Las peregrinaciones a Santiago de Compostela,* 1:124–43.

35. On the miserabiles personae see R. Génestal, *Le Privilegium fori en France du Décret de Gratien à la fin du XIV⁰ siècle,* 1:57–59.

36. The most important recent work on the subject of the peace movement is Hartmut Hoffman, *Gottesfriede und Treuga Dei, MGH, Schriften,* 20 (Stuttgart, 1964) which includes an extensive bibliography. See also: Sir Steven Runciman, *A History of the Crusades;* Marc Bloch, *Feudal Society,* trans. L. A. Manyon, pp. 412–20; Loren C. Mackinney, "The People and Public Opinion in the Eleventh Century Peace Movement," *Speculum,* 5(1930), 181–206; R. Bonnaud-Delamare, "La Paix en Flandre pendant la première croisade," *Revue du Nord,* 39(1957), 147–52; and the excursus on the councils dealing with the peace movement in Erdmann, *Die Entstehung des Kreuzzugsgedankens,* pp. 333–38. For additional references see Mayer's *Bibliographie,* 1741–48.

37. For the canons of the Synod of Charroux see Mansi, *Concilia,* 19:89–90; also Hoffmann, *Gottesfriede und Treuga Dei,* pp. 25–26, 70.

attempts were made by churchmen to secure travellers against the more outrageous forms of attack,[38] but the eleventh century saw for the first time a concerted series of efforts to bring them under ecclesiastical protection. At a Roman council of 1059, Pope Nicholas II (1058–61) adopted the policy of protecting both the persons and the possessions of travellers, especially pilgrims to sacred shrines, as an obligation of the papacy.[39] Later papal and conciliar enactments confirmed this stand[40] and the peace movement assumed its definite form in the canons of the three general councils of the Lateran during the twelfth century.[41]

The adoption of canons decreeing the extension of ecclesiastical protection to travellers and even the promulgation of similar declarations by secular princes, however, was not in itself a sufficient guarantee that the immunities of travellers would be respected in actual fact.[42] Indeed, the

38. Thus the *Decreta* of Burchard of Worms, 1.94 (*PL*, 180:573–80) include a list of inquiries to be made by bishops, two of which (*interrogationes* 41 and 76) relate to the abduction and enslavement of travellers. The bishop is directed to inquire "si aliquis hominem liberum aut servum alterius, aut peregrinum aut adventitium furatus fuerit, aut eum blandientem seduxerit et vendiderit, et extra patriam in captivitatem duxerit. . . ." and also "si aliquis peregrinum, qui de sua patria propter paganorum infestationem, vel persecutionem fugit, hac de causa quia in domo ejus mansit et diebus aut annis loco mercenari illi servivit, pro proprio servo velit habere, et vendere, aut dare alicui praesumat." The list of questions is attributed, almost certainly falsely, to Pope Eutychianus (275–83). Again, Ivo of Chartres, *Decretum* 4.60 (*PL*, 161:276) reproduces a decree of the Council of Erfurt (932) prohibiting measures which would impede the access of travellers to churches, while Ivo's *Panormia* 8.147 (*PL*, 161:1343) forbids attacks on travellers (among others) at all seasons of the year. See also Garrisson, "A propos des pèlerins," pp. 1178–79.

39. Ivo of Chartres, *Panormia* 5.114 (*PL*, 161:1238). Save for the concluding sentence, this canon was incorporated by Gratian in the *Decretum* C. 24 q. 3 c. 25.

40. In particular, Pope Urban II reaffirmed the peace and truce of God at the Councils of Melfi and Troia and especially at the Council of Clermont: Mansi, *Concilia*, 20:790 (Council of Troia, can. 2) and 20:816 (Council of Clermont, can. 1). On Pope Urban and the peace movement, see also Francis J. Gossman, *Pope Urban II and Canon Law*, pp. 181–83; Hoffmann, *Gottesfriede und Treuga Dei*, pp. 221–24.

41. First Lateran Council (1123), can. 14 (= C. 24 q. 3 c. 23) and 15, in *COD*, p. 169; Second Lateran Council (1139), can. 11–12 (*COD*, pp. 175–76); Third Lateran Council (1179), can. 21 (= *X* 1.34.1) and 22 (= *X* 3.39.10) in *COD*, p. 198. On the significance of this last in particular, see F. Poggiaspalla, "La condotta della guerra secondo una disposizione del III concilio Lateranense," *Ephemerides iuris canonici*, 12(1956), 371–86.

42. Thus in the *Consuetudines et iusticie* of William the Conqueror, which were set down after William's death by Robert Curthose and William Rufus, § 12 provides that "Nulli licuit peregrinum disturbare pro aliquo forisfactio. Et si aliquis fecit, de corpore suo fuit in misericordia domini Normannie" (ed. Charles Homer Haskins in *Norman Institutions*, p. 283). For earlier examples, see the *Lex Baiwariorum* (742–44) 4.31 (ed. E. de Schwind, *MGH, LL*, 5/2:335–36); Capitulary

frequent reiteration of such guarantees is probably an adequate indication that travellers continued to be molested uncomfortably often on the roads. Some additional guarantee of protection for the individual traveller might be afforded by a letter of introduction and safe-conduct to the authorities through whose lands the journey was planned. Efforts were sometimes made, too, to assist and safeguard travellers in general and pilgrims in particular by seeking assurances of their safety and special arrangements for their well-being from individual rulers.

HOSPITALITY FOR PILGRIMS. In addition to the protection which the Church sought to extend to travellers of all sorts, the canonistic writers, taking their inspiration from Matt. 25.35, frequently adverted to the further obligation of hospitality toward them. At least as early as the end of the fifth century, the *Statuta ecclesiae antiqua* acknowledged the obligation of the bishop to look after the needs of pilgrims and directed that this function be delegated to his archpriest or archdeacon.[43] The particular obligations of monks in this regard were most emphatically set forth by St. Benedict (ca.480–550/53) in his *Rule*. His monks were directed to receive travellers in the monastery and to entertain them as if they were Christ Himself. The monks were to behave with all humility toward their wayfaring guests and to prostrate themselves in adoration of the Christ who is in them. The abbot himself should help to wait upon them and they were to dine at the abbot's table in refectory.[44] The Irish penitentials insisted upon the obligation of hospitality toward travellers and directed that penance be imposed upon those who neglected this obligation.[45] Both royal and ecclesiastical legislation of the Carolingian period likewise repeatedly directed clerics to assist, feed, and house pilgrims who were travelling to worship at sacred shrines.[46] In the eleventh-

---

of Pipin of Italy (782–86), ch. 10 (*MGH, Capit.* 1:193); Capitulary of 802, ch. 5 (*MGH, Capit.,* 1:93). See also Vázquez de Parga et al., *Las peregrinaciones a Santiago de Compostela*, 2:255–79, although most of the instances cited postdate the first crusade.

43. *Les Statuta ecclesiae antiqua*, can. 7 (ed. Charles Munier, p. 80). Munier dates the collection ca.476–85.

44. *Regula monachorum*, ch. 53, 56 (ed. Rudolf Hanslik, pp. 123–26, 131).

45. Finnian, *Penitentiale* 33 (ed. Bieler, p. 86; trans. McNeill and Gamer, p. 93). Columban, *Regula coenobialis* (trans. McNeill and Gamer, p. 263).

46. Thus, *Capitularium a sacerdotibus proposita* (802?), ch. 7 (*MGH, Capit.,* 1:106); Capitulary of 802. ch. 27 (*MGH, Capit.,* 1:96); *Instructio pastoralis* of

century canonistic collections priests were enjoined to labor in order that they might be better able to give hospitality to travellers[47] and were even allowed to entertain them in the churches if need be,[48] or to alienate the goods of the Church in order to minister to their wants.[49]

OTHER PRIVILEGES OF PILGRIMS. Pilgrims commonly benefitted from other privileges, more or less extensive and important. Exemptions from tolls and immunity from taxes were certainly conceded to them with some regularity, at least in theory.[50] Immunity from arrest or seizure was promised to them by the Church at least from the time of Gregory VII,[51] and later pilgrims enjoyed the right to appoint an attorney to safeguard their interests during their absence and to a suspension of legal proceedings against them while they were engaged in their journeys.[52]

PILGRIM CLERICS. One large and important group of travellers received very special and detailed treatment in the eleventh-century canonistic treatises: these were clerical travellers or pilgrims. The canon law assumed that in normal circumstances all clerics and monks would reside and remain permanently in the places where they were professed or ordained. Priests or deacons who left must first seek the permission of

Archbishop Arno of Salzburg (798?), ch. 10 (*MGH, Conc.*, 2:200); Council of Tours (813), ch. 6 (*MGH, Conc.*, 2:287); Council of Aachen (816), ch. 41 (*MGH, Conc.*, 2:416–17).

47. Burchard of Worms, *Decreta* 2.104 (*PL*, 140:644), citing the Council of Nantes (895). This same canon was later incorporated as one of the *paleae* in the *Decretum Gratiani*, D. 91 c. 2 and also appears in X 3.41.1, where the source is cited as the Council of Agde (506).

48. Burchard, *Decreta* 3.83 (*PL*, 140:690); Ivo, *Decretum* 3.74 (*PL*, 161:214); *Decretum Gratiani* D. 42 c. 5; the source of this canon is c. 30 of the third Council of Carthage (397); see *Die Kanones der wichtigsten altkirchlichen Concilien*, ed. F. Lauchert.

49. Ivo, *Decretum* 3.167 (*PL*, 161:236), citing c. 3 of the third Council of Toledo (589). On this whole matter see also Garrisson, "A propos des pèlerins," pp. 1185–87.

50. Pepin the Short, Capitulary of 754/55, ch. 4 (*MGH, Capit.*, 1:32); Charlemagne, letter to King Offa of Mercia, 796, in *Alcuini epistolae* 100 (*MGH, Ep.*, 4:145); other references in Garrisson, "A propos des pèlerins," pp. 1179–80.

51. *Acta pontificum Romanorum inedita*, ed. Julius von Pflugk-Harttung, 2:126, c. 15 of the Roman Council of 1074–75; other references in Garrisson, "A propos des pèlerins," pp. 1180–81.

52. Garrisson, "A propos des pèlerins," pp. 1180–88; Eugen Wohlhaupter, "Wallfahrt und Recht," in Georg Schreiber, ed., *Wallfahrt und Volkstum*, pp. 239–41.

their bishop, who was to grant leave only for a short time and in urgent cases.[53] Bishops wishing to travel were required to secure the prior approval of their metropolitans,[54] and an invitation from the bishops of the province to which they were journeying, *ne videamur ianuam claudere caritatis.*[55] Upon their arrival, the bishop of the place must pass on the validity of their reasons for making the journey.[56] Monks were strictly enjoined by the Benedictine rule from leaving their monasteries save at the command of their superior, a ban reinforced by the general law of the church, which demanded that monks remain within their cloisters.[57] The same rules, it is clear, applied also to nuns.[58] Clerics infringing these rules were, at least technically, subject to severe penalties.

Clerical travellers were not to say Mass or otherwise to exercise their orders, unless they could furnish proof of ordination and clerical status, in the form of credentials issued by the bearer's bishop under his official seal and sometimes fortified with the seals of other bishops as well.[59] The canonists prescribe in great detail the forms and safeguards to be used in composing these letters, which are variously known as *litterae formatae, litterae commendatitiae, litterae testimoniales,* or *litterae dimissoriae.*[60] A major purpose of these detailed prescriptions was to prevent, or at least to detect, forgeries of the letters. Notwithstanding such regulations, clerical

53. First Council of Nicaea (325), can. 15 (*COD*, p. 12). Ivo of Chartres, *Decretum* 6.170 (*PL*, 161:484–85) = *Panormia* 3.71 (*PL*, 161:1146) and *Decretum* 6.172 (*PL*, 161:485) = *Panormia* 3.72 (*PL*, 161:1146). Jean Gaudemet, *L'Eglise dans l'empire romain (IVᵉ–Vᵉ siècles),* pp. 347–49. A useful collection of admonitions against wandering monks and clerics, from the fourth to the fourteenth centuries, is in Helen Waddell, *The Wandering Scholars,* Appendix E, pp. 269–99.

54. Third Council of Carthage (397), can. 28, in *Kanones,* ed. Lauchert, p. 167.

55. Council of Sardica (343), can. 3 in ibid., pp. 52–53.

56. Council of Sardica, can. 10 in ibid., p. 60; Ivo, *Decretum* 6.213 (*PL*, 161:491), citing can. 35 of the third Council of Carthage.

57. *Regula monachorum,* ch. 51 (ed. Hanslik, pp. 121–22); a letter of Alexander II (1061–73) in 1064 commanded monks to remain within the monastery and to stay out of towns, castles, and other non-claustral resorts, even for purposes of preaching (*JL*, 4,552 = Ivo of Chartres, *Decretum* 7.15 [*PL*, 161:582] and C. 16 q. 1 c. 11).

58. Ivo of Chartres, *Decretum* 7.77 (*PL*, 161:563–64), citing the second Council of Chalon-sur-Saône (813), can. 62.

59. Burchard, *Decreta* 1.116 (*PL*, 140:583) = Ivo, *Decretum* 5.216 (*PL*, 161:388), citing can. 19 of the Council of Arles (314), in *Kanones,* ed. Lauchert, p. 29. Also, Ivo, *Decretum* 5.222 (*PL*, 161:390), from can. 23 [68] of the Council of Rouen; Burchard, *Decreta* 1.121 (*PL*, 140:585) = C. 1 q. 1 c. 13 (part), citing a letter of Gregory the Great assigned by Jaffé to July, 599: *JL*, 1,747.

60. For these letters, see George F. Schorr, *The Law of the Celebret;* E. Jombart, "Celebret," *DDC,* 3:126–31; R. Naz, "Testimoniales (Lettres)," *DDC,* 7:1207–10; Antonio Poli, *De litteris commendatitiis ad sacra facienda in jure canonico.*

impostors sometimes did manage to escape detection for considerable periods of time, especially when the canonical safeguards were for some reason ignored.[61]

The clerical traveller, like all travellers, was to some extent freed from the observance of purely local ecclesiastical regulations and customs while making his journey. There seems, however, to have been no clear consensus in the period before Gratian as to the extent of his exemption, save that under any circumstances the traveller should avoid giving rise to scandal in the places he visited.[62] In addition, travelling clerics were freed from a few obligations in the common law of the Church. Thus, although clerics were in general prohibited from entering taverns and eating or drinking there, travelling clerics were explicitly exempted from this rule.[63]

THE PILGRIM VOW. Although there is no formal canonical regulation on the matter, it is apparent that in the era before the beginning of the crusades some pilgrims made their journeys as a result of a vow which they had taken.[64] No text or notarial attestation of any pre-crusade pilgrimage vow has, to my knowledge, survived, and it is difficult to say exactly what was promised in them and what obligations may have been entailed. There is no indication that any well developed canonistic theory

61. An egregious case is reported s.a. 1093 by Cosmas of Prag, *Chronica Boemorum* 2.51 (*MGH, SS,* 9:101).

62. The texts bearing on the traveller's obligation to observe local regulations are fully cited and discussed by Hammill, *The Obligations of the Traveler,* pp. 7-24.

63. Burchard, *Decreta* 2.130 (*PL,* 140:647-48) = Ivo, *Decretum* 6.204 (*PL,* 161:490) and D. 44 c. 4, citing the third Council of Carthage (397), can. 27 (*Kanones,* ed. Lauchert, p. 167).

64. Kötting, *Peregrinatio religiosa,* p. 205, notes a pilgrimage vow of Sophronius of Jerusalem, who promised to make a journey to Alexandria (*PG,* 3:336) and Leclercq, "Mönchtum und Peregrinatio," p. 216, mentions a "votum peregrinationis" ascribed to St. Silvinus of Thérouanne (d. 720) in a ninth-century biography (*Acta Sanctorum Ordinis s. Benedicti,* ed. Mabillon et al., 3/1:296), as well as the reference to a pilgrimage vow of St. Egbert in Bede, *Historia ecclesiastica* (ed. Charles Plummer, p. 193). Another early mention of this practice occurs in connection with the pilgrimage of a French knight, Josselin, after 954 (*AASS,* 17 Jan. [Jan. 2:516-17], summarized by Lalanne, "Des pèlerinages," p. 27). Apparently the participants in the great German pilgrimage of 1064-65 made their journey under vows, as the *Annales Altahenses maiores,* s.a. 1065 (*MGH, SS,* 20:817; trans. in CDS, p. 7) mention the fulfillment of their vows upon their arrival at Jerusalem. The epitaph of Bishop Gunther of Bamberg, one of the leaders of the expedition, also mentions this: "Dum solvit votum, quo se vovit dare totum, / Exul abit Soliman, repperit et patriam" (quoted by Joranson, "Great German Pilgrimage," p. 9, n. 17).

of the binding power and implications of pilgrimage vows had been worked out before the beginning of the twelfth century. Rather, the development of the juridical implications of the pilgrimage vow was in part a result of the maturation during the twelfth and thirteenth centuries of the canon law itself and in part, also, of the need for clarification of the canonistic doctrine of the vow brought on by the crusade movement.

By the end of the eleventh century, however, pilgrims certainly had at least a rudimentary sense that certain formal actions were necessary to acquit themselves of their vows. The most important of these actions for pilgrims to the Holy Land, apparently, was the offering of prayer at the Holy Sepulchre, without which no such pilgrimage was deemed complete. In addition, other formal rituals were usual for pilgrims to Jerusalem, especially the giving of alms, and the taking of a ritual bath, commonly in the River Jordan.[65] Returning pilgrims were accustomed to bear back with them palms from Jericho as a symbol of the fulfillment of their obligations—hence the term "palmer."[66] The palms symbolized the pilgrim's victory over the obstacles in his path and his renewal in grace by the penance performed on his journey.[67]

Thus, on the eve of the proclamation of the first crusade in 1095 pilgrims had already secured a special status in medieval society, a status which as yet, however, had not been sharply defined or closely regulated by the existing canon law. The pilgrim was a recognized figure in ecclesiastical discipline and was acknowledged to be possessed of some privileges and to be subject to some obligations, however indefinite these notions may have been. It was this status, this loose set of obligations and privileges, which the crusaders inherited, and it is upon this basis that the Church in the twelfth and thirteenth centuries built the more complex and much better defined structure of crusader status. But if the crusader was from the outset a pilgrim and thus possessed legally of the obligations and privileges belonging to that class of persons in the canon law, he was also something more: he was a fighter in a holy war. This fact further modified and influenced the development of the canonistic concept of the crusader.

65. Edmond-René Labande, "Recherches sur les pèlerins dans l'Europe des XIe et XIIe siècles," *Cahiers de civilisation médiévale*, 1(1958), 341–43; on votive offerings by pilgrims, see Kötting, *Peregrinatio religiosa*, pp. 398–402, and U. Berlière, "Anciens pèlerinages bénédictins au moyen-âge," *Revue liturgique et monastique*, 11(1925–26), 205–13, 247–53.
66. For examples of the usage, see the *Oxford English Dictionary*, s.v. "Palmer."
67. Labande, "Recherches sur les pèlerins," pp. 343–44.

The Holy War Tradition

JUST WAR AND WAR JUSTIFIED. The theology of war in the Western Christian tradition was first propounded by St. Augustine, whose doctrine rests fundamentally upon the classic distinction between just and unjust wars.[68] Although he deplored the necessity of warfare at all, Augustine maintained that the righteous are forced to wage just wars because the wrongdoing of the wicked forces the just man to repress them.[69] Both the righteous and the wicked wage war in order to secure peace, since peace is the ultimate goal of all warfare: "For every man seeks peace by waging war, but no man seeks war by making peace. For even they who intentionally interrupt the peace in which they are living have no hatred of peace, but only wish it changed into a peace which suits them better."[70] Thus the general aim of securing peace cannot be a justification for war, unless every war is to be considered just. St. Augustine posited, instead, certain criteria which distinguished a just war from an unjust one; later commentators reduced these to three: *auctoritas principi,* a *causa iusta,* and an *intentio recta.*[71] Briefly, the first of these principles requires that a

68. On the Christian idea of war in general, see Robert Regout, *La Doctrine de la guerre juste de saint Augustin à nos jours;* Kurt Georg Cram, *Iudicium belli: Zum Rechtscharakter des Krieges in deutschen Mittelalter;* and especially Erdmann, *Die Entstehung des Kreuzzugsgedankens.* Other treatments may be found in P. Bierzanek, "Sur les origines de la guerre et de la paix," *RHDF,* 4th ser., 38(1960), 83–123; Ernst Nys, *Le Droit de la guerre et les précurseurs de Grotius;* A. Vanderpol, *La Doctrine scolastique du droit de guerre;* G. S. Windass and J. Newman, "The Early Christian Attitude to War," *Irish Theological Quarterly,* 29(1962), 235–47; G. Hubrecht, "La 'juste guerre' dans le Décret de Gratien," *Studia Gratiana,* 3(1955), 162–77.

69. *De civitate Dei* 19.7 (ed. Dombart and Kalb 2:672).

70. Ibid., 19.12 (ed. Dombart and Kalb 2:675): "Omnis enim homo etiam bello gerando pacem requirit; nemo autem bellum pacificando. Nam et illi qui pacem, in qua sunt, perturbare uolunt, non pacem oderunt, sed etiam pro arbitrio suo cupiunt commutari."

71. Cram, *Iudicium belli,* p. 13; Regout, *La Doctrine de la guerre juste,* pp. 49–50; Erdmann, *Die Entstehung des Kreuzzugsgedankens,* pp. 5–6; see also the article "Guerre" by T. Ortolon in the *Dictionnaire de théologie catholique,* 3d ed., 6:1899–1962. The threefold classification, however, involves a certain simplification of Augustine's thought, for which see especially *Epist.* 189 (C. 23 q. 1 c. 3), *Contra Faustum* 22.74–75 (C. 23 q. 1 c. 4), and *Liber quaestionum* 6.10 (C. 23 q. 2 c. 2). See also Juan Fernando Ortega, "La paz y la guerra en el pensamiento agustiniano," *Revista española de derecho canónico,* 20 (1965), 5–35.

just war be lawfully proclaimed by a legitimate ruler, whether ecclesiastical or secular, and of whatever rank or dignity, as long as the proclamation of war falls within the scope of his jurisdiction. The second condition requires that a justifiable purpose be intended. Under the heading of just causes for war, Augustine would include the defense of one's country, laws, and traditional ways of life, the recovery of land or other property which has been unlawfully appropriated by another, or the enforcement of a judicial sentence. The third condition requires that a just war not involve any ulterior motives and that war must be the only feasible means of achieving the righteous purpose in question. Medieval canonists found this Augustinian doctrine of just war neatly summed up in a citation from the *Etymologies* of Isidore of Seville (ca.560–636): "That war is just which is waged upon command in order to recover property or to repel attack." This passage was subsequently incorporated by Ivo of Chartres into both his *Decretum* and his *Panormia,* and passed from these collections into the *Decretum* of Gratian.[72]

The canonists also contended that the participants in a just war were not morally guilty of murder should they slay one of the enemy. There is a distinction, they argued, once again on an Augustinian basis, between those who slay other men with rightful authority in a just cause and the murderer who kills without lawful sanction.[73] The soldier in a just war acted as a minister of the law and by slaying the enemy carried out the commands of justice and lawful authority.[74] Not only was it not wicked to chastise wrongdoers,[75] but the person who punished them acted as a servant and minister of God Himself.[76] Before the end of the eleventh

72. Isidore of Seville, *Etymologiae* 18.1.2, ed. W. M. Lindsay; Ivo, *Decretum* 10.116 (*PL,* 161:727); *Panormia* 8.54 (*PL,* 161:1315); C. 23 q. 2 c. 1.

73. Ivo, *Decretum* 10.65 (*PL,* 161:77) = *Panormia* 8.18 (*PL,* 161:1309) = C. 23 q. 8 c. 14; Ivo, *Decretum* 10.101 (*PL,* 161:722–23) = *Panormia* 8.38 (*PL,* 161:1313) = C. 23 q. 5 c. 41.

74. Ivo, *Decretum* 10.104 (*PL,* 161:724) = *Panormia* 8.41 (*PL,* 161:1313); Burchard, *Decreta* 6.43 (*PL,* 140:775–76) = Ivo, *Decretum* 10.115 (*PL,* 161:726–27) = *Panormia* 8.51–52 (*PL,* 161:1315) = C. 23 q. 5 c. 29–30; Ivo, *Decretum* 10.78 (*PL,* 161:717–18); Ivo, *Decretum* 10.98 (*PL,* 161:721–22) = *Panormia* 8.35 (*PL,* 161:1312) = C. 23 q. 5 c. 13; Ivo, *Decretum* 10.4 (*PL,* 161:691–92) = *Panormia* 8.2 (*PL,* 161:1305–6) = C. 23 q. 5 c. 9; Ivo, *Decretum* 10.110 (*PL,* 161:725–26) = *Panormia* 8.44 (*PL,* 161:1314) = C. 23 q. 4 c. 36.

75. Ivo, *Panormia* 8.36 (*PL,* 161:1312); Ivo, *Decretum* 10.113 (*PL,* 161:726) = *Panormia* 8.50 (*PL,* 161:1315) = C. 23 q. 3 c. 6; Ivo, *Decretum* 10.72 (*PL,* 161:713) = *Panormia* 8.21 (*PL,* 161:1310) = C. 23 q. 8 c. 13; Ivo, *Decretum* 10.112 (*PL,* 161:726) = C. 23 q. 5 c. 18.

76. Ivo, *Decretum* 10.111 (*PL,* 161:726) = *Panormia* 8.48 (*PL,* 161:1315) = C.

century, as the canonistic collections of the period make clear, papal teaching on the justification for killing had broadened sufficiently so that those who slew excommunicated persons, even if they were not engaged in a just war, were not counted guilty of homicide, although they might be subject to ecclesiastical penance for their deeds.[77] On the other hand, the canonists taught that non-Christians should not be set upon violently, nor should they be coerced to accept baptism,[78] although in this connection a distinction was drawn between Jews and Saracens. Against the latter, force might be used, since they were already persecuting Christians and driving them from their homes.[79] A defensive war against attacking Saracens would, of course, constitute a just war if it were lawfully proclaimed, and under such circumstances a pope might consider it his duty as protector of his flock to authorize the use of force to protect them from attack.[80]

WAR AS JUSTIFICATION. It is one thing, however, to hold that war may, under certain circumstances, be considered just; it is quite another matter to consider the waging of war as something positively meritorious, as a way to personal salvation. In antiquity, the soldier who died while fighting in defense of his homeland was frequently considered a civic hero and the honors paid to him might occasionally approach the worship accorded to a deity,[81] but the notion of death in battle for one's fatherland as a means of sanctification was one which the early middle ages generally found repugnant.[82] The attitude was different, however, when it was a

---

23 q. 5 c. 27; Burchard, *Decreta* 6.43 (*PL*, 140:755–76) = Ivo, *Decretum* 10.114 (*PL*, 161:726) = *Panormia* 8.51 (*PL*, 161:1315) = C. 23 q. 5 c. 29.

77. This point was made in a letter of Pope Urban II, dated by Jaffé between 1088 and 1095: *JL*, 5,536; it was used by Ivo and later by Gratian as well: Ivo, *Decretum* 10.54 (*PL*, 161:706) = *Panormia* 8.11 (*PL*, 161:1308) = C. 23 q. 5 c. 47.

78. Gregory I, *Epist.* 1.34, 16 March 591 (*JL*, 1,104) = Ivo, *Decretum* 1.285 (*PL*, 161:125); also, Ivo, *Decretum* 1.182 (*PL*, 161:106).

79. Alexander II (1063) in *JL*, 4,528 (Mansi, *Concilia*, 19:980) = Ivo, *Decretum* 13.114 (*PL*, 161:824–25) = *Panormia* 8.29 (*PL*, 161:1311) = C. 23 q. 8 c. 11.

80. Thus Leo IV justified his attempt to raise defensive forces to ward off threatened Saracen attacks on Rome (*JL*, 2,627) = Ivo, *Decretum* 10.84 (*PL*, 161:719) = *Panormia* 8.28 (*PL*, 161:1311) = C. 23 q. 8 c. 8 and *JL*, 2,620 = Ivo, *Decretum* 10.83 (*PL*, 161:719) = *Panormia* 8.27 (*PL*, 161:1311) = C. 23 q. 8 c. 7.

81. Cf. the *Institutes* of Justinian, which states that "hi enim, quia pro re publica ceciderunt, in perpetuum per gloriam vivere intelliguntur" (*Inst.* 1.25 pr.).

82. The history of this idea is dealt with by Ernst H. Kantorowicz in *"Pro patria mori* in Medieval Political Thought," *AHR*, 56(1951), 472–92, and at greater

question of death in defense of the heavenly fatherland of all Christians, for this was martyrdom—a universally acknowledged path to salvation. Obviously martyrdom might be earned in a number of different ways; but from the mid-ninth century a new path to the martyr's crown appears.

Pope Leo IV (847–55) in December 853 addressed to the Frankish army an appeal for aid against the Saracen marauders who had pillaged Rome and desecrated St. Peter's in 846 and who were still ravaging the area. Reminding the Franks of their earlier victories against the same foe, the pope held out a promise that those who died in the struggle would find a reward laid up for them in heaven.[83] The promise of eternal life in Pope Leo's letter was certainly neither a proclamation of doctrine nor a remission either of sins or of the penalties of sin. Rather it was a hortatory expression of pious hope and prayer, comparable to the *absolutio super tumulum* of the burial service.[84] Nonetheless, Pope Leo made a vital link between the act of fighting against the infidel in defence of the faith and the prospect of salvation. War against the infidel is treated as a praiseworthy act, one which will gain merit in heaven; it is treated, in fact, as a holy war.

Two decades later, in 878, this idea was reiterated and amplified by Pope John VIII (872–82). In reply to a question posed by a group of bishops who asked whether those who died in defense of the Church, the Christian religion, and their government were granted remission of their sins (*indulgentiam possint consequi delictorum*), the pope answered with an assurance that these warriors would surely receive eternal life, as had the good thief on the cross with Christ (Luke 23.40–43). Moreover, the

---

length in *The King's Two Bodies: A Study in Medieval Political Theology*, pp. 232–72. See also Gaines Post, *Studies in Medieval Legal Thought: Public Law and the State, 1100–1322*, ch. 10, especially pp. 435–53.

83. Leo IV, *Epist.* 1 (*PL*, 115:655–57) = *JL*, 2,642 = Ivo, *Decretum* 10.87 (*PL*, 161:719–20) = *Panormia* 8.30 (*PL*, 161:1311, where the text is erroneously ascribed to Pope Nicholas I) = C. 23 q. 8 c. 9 and C. 23 q. 5 c. 46: "Omnium vestrum nosse volumus charitatem, quoniam quisquis (quod non optantes dicimus) in hoc belli certamine fideliter mortuus fuerit, regna illi coelestia minime negabuntur. Novit enim Omnipotens, si quilibet vestrum morietur, quod pro veritate fidei, et salvatione patriae, ac defensione Christianorum mortuus est; ideo ab eo praetitulatum praemium consequetur." On this passage see also Kantorowicz, "*Pro patria mori*," pp. 481–82; Gottlob, *Kreuzablass*, pp. 18–19; Erdmann, *Die Entstehung des Kreuzzugsgedankens*, p. 248. For some earlier examples of the idea see Albrecht Noth, *Heiliger Krieg und heiliger Kampf in Islam und Christentum*, pp. 92–109.

84. Thus in the four prayers of the modern *absolutio: Missale Romanum ex decreto sacrosancti concilii Tridentini restitutum*, 7th ed. (New York, 1949), pp. (116)–(120).

pope granted them absolution,[85] but this again was a general absolution, not an indulgence as sometimes maintained.[86] While John VIII dealt with the matter more explicitly and in slightly greater detail than did Leo IV, there was no essential difference between their two statements. Both affirmed clearly the salvific value of fighting against the enemies of Christendom. Both granted general absolutions to those who were killed in these struggles; Pope John in this connection explicitly invoked the Petrine power of binding and loosing, while Leo IV did not. In neither letter, however, do we have any mention of the remission of the punishment for sin that is essential to the concept of an indulgence.[87] What these two letters do show, and that very clearly, is the doctrine that war against the infidel is sanctified and sanctifying for those who participate in it—at least if they have the misfortune to be killed in the struggle.

Aside from a spurious letter attributed to Sergius IV (1009–12),[88] it was not until the mid-eleventh century that the papacy again took up the idea of holy war—at a time coinciding, significantly, with the rise to power of the reform party in the Western Church. Pope Leo IX (1049–54), the first of the reform party to occupy the Chair of St. Peter, found himself in military difficulties almost from the outset of his pontificate. Two months after his consecration, Leo held a synod in Rome at which he urged military action against the Tuscan rebels who were disrupting the peace of Campania. Also significant was the position which the pope took in the struggle with the Normans over Benevento, which in 1051 had placed itself under papal protection. Thus when the Norman invaders of southern Italy attacked the city, papal interests were immediately and directly involved. The pope appealed to the emperor for aid and, with the help of a small troop of German knights, personally took the field against the Normans in 1053. The campaign was a military disaster. At the battle of Città the papal army was routed; Leo himself was taken prisoner by the Normans, and was held at Benevento for nearly a year. Released in March 1054, he returned to Rome, where he died a month later. The interest of

---

85. *JL*, 3,195 (September 878); *PL*, 126:816.
86. Gottlob, *Kreuzablass*, pp. 23–27.
87. See below, ch. V, pp. 145–46.
88. *JL*, 3,972; the text is in *PL*, 139:1498–1502 and, in a better edition by J. Lair, in the *Bibliothèque de l'Ecole des Chartes*, 18(1856–57), 246–53. In a detailed, critical study of this text, however, Alexander Gieysztor has concluded that the letter is a forgery, probably originating at Moissac in 1095/96, as part of the propaganda for the first crusade: "The Genesis of the Crusades: the Encyclical of Sergius IV (1009–1012)," *Medievalia et Humanistica*, 5(1948), 3–23 and 6(1949), 3–34.

these events for the developing idea of holy war lies in the active role played by the papacy in the conduct of military operations to safeguard the territory of the Church. Apparently the pope regarded his campaign not only as a just war, but also as a holy war in defense of the Church itself.

A more important step occurred in 1063, when Pope Alexander II granted to the Christian warriors against the Moors in Spain not merely a general benediction, but a remission of the penance required for their sins. His action was part of a general encouragement of the *reconquista,* which was a major interest of his pontificate. In one letter, addressed to the archbishop of Narbonne, Alexander specifically excepted the slaying of Saracens by those fighting in Spain from the general prohibition of homicide and made quite plain his approval and encouragement of the Spanish campaigns.[89] In a second letter, to the clergy of Volturno, the pope specified the spiritual favors to be enjoyed by participants in these wars:

> With fatherly affection we urge those who have resolved to go to Spain that they take the greatest care to complete that task which with divine counsel they have set out to accomplish. Let each soldier confess, according to the character of his sins, to his bishop or spiritual father and let the confessor impose suitable penance upon him, lest the devil be enabled to accuse him of impenitence. We, however, by the authority of the holy apostles Peter and Paul, relieve them of their penance and grant them remission of sins, while our prayers go with them.[90]

89. *JL,* 4,533. A fragment of this letter was cited by Ivo of Chartres, *Decretum* 13.115 (*PL,* 161:825).

90. *JL,* 4,530; text in *Epistolae pontificum Romanorum ineditae,* ed. Löwenfeld, no. 82, p. 43: "Eos qui in Ispaniam proficisci destinarunt, paterna karitate hortamur, ut, que divinitus admoniti cogitaverunt ad effectum perducere, summa cum sollicitudine procurent; qui iuxta qualitatem peccaminum suorum unusquisque suo episcopo vel spirituali patri confiteantur, eisque, ne diabolus accusare de inpenitentia possit, modus penitentiae imponatur. Nos vero auctoritate sanctorum apostolorum Petri et Pauli et penitentiam eis levamus et remissionem peccatorum facimus, oratione prosequentes." On this letter see Francis E. Hagedorn, *General Legislation on Indulgences,* pp. 36–37; Nikolaus Paulus, *Geschichte des Ablasses im Mittelalter vom Ursprunge bis zur Mitte des 14. Jahrhunderts,* 1:195; Dom Edmond Bernardet, "Croisade (Bulle de la)," *DDC,* 4:774; Paul Rousset, *Les Origines et les caractères de la première croisade,* pp. 49–50; Willibald Plöchl, *Geschichte des Kirchenrechts,* 2:242; Erdmann, *Die Entstehung,* p. 125; Runciman, *A History of the Crusades,* 1:90–92; Noth, *Heiliger Krieg und heiliger Kampf,* pp. 109–20; Hans Eberhard Mayer, *Geschichte der Kreuzzüge,* pp. 26, 34–35. M. Villey, *La Croisade,* pp. 143–44, has questioned the authenticity of this letter and Rousset apparently shares his misgivings about it. The text is preserved in the *Collectio Brittanica,* ed. P. Ewald,

Participation in the expedition to Spain is thus specifically declared to be an adequate satisfaction for whatever penance may have been imposed upon the participants by their confessors. The commutation, furthermore, is directly linked to the apostolic authority of the pope. The penitent is required to receive sacramental absolution first and, to judge from the literal meaning of the text, the commutation would apply only to the penance specifically imposed for absolved sins. It might be presumed that actual participation in the reconquista was expected of those who availed themselves of this spiritual favor, although the pope's language specified only the intent (*proficisci destinerunt*). Be that as it may, it is amply evident that the pope's purpose in this letter was to encourage the enlistment of soldiers in the ranks of the reconquista and to assist the vigorous prosecution of the holy war. As a means to achieve this end, he was willing to grant those prosecuting the war a signal spiritual privilege.

Thus by the time that Gregory VII (1073–85) succeeded Alexander II on the papal throne, many of the basic principles of the crusade idea had already been stated in papal declarations and incorporated in canonistic collections—the bulk of them in connection with the campaigns in Spain, although the Spanish expeditions clearly differed from the crusades themselves in a great many significant ways.[91] During Gregory's harried

---

"Die Papstbriefe der Brittischen Sammlung," *Neues Archiv*, 5(1879–80), 338–39, *Epist.* 58. The collection was probably compiled at Rome ca.1090, most likely from the papal registers, and contains some 233 papal letters, dating from Gelasius I (492–96) to Urban II (1088–99). See also Alfons M. Stickler, *Historia iuris canonici latini institutiones academicae*, I, *Historia fontium*, p. 175.

91. Pissard, *La guerre sainte en pays chrétien*, p. 26, goes too far when he states that "il n'est pas exagéré de dire que tous les principes de la croisade étaient déjà contenus en germe dans le droit canonique du temps de Grégoire VII." Elements in common were the fact that participants in the Spanish campaigns enjoyed papal blessings and were rewarded with a remission of penance, that the reconquista involved a war against the Saracens for the defence of Christendom and the reconquest of formerly Christian territories, and that its heroes might even be considered martyrs—but it is a perversion of terms to call the Spanish campaigns at that point "crusades." One of the most essential characteristics of the crusades is the fusion in them of the holy war and pilgrimage traditions; of this there is no sign in the Spanish wars of the eleventh century. Certainly they were holy wars; just as certainly they were not pilgrimages. The warriors in the Spanish campaigns apparently did not enjoy the promises of personal protection which were given to pilgrims at this time and later to crusaders, nor did they have the explicit papal protection for their wives, families, and possessions later given to crusaders. There is no trace, so far as I am aware, of anything like the crusader's vow, which was to become one of the most significant and characteristic legal considerations in the canonistic concept of the crusader. Also lacking in the Spanish expeditions are the insignia of the cross,

pontificate, the holy war principle was further invoked and it is tempting to interpret the scanty texts bearing upon the pope's projected Eastern campaign as a crusade in embryo.

Three texts in Gregory's *Register* bear upon the project for a papal campaign in the East. The first of them is a letter, dated at Rome, 2 February 1074, directed to Count William of Upper Burgundy. In this letter the pope asked William to raise a levy of troops who might be used to preserve the liberties of the Roman Church; evidently he had in mind another expedition against the Normans, but this time one which would frighten them into submission. The pope, however, had a further object in view. He intended, he told Count William, to cross over with this army to Constantinople "in aid of the oft-beset Christians, who cry out in vain under the repeated assaults of the Saracens, that we might stretch out a helping hand to them."[92] Apparently, then, Gregory envisioned the inauguration of another holy war against the Saracens, one which would this time carry the action against them into the Near East and which would specifically aim to assist the Byzantine empire in its struggle against the Seljuk Turks, who were pressing hard and successfully against its frontiers in Asia Minor.[93]

A month later, on 1 March, Gregory made a more general appeal for military aid to Byzantium. Addressing himself to "all those willing to defend the Christian faith," the pope related that the bearer of his letter had brought further news of military disaster in the East and, in relatively vague terms, admonished recipients of the letter not only to join in bewailing the recent reverses, but also to prepare themselves to help redress the situation.[94]

the financial privileges which crusaders came to enjoy, the *privilegium fori* and related legal and jurisdictional privileges. So far as can be seen, there was not even a formal papal proclamation of the war, of the type which was common to the crusade expeditions. In short, the crusades, properly speaking, represent a considerably broader synthesis of ideas and institutions than we find in the eleventh-century reconquista.

92. ". . . in adiutorium christianorum, qui nimium afflicti creberrimis morsibus Saracenorum inaniter flagitant, ut sibi manum nostri auxilii porrigamus." *Das Register Gregors VII* 1.46, ed. Erich Caspar, 2 vols. (*MGH, Ep. sel.,* 2), 1:70–71; partial translation in *CDS,* pp. 8–9.

93. The Seljuk invasion and the collapse of Byzantine defences against them are described by Claude Cahen, "The Turkish Invasions: The Selchükids," and Peter Charanis, "The Byzantine Empire in the Eleventh Century," in *Crusades,* ed. Setton, 1:135–219; Runciman, *History of the Crusades,* 1:51–79; A. A. Vasiliev, *History of the Byzantine Empire,* 1:351–61, 2:375–89.

94. Gregory VII, *Register* 1.49 (ed. Caspar, 1:75–76; trans. in *CDS,* pp. 9–10).

What results these two appeals may have had is hard to determine, but the pope was apparently sufficiently encouraged by the reaction during the spring and summer of 1074 to carry his plans a step further. On 7 December 1074 he wrote a long, intimate letter to the German king, Henry IV (1050–1106), outlining his proposal in greater detail. Christians overseas, he told the king, "are daily being butchered like herds of cattle." Appeals had come to him, begging for assistance, and he had "taken steps to rouse and stir up certain Christians who long to lay down their lives for their brethren by defending the law of Christ." The results to date he found encouraging, for he asserted that more than fifty thousand men (!) were prepared to undertake the expedition. Most interesting are two further assertions. Gregory indicated, first, that it was his intention to lead the expedition himself, and second, that his men were prepared to go all the way to the Lord's sepulchre. Moreover the pope stated that it was his hope that this expedition might be of help in reuniting the Eastern and Western Churches under papal leadership. He closed his letter by asking King Henry's counsel in this enterprise and by affirming his intention, should the expedition materialize, of naming the German king protector of the Roman Church during his absence.[95]

All these plans came to nothing. A year later the pope was embroiled in the investiture struggle with the empire and the projected military intervention in the East was carried no further. Still, even though abortive, this project is of considerable interest for the development of the crusade idea. For the first time, the idea of carrying a holy war into the Near East at the instigation and under the command of the papacy had been broached. Further, although the primary reason for the plan was originally said to be the bolstering of Byzantine defenses against the Muslims, it was clear that by the end of 1074 Gregory was toying with the idea of carrying the war further—all the way to Jerusalem, in fact. In this proposal lay the germ of the idea of bringing together the institutions of holy war and pilgrimage. That synthesis was never made, so far as is known, in the mind of Gregory VII, but it was brought to realization by the canny genius of Urban II.[96]

Gregory VII's pontificate is important in yet another way for the

95. Ibid., 2.31 (ed. Caspar, 1:165–68; trans. in *CDS*, pp. 10–11).
96. On the relationship of Gregory's Eastern project to the crusade as it took shape under Urban II, see especially the conclusions of Erdmann, *Die Entstehung des Kreuzzugsgedankens,* pp. 308–9, and Mayer, *Geschichte der Kreuzzüge,* pp. 26–28.

developing background of the crusade. Under him the holy war became a
central theme of papal policy—most clearly, of course, during the quarrel
with Henry IV. But the military rhetoric of the holy war permeated
Gregory's thought and expression. In his correspondence, those fighting in
the papal cause are individually dignified as Christ's own soldiers, and, as
a group, they are commonly referred to as the *militia Christi*. Conversely,
the bishops and even the Church as a whole are normally referred to in
Gregory's correspondence under military metaphors.[97]

During the brief pontificate of Gregory's immediate successor, Victor
III (1086–87), the holy war idea lay dormant, save perhaps for a dubiously
documented call to holy wars in Italy and Africa.[98] Nonetheless it is
evident that by the beginning of the pontificate of Urban II the idea of
sanctified war had already become well established in ecclesiastical
thought. The papacy had repeatedly recognized and even proclaimed the
waging of wars which were not only considered just, but which might
actually be counted toward the eternal merit of their participants. True,
no formalized general doctrine of holy war had yet been advanced, but
the de facto existence of this species of war had been acknowledged.
Implicit in the acknowledgment was a sense that some sort of papal
sanction was required to sanctify warfare and it was assumed as a matter
of course that a holy war must necessarily be a just one. Given these
conditions it was seemingly clear by 1095 that laymen might fight in a
holy war, not only licitly, but even with reasonable expectation that their
labors would be blessed.

CLERICS AND HOLY WAR. The relation of clerics to the holy war was,
however, more dubious than that of laymen. In theory at least, clerics
were forbidden to bear arms or to fight in person against Christians or
pagans; this point was often reiterated in the most frequently used
eleventh-century canonistic collections.[99] Bishops might not even do auxil-

97. This theme is explored at length by Erdmann, *Die Entstehung des Kreuzzugsgedankens*, pp. 185–96.

98. Evidence for this is furnished by Petrus Diaconus, *Chronica Montis Cassinen-
sis (MGH, SS, 7:751)*. Erdmann, *Die Entstehung des Kreuzzugsgedankens*, pp.
284–85, is inclined to accept this testimony, but Paulus, *Geschichte des Ablasses*,
1:196, is more skeptical of it.

99. Thus Burchard, *Decreta* 2.211 *(PL, 140:661)* = Ivo, *Decretum* 6.286 *(PL,
161:505)* = C. 23 q. 8 c. 6; Ivo, *Decretum* 6.287 *(PL, 161:505)*, 10.34 *(PL, 161:701)*,
10.45 *(PL, 161:702)*. Another much repeated canon directed not only that clerics
might not take arms, but also that any who were killed in battles or in brawls
should not be prayed for and that those who voluntarily took up arms should be

iary duty, for example as lookouts against pirates.[100] Although some modifications and exceptions to these established positions were later admitted, these doctrines were not much controverted on the theoretical level in the period prior to the crusades. Practice, of course, was something else again.[101] Less obvious was the canonistic position of clerics who accompanied an army not as fighters but as counsellors and spiritual guides. It was accepted that clerics should not be allowed to do so indiscriminately, but that a few might fittingly be permitted to travel with the soldiers in order to minister to their spiritual needs. Those who did so were to be selected by the bishops.[102] Pope Gelasius I was inclined to think that the pope should also be consulted, at least before a bishop was allowed to accompany any army.[103] Here again, there was a serious gap between canonistic theory and actual practice, both in the eleventh century and later.

By the late eleventh century, therefore, Western Christendom had arrived at a concept of war, the holy war, which was both novel and important.[104] Although it was built upon the Augustinian notion of the just war, the holy war went well beyond the positions which Augustine had set forth. Not only was the holy war considered not offensive to God, but it was thought to be positively pleasing to Him. Participants were not merely held to act in a morally acceptable fashion, but their fighting in a blessed cause was believed to be a virtuous act which merited God's special favor, as embodied in the commutation of penance granted by papal proclamation.

It is to the fusion of this tradition with the much older tradition of Christian pilgrimage that we now turn.

---

degraded and confined in a monastery: Burchard, *Decreta* 2.233 (*PL,* 140:664) = Ivo, *Decretum* 6.308 (*PL,* 161:508) = C. 23 q. 8 c. 4. The whole matter is reviewed by F. Poggiaspalla, "La chiesa e la partecipazione dei chierici alla guerra nella legislazione conciliare fino alla Decretali di Gregorio IX," *Ephemerides iuris canonici,* 15(1959), 140–53.

100. *JL,* 2,788 = Ivo, *Decretum* 5.334 (*PL,* 161:424) = C. 23 q. 8 c. 19.

101. For an account of the military involvements of German bishops in the tenth and early eleventh centuries, see Edgar N. Johnson, *The Secular Activities of the German Episcopate, 919–1024,* pp. 206–18.

102. Burchard, *Decreta* 1.218–19 (*PL,* 140:612–13) = Ivo, *Decretum* 5.332–33 (*PL,* 161:424).

103. *JL,* 735 = C. 23 q. 8 c. 26.

104. It was novel, at any rate, in Western Christian thinking, although already well developed in Muslim doctrine; on this see especially Noth, *Heiliger Krieg und heiliger Kampf,* pp. 13–92. Noth is able to point to an impressive list of parallels between Muslim and Christian ideas of holy war (pp. 139–46), but no direct connection between the two sets of ideas can be shown.

CHAPTER II

The Crusade Vow to the Early Thirteenth Century

Vovete et reddite Domino Deo vestro,
Omnes qui in circuitu ejus affertis munera terribili.

Ps. 75.12

THE CRUSADE: HOLY WAR AND PILGRIMAGE. As a canonical basis for the crusades, the eleventh-century Church made use of two established institutions: the pilgrimage and the holy war. The crusader combined in his person characteristic features of the participants in both these enterprises. Like the pilgrim, he was bound by a vow to make a journey to a sacred shrine; he enjoyed the benefits of a privileged personal status in ecclesiastical law, of guarantees of immunity, of hospitality. Like a soldier in a holy war, he was bound to fight for the declared objectives of the campaign in which he volunteered his services, and was promised a spiritual reward which took the form of a remission of the punishment merited by his sinful past. He might, too, at least in popular belief, be considered a martyr if he died on campaign.[1]

1. References to slain crusaders as martyrs are common in the crusade chroniclers; e.g., *Gesta Francorum et aliorum Hierosolimitanorum,* ed. and trans. Rosalind M. T. Hill and Sir Roger Mynors: "Isti primo felix acceperunt martirium pro nomine Domini Iesu. . . . quem statim super altare martirizauerunt. [1.2, p. 4]" "Fuimusque in obsidione illa per septem ebdomadas et tres dies, et multi ex nostris illic receperunt martyrium, et letantes gaudentesque reddiderunt felices animas Deo; et ex pauperrima gente multi mortui sunt fame pro Christi nomine. Qui in caelum triumphantes portarunt stolam recepti martyrii. . . . [2.8, p. 17]" "Fueruntque in illa die martyrizati ex nostris militibus seu peditibus plus quam mille, qui ut credimus in caelum ascenderunt, et candidati stolam martyrii receperunt. [7.18, p. 40]" Cf. Norman Daniel, *Islam and the West: The Making of an Image,* pp. 314–15; Kantoro-

The term "peregrinus" was consistently, indeed almost invariably, used to describe crusaders from the time of the first crusade up to the end of the twelfth century, when more specific terms, of which *crucesignatus* was the most common, began to come into use. Even so, "peregrinus" continued to be applied indiscriminately both to unarmed pilgrims and to crusaders throughout the thirteenth and fourteenth centuries. Nor was this merely an accident of speech or a mistaken notion reflected in popular language. Juridically, the crusader was first and foremost a pilgrim, although a pilgrim of a special type, inasmuch as he was pledged to fight a holy war in the course of achieving his pilgrimage goal.[2]

This momentous combination of the roles of pilgrim and participant in a holy war was first spelled out in the famous speech of Pope Urban II at Clermont on 27 November 1095.

THE PROCLAMATION OF THE FIRST CRUSADE. The thematic relations of the five principal accounts of Pope Urban's exhortation at Clermont have been analyzed in detail by D. C. Munro.[3] There is a solid core of agreement among the various writers who preserve versions of the pope's address, even though no account is strictly contemporary with the event and obviously none relates verbatim what the pope actually said. Furthermore, their evidence is supplemented and reinforced to some degree by the pope's letters to the princes of Flanders and to the people of Bologna, as well as by the canon of the Council of Clermont concerning the crusade. The evidence from all of these sources concerning the canonistic mechanisms governing the crusade is relatively slight. Some mention, however, was apparently made, either in the pope's public address on 27 November or, more likely, in his allocution on the following day to the clergy, of the character of those who should participate in the expedition. This element in the pope's speech is most fully related by Fulcher of Chartres and Robert the Monk, who agree that Urban outlined the

wicz, *The King's Two Bodies*, pp. 238–39; Rousset, *Les Origines et les caractères*, pp. 81–84, where further examples are cited.

2. Crusaders were so different from the usual pious travellers that the author of the *Gesta Francorum* notes that the Byzantines refused to regard them as pilgrims at all: "ualde timebant nos, non putantes nos esse peregrinos, sed uelle populari terram et occidere eos" (*Gesta Francorum* 1.4, ed. Hill, p. 8). There was doubtless much to be said for the Byzantines' fears—especially as the narrator continues: "Quapropter apprehendemus boues, equos et asinos, et omnia quae inueniebamus."

3. "The Speech of Pope Urban II at Clermont, 1095," *AHR*, 11(1906), 231–42.

juristic mechanism of the crusade vow at some point in his discussion at Clermont, and directed those who had vowed to participate to sew crosses to their apparel as a symbol of their commitment.[4] Robert the Monk testifies that the pope sought to dissuade the elderly and feeble, and all noncombatants in general, from accompanying the armies of the crusade. Women were not to join the expedition, unless they were accompanied by husbands, brothers, or guardians. Priests and monks were to come only if they had previously secured the permission of their bishops. The expedition, in short, was to be composed of able-bodied fighting men, and even they were advised to secure the blessings of their priests before committing themselves to the venture.[5] Finally, the pope appointed Adhémar of Monteil, Bishop of Le Puy, as papal legate to accompany the crusade army[6] and commissioned the bishops at the council to preach the crusade upon their return to their dioceses.[7]

Brief and scanty as these accounts are, they nonetheless outline a basic juridical structure which marked the crusade ever after. The first and most fundamental element in this structure was the crusade vow. This, as Michel Villey has pointed out, was the means by which the papacy was able to convert the immediate enthusiasm of would-be crusaders into a permanent obligation which could be enforced, if need be, by formal, legal sanctions.[8] While the momentary enthusiasm of a crowd fired up by a crusade preacher might evaporate, the juristic mechanism of the vow made it possible for the Church to turn this enthusiasm into a binding

---

4. Fulcher of Chartres, *Historia Hierosolymitana* 1.4.4 (ed. Hagenmeyer, pp. 140–42; also trans. Martha E. McGinty, p. 18). Robert the Monk, *Historia Iherosolimitana* 1.2 (*RHC, Occ,* 3:729–30; trans, in *CDS,* pp. 17–21). Cf. the accounts of Baldric of Dol, *Historia de peregrinatione Jerosolimitana* 1 (*RHC, Occ,* 4:16) and Guibert of Nogent, *Gesta Dei per Francos* 2.5 (*RHC, Occ,* 4:140). The pope himself mentioned the vow casually in his letter of December 1095 to the Flemings: *Epistulae et chartae ad historiam primi belli sacri spectantes,* ed. Heinrich Hagenmeyer, p. 137. Noth, *Heiliger Krieg und heiliger Kampf,* pp. 120–39, has recently questioned the part played by the vow in the first crusade.

5. Robert the Monk, *Historia* 1.2 (*RHC, Occ,* 3:729–30; trans. in *CDS,* p. 20). See also Urban's own comments on this matter in his letter to the Bolognese, dated 19 September 1096 (*Epistulae et chartae,* ed. Hagenmeyer, pp. 137–38).

6. Baldric of Dol, *Historia* 1.5 (*RHC, Occ,* 4:15–16); Robert the Monk, *Historia* 1.4 (*RHC, Occ,* 3:731); and especially Pope Urban's own letter to the people of Flanders (*Epistulae et chartae,* ed. Hagenmeyer, pp. 136–37).

7. Fulcher of Chartres, *Historia* 1.4.2–3 (ed. Hagenmeyer, pp. 139–40; trans. McGinty, pp. 17–18); Robert the Monk, *Historia* 1.2 (*RHC, Occ,* 3:729–30); Guibert of Nogent, *Gesta* 2.6 (*RHC, Occ,* 4:140).

8. Villey, *La Croisade,* pp. 119–20, and more recently in "L'Idée de la croisade."

commitment, of the highest importance for preventing the crusade armies from dwindling into insignificant forces as they went along. The perception of this was one of Pope Urban's most important contributions to the shaping of the crusade.

THE ORIGINS OF CHRISTIAN VOWS. The idea of the vow itself was, of course, scarcely a novelty in 1095. Some sort of system of vows (taken in the general sense of a promise or commitment made to a deity) is found in virtually every religious system. The Old Testament abounds in references to vows of various kinds and one whole chapter of Leviticus is devoted to an elaborate discussion of the obligations arising from them and the means of satisfying those obligations.[9] The Church fathers, too, spoke on occasion of vows, though generally not in the specifically juristic sense of an undertaking which entailed enforceable moral or legal obligations.[10]

Certainly no monk or priest, even if not a profound student of the Mosaic law or the fathers, could have escaped some acquaintance with the notion of the obligations arising from vows, when, for example, he read or chanted every Monday at Vespers: "Vota mea Domino reddam in conspectu omnis populi eius; in atriis domus Domini, in medio tui, Jerusalem."[11] As persons bound by vows themselves, moreover, members of

9. Lev. 27. The problem of vows and the obligations resulting from them also occupies an important place in the New Testament, for Jesus took serious issue with the Pharisees on the question of the binding force of votive obligations and dispensations from vows: Matt. 15.3–6, Mk. 7.9–14; cf. Samuel Belkin, "Dissolution of Vows and the Problem of Anti-Social Oaths in the Gospels and Contemporary Jewish Literature," *Journal of Biblical Literature*, 55(1936), 227–34, and George W. Buchanan, "Some Vow and Oath Formulas in the New Testament," *Harvard Theological Review*, 58(1965), 319–26. The Talmudic literature is also rich in its treatment of the law of votive obligations and the annulment of vows. The lengthy tractate *Nedarim* ("Vows") of *Seder Nashim* in the *Babylonian Talmud* is entirely devoted to the subject, which also crops up elsewhere, e.g. *Kettuboth* 62b–63a, *'Arakin* 19a–21b (references are to the Soncino edition by Isidore Epstein). (I am much indebted to Professor Jacob Neusner of Dartmouth College for information about problems of Talmudic law.)

10. Germaine Capelle, *Le Voeu d'obéissance dès origines au XIIᵉ siècle*, pp. 5–32, discusses the usage of the term "vow" and related words in antiquity and by the fathers.

11. Ps. 115.18–19; St. Benedict, *Regula monachorum* 18 (ed. Hanslik, p. 71) prescribes this psalm for Vespers. Other references to vows and the satisfaction of votive obligations are frequent in the Psalter, which the Rule prescribes must be sung in its entirety each week: ibid., 18 (ed. Hanslik, p. 71).

monastic communities throughout the medieval world must have been rather keenly aware of the binding force of obligations arising from these promises.[12]

The notion of the vow as an act which produced a legally binding obligation was not unknown, either, to the teachers and scholars who, at just about the period when Pope Urban II proclaimed the crusade, were beginning to investigate and expound the Roman law.[13] The Roman law notions that the obligation arising from a vow rested upon the person making the vow, not upon the thing which was vowed, and that the vow created an heritable obligation, were to play a major role in the development of the canonistic doctrines of the vow during the twelfth and thirteenth centuries.[14] And not only were the strictly legal notions of the vow familiar in the technical literature studied by the jurists, but also the notion of the vow and its binding consequences was widely reflected in nontechnical Latin literature—notably in Cicero, Virgil, and Ovid, to mention only three of the more frequently read authors who were likely to be known to literate Europeans in the eleventh and twelfth centuries.[15]

12. St. Benedict nowhere in his Rule uses the term "votum," however. Ch. 58, which deals with the profession of monks, consistently uses the verb *promittere* to describe the act by which monks bind themselves to the observance of the Rule and its precepts; the same verb is used to describe the dedication of an oblate (c. 59) and the reception of a priest in the community (c. 60). These promises seemingly were made to the abbot, not to God, and hence they were not vows in a proper sense at all. A promise of chastity was required of candidates for ordination to the subdiaconate and higher orders from the sixth century onwards, but again this promise did not technically constitute a vow. L. Hertling, "Die Professio der Kleriker und die Entstehung der drei Gelübde," *Zeitschrift für katholische Theologie,* 56(1932), 148–74. Monastic vows in the strict, juridical sense of the term appear only toward the end of the eighth century; see Capelle, *Le Voeu d'obéissance,* p. 239.

13. Irnerius, for example, had begun to lecture at Bologna just a few years prior to the Council of Clermont—Sir Paul Vinogradoff, *Roman Law in Medieval Europe,* p. 56, would date the commencement of his lectures ca.1088. See also Kantorowicz, *Studies in the Glossators of the Roman Law,* pp. 33, 69.

14. *Dig.* 50.12.2 pr., 2. The whole subject of the Roman law concerning vows has been studied by Juliette Turlan, "L'Obligation 'ex voto'," *RHDF,* 4th ser., 33(1955), 502–36.

15. The vows referred to in the literature are basically of two kinds: one of them is the active vow, by which a person promised the performance of an act, the gift of an object, or the accomplishment of some specific deed in return for a favor to be granted by the deity. This type of vow is the ancestor of the pilgrimage or crusade vow. The other type, which also persists in Christianity, is a vow to live a life of dedication to the deity, a type which is the ancestor of the monastic vows. See Capelle, *Le Voeu d'obéissance,* p. 2. See, for example, *De legibus* 2.9, 12, *De natura deorum* 3.37, *In Verrem* 2.4.55.123, *Pro Milone* 15, and *Ad Atticum* 12.18,43; *Aeneid*

DISPENSATIONS FROM VOWS. A persistent problem with vows, both for those who had made them and found their fulfillment unexpectedly difficult or even impossible, and for canonists who sought to understand and explain their juridical character, was the question of dispensation. While it is clear that in a general way some forms of relaxation of the prescriptions of law in special cases were in use in the Church from quite early times,[16] nevertheless dispensation from the obligations flowing from vows presented particular difficulties for the canonists. The most perplexing of these arose from the fact that votive obligations were not usually considered to be a creation of the positive law, but were believed to originate rather in the natural law. While the canonists could find ample grounds for allowing dispensations from the provisions of the positive law,[17] it was quite another matter to justify relaxation of natural law obligations. From the time of Pope St. Leo I (440–61), however, the popes had often been described as enjoying a *plenitudo potestatis*.[18] Gradually this term came to denote a kind of spiritual sovereignty, from which the canonists could then deduce the most sweeping powers, including the

---

5.53, 5.234–43, 7.471, 9.624–41; *Metamorphoses* 7.594, 8.80, *Ars amatoria* 1.486, 737–38.

16. For a general review of dispensation in the early Church, see J. de Brys, *De dispensatione in iure canonico*, pp. 25–30.

17. Canonistic treatment of dispensations found its roots particularly in the Roman law, where the emperor's prerogatives clearly included the right to dispense from the prescriptions of positive law: *Inst.* 1.2.6; *Dig.* 1.4.1; *Cod.* 1.14.9, 12; 1.17.1, etc. Buckland, *Textbook of Roman Law*, pp. 13–15. The canonists came to ascribe these imperial prerogatives to the popes with increasing frequency from the eleventh century onward. On this development, see especially Walter Ullmann, *The Growth of Papal Government in the Middle Ages*.

18. Leo I, *Epist.* 14.1, 11 (*PL*, 54:671, 676), is the earliest occurrence of the term. On the evolution of this term and its correlative, *pars sollicitudinis*, see especially Jean Rivière, "In partem sollicitudinis: Evolution d'une formule pontificale," *Revue des sciences religieuses*, 5(1925), 210–31; Gerhard B. Ladner, "The Concepts of 'Ecclesia' and 'Christianitas' and Their Relation to the Idea of Papal 'Plenitudo potestatis' from Gregory VII to Boniface VIII," *Miscellanea historiae pontificiae*, 18(1954), 49–77; Gaines Post, "*Plena potestas* and Consent in Medieval Assemblies," *Traditio*, 1(1943), 355–408 (revised version in his *Studies in Medieval Legal Thought*, pp. 91–168); Yves Congar, "L'Ecclésiologie de S. Bernard," in *Saint Bernard théologien*, pp. 136–90; John A. Watt, "The Use of the Term 'Plenitudo Potestatis' by Hostiensis," in *Proceedings of the Second International Congress of Medieval Canon Law*, pp. 161–87 (also "Summary of Discussions," pp. 205–6), and "The Theory of Papal Monarchy in the Thirteenth Century: The Contribution of the Canonists," *Traditio*, 20(1964), 179–317; R. L. Benson, "Plenitudo Potestatis: Evolution of a Formula from Gregory IV to Gratian," *Studia Gratiana*, 14(1967), 193–217.

power to abrogate votive obligations. The developing discussion of the power of dispensing from vows thus paralleled the developing idea of the plenitude of papal power itself.

THE VOW IN CANON LAW BEFORE 1140. Before 1095 a well-defined doctrine of the vow and its resultant obligations did not exist in Western canon law. The most important of the late eleventh-century canonistic writers, Ivo of Chartres, whose major canonistic collections were compiled at almost exactly the time when Urban II was proclaiming the first crusade at Clermont,[19] reflects the inchoate state of canonistic doctrine on this point. Essentially, Ivo's collections set forth five principles concerning vows: first, a vow creates an enforceable obligation or, in other words, what is vowed must be done lest punishment follow;[20] second, actions which were lawful before taking a vow may become unlawful afterwards if they tend to vitiate the vow;[21] next, foolish vows should not be kept;[22] fourth, a monk may not take vows without the permission of his abbot;[23] and finally, a married person may not lawfully make a vow without the consent of his spouse.[24] However basic these concepts may have been—to-gether, of course, with the underlying theological notion that vows were in themselves effective aids to salvation—they are far from constituting a coherent juridical theory of the vow. For one thing, the notion of dispen-sation from vows—at least in a proper sense of the word—plays no part in Ivo's teaching, although he occasionally uses the word "dispensatio" to mean an alteration of the law.[25] For another thing, the doctrine of votive obligations is only partially developed, although the rudiments of a

19. Ivo's three canonistic collections—the *Decretum*, the *Panormia*, and the *Tri-partita*—all date from the years 1094–96. See Paul Fournier and Gabriel Le Bras, *Histoire des collections canoniques en occident depuis les fausses décrétales jusqu'au Décret de Gratien*, 2:55–57, 105–6; also Rolf Sprandel, *Ivo von Chartres und seine Stellung in der Kirchengeschichte;* Capelle, *Le Voeu d'obéissance*, pp. 210–11.

20. Ivo, *Decretum* 7.19 (*PL*, 161:549) = *Panormia* 3.183 (*PL*, 161:1173) = C. 20 q. 3 c. 1; 7.20 (*PL*, 161:549) = C. 20 q. 1 c. 8; 7.146 (*PL*, 161:580) = C. 27 q. 1 c. 16; 8.137 (*PL*, 161:614). *Panormia* 3.192 (*PL*, 161:1175–76) = D. 27 c. 5; 3.199 (*PL*, 161:1177) = C. 27 q. 5 c. 34.

21. Ivo, *Decretum* 8.73 (*PL*, 161:599) = C. 32 q. 8 c. un.; *Panormia* 3.200 (*PL*, 161:1177) = C. 27 q. 1 c. 33.

22. Ivo, *Decretum* 12.64 (*PL*, 161:796) = C. 22 q. 4 c. 14.

23. Ibid., 7.32 (*PL*, 161:553) = C. 20 q. 4 c. 2.

24. Ibid., 8.136 (*PL*, 161:614) = C. 33 q. 5 c. 4.

25. Ibid., prol. (*PL*, 161:51, 57). On Ivo's idea of dispensation see Sprandel, *Ivo von Chartres*, pp. 77–85.

coherent theory are formulated in a passage of the prologue to his *Decretum* in which he discusses the necessity of observing the terms of a vow and the change in status resulting from the making of a vow.[26] He does not use the term *obligatio* in a restricted, technical sense here, however, and his whole treatment of vows lacks a well-developed theoretical structure. Indeed, it was only after the first crusade that a comprehensive theory of the vow in general and the crusade vow in particular developed in canonistic literature.[27]

Although the nature of votive obligations was not clearly defined by the canonists at the time of the first crusade, this is not to say that there was no generally accepted belief in the binding power of the crusade vow from the very beginning. On the contrary, comparatively early in the history of the first expedition we meet with pejorative references to discouraged crusaders who had turned back to their homes. Thus, when the Norman princes determined to spend the winter of 1096–97 in Calabria, Fulcher relates that:

> Many of the commoners were discouraged at that point, fearing that they would be poverty-stricken. Accordingly they there sold their bows, took up again the staff of pilgrimage, and returned like cowards to their homes. For this reason they became outcasts before God and man and their action became a reproach to them.[28]

At least according to Ordericus Vitalis (whose credibility on the point leaves something to be desired), Pope Urban II had pronounced excommunication upon any crusaders who left the ranks of the expedition be-

---

26. Ivo, *Decretum, prol.* (*PL*, 161:49). Basing his argument on this passage, H. Hoffmann, *Gottesfriede und Treuga Dei*, pp. 199–200, concludes that Ivo accepted the view that a vow to observe the Truce of God gave rise to an enforceable obligation. The enforcement of the Truce might take the form of a military campaign—almost a "crusade" in a very loose sense—against those who failed to observe the terms of their vows. For examples, see ibid., pp. 211–21.

27. There may be some marginal significance in the use by Robert the Monk, reporting Pope Urban's speech at Clermont, of the term *sponsio Deo* to describe the taking of the crusade vow: *Historia* 1.2 (*RHC, Occ*, 3:729). In the terminology of Roman law, the *sponsio voti* denotes a promise or oath pronounced during ceremonial libations that created a solemn and irrevocable obligation to the deity to whom it was addressed. See Turlan, "L'Obligation 'ex voto'," pp. 515–20; Kaser, *Das römische Privatrecht*, 1:150–52, 2:330–31.

28. Fulcher, *Historia* 1.7.5 (ed. Hagenmeyer, p. 168): "tunc vero plurimi de plebe desolati, inopiam etiam futuram metuentes, arcubus suis ibi venditis et baculis peregrinationis resumptis, ad domos suas ignavi regressi sunt. Qua de re tam Deo quam hominibus viles effecti sunt et versum est eis in opprobrium."

fore reaching Jerusalem.[29] Other and more reliable evidence also points to a very similar conclusion, namely that the crusader, once he had made his vow, was considered to be permanently committed to accompany the crusade expedition until its goal had been reached. The papal legate with the crusade army, Bishop Adhémar of Le Puy, the Patriarch Simeon of Jerusalem, and other bishops also denounced those renegades who had deserted the expedition prematurely and demanded that they be compelled to fulfill the obligation arising from their vows.[30] Writing from Jerusalem after the capture of the city by the crusaders in 1099, Archbishop Manasses of Reims instructed his correspondent, Bishop Lambert of Arles, to take measures against those who had made the crusade vow but had not fulfilled their obligation, so that they might be constrained to discharge their commitment, at least if they were physically and financially capable of doing so.[31] Toward the end of the year 1099, too, Pope Paschal II instructed the prelates of France that crusaders who had not fulfilled the obligation arising from their vows were to be compelled to do so under pain of infamy:

> You are to compel those especially who, having vowed this service, have taken the sign of the cross, to proceed to that place, unless they are hindered by the stumbling-block of poverty. Otherwise, we decree that they be treated as infamous persons. Those of timid and feeble faith who turned back from the siege of Antioch shall remain excommunicate unless they pledge upon reliable security that they will return.[32]

The last sentence of the pope's letter refers to the notable desertion of Count Stephen of Chartres and Blois from the ranks of the crusading army on 2 June 1098. Stephen's career, moreover, indicates that papal sanctions against those who failed to fulfill their crusade obligations could be reasonably effective. Upon Stephen's return to the West, he met with a hostile reception, not only from the Church, but also from his peers, including most especially his wife, Adèle, so that his position finally

29. Ordericus Vitalis, *Historia ecclesiastica* 10.11 (ed. A. Le Prévost, 4:67–68).
30. *Epistulae et chartae* (ed. Hagenmeyer, pp. 142, 148–49).
31. Ibid., p. 176.
32. Ibid., p. 175: "Eos praesertim, qui huius militia uoto crucis signa sumpserunt, illuc properare compellite, nisi paupertatis retineantur obstaculo: alioquin eos infames haberi decernimus. qui uero de Antiochena obsidione fide pusillanimi et ambigua recesserunt, in excommunicatione permaneant, nisi se redituros certis securitatibus confirmauerint." On the penalty of *infamia* see Peter Landau, *Die Entstehung des kanonischen Infamiebegriffs von Gratian bis zur Glossa Ordinaria.*

became intolerable.[33] As a result, when a new expedition to the East was forming in 1100, Stephen joined forces with this group to make the journey to Palestine once again and to complete his pilgrimage. It was only on Palm Sunday, 30 March 1102, that Stephen finally reached Jerusalem where, after his many grim adventures, he was at last able to fulfill his crusade vow by worshipping at the Holy Sepulchre. A few weeks later he was captured and slain by the Muslims at Ramleh while fighting in defence of the Holy Land.[34]

Still, even after the first crusade it can scarcely be said that the juristic notion of the vow had been well worked out or analyzed in detail by western legal writers. Rather, this was to be the accomplishment of the twelfth- and thirteenth-century canonists.

THE DOCTRINE OF VOWS IN THE DECRETUM GRATIANI. The canon law may be said to have come of age with the appearance ca.1140 of the *Concordia discordantium canonum* (usually known as the *Decretum*), compiled and edited by the Camaldolese monk, Gratian of Bologna. In Gratian's work, for the first time, not only was a comprehensive collection of the whole complex body of the ecclesiastical legislation of the Church assembled in one treatise, but the collected materials were also subjected to a rigorous dialectical analysis. Although Gratian's work was not an "official" collection, it became almost immediately upon its appearance the fundamental and universally used canonistic collection, upon which all subsequent studies of the canon law depended.[35]

Somewhat surprisingly, Gratian nowhere deals in the *Decretum* explicitly with the juristic problems posed by the crusade or with the status of crusaders. He does, however, treat in several different contexts some of the

33. Ordericus Vitalis, *Historia* 10.19 (ed. Le Prévost, 4:118–19).

34. See Brundage, "An Errant Crusader: Stephen of Blois," *Traditio*, 16(1960), 380–95, and Paul Rousset, "Etienne de Blois, croisé, fuyard et martyr," *Genava*, new ser., 11(1963), 183–95.

35. The literature dealing with the work of Gratian is enormous, but perhaps the best brief study is Stephan Kuttner, *Harmony from Dissonance: An Interpretation of Medieval Canon Law*. The traditional date of 1140 for the *Decretum* has been vigorously questioned, but is convincingly defended by Gérard Fransen, "La Date du Décret de Gratien," *Revue d'histoire ecclésiastique*, 51(1956), 521–31. See also R. Gansiniec and G. Fransen, "Le premier abrégé du Décret de Gratien," *Revue d'histoire ecclésiastique*, 52(1957), 865–70; G. Le Bras, "Le Triomphe de Gratien," *Studia Gratiana*, 1(1953), 3–14.

fundamental problems and doctrines involved, including the problem of the vow.

Gratian's most extensive treatment of the vow and its canonistic implications occurs in Causa 17 of the *Decretum*. The case proposed as a basis for the exposition of this *causa* is that of a priest who, during a grave illness, professed a desire to become a monk and in consequence released his church and benefice to an *advocatus*. Upon recovery from his illness, however, the priest revoked his decision, and sought to recover his church and benefice.

Upon this not entirely hypothetical situation, Gratian bases his discussion of the nature of vows and of the obligations which arise from them. The discussion commences with a *questio* in which Gratian poses the problem: *Utrum reus uoti teneatur, an liceat ei a proposito sui cordis discedere?* It is noteworthy that the way in which the question is framed reflects a certain confusion of terms, since the question itself refers to the undertaking at issue as a *propositum,* while the body of the text refers to a votum.[36]

The treatment of this question opens with a dictum in which Gratian states the basic contention (grounded upon the Psalmist's injunction, "To the Lord your God let vows be made and paid") that it is unlawful to fail to do what has been vowed.[37] In support of this position, Gratian cites four canons: one from Cassiodorus (c. 1; wrongly attributed to St. Augustine), one from the *Liber de bonis uiduitatis* attributed to St. Augustine (c. 2), and two from St. Gregory the Great (c. 3–4). Only one of these canons (c. 3) appeared in any of the earlier canonistic collections, and that one occurred but a single time, in the *Tripartita* of Ivo of Chartres.[38]

36. On the significance of these terms see Capelle, *Le Voeu d'obéissance,* pp. 31–32. Essentially a vow means a promise made to God, while in patristic Latin a propositum means a firm, definite resolution to accomplish some objective.

37. "Quod a uoto discedere non liceat, multis auctoritatibus probatur. Ait enim Propheta: 'Vouete et reddite Domino Deo uestro' [Ps. 75.12]." This basic position was also enunciated earlier in the *Decretum,* C. 12 q. 1 c. 9: "Quicumque uestrum communem uitam susceptam habet, et uouit se nichil proprium habere, uideat ne pollicitationem suam irritam faciat, sed hoc, quod Domino pollicitus est, fideliter custodiat, ne dampnationem sibi, sed premium acquirat, satius [*lect. al.:* sanctius *vel* melius] est non uouere, quam uotum, prout melius potest, non perficere. Grauius enim puniuntur qui uotum perfecerunt aut in malis uitam finierunt, quam illi, qui siue uoto aut fide mortui sunt, et tamen bona egerunt opera."

38. On Ivo and the *Tripartita,* see Stickler, *Historia iuris canonici latini,* pp. 180–81; Fournier and Le Bras, *Histoire de collections canoniques,* 2:55–57, 105–6.

The first of the four canons cited by Gratian enunciates the basic premise that the making of a vow creates an enforceable obligation to perform the action vowed, although the sanctions for enforcement are not specified.[39] The second canon relates to the vow of virginity in particular and states that for those who have taken this vow it is grievously sinful (*dampnabile*) even to desire marriage. This point might be further generalized to mean that the wish to break any vow is morally wrong.[40] Canon three makes the point that those who are under a votive obligation and who fail to fulfill their vows are in danger of divine judgment.[41] The fourth canon further takes the position that *deliberatio* on a proposed course of conduct creates an obligation to follow through that course, and that failure to do so is gravely sinful.[42]

In his dictum at the end of the first questio, Gratian summed up the principles enunciated in the canons he had cited: a vow creates an obligation which is enforceable and must be absolved; even the wish not to fulfill a votive obligation is sinful; a vow becomes binding when it is mentally resolved upon, even if it is not pronounced orally. To the last of these principles, however, Gratian proposes a dialectical distinction: it is one thing to entertain (*concipere*) a proposal mentally and even to pronounce it aloud; but it is quite another thing to place oneself under the obligation of a vow.[43] Applying this distinction to the case in point, Gratian went on in *questio secunda* to pose authorities who supported the view that one does not become bound by a vow to enter a monastery until

---

39. "Sunt quedam, que etiam non uouentes debemus; quedam etiam, que nisi uouerimus, non debemus, sed postquam ea Deo promittimus, necessario reddere constringimur." The canon is a paraphrase of Cassiodorus' commentary on Ps. 75.11.

40. "Vouentibus [*scil.*: uirginitatem] non solum nubere, sed etiam uelle dampnabile est." This canon also appears earlier in the *Decretum* as D. 27 c. 4.

41. "Ananias Deo pecunias uouerat, quas post diaboli uictus persuasione subtraxit. Sed qua morte mulctatus est, scis [Acts 5.1–5]. Si ergo ille mortis periculo dignus fuit, qui eos, quos dederat, nummos Deo abstulit, considera, quanto periculo in diuino dignus eris iudicio, qui non nummos, sed temetipsum omnipotenti Deo (cui te sub monachali habitu deuoueras) subtraxisti." This canon is taken from the letters of Gregory I, *Ep.* 1.33 (*JL,* 1,103, dated 16 March 591).

42. "Qui bona agunt, si meliora agere deliberant, et post deliberata non faciunt, licet in bonis prioribus perseuerent, in conspectu tamen Dei ceciderunt ex deliberatione. *Item* 1. Sunt qui cuncta relinquere, et Dei servicio se subdere, et freno castitatis se restringere deliberant; sed cum post castitatem alios cecidisse conspiciunt, se retrahando meritum perdunt." The canon is a paraphrase of Gregory I, *Super Ezechielem* 1.3.

43. "His ita respondetur; aliud est propositum corde concipere, et etiam ore enunciare; aliud est subsequenti obligatione se reum uoti facere."

one has actually entered the community or subjected oneself to the abbot or made a written promise to do so.[44] Of the three canons cited, the first is a decretal of Alexander II, the second an excerpt from a letter of St. Augustine, and the third is ascribed to a Council of Toledo. Only the first two are relevant to the problem of vows. Canon 1 makes the point that it is not sufficient for a person simply to announce a desire to become a monk, but rather that he must enter a monastery and spend a year as a novice on probation before he becomes bound by an obligation to lead the monastic life.[45] The second canon deals with a situation in which an individual who has expressed a desire to enter the monastic life is unable to do so because of his marriage.[46] On this point, Gratian commented that even though an individual had conceived the notion of becoming a monk and had expressed orally his desire to do so, he was nevertheless not bound to carry through the proposal.[47]

Gratian nowhere dealt with the specific problem of dispensation from vows and votive obligations, although he did present a general doctrine of dispensation from ecclesiastical law. The clear teaching of his own dicta and of the canons which he cited in support of his view was that

44. "Quia ergo iste propositum sui cordis ore simpliciter enunciauit, non autem monasterio aut abbati se tradidit, nec promisionem scripsit nequaquam reus uoti habetur." C. 17 q. 1 d. p. c. 4.

45. "Cosaldus presbiter, quondam infirmitate feruore passionis pressus, monachum se fieri promisit, non tamen monasterio aut abbati se tradidit, nec promissionem scripsit, sed beneficium ecclesiae in manu aduocati refutauit. At postquam conualuit, mox se monachum negauit fieri. Quopropter quia et B. Benedicti regula et precipue patris et predecessoris nostri S. Gregorii papae canonica institutio interdicit monachum ante unius anni probationem effici, iudicamus et auctoritate apostolica precipimus, ut prefatus presbiter beneficium et altaria recipiat, habeat, et quiete retineat." This is, obviously, the situation described in the causa upon which the whole discussion of vows is based.

46. "Nos nouimus, nos testes sumus, quod omnes actus publicos, quibus occupatus eras, relinquere cupiebas, et te in otium sanctum conferre, atque in ea uita uiuere, in qua serui Dei monachi uiuunt. Cum ergo te esse in hoc proposito gauderemus, nauigasti, uxorem duxisti. Si coniugem non haberes, dicerem tibi quod et Tubanis diximus, ut in castitate continenter uiueres. Sed ut te ad istam uitam non exhorter, coniunx est inpedimento, sine eius consensu continenter tibi uiuere non licet, quia et si tu eam post illa uerba Tubanensia ducere non debueras, illa tamen nichil eorum sciens innocenter tibi et simpliciter nupsit."

47. "Ecce iste se corde concepit monachum fieri, et ore pronunciauit, se uelle in otium sanctum conferre, non tamen postea coactus est suscipere quod corde concepit, et ore pronunciauit." C. 17 q. 2 d. p. c. 2. (The third and fourth questiones of Causa 17 deal with other facets of the monastic profession—residence obligations and loss of property—and are not relevant to the present discussion.)

dispensations from the law are frequently required and must be granted,[48] in order to adjust the law to changes in the times and to the various conditions of men.[49] There are, however, limits beyond which the dispensing power may not go. No one may dispense from the gospel precepts or from the requirements of the natural law, although even here some latitude is conceded where it might be necessary to choose the lesser of two evils.[50] Gratian apparently found it unnecessary to distinguish between dispensation, by which a vow or other legal obligation was entirely absolved without the imposition of any further obligation, and redemption or commutation, by which another obligation was substituted in place of the one originally assumed.[51]

Elsewhere in the *Decretum,* Gratian dealt with some of the special problems posed by the vows made by persons who were subject to others, such as minors, monks, and married persons. Essentially, his teaching was that vows and other commitments generally were not binding when made by minors without consent of their parents or guardians[52] and might be revoked by the parent or guardian if timely action was taken.[53] On the other hand, minors might be held bound by commitments made for them by their parents.[54] His position on this matter generally followed the teaching of the Roman law.[55] Likewise monks were forbidden to make vows without the consent of their abbots; should they do otherwise, the vow was to be broken.[56] The rationale for this, Gratian explained, was

48. C. 1 q. 7 d. a. c. 6: "Multorum enim crimina sunt damnabilia; que tamen eccesia tolerat pro tempore, pro persona, intuitu pietatis, uel necessitatis, siue utilitatis, et pro rei euentu." See also c. 6, 15, 16, 17, and 23 of this questio.

49. C. 32 q. 4 d. p. c. 2.

50. D. 13 d. a. c. 1: "Item aduersus naturale ius nulla dispensatio admittitur, nisi forte duo mala ita urgeant ut alterum necesse sit elegi." See also D. 14, especially c. 2.

51. A well-developed system of commutation had long since appeared in the Church's penitential discipline and the redemption of vows was already a feature of the Mosaic law; see Lev. 27, which treats the matter at length. On the notion of commutation in early medieval contractual law, see J. Balon, *Ius medii aevi,* 1/2:398. Commutation of penance is discussed in detail by Cyrille Vogel, "Composition légale et commutations dans le système de la pénitence tarifée," *Revue de droit canonique,* 8(1958), 289–318 and 9(1959), 1–38, 341–59. See also J. Creusen, "Commutation de voeu," *DDC,* 3:1184–86; J. de Brys, *De dispensatione in iure canonico;* Le Bras, Lefebvre, and Rambaud, *L'Age classique,* pp. 514–32.

52. C. 20 q. 2 c. 1–2, C. 22 q. 5 c. 14–16.

53. C. 22 q. 5 c. 15.

54. C. 22 q. 2 d. p. c. 2.

55. *Dig.* 50.12.2.1; cf. Turlan, "L'Obligation 'ex voto'," pp. 529–30.

56. C. 20 q. 4 c. 2 and d. p. c. 3.

that it would prevent monks and other clerics from taking pilgrimage vows in order to escape from the regular discipline of their orders.[57]

Gratian discussed the vows of married persons specifically with reference to the vow of chastity,[58] following essentially here the basic positions of the Mosaic law, although without explicit reference to the Old Testament parallels.[59] Gratian's basic principles may be reduced to these: first, neither party to a marriage might licitly make a vow without the consent of the other party.[60] Second, a vow made by one party without the other's consent was not binding and might, at the insistence of either party, be broken.[61] Third, a vow made with the consent of the other party was binding and must be kept.[62] Fourth, once a vow of chastity had been made in this fashion, it remained binding on both, even if the consenting party should subsequently withdraw consent. Finally, other vows (specifically vows to enter religion or vows of abstinence) made by the wife with her husband's consent might be revoked should the husband subsequently withdraw his consent.[63]

Gratian thus developed in his *Decretum* a reasonably coherent doctrine of the vow *in genere,* even though there was no consideration of the special problems posed by the crusade vow in particular. Still, Gratian's treatment left a number of problems still open, or at least not clearly resolved. The character of the vow itself, for example, was not clearly defined anywhere in the *Decretum,* nor was there any rigorous distinction between different types of vows, even though Gratian obviously thought it possible to distinguish more than one species of them. Likewise the problem of dispensation from vows, though hinted at by some of Gratian's canons and dicta, was nowhere clearly faced and resolved in the *Decretum.*[64] These aspects of the doctrine of the vow, however, were

57. C. 20 q. 4 d. p. c. 3.

58. The whole of C. 33 q. 5 is devoted to this problem in its various aspects.

59. Num. 30 deals with this matter at length.

60. C. 33 q. 5 c. 1 and especially d. p. c. 11: "Ex premissis apparet quod continentiae uota nec mulier sine uiri consensu, nec uir sine mulieris consensu Deo reddere potest."

61. C. 33 q. 5 c. 2–3, 5–6, and d. p. c. 11, which sums up Gratian's position: "Quia uero in ceteris uir est caput mulieris, et mulier corpus sui, ita uota abstinentiae uiro permittente mulier potest promittere, ut tamen eodem prohibente repromissa non ualeat inplere, et hoc, ut diximus, propter condicionem seruitutis, quia uiro in omnibus debet subesse."

62. C. 33 q. 5 c. 4 and d. p. c. 11.

63. C. 33 q. 5 d. p. c. 20.

64. On the general topic of canonical doctrines of dispensation, see also A. Van Hove, *De privilegiis; de dispensationibus,* tit. 6, especially pp. 293–304, 312–30, 355–62, 406–29.

taken up and discussed by the theologians and decretist writers in the period following the publication of the *Decretum*.

THE DOCTRINE OF THE VOW IN THE SENTENTIAE OF PETER LOM-
BARD. Another major work which, although not formally canonistic in character, had a considerable influence upon both canonists and theologians in the twelfth century and later was the *Sententiae* of Peter Lombard. Written ca.1158, the *Sententiae* quickly became, after the Bible, the most essential textbook of the medieval theologians; not until the sixteenth century was it finally supplanted by the *Summa theologica* of Aquinas as the text par excellence of Catholic theological faculties.[65]

The treatment of vows in the *Sententiae* is a relatively short subsection of the Lombard's treatment of the sacrament of matrimony. The discussion begins with a definition of the vow as the evidence (*testificatio*) of a freely-made promise—a highly specific promise to do something which might properly be done for God and in matters which pertained to God.[66] The terms of the definition were constructed so as to exclude promises exacted under force or duress, promises of illicit or sinful acts, or promises of any kind which were not related directly to God or spiritual concerns. The Lombard also excluded from his consideration vows made by fools; these, he curtly stated, should be broken.[67] He then proceeded to distinguish various kinds of vows. The first distinction was between a common vow—the one made by all Christians at baptism to renounce the devil and his works—and a singular vow, made by some Christians but not by all— e.g., a vow of sexual continence or of virginity.[68] The second distinction was between private and solemn vows, the former defined as one made without public knowledge (*in abscondito*), the latter as one made with the knowledge of the Church. To violate either species of vow would be mortally sinful but to violate a solemn vow would be the more serious, for it would involve scandal as well as serious sin.[69] The discussion then

---

65. On the influence of Peter Lombard's *Sententiae* see M. Grabmann, *Geschichte der scholastischen Methode*, 2:392–98.

66. *Sententiae* 4.38.1 (*PL,* 192:932): "Votum est testificatio quedam promissionis spontanee que Deo, et de his que Dei sunt, proprie fieri debet."

67. Ibid.: "Sunt tamen et vota stultorum, que frangenda sunt."

68. Ibid., 4.38.2 (*PL,* 192:932).

69. Ibid.: "Idem singulare votum, aliud est privatum, aliud solemne. Privatum est, in abscondito factum; solemne vero, in conspectu ecclesiae factum. Item privatum votum si violetur, peccatum est mortale; solemne vero violare, peccatum et scandalum est."

proceeded to deal specifically with vows of chastity and marriage vows, to the details of which all the rest of the Lombard's treatment of vows was particularly directed.

DECRETIST DISCUSSIONS OF THE VOW. The brief *Summa* of Gratian's disciple and earliest commentator, Paucapalea, added substantially nothing to the texts dealing with vows and did nothing to clarify Gratian's position on the subject.[70] Far more important for the doctrine of vows is the *Stroma* of Rolandus Bandinelli, who was later to become Pope Alexander III (1159–81).[71] Rolandus was apparently a pupil of Gratian and was teaching at Bologna about the time of the publication of the *Decretum*. In his *Stroma* (written before 1148) he added some important nuances to Gratian's treatment of vows. First, he drew a distinction between two species of vow: using the same terminology as Peter Lombard, Rolandus called these species respectively private and solemn. The meaning he assigned to these terms, however, was quite different from that adopted by Peter Lombard. In Rolandus' terminology a private vow was one which was mentally determined upon and which might even be pronounced aloud, but which was made without formalities (*simpliciter*). It might be binding in God's eyes, but it created no obligation so far as the Church was concerned. Rolandus distinguished, in other words, between the binding power of a vow *in foro interno* and *in foro externo*.[72] A simple vow, in his estimation, was binding only in conscience, not in the external forum.[73] Rolandus did not attempt to define the formalities which

70. Paucapalea's commentary was published as *Die Summa des Paucapalea über das Decretum Gratiani*, ed. J. F. von Schulte.

71. On Rolandus, see especially M. Pacaut, *Alexandre III: Etude sur la conception du pouvoir pontifical dans sa pensée et dans son oeuvre.*

72. This terminology, though late, is useful. The thirteenth-century terms were *ius fori* (= *forum externum*) and *ius poli* (= *forum internum*); see Stephan Kuttner, *Kanonistische Schuldlehre von Gratian bis auf die Dekretalen Gregors IX*, pp. 324–25; R. Naz, "For," *DDC*, 5:871–73; P. M. Quantin, "A propos des premières summae confessorum," *Recherches de théologie ancienne et médiévale*, 26(1959), 305. For a clear, concise statement of the difference between the two fora, see A. Ottaviani, *Institutiones iuris publici ecclesiastici*, 1:189. A more extended analysis is P. Capobianco, "De ambitu fori interni in iure ante codicem," *Apollinaris*, 8(1935), 591–605, and "De notione fori interni in iure canonico," *Apollinaris*, 9(1936), 364–74; also G. D'Ercole, "Foro interno e foro esterno nella penitenza delle origine cristiane," *Apollinaris*, 22(1959), 273–304.

73. *Die Summa magistri Rolandi, nachmals Papstes Alexander III*, ed. Friedrich Thaner, p. 58 (to C. 17 q. 1).

would make a vow solemn, but he apparently held that a solemn vow would be binding both in foro interno and in foro externo.[74] It should be noted, too, that in his discussion of the vows of minors, Rolandus applied the Roman law rule which fixed the age of puberty for boys at fourteen, for girls at twelve, thus carrying its application a step beyond that advanced in Gratian's text.[75]

Another important early treatment of the vow was that of Rufinus. In his *Summa* (written between 1157 and 1159),[76] Rufinus commenced his principal discussion of the subject of vows in his commentary to C. 27 q. 1 by quoting Peter Lombard's definition of the term. Rufinus differed from the Lombard, however, in his concept of the extent of the term's meaning. The general notion of the vow, Rufinus held, might apply equally well to a promise to perform an evil act as to a promise to perform a good act. This latter he would distinguish as a special meaning of the general term. Rufinus followed the Lombard in distinguishing two types of vows, the general vow binding on all Christians, and the special vow, which bound only those who undertook it voluntarily (in this context, he discussed only the special vow of continence and the vow to enter the religious life). The special vow might be either simple or solemn in form: a simple vow might be pronounced either in public or in private, but it was made without special ceremony and no solemn obligation resulted from it; a solemn vow, on the other hand, must be made with some sacred ceremony and witnessed by at least two or three persons.[77]

In his commentary to C. 17 q. 1, Rufinus carried further the analysis of the binding power of vows begun by Gratian. He followed in his discussion the distinction made by Rolandus between the binding power of a vow in God's eyes and its binding power in the eyes of the Church, but in Rufinus' treatment the greatest emphasis was laid upon the notion of deliberatio, which stands out as an essential element of a binding vow.

---

74. Ibid.; also to C. 12 q. 1 (ed. Thaner, p. 26).

75. C. 20 q. 2 c. 2 indicates that twelve is to be reckoned the age of puberty for girls, but fails to mention the age for boys. The Roman law rule may be found at *Cod.* 5.60.3, summarized in *Inst.* 1.22.pr. Girard, *Manuel*, p. 171, n. 2, discusses the various rules elaborated by Roman legal writers to establish the legal age of puberty; see also Buckland, *Textbook of Roman Law*, p. 159, and Adolf Berger, *Encyclopedic Dictionary of Roman Law*, s.v. "Impubes," at p. 495; Kaser, *Das römische Privatrecht*, 1:74-75, 238-40; 2:78-81.

76. On the date of Rufinus' *Summa* see the introduction to *Die Summa magistri Rufini zum Decretum Gratiani*, ed. H. Singer, pp. cxv-cxviii.

77. Rufinus, *Summa* to C. 27 q. 1, ad v. "Quod vero voventes" (ed. Singer, p. 435).

Vows made in haste, without deliberatio, were not binding *quantum ad ecclesiam,* even though they might bind the individual in conscience, *quantum ad Deum.*[78]

At some length, Rufinus discussed dispensation, as an alteration (*derogatio*) of the rigorous application of a canon for just cause by a person empowered so to do. Following Gratian, he distinguished between those rules which might be dispensed from and those which might not; but to these categories he added a third, that of canons whose application might be altered by the precedent either of a contrary custom or a contrary enactment. Those canons which might not be dispensed from were said to derive their special force from their origin; thus Rufinus held that dispensations might not be granted against the rules of the moral law or those regulations prescribed in the gospels or by the apostles. As examples of indispensable rules, Rufinus explicitly named the obligation to fulfill an unqualified vow, as well as the law that a man whose wife is living may not take another wife, that an unconsecrated man may not consecrate another, that offerings made to the Church may not be sold, *et cetera que prudenti meditatori facillime occurrunt.* Fundamentally Rufinus would ground the indispensability of a rule on the natural law, against which absolutely no dispensation might be granted.[79] He taught further that there were two factors which argued for the granting of a dispensation: the necessity of the times and the usefulness of the dispensation for the general welfare of the Church. There were likewise two factors which might argue against the granting of a dispensation in a particular situation: if there were a gross irregularity in the person for whom the dispensation was requested or if there were gross irregularity in the actions which would flow from the dispensation. In any event, dispensations should only be granted with discretion.[80]

Another early commentary of considerable importance is the *Summa Parisiensis,* written about 1160.[81] This anonymous commentary, which was one of the earliest products of the French school of decretist writers, followed Rolandus' analysis of the two species of vows, but used a

78. Ibid. to C. 17 q. 1, ad v. "Quod a voto discedere non liceat" (ed. Singer, p. 372).

79. Ibid. to C. 1 q. 7 d. a. c. 6 (ed. Singer, p. 234). The rule of indispensability is also further elaborated and explained in Rufinus' commentary to D. 14 c. 2 (ed. Singer, pp. 34–35).

80. Ibid. to C. 1 q. 7 (ed. Singer, pp. 235–36).

81. See especially the introduction by Terence P. McLaughlin to his edition of the text, *The Summa Parisiensis to the Decretum Gratiani,* pp. vii–xxxiii.

different terminology for them. What Rolandus had called a solemn vow became a public vow in the *Summa Parisiensis* and this slight alteration in terminology was significant. Private vows, according to the *Summa Parisiensis,* were binding quantum ad Deum, but not quantum ad ecclesiam, while public vows were binding both before God and the Church. What distinguished these two species of vows for the author of the *Summa Parisiensis* was specifically the fact of publicity. It was the public knowledge of a vow which made it binding in the forum externum and would subject its author to public sanctions should he fail to keep the promise which he had made, while the same vow, if made privately, might be broken with impunity, at least so far as the coercive power of the Church was concerned.[82] Further, the *Summa Parisiensis* seems to imply that deliberatio is a quality of public vows alone, not of private vows; this position would provide a consistent basis for the denial of binding obligations in foro externo resulting from private vows.[83] In his discussion of the vows of minors, the author of the *Summa Parisiensis* recapitulated essentially the doctrine taught by the *Decretum;* he did so, however, much more vividly, portraying a lively scene in which a father unexpectedly sees his son in monastic garb taking part in a procession and, in order to protect his legal rights, must protest immediately and publicly.[84]

In dealing with vows made by women, the author drew an interesting distinction between the power of a husband or father to quash a vow of abstinence or a pilgrimage vow, even if he had earlier given his consent, and his absolute inability to revoke a vow of continence once his consent had been given.[85]

Stephen of Tournai, writing in the 1160's, had some further important observations to contribute to the discussion of the vow by the early decretist writers.[86] Stephen distinguished three types of vows: the solemn vow, the private vow, and the implicit vow (*votum adnexum*). A solemn

82. *Summa Parisiensis* to C. 17 q. 1 (ed. McLaughlin, p. 188).
83. Ibid. to C. 17 q. 1 c. 4 (ed. McLaughlin, p. 188).
84. Ibid. to C. 20 q. 2 (ed. McLaughlin, p. 197).
85. Ibid. to C. 33 q. 5 c. 16, ad v. "Noluit itaque lex" (ed. McLaughlin, p. 255).
86. The date of Stephen's *Summa* cannot be definitely fixed. It was finished before 1171, as Joannes Faventinus made use of it, and it is certainly later than the work of Paucapalea, Rufinus, and Rolandus, all of whom Stephen quotes. On Stephen, see especially the introduction to Schulte's partial edition of the *Summa,* and S. Kuttner, "Les Débuts de l'école canoniste française," *Studia et documenta historiae et iuris,* 4(1938), 193–204.

vow he described as a vow taken publicly at the hands of a bishop, abbot, or priest in a ceremony which was sometimes marked by the imposition of a cross—conceivably a reference to the taking of the cross for the crusade—or a sacred relic. A private vow was one made either silently or at least without any formal public ceremony. An implicit vow was one which was not expressed formally or explicitly, but which was implied by some other action—as a vow of chastity might be implied by taking holy orders or by investiture with the monastic habit. The binding force of a solemn or implicit vow of chastity, Stephen added, was sufficient to impede the subsequent contracting of marriage and to nullify a previous marriage; the vow would take precedence over the marriage bond in either case. A simple vow of chastity, however, would not have quite the same force. It would create an impediment to a subsequent marriage, according to Stephen's teaching, but it would not nullify an existing marriage.[87]

The *Summa* of Joannes Faventinus, written ca.1171,[88] shows a further refinement of the decretist analysis of the vow. Joannes makes a threefold distinction between deliberatio or propositum,[89] *desiderium,* and votum. The process of making a vow, as Joannes describes it, must begin with deliberatio, a pondering and consideration of a possible course of action. The next stage is one in which the notion is carefully considered and might be mentioned aloud. At this stage Joannes would term the project a desiderium; it is decided upon, but the decision is not final and no precisely formulated undertaking is formally embraced. In the third stage a definite promise is made to pursue the course intended; this is a vow properly speaking. The binding force of the projected course of action and the seriousness of the obligations involved vary with the different stages of the process, as Joannes conceives of it. There is no sin involved in setting aside a deliberatio, and thus at that stage no obligation to carry through the project. To set aside a desiderium, however, is slightly sinful, for there is an obligation, though a relatively minor one, to follow through the course of action which has been tentatively decided upon. To set aside a vow, on the other hand, is a most serious matter. Joannes counts such an

87. Stephen of Tournai, *Summa* to C. 27 q. 1 *pr.* (ed. Schulte, p. 233).

88. On Joannes, see especially Giovanni Argnani, "Ioannes Faventinus glossator," *Apollinaris,* 9(1936), 418–43, 640–58.

89. This usage of "propositum" is somewhat confusing, but it is clearly different from that discussed by Hertling, "Die Professio der Kleriker," pp. 149, 155–57, for he would equate "propositum" with *professio* and concludes that both terms denote a definite, binding commitment to a proposed course of action.

action mortally sinful, and clearly believes that an obligation of major importance is created by the utterance of a full-fledged vow.[90]

It is noteworthy that Joannes seems to have been the first of the decretists to use the pilgrimage to Jerusalem specifically as an example of the kind of vow which a monk might not make without the permission of his abbot.[91]

A further refinement to the decretists' theory of the vow was added in the *Summa* of Sicardus of Cremona, written between 1179 and 1181.[92] Sicardus adopted the tripartite scheme (propositum, desiderium, votum) of Joannes Faventinus, although he held (in contrast to Rolandus and Rufinus) that both simple and solemn vows were binding under pain of mortal sin. He added the further qualification that a vow was rendered invalid if the person making it was mentally disturbed.[93] In his discussion of the distinction between simple and solemn vows, Joannes specified four means by which vows were solemnized: (1) by writing or by witnesses, although these, he added, could properly be said only to publicize, not to solemnize a vow; (2) by actual entrance into a monastery; (3) by formal profession to a religious superior (both these were applicable only to religious vows); (4) by the use of the appropriate habit or garb.[94] For

90. Joannes Faventinus, *Summa* to C. 17 q. 1, in Oxford, Bodleian Library, MS. Tanner 8, p. 494: "Preterea distinguendum censemus inter deliberationem et uoluntatem et uotum. Incipit enim uotum in deliberationem; augmentatur in uoluntatis delectatione et pronunciatione; perficitur in promissione: ex primo propositum, ex secundo desiderium [*ms.:* desiderii], ex tertio dicitur uotum. A primo recedere non est mortiferum, alioquin recedens in priore fide et caritate non remaneret, ut infra causa quarta dicitur. Nec a secundo recedere uidetur mortale peccatum, in quo casu loquitur C. q. ii. A tertio tamen recedere mortale peccatum est, ut eiusdem cap. fine perpenditur."

91. Ibid. to C. 20 q. 4, in Bodleian, MS. Tanner 8, p. 502; British Museum, MS. Royal 9.E.VII, fol. 117ra: "Sine licentia abbatis non potest [*scil.:* monachus] uouere aliquid peregrinationis, sicut eundi Ierosolimam uel ad sanctum Iacobum."

92. See especially S. Kuttner, "Zur Biographie des Sicardus von Cremona," *ZRG, KA,* 25(1936), 476–78.

93. Sicardus, *Summa* to C. 17 q. 1, in British Museum, MS. Add. 18367, fol. 45ra: "Nota quod uotum mente concipitur: hoc est propositum; concepti uoluntas editur: hoc est desiderium denique uerborum obligatione perficitur: hoc est proprium uotum. A proposito et desiderio recedere potes sine mortali peccato; a uoto nequaquam, siue sit simplex, siue solempne, si tamen ex sana mente processit."

94. *Summa* to C. 20 q. 3, in British Museum, MS. Add. 18367, fol. 46vb: "Nota quod sub plurium testimonio et cum scriptura facienda est professio [*scil.:* religionis]. Hec et enim ⟨solempnitatis⟩ sunt et solempne uotum faciunt.
Solempnitates—Scriptura, ut q. i uidua [C. 20 q. 1 c. 16] et C. xxvii q. i
       —Testimonium populi, vt q. ii oportet [C. 20 q. 2 c. 4]. Hoc tamen proprie publicum facit et non solempne.

Sicardus, it seems, publication of a vow was not directly related to its binding power. What was essential was the intention and degree of determination of the person making the vow, not the publicity of the act. Once a person had proceeded to the point of making a vow, public or private, simple or solemn, he was bound to fulfill the obligation thereby incurred under pain of serious sin. However, since Sicardus did not invoke (as Rolandus and Rufinus did) the distinction between the binding power of a vow quantum ad ecclesiam and quantum ad Deum, we are left in the dark as to his teaching on the enforcibility of vows in foro externo.

The greatest of the twelfth-century decretists, Huguccio of Pisa, in his *Summa* (written ca.1188–90)[95] summed up the doctrines of his predecessors concerning vows. The doctrine of Rolandus, Rufinus, and the *Summa Parisiensis* he found unsatisfactory; for, he asked, how could an action, such as breaking a private vow, which is sinful in God's eyes, be held licit by the Church, especially when it is a matter of a promise made to the Church? Such a doctrine he rejected as a snare, which might deceive men's souls by giving them a false sense of security. Further, he was inclined to think that even a simple promise, without formalities, would be morally binding, although it was not technically a vow at all.[96] He then summarized, with apparent approval, the tripartite scheme of Joannes Faventinus and Sicardus. To reject a deliberatio he held to be a very slight sin (*levissimum peccatum*); to reject a propositum was like-

---

—Ingressus cenobii, ut C. xix Quia [C. 19 q. 3 c. 7].
—Traditio in manus prelati uel eius ministri, ut infra Q. e. uidua [C. 20 q. 1 c. 16] et C. xvii q. i i Consaldus [C. 17 q. 2 c. 1].
—Habitus uestitum et ueli, ut C. ⟨x⟩xvii q. i uidua [C. 27 q. 1 c. 34]."
95. On Huguccio, see especially Le Bras, Lefebvre, and Rambaud, *L'Age classique*, pp. 279–81.
96. Huguccio, *Summa* to C. 17 d. a. c. 1, in Paris, Bibliothèque Nationale, MS. lat. 3892, fol. 243vb: "*Quod a uoto*. Hic intitulatur prima questio, scilicet an liceat alicui discedere a uoto. In hac questione magister sic distinguit, scilicet quod aliud est uotum corde conceptum simpliciter ore pronunciare, aliud est subsequente obligatione se reum uel obnoxium facere. Quocumque horum modorum quis uotum faciat, non licet ei discedere a uoto quantum ad deum, alioquin reus erit; sed quantum ad ecclesiam licet ei discedere a priori uoto, non autem a secundo. Sed si peccatum est apud deum, qualiter erit licitum apud ecclesiam, presertim cum notum sit ecclesie, sicut sanctum Consaldi uotum erat apostolico [C. 17 q. 2 c. 1]? Nonne hoc esset laqueum inicere talibus et decipere animas eorum falsa securitate, quod non est faciendum, ut xxvii q. i de uiduis [C. 27 q. 1 c. 42] et de penitentia di. v fratres [c. 8]? Sed numquid non tenetur quis de simplici promissione? Utique: non enim dominus uoluit differentiam esse inter communem loquelam et iuramentum, ut xxii q. v iuramenti [c. 12]."

wise sinful, but not mortally so; but to violate a vow which had been pronounced aloud, whether with or without solemnity, was mortally sinful, unless perchance the vow was made in the heat of passion.[97] Huguccio's opinion on this, as on many other matters, was extremely influential and was adopted by most of his successors; it was repeated by the Anglo-Norman *Summa "Prima primi"* and the *Apparatus "Ecce vicit leo"* of the French school.[98] *"Ecce vicit leo"* defines a vow as the concep-

97. Ibid.: "Alii faciunt distinctionem inter deliberationem et uoluntatem et uotum. Incipit enim uotum in deliberatione; augmentatur in uoluntate; perficitur in promissione. Et scilicet hunc triplicem progressum triplex sortitur uocabulum. Primo enim dicitur deliberatio, cuius fractio est leuissimum peccatum, quia potest homo deliberata non facere et in prioribus bonis permanere, quod non esset si illa fractio esset mortale peccatum, ut i. e. ⟨Qui⟩ [*ms.:* non] bona [C. 17 q. 1 c. 4]. Tandem quod quis tepide deliberauerat firmiter se facturum in animo proponit et dicitur propositum, ut i. e. q. ii nos nouimus [C. 17 q. 2 c. 2]; huius propositi uiolatio est ueniale peccatum, sed grauius quam primum peccatum. Idem quod in animo quis proposuerat ore promittit, uel sollempniter uel sine sollempnitate et dicitur uotum, a quo recedere est mortale peccatum, nisi pro passionis feruore promittatur, ut dicitur de Consaldo [C. 17 q. 2 c. 1]."

98. See Kuttner, *Repertorium,* pp. 59–66, 205–6, and, on the *Summa "Prima primi"* (written between 1191 and 1210), see also B. Tierney, "Two Anglo-Norman Summae," *Traditio,* 15(1959), 483–91. The commentary of this *Summa* to C. 17 q. 2 in British Museum, MS. Royal 11.D.II, fol. 329ʳᵃ, reads: "Venire contra uotum quod est tantum in proposito, cum nondum uel uoce uel animo aliquam cum deo contracta est obligatio, aut nulla aut ueniale peccatum est, ut i. e. c. i. Si uero post deliberationem firmatum est in animo et siue per uocis expressionem, siue sine uocis fama in animo Deo promissum, est obligatorium et eius transgressio mortalis, ut in sequentibus c.; nisi feruore passionis factum sit, ut i. e. q. et c. i. Deus enim cor attendit: quod habetur tamen intelligit. De passione alienationem mentis inducente et de talibus legit⟨ur⟩ primum c. secunde questionis."

The *Apparatus "Ecce vicit leo"* was written between 1202 and 1210. The gloss to C. 17 q. 1 *pr.,* in Paris, Bibliothèque Nationale, nouvelles acquisitions latins 1576, fol. 219ʳᵇ, is a close paraphrase of Huguccio: *"Quod autem.* hic intitulatur prima questio, utrum scilicet quis a uoto possit discedere et reuera non potest in questio ista et c. i; sed nota quod circa uota tria debes attendere: primo deliberatione, quando scilicet homo cogitat intra se bonum esset, quod illud faceret uel uoueret; si uero tunc hic bonum ⟨non⟩ faciat, peccat uenialiter; secundum quosdam non, ut s. e. q. i. qui bona [C. 17 q. 1 c. 4]. Postea secunda quando scilicet primo deliberauerit propositum et si non servet propositum ex quo in aliam partem consentit, peccat mortaliter, ut i. c. uouentibus [C. 17 q. 1 c. 2], xx q. iii [i] propositum [c. i]; sed per his uenialiter; infra, qui bona [c. 4]. Item quando postea expressio per uocem; scilicet prima promissio, etiam sine uoce, et equipollet uoto, a quo non est recedendum a uouentibus; et si contra tunc non seruetur ex quo uoce expressum est, grauius peccatur quam in secundo casu, id est mortaliter, ut i. e. q. ii nos [c. 2]. Simplici uoto quod obligat ubi et sollempnia; de e. s. c. iii laudabilem [*Comp. II* 4.4.2 = X 4.6.6 = *JL,* 17,649] rursus." The version of this passage in Florian, Stiftsbibliothek, MS. XI.605, fol. 76ʳᵃ, is considerably shorter than that in the Paris MS.

tion of a better good, which is confirmed by deliberation or by an act of oblation.[99] A vow according to this view cannot properly be said to be made for an evil purpose or, the author adds, a frivolous one. *"Ecce vicit leo"* also discussed the solemnization of religious vows and added, by way of example, two forms of words for the making of a vow of continence.[100] The author distinguished carefully in this discussion between a promise in the present tense, which would constitute a vow, and a promise in the future tense, which would not. Finally, he noted that it was the intention of making a vow, not the form of words employed, which resulted in a binding obligation.[101]

An interesting attempt to compare the guilt involved in breaking a vow with that incurred by other acts is found in the anonymous early gloss to the *Decretum* in a manuscript of Corpus Christi College, Cambridge. The unknown writer held that the sin involved in breaking any vow was more serious than the sin of adultery, at least if it were a question of a vow voluntarily made.[102] This position contrasts strikingly with that expressed

99. Gloss to C. 27 q. 1 in St. Florian, Stiftsbibliothek, MS. XI.605, fol. 99[rab]: "Votum est conceptio melioris boni cum deliberatione firmata uel oblata. Conceptio dicitur quia non ualet si fiat ex impetu, immo operat ut prius concipiatur, ar. xvii q. iia Consaldus [c. 1] uel extra de regularibus transeuntibus ad religionem, ad nostram [*Comp.* I 3.27.8 = X 3.31.8]. Melioris boni dicitur quia non est [*cancelled in ms.:* bonum] uotum si fiat de malo et huius friuolis uel fatuis immo non est tenendum, ut hic xxii q. iiii in malis [c. 5]. Firmata dicitur quia debet uouens firmiter proponere se non facturum ceterum contra uotum. Oblata dicitur quia non est uotum nisi uoce uel signis exterius exprimatur. Quod si habeat propositum illud obseruandi de cetero [*cancelled in ms.:* non] tamen ueniendo tunc contra peccat mortaliter, ut xxii q. iiii qui bona [C. 17 q. 1 c. 4]. Aliter tamen bene describitur uotum in sententiis sic [*Sent.* 4.38.1]: uotum est quidam protestatio spontanee promissionis que de his que dei sunt deo fieri debet [*corr. in ms. ex:* debent]."

100. Ibid., fol. 99[rb]: "Solempnizatur autem tribus modis: abbatis susceptione, ut j. e. c. i et ii; per ordinis sacri susceptionem, quia eo ipso presumitur uouere, ut lxxxiii i cum in preterito [D. 84 c. 3]; tercio modo per professionem [*add. marg.:* in manu] publice pare factam, ut extra ne clerici uel uouentes matrimonium contrahere possint, meminimus [*Comp.* I 4.6.6 = X 4.6.3]."

101. Ibid.: "Quando contrahitur autem his uerbis uotum: 'uoueo continentiam', 'obstringo me ad continentiam', 'do deo meam continentiam', sed non [*add. marg.:* 'sic promitto uel iuro quod continebo', quia qui uouet se ⟨. . .⟩ deo tradit, sed non] talis, immo qui promittit uerbo ⟨de futuro⟩ unde non [*repeated and cancelled in ms.:* non] est uoto obligatus, nisi intendat uouere, quia tunc tenetur uoto, non exemplo [*ms.:* exm̄] uerborum, sed ex intentione."

102. Cambridge, Corpus Christi College, MS. 10, fol. 271[rb], gloss to C. 27 q. 1 c. 41: "Grauius est labi a quolibet uoto quam adulterari; id est uotum quod non cogit uouere; sed postquam uoueritis, reddere." This manuscript seems from several viewpoints a particularly interesting one. The script is of the late twelfth century and the glosses are of an early type, with considerable dependence upon Paucapalea;

ca.1186 by the author of the *Summa Lipsiensis*,[103] who airily dismissed the
notion that there was any grave sin involved either in not fulfilling a
simple vow or in entertaining an adulterous desire. "Who, indeed," he
asked rhetorically, "will reproach the breaking of a simple vow or an
adulterous inclination?"[104]

The notion of simple and solemn vows was put in a slightly different
light by another anonymous work of the twelfth-century Anglo-Norman
school, the *Summa "De iure naturali"* preserved in a unique manuscript
at Durham University.[105] For the author of this *Summa,* writing between
1171 and 1179, the solemnity or simplicity of a vow was defined by the
character of the witnesses to it: a vow became solemn when it was
professed before the Church in the presence of a priest or bishop, while a
simple vow, *e converso,* was one which was witnessed only by very few
persons or by no one at all.[106] This position was, of course, closely akin to
that of the *Summa Parisiensis,* which took the publication of a vow to be
the decisive factor in determining its solemnity and hence its binding
power, although *"De iure naturali"* linked the publication of a vow and
its consequent solemnity rather more directly to the official, pastoral
character of the witnesses. Another Durham manuscript of the late
twelfth century containing glosses of the Anglo-Norman school[107] provides evidence in its treatment of the topic of vows that its author was
considerably influenced by the teaching of Rufinus. According to its
definition of the vow—which also echoes the *Sentences* of Peter Lom-

---

see Kuttner, *Repertorium,* p. 23. Both text and glosses are neatly written on a
high-grade vellum and there are a number of beautifully illuminated initials, which
have been carefully laid into the text. The *siglum* "j" occurs fairly frequently in the
glosses (e.g., fol. 60[vb], 62[ra], 62[vb], 63[rb]).

103. See Kuttner, *Repertorium,* pp. 196–98.

104. *Summa Lipsiensis* to D. 81 c. 1, cited by Kuttner, *Kanonistische Schuldlehre,*
p. 19, n. 3: ". . . 'grave' ideo dicit ad differentiam illius, quod tantum in voluntate
consistit . . . quis enim accusat fractionem simplici voti vel adulterium voluntatis?"

105. Pierre Legendre, "Miscellanea Brittanica," *Traditio,* 15(1959), 494, first
called attention to this *Summa,* which has since been studied by Kurt Nörr, "Die
Summen 'De iure naturali' und 'De multiplici iuris diuisione'," *ZRG, KA,* 79(1962),
138–63.

106. *Summa "De iure naturali"* to C. 17 q. 1, Durham University Library, MS.
Cosin V.III.3, fol. 64rb: "Votum ⟨est⟩ tamen corde conceptum sed ore non prolatum
uel ore prolatum, sed simpliciter, id est coram nullo uel paucis enunciatum, nullum
apud ecclesiam ⟨reum⟩ constituit, licet apud deum. Si uero solempniter, id est coram
facie ecclesie presente episcopo uel sacerdote fuerit pronunciatum, tam apud ecclesiam quam apud deum uouentem reddit obligatum et transgredientem constituit
reum."

107. On Durham Cathedral, MS. C.II.1, see Kuttner, *Repertorium,* pp. 25–26.

bard[108] and the definition of *"Ecce vicit leo"*—a vow is a proposal to perform a good deed (or, according to the more common opinion, either a licit or an illicit deed) which has been confirmed by mindful deliberation.[109] The source of the "more common" opinion here was clearly Rufinus. It is obvious, too, that the author of this Durham gloss was also influenced by the discussion of the nature of the vow among the canonists of the French school, particularly by the emphasis of Rufinus and his followers upon deliberatio as a necessary constituent of a binding vow. The influence of Rufinus is less apparent in the treatment of the grounds for dispensation, of which four are enumerated: the character of the person dispensed, the provision of good example, the avoidance of scandal, and sacramental considerations.[110]

Richardus Anglicus in his *Distinctiones decretorum* (written ca.1196)[111] gives an interesting list of instances in which dispensations may be granted against authorities whose precepts were commonly supposed to be indispensable—the natural law, sayings of the Apostles, statutes of the universal Church, the gospels, and canons of the Apostles, and the canons of the first four general councils.[112] The *Summa "Prima primi"* added

108. *Sent.* 4.38.1 (*PL*, 192:932).
109. Durham Cathedral, MS. C.II.1, gloss to C. 17 q. 1 *pr.*, fol. 200[rb]: "Votum est conceptio boni cum anime deliberatione confirmata; uel uotum testificatio quidam spontanee promissionis, secundum primam diffinitionem de licitis, tamen secundum secundam tam de licitis quam de illicitis communius accipitur."
110. Durham Cathedral, MS. C.II.1, fol. 223[vb]:

"Dispensatio fit—propter qualitatem persone—honeste
                                              —potentis
                                              —utilis
            —propter exemplum salutis
            —propter scandalum vitandum
            —propter sacramentum—ordo enim cum admitti non possit dispensatio non reperitur"

111. On Richardus, see especially Glorieux, *Répertoire des maîtres en théologie,* 1:280–81; Charles E. Lewis, "Ricardus Anglicus: A 'Familiaris' of Archbishop Hubert Walter," *Traditio,* 22(1966), 469–71.
112. Richardus, *Distinctiones,* in British Museum, MS. Royal 10.C.III, fol. 13[v]:

"i Q. vii Multorum
Nota dispensationem—Contra apostolum qui dixit: oportet episcopum esse mono-
        factam   gamum; contra in archiepiscopo panormitano
            —Contra ius naturale, ubi dicitur uovete et reddite; item
                xxxiii Q. v Manifestum [c. 11] et extra de uoto ⟨et uoti⟩
                redim ⟨endo⟩
            —Contra statutum universalis ecclesie ubi in spiritualibus pro-

infirmity as a further reason for granting dispensations from vows, an addition which is significant for the crusade vow in particular.[113]

Another definition of a vow was attempted in the *Glossa Palatina,* written between 1210 and 1215 by Laurentius Hispanus,[114] who described a vow as the conception of a proposal for a better way of life, determined upon by mental deliberation, through which one places oneself under an obligation to God.[115] In his discussion of the origin and binding power of vows, Laurentius adopted the tripartite scheme of Joannes Faventinus and Huguccio, whom he paraphrased very closely and in contrast to whom he presented the rather different views of a *magister B,* identified by Kuttner as Bernardus Compostellanus antiquus.[116] Laurentius, however, apparently misunderstood Huguccio's position, for he restated it incorrectly at one point.[117] He also added a further note concerning the impediments to

---

hibetur successoris designatio, viij Q. i apostolica [c. 7]; sed contra vii Q. i petisti [c. 17]

—Contra evangelium et ius naturale que precipiunt decimas dari; sed contra de decimis per totum [*Comp. I* 3.26], xvi q. i Questi [C. 17 q. 4 c. 41].

—Contra canones apostolorum quibus deponitur presbiter fornicator, sed contra Presbiter si fornicationem [D. 82 c. 5]

—Contra quatuor principalia concilia in simoniacis condempnandis i Q. iii Calcedonense [?], sed contra i Q. v Quicumque [c. 1] et c. ult."

113. *Summa "Prima primi"* to C. 17 q. 2 in British Museum, MS. Royal 11.D.II, fol. 329[va]: "Si enim ex multis causis licet contra proprium uotum uenire, ut solet dici infra eodem capitulo et alibi, secundum magistrorum uoluntatem, licitum erit similiter uenire contra uotum propter infirmitatem factam, si tamen id papa concesserit, ut hic in primo capitulo secunde questionis; et intellige quod hic fuit dispensatum; pro hac opinione ar. in extra de regularibus ad religionem ⟨transeuntibus⟩ [*ms.:* transire] super eo [*Comp. I* 3.27.9 = X 3.31.9]. Ad hec pertinerunt que dicta sunt 14 Q. 6 Auctoritatem [C. 15 q. 6 c. 2]."

114. A. M. Stickler, "Il decretista Laurentius Hispanus," *Studia Gratiana,* 9(1966), 463–549, has shown that the *Glossa Palatina* was almost certainly written by Laurentius. See also Gaines Post, "The So-Called Laurentius Apparatus to the Decretals of Innocent III in Compilatio III," *The Jurist,* 2(1942), 5–31; Kurt Nörr, "Der Apparat der Laurentius zur Compilatio III," *Traditio,* 17(1961), 542–43; Antonio García y García, *Laurentius Hispanus: Datos biográficos y estudio crítico de sus obras.*

115. *Glossa Palatina* to C. 27 q. 1 c. 1 in Bibliotheca Apostolica Vaticana, MS. Pal. Lat. 658, fol. 76ra: "Est autem uotum prout hic accipitur: conceptio melioris propositi, animi deliberatione firmata, qua quis se deo obligat."

116. "Bernardus Compostellanus antiquus: A Study in the Glossators of the Canon Law," *Traditio,* 1(1943), 277–340.

117. *Glossa Palatina* to C. 17 q. 1 pr. in Vat. Pal. Lat. 658, fol. 60[va]: "*Quod a uoto discedere.* Hic intitulatur prima questio: an liceat alicui discedere a uoto. Quid

marriage created by vows of chastity.[118] The treatment of simple vows in the *Glossa Palatina* is taken over verbally from the *Distinctiones decretorum* of Richardus Anglicus. Richardus and the author of the *Glossa Palatina* took the view (earlier reflected in *"Ecce vicit leo"*) that a vow, properly speaking, must be a promise of present action, not of a future undertaking, which would not be binding.[119] This construction of the vow was based upon an analogy with the law of *sponsalia,* in which a promise of future marriage might be rescinded, while a promise of marriage *de presente* was held binding.[120] According to this author's

---

autem sentiat de hac materia omnia habes infra eadem his ita [*d. p. c.* 4] quia refert [an] uotum corde conceptum, ore exprimat tantum an sequenti obligatione se reum uoti faciet. In ⟨secundo⟩ casu utroque tenetur quoad deum; extra qui clerici uel uouentes, rursus [*Comp. II* 4.4.2 = *X* 4.6.6]; et peccat mortaliter contraueniendo. Sed quoad ecclesiam non tenetur in primo, sed tantum in secunda: extra de uo. et uo. redemp., litteraturam [*Comp. II* 3.21.1 = *X* 3.34.3]. Sed si in primo peccatum est quoad deum, quomodo licitum erit quoad ecclesiam? Preterea cum notum sit ecclesie. Hic notum erit domino pape secundum consalii [*C.* 17 q. 2 c. 1]. Nonne hic est laqueum talibus inicere, ar. xxvii q. j de uiduis [c. 42]? Immo non est differentia inter simplicem promissionem et iuramentum: b. uero dicit quod uotum quandoque dicitur deliberatio que uersatur in animo, cum scilicet secum quis reuoluit et fluctuat; si quis uenit contra hoc, non peccat. Quandoque dicitur propositum, cum alterum scilicet elegit et proponit, [et] ueniendo contra tale propositum secundum b. peccat uenaliter; secundum h. mortaliter, nam h. dicit tale propositum esse uotum, nec facit nisi bimembrem distinctionem: quandoque dicitur uotum proprie prout corde uel ore exprimitur, et tunc contrauenire est mortale peccatum secundum hanc distinctionem: 2 i. e. qui bona [c. 4] H. dicit quod cum quis [dicit] uouet uel promittat se monachum fieri uel aliud, si est sane mentis, tenetur; si alienate propter furorem uel infirmitatem, non tenetur: uide i. e. Consaldus [*C.* 17 q. 2 c. 1] *Vouete;* hic consilium est; quod sequitur preceptum." For Huguccio's view, cf. n. 96 above.

118. *Glossa Palatina* to C. 27 q. 1 c. 3 in Vat. Pal. Lat. 658, fol. 76rb: "Cum quis disponit aliud boni facere, tunc dicitur deliberatio, ut xxvii q. i qui bona [c. 4]; et hoc frangere ueniale est. Quando procedit et proponit firmiter idem se facturum, et dicitur propositum, ut xvii q. i c. i et q. ii nos nouimus [c. 2]; huius fractione est uenialis sed grauis, et hec matrimonium contrahendum impediunt, sed non grauant contractum. Si uero accedat obligatio, dicitur uotum, cuius fractio mortale peccatum est, et impedit matrimonium contrahendum et dirimit contractum, si solle⟨m⟩pne fuerit."

119. Ibid. to D. 27 c. 8 in Vat. Pal. Lat. 658, fol. 7rb–va: "Hinc argue quod uotum dicatur sollempne, ut extra ii qui clerici uel uo. rursus [*Comp. II* 4.4.2 = *X* 4.6.6]. . . . Ergo uotum de futuro non est uotum simplex, quia non proprie dicitur uotum, cum fit uoti quedam promissio sicut sponsalia futurum nuptiarum, quia non tantum obligat; et ita uotum simplex est uotum de presente sine solle⟨m⟩pnitate."

120. This doctrine, in turn, was largely borrowed from the Roman law of betrothal; see *Dig.* 45.1.134 and 23.1; *Cod.* 5.1; also Berger, *Encyclopedic Dictionary,* s.v. "Sponsalia," p. 713; Buckland, *Textbook of Roman Law,* p. 112, n. 5; Girard, *Manuel,* pp. 163–64; Kaser, *Das römische Privatrecht,* 1:274–75; 2:109–10.

scheme of things, then, a vow was first conceived as a *deliberatio,* which was binding neither before God nor before the Church. At the next stage it became a *propositum,* which was binding before God, but not before the Church. In the last stage of its development, it was expressed in precise terms in *verba de presenti.* This expressed vow was binding before both God and the Church, unless it was nullified by reason of age, of marriage (evidently applicable primarily to vows of chastity and entrance into the religious life), or of an excess of enthusiasm (*feruor passionis*).[121]

Another viewpoint still is represented in the late twelfth-century glosses of an Innsbruck manuscript of the *Decretum.*[122] The author of these glosses, while apparently aware of the position represented by the *Glossa Palatina,* sought to distinguish between the enforcibility of simple vows which were known (*manifestum*) to the Church and those which were not. One might be compelled to observe a manifest vow, even if it was a

---

On the canonists' adaptation of the Roman system of *sponsalia* see especially C. 30 q. 5 c. 3 and C. 31 q. 2–3; also Plöchl, *Geschichte,* 2:268–70; Hans Erich Feine, *Kirchliche Rechtsgeschichte,* 1:381–82; F. X. Wernz, *Ius decretalium,* 4/1:155–66; Z. B. Van Espen, *Jus ecclesiasticum universum* 2.1.12.1–2 (Louvain, 1753, ed., 1:554–58).

121. *Glossa Palatina* to C. 17 q. 1 in Vat. Pal. Lat. 658, fol. 60ᵛᵃ, and Richardus Anglicus, *Distinctiones decretorum* to C. 17 q. 2 c. 1 in British Museum, MS. Royal 10.C.III, fol. 28ʳ (italicized passages are omitted in the *Glossa Palatina*):

Votum—Expressam per uerba de presenti precise obligat; uide xxvii q. i per totum; *per uerba de futuro hoc obligat, sed matrimonium contractum non dissoluit*

   —Conceptum—deliberando: *hic non obligat* nec apud deum, nec apud ecclesiam obligat; xxvii q. i Nubendi [c. 20]

     —proponendo: hec apud deum obligat, sed non apud ecclesiam; unde hic etc. qui bona [C. 17 q. 1 c. 4] et secundum h⟨uguccio⟩ peccat mortaliter qui contrauenit; sed b⟨ernardus⟩ uenialiter.

Nisi impediat

etas: xx q. ii Puella [c. 2]

Publica utilitas: vii q. i Qualiter

Matrimonium: xxxvi Agathosa [C. 27 q. 2 c. 21]

Doli spes: di. liiij Generalis Maioris uoti susceptio: xix q. ii due

Contraria constitutio: xxiii q. ult. Manifestum

Feruor passionis; uide hic Consaldus

122. Kuttner, *Repertorium,* p. 51.

simple vow, and a violation of the vow would, in any event, be mortally sinful.[123] Here again it was the element of publicity which was held to determine the binding force of the vow, although in this gloss the binding power seems to be distinct from the classification of the vow as simple or solemn.

THE GLOSSA ORDINARIA. Shortly after the conclusion of the Fourth Lateran Council, probably between 1215 and 1217, the work of the more important earlier commentators on the *Decretum* was compiled and edited by a Bolognese canonist of German origin, Johann Zemeke, who is usually known as Joannes Teutonicus (ca.1170–1245/46).[124] The gloss apparatus of Joannes Teutonicus was subsequently reedited and enlarged ca.1245 by another Bolognese professor, Bartholomaeus Brixiensis (d. ca.1258). This revised version of the apparatus of Joannes came to be accepted in the universities as the standard exposition of the *Decretum* and, as the *glossa ordinaria,* came to possess a special authority for later commentators and expositors.

The treatment of vows in the *glossa ordinaria* strongly reflects the teachings of three earlier decretist writers: the *Summa* of Huguccio, the *Apparatus* attributed to Laurentius Hispanus (d. 1248),[125] and the *Glossa Palatina.* The *glossa ordinaria* adopted Huguccio's analysis of the process by which a vow was made: the three-stage scheme (deliberatio, *voluntas,* votum) was spelled out by Joannes Teutonicus in a gloss which followed Huguccio almost verbatim, although Joannes also noted that Huguccio's assessment of the seriousness of violating a propositum was disputed by

123. Innsbruck, Universitätsbibliothek, MS. 90, fol. 146rb, gloss to C. 17 q. 2 c. 1: "Quidam dicunt eum qui simpliciter uouet ad uoti obseruationem non compellendum, cum quantum ad deum tantum, non quantum ad ecclesiam teneatur. Vnde dicunt Consaldum istum simpliciter uouisse. Alii dicunt eum nec sollempniter nec simpliciter uouisse. Si enim uouisset [*cancelled in ms.:* quantum] quis simpliciter cum manifestum esset ecclesie uotum eius, omnino compelleretur. Mortaliter enim peccaret uotum non implendo, foret ergo cum uotum esset merito corripiendum." Also ibid., gloss to C. 17 q. 2 c. 3: "Votum priuatum esse etiam quod testibus probari potest. j."

124. See especially Franz Gillmann, "Hat Johannes Teutonikus zu den Konstitutionen des 4. Laterankonzils (1215) als solchen einen Apparat verfasst?" *Archiv für katholisches Kirchenrecht,* 97(1937), 453–66; and S. Kuttner, "Johannes Teutonicus, das vierte Laterankonzil und die Compilatio Quarta," *Miscellanea Giovanni Mercati,* 5:608–34.

125. See above, n. 114.

some.[126] Even a simple promise made to God or to a public authority, however, was likewise held to be enforceable, although the means and techniques for so doing were only vaguely indicated.[127] It is clear, how-

126. *Glos. ord.* to C. 17 q. 1 pr., ad v. *a uoto:* Hic queritur an liceat alicui discedere a uoto. Et in hac questione magister distinguat quod aliud est uotum conceptum corde ore simpliciter pronunciare et aliud est obligatione aliqua se obnoxium facere; sed tamen quocunque istorum modorum quis uoueat, non liceat ei recedere a uoto quoad Deum: sed quoad ecclesiam licet a primo uoto ei recedere, sed non a secundo. Sed mirum uidetur, cum hoc sit peccatum quoad Deum, quare ecclesia illud tolerat: cum hoc sit laqueum iniicere talibus, et decipere animas eorum: quod non est faciendum, ut 27 q. 1 de uiduis [c. 7]; cum dominus ipse noluit facere differentiam inter iuramentum et simplicem loquelam, ut 22 q. 5 iuramenti [c. 12]. Potest melius distingui inter deliberationem et uoluntatem et uotum. Si quis recedit a deliberatione, non peccat mortaliter. Si quis autem recedat a proposito quod firme fixerat in animo suo, peccat: sed uenialiter secundum quosdam, ut extra de uoto et uoti redemptione, litteraturam [*X* 3.34.3]; secundum Hug. uero peccat talis mortaliter, ac si uerbis uouisset, ut infra, eadem, qui bona [c. 4]. Sed a uoto quod uerbis exprimitur sine mortale peccato secundum omnes, ut extra qui clerici uel uouentes, rursus [*X* 4.6.6]; licet Alexander uideatur dicere, quod post uotum simplex potest contrahi matrimonium, ut extra qui clerici uel uouentes, ueniens [*X* 4.6.5]. Sed illud intelligas de comparativa promissione. Joan." Likewise, ibid. to C. 17 q. 1 c. 4, ad v. *deliberant:* "Firmiter proponendo, et tunc secundum Hu. peccant mortaliter, secundum alios uenialiter"; to which a later marginal gloss added: "Hec sententia Hu. approbatur per Lau. Gof. et B., extra de uoto, litteraturam." Again, ibid. to C. 17 q. 1 d. p. c. 4, ad v. *pronunciat:* "Ergo obligatur quis ex solo proposito cordis quod Hug. concedit."

127. Ibid. to C. 12 q. i c. 9, ad v. *Pollicitationem:* "Nota quod ex nuda pollicitatione, quam quis facit Deo, potest contrauenire, 22 quest. 5 capitu. iuramenti [c. 12]; sic ex nuda pollicitatione facta Reipublice, ut ff de pollicitationibus [*Dig.* 50.12] l. 1." Ibid. to C. 22 q. 5 c. 12, ad v. *iuramenti:* "Adhuc probat Gratianus per hoc capitulum quod iuramentum debet intelligi secundum intentionem proferentis. Dicit ergo Chromatius [of Aquileia: *Tractatus in Matth.* 10, in *PL,* 20:352. Both Gratian and the gloss give the name as Chrysostomus; the emendation comes from the *Correctores Romani.*] quod quicunque iurat, ideo iurare debet, ut uerum loquatur; unde Deus inter iuramentum et communem loquelam differentiam non facit: quia sicut in iuramento non debet esse perfidia, ita nec in loquela nostra: et si quis contrafecerit, poena diuini iudicii damnabitur, et hoc probat auctoritate domini dicentis: 'Os quod mentitur' etc. [Wisd. 1.11]." Ibid., ad v. *Distantiam:* "Quantum ad hoc, cum mortaliter peccat qui simpliciter dicit falsum, magis tamen peccat periurando quam mentiendo solidius subsistit ubi iuramentum interponitur, ut supra eadem q. 1 c. 1; sed tamen plus operatur sacramentum, quam simplex promissio, ut extra de iureiurando, debitores [*X* 2.24.6]. Item hic est arg. quod ex nudo pacto oritur actio, ut 12 q. 2 quicumque suffragio [c. 66] et q. 5 quia Joannes [c. 3]. Jo." A later marginal gloss adds: "Dic ergo quod licet Deus non faciat differentiam inter loquelam et iuramentum, ecclesia tamen facit, quia mendax simplex non patitur poenam quoad infamiam et repulsionem testimonii, uel quin possit promoueri: sed secus in mendace iuramento et hoc intelligas, ex quo simpliciter mendax est de crimine emendatus, secundum Decretales, extra de testibus, testimonium [*X* 2.20.54], secundum H⟨ostiensem⟩."

ever, that Joannes held that a vow, to be enforceable at all, must be pronounced aloud, not merely settled upon in the mind.[128] The means of solemnizing vows, on the other hand, were described in some detail, although with specific reference to vows of continence and religion.[129] Joannes held that solemnization should generally take place before a priest or other ecclesiastical authority, but this was not absolutely essential, and vows might even be solemnized before a private person.[130] Accordingly, it appears that the *glossa ordinaria* would define solemnization of a vow in terms of the bestowing or investiture with religious garb or other symbol of the votive act, together with a formal declaration of the terms of the vow publicly made before witnesses, preferably before a priest. The formal declaration of the vow, moreover, should be expressed in verbis de presenti, as this form of expression binds more strictly than an expression in *verbis de futuro*.[131] In any event, it was the intention of the person making the vow, rather than the form of words which he used to express that intention, which was to be considered in assessing the character and binding nature of the vow.[132] While Joannes admitted as a general

128. Ibid. to C. 27 q. 2 d. p. c. 2, ad v. *Ore:* "Expressio enim oris in uoto multum operatur, ut extra de uo. et uo. rede. literaturam [X 3.34.3]; ar. infra eodem duobus [c. 5] in fi.; arg. de pe. dist. 1 magna [c. 5] in prin.; utrum tamen quoad Deum non sit necessaria oris confessio, 22 q. 5 humane [c. 11] et cap. cauete [c. 20] et 24 [*recte:* 14] q. 5 si quid [c. 6]. Sed tamen secus est in uoto tacito, quam expresso. Nam dicit lex, quod si legaui tibi decem, si uolueris, tale legatum non transmittes ad heredes, nisi primo expresseris te uoluisse; secus uero est si legauero tibi X pure: quia illud transmittes, ff de legatis I si item legatum sit § illi si volet [*Dig.* 30.65.1]. Immo nec uotum dicitur conditionale ubi conditio subintelligitur, ut ff de condicionibus ex demonstrationibus, conditiones, que [*Dig.* 35. 1.99]. Ioan."

129. Ibid. to C. 27 q. 1 c. 1, ad v. *Sub testimonio.*

130. Ibid. to C. 20 q. 1 c. 16, ad v. *uel ministro:* "Arg. quod uotum solenne potest fieri coram priuata persona; sed ad quid facit mulier professionem sacerdoti? Potius enim deberet facere abbatisse. Sed hoc ideo fit, quia feminis non licet imponere uelum alicui, ut infra eodem q. 2 statuimus [c. 3]."

131. Ibid. to D. 3 *de pen.* c. 26, ad v. *Quanto:* "Arg. uotum de presenti magis obligare quam uotum de futuro, arg. contra extra qui clerici uel uouentes, rursus [X 4.6.6], ubi dicitur, quod simplex uotum non minus obligat quam solenne."

132. Ibid. to C. 22 q. 2 c. 4, ad v. *Instituta:* "Semper ergo in priuilegiis, uel in rescriptis interpretabuntur uerba ad id quod instituta sunt, ut hic et 37 distinct., relatum [c. 14]; et semper ad communem intelligentiam, etc.: extra de sponsalibus, ex litteris [X 4.1.7] et ff de legatis 3, non aliter [*Dig.* 32.69.pr.]. Sed contra plerumque dum proprietas uerborum attenditur, ueritas sensus amittitur, extra de uerborum significatione, propterea [X 5.40.8]; nam potius mens attenditur, quam uerba consideranda sunt, ut infra eadem q. 5 humane [c. 11], et contra uerum intellectum sit interpretatio, extra de postulatione, ad hec, circa finem [X 1.5.1]; et potius considerandum est quod testator senserit, quam ipsa uocis significatio, ut

principle that any undertaking might, under some circumstances, be licitly broken,[133] the *glossa ordinaria* discussed only a limited range of such circumstances, and all of those discussed arose from defects in the vow itself. Thus, vows made by minors were held not binding if they were repudiated upon attaining majority; a vow might be quashed by order of a superior or by one whose wishes were binding upon the person making the vow; hasty or improvident vows, or those taken under compulsion, might be repudiated.[134] The only apparent exception to this general discussion of the rescinding of vows by virtue of some inherent defect in the vow is the discussion of the abrogation of a vow by reason of the obligations arising from a greater or more serious vow.[135]

Dispensation, in the *glossa ordinaria,* was a relaxation of the general law in favor of an individual by a person properly empowered so to do, provided that he who conferred the dispensation had adequate knowledge of the facts of the case.[136] Dispensations might not be granted as a matter of law or of right, but only as exceptions to the law, specially granted in an individual case[137] and even then only in matters which were properly dispensable, for the *glossa ordinaria* followed Gratian in holding that on

---

ff de fundo instru. [*recte:* De instructo vel instrumento legato], 1 cum de lanionis § asinam [*Dig.* 33.7.18.2]; et hec uera sunt nisi interpretatio a iure habeatur, ut 20 questio 2, puella [c. 2]."

133. Ibid. to C. 22 q. 2 c. 5, ad v. *Diuina:* "Quod omnia uincula humana franguntur, 19 q. 2 due sunt [c. 2], et secundum quam dispositionem est licitum, quod alias est illicitum, ut 14 q. 5 dixit [c. 12]. Et est arguendum hic, quod in omni uoto uel sacramento intelliguntur huiusmodi generales conditiones, 'Si Deus uoluerit,' 'Si uixero,' 'Si potero,' ut infra eadem questio, ne quis [c. 14], et 27 q. 2 § cum ergo [d. p. c. 28], et ff qui satisdare cogantur, 1. ultima [*Dig.* 2.8.16], et etiam hec, 'Si marito placuerit,' 33 q. 5 noluit [c. 16]; argumentum contra, 22 quest ult., ubi de hoc notaui."

134. These points are made at the following glosses, respectively: *Glos. ord.* to C. 20 q. 1, ad v. *Quod intra annos;* to C. 17 q. 1 c. 1, ad v. *Necessario;* to C. 22 q. 4 c. 17, ad v. *Emendatio;* to C. 17 q. 4 c. 3, ad v. *Non iudicio perpetuo.*

135. Ibid. to C. 22 q. 2 c. 5, ad v. *Maioribus:* "Nota quod secundum canones excusatur quis iuramento propter maiora negocia, ut extra de iureiurando [*X* 2.24.17] et cap. querelam [*X* 2.24.10]; secus secundum leges, quia difficultas prestationis non reddit stipulationem inutilem, ut ff de uerborum obligationibus, continuus, § illud [*Dig.* 45.1.137.4]."

136. Ibid. to C. 1 q. 7 d. p. c. 5, ad v. *Ut plerisque:* "Dispensatio est iuris communis relaxatio facta cum cause cognitione ab eo, qui ius habet dispensandi."

137. Ibid. to C. 1 q. 7 c. 16, ad v. *A debito:* "Id est a iure communi, quod omnibus equaliter debetur, et ita dispensatio non est ius, ut 31 q. i hac ratione [c. 9], quandoque tamen dispensatio debetur, ut 50 dis. constitueretur." See also ibid. to D. 50 c. 24, ad v. *Detrahendum est.*

some matters no dispensation at all might be granted.[138] Elsewhere, the gloss (drawing upon the categories outlined in the *Distinctiones* of Richardus) noted some exceptional instances in which dispensations were granted even against the most sacred authorities.[139] While Joannes held the general principle, as has been said, that any human bond might under certain conditions be nullified or dispensed,[140] he grounded his theory of dispensation from votive obligations upon the principle that every vow involves the positing of certain unexpressed conditions. If these necessary conditions are not fulfilled, then the vow does not become binding. Further, so far as the obligations resulting from pilgrimage vows were concerned, Joannes held that what were commonly called dispensations from vows of this type were not true dispensations, by which the obligations arising from the vow were nullified, but were really commutations, by which the pilgrimage obligations flowing from the vow were transmuted into a different and "better" set of obligations.[141] The exercise of the dispensing power was treated by Joannes as a kind of residual power of the bishop, who might dispense from any matter in which episcopal dispensation had not been expressly prohibited.[142]

THE DECRETISTS AND THE VOW. In summary it may be said that the decretists carried the analysis of the vow considerably further than Gra-

---

138. Ibid. to C. 1 q. 7 c. 23, ad v. *Et si ea ipsa:* "Si in dispensationibus non debet iudex dispensare nisi ex magna causa, quanto magis in iis que sunt indispensabilia, nullo modo debet iudex dispensare."

139. Ibid. to C. 25 q. 1 c. 6, ad v. *Apostoli:* "Hii uidetur quod papa non possit dispensare contra Apostolum, uel Dominum qualiter ergo Martinus dispensauit cum bigamo contra Apostolum, ut 34 dist. lector [c. 18]? Item cum canones Apostolorum dicat, presbyter si fornicator fuerit, deponatur, 81 dist. presbyter [c. 12], quomodo ergo Gangrense concilium dispensat in tali casu, ut di. 82 presbyter [c. 5]? Item contra Dominum dispensauit, qui dixit, 'Vouete, et reddite,' et tamen absoluit a iuramento et a uoto, 15 questio 6 iuratos [c. 5], extra de uoto et uoti redemptione per totum? Satis potest sustineri quod papa contra Apostolum dispensat in Euangelio: non tamen in his, que pertinent ad articulos fidei, eodem modo dispensat in Euangelio interpretando ipsum, extra de testibus, licet, in fin. [X 2.20.23]."

140. See the gloss cited in n. 134 above.

141. *Glos. ord.* to C. 25 q. 1 c. 6, ad v. *Apostoli:* "Item non est uera dispensatio que fit in uoto peregrinationis quia non dicitur uouens liberari ab illa obligatione: sed potius dicitur in melius commutari, ut extra de iureiurando, peruenit [X 2.24.2]; sed circa uotum continentie non posset dispensare, quia uix inueneretur melius in quo posset commutari, ut extra de statu regularium, cum ad monasterium, in fi. [X 3.35.6]. Ioann."

142. Ibid. to C. 1 q. 7 d. p. c. 5, ad v. *Ut plerisque.*

tian did and that they discussed and clarified some of the areas of uncertainty which he left open. By the early thirteenth century the tripartite analysis of the process of making vows had clearly become the accepted teaching of the canonists, despite disagreement concerning the degree to which each of the three stages of commitment was binding. The notion of simple and solemn vows, and the character of the solemn vow as a formal public act, expressed in verbis de presenti, usually witnessed by a priest or prelate, and binding both in foro externo and in foro interno, had been spelled out. There was general agreement, too, that the solemn vow might be judicially enforced by the ecclesiastical courts and that the person who voluntarily made a solemn vow could, if necessary, be coerced into satisfying the obligations resulting from his vow. On the other hand, vows might be held to be invalid for a variety of reasons, including the failure to obtain the consent of a superior, parent, or spouse, the influence of compulsion in taking the vow, or the lack of an adequate and responsible intention of binding oneself by the vow. A vow, although valid, might be rescinded under certain exceptional circumstances, notably when the conditions posited as necessary for the fulfillment of the vow ceased to exist, or when a greater obligation than that involved in the vow was assumed.

Up to this point, however, the crusade and the crusade vow in particular did not figure at all in the substantive law of the *Decretum* or in the commentaries of the decretists. As a particular species of vow with characteristics of its own differentiating it from other vows, the crusade vow first received specific canonistic consideration only in the thirteenth century.

CHAPTER III

The Crusade Vow in the
Works of the Decretalists

> *. . . ease would recant*
> *Vows made in pain, as violent and void.*
>
> *Paradise Lost 4.96–97*

By the end of the twelfth century, the character of the canon law as reflected in the *Decretum* of Gratian was already undergoing drastic modification, principally as a result of the increasing volume of legislation and authoritative canonistic interpretation which was beginning to flow from the papal curia and the universities. The main vehicle of this papal legislation was the steady stream of rescripts issued in ever larger numbers by the popes of the late twelfth and thirteenth centuries.

Writing toward the end of the twelfth century, Stephen of Tournai complained to the pope of these developments:

> Again, if a case comes up which should be settled under the canon law either by your judges delegate or by the ordinary judges, there is produced from the vendors an inextricable forest of decretal letters presumably under the name of Pope Alexander of sacred memory, and older canons are cast aside, rejected, expunged. When this plunder has been unrolled before us, those things which were wholesomely instituted in councils of holy fathers do not settle the case, nor is the conciliar prescription followed, since letters prevail which perchance advocates for hire invented and forged in their shops or cubicles under the name of Roman pontiffs. A new volume composed of these is solemnly read in the schools and offered for sale in the market place to the applause of a horde of notaries, who rejoice that in copying suspect opuscula both their labor is lessened and their pay increased.[1]

1. Adapted from the translation by Lynn Thorndike, *University Records and Life in the Middle Ages,* pp. 23–24; text in Heinrich Denifle, *Die Entstehung der Uni-*

Despite the protests and resistance of Stephen and others who may have felt as he did, the multiplication of rescripts and the growing importance of the regulations which they contained made the collection and publication of decretals an indispensable activity of the schools and the canonistic scholars of the time. Although such collections were, in the early stages, relatively miscellaneous and unstructured—containing only those few decretals which happened to be available to the compiler and of interest for his particular concerns—in the space of about fifteen years, from 1174/75 to 1191, they spanned the course of development from small, disorganized, local collections to such large, well-structured works as the *Compilatio prima* of Bernard of Pavia.[2]

From the time this work appeared in 1191, the decretal collections generally followed a uniform pattern of organization. The decretals as a whole were divided into five books, each of which treated a relatively well-defined field of canonistic legislation. The topics of the five books were indicated by the words of a mnemonic line: *Iudex, iudicium, clerus, connubium, crimen.* That is, the first book dealt with the sources of the law and the jurisdictional structure of the Church; the second with the canonistic courts and court procedures; the third with the law governing the lives of the clergy and related groups, as well as with ecclesiastical property; the fourth with matrimonial law; and the last book treated the canonistic penal law.

THE VOW IN THE DECRETAL COLLECTIONS. At first glance two things are striking about the treatment of the vow in the six great decretal collections—the *Quinque compilationes antiquae* and the *Decretales Gregorii IX*—of the late twelfth and early thirteenth centuries. In the first place, all but one contain a separate *titulus* of Book III which is devoted to the subject of vows; in the second, there is for the first time specific treatment of the crusade and pilgrimage vow.

---

versitäten des Mittelalters bis 1400, p. 745 n. 1, and *Chartularium Universitatis Parisiensis,* 1:47–48. For an estimate of the numerical rate of increase of papal *acta* in the eleventh and twelfth centuries, see Alexander Murray, "Pope Gregory VII and His Letters," *Traditio,* 22(1966), 149–202.

2. The juristic basis of decretal authority and the technical development of the collections are well described by Charles Duggan, *Twelfth-Century Decretal Collections and Their Importance in English History,* chs. 1–3.

THE TREATMENT OF VOWS IN THE COMPILATIO PRIMA. The *Breviarium extravagantium* or *Compilatio prima,* the earliest of the six major decretal collections, was compiled by Bernardus Papiensis [Bernard of Pavia], a Bolognese master and a one-time student of Huguccio, between 1187 and 1191.[3] Bernard's collection expressly treated the vow in title 29 of Book III of *Compilatio I,* under the heading *De voto et voti redemptione.* This title comprised only two decretals, both of them issued by Alexander III. The first decretal replied to a query of Bishop Bartholomew of Exeter as to whether a pilgrimage vow might be redeemed by almsgiving or, in case of necessity, commuted to some other good work. The pope stated that the answer to the question must lie with the person in charge (*qui presidet*), who was to consider diligently the position of those petitioning for alteration of the votive obligation and the reasons alleged for the request. Further, the party responsible for the decision must determine whether it would be better and more pleasing to God to accept a settlement (*recompensatio*) than to require the fulfillment of the pilgrimage obligation. Should a settlement seem more suitable, the pilgrimage vow might be dispensed from.[4]

The second decretal of this titulus also dealt with the problem of the commutation of a pilgrimage vow, specifically the vow to visit the Holy Sepulchre. In his letter to the bishop of Norwich on this matter, Alexander III granted a dispensation from the vow to one R., who had as a minor vowed to make the pilgrimage to Jerusalem and who had, moreover, pledged to accompany another person on the journey there. The dispensation from the vow was grounded on R.'s undertaking to redeem his vow by almsgiving and to provide during the balance of his life (if his funds were sufficient) for the support of one poor person.[5]

Both of these decretals, then, were concerned with the methods by which a vow might be dispensed, the circumstances under which it might be redeemed, and the possibility of commuting it to some other religious

3. *Compilatio prima* is analyzed by E. Friedberg in *Quinque compilationes antiquae,* pp. 1–65.

4. *Comp. I* 3.29.1 = *X* 3.34.1 (*JL,* 13,916). This decretal also appeared in the earlier Canterbury and Rochester collections, analyzed by Duggan, *Twelfth-Century Decretal Collections,* pp. 165, 180, and in the *Collectio Tanner* (Oxford, Bodleian Library, MS. Tanner 8, fol. 638ᵛ), analyzed by Walther Holtzmann, "Die Dekretalensammlungen des 12. Jahrhunderts," in *Festschrift zur Feier des Zweihundert-jährigen Bestehens der Akademie der Wissenschaften in Göttingen,* p. 119; Holtzmann also notes that it is found as well in the St. Germain and Bamberg collections.

5. *Comp. I* 3.29.2 = *X* 3.34.2 (*JL,* 11,339).

observance. These three matters—dispensation, redemption, and commutation—were to receive major emphasis in subsequent decretalist legislation concerning the vow and were further refined and extended by the decretalist commentators. With specific reference to the crusade vow, this new emphasis on the methods of avoiding fulfillment of the act vowed seemed to reflect the papacy's recent experience. The end of the twelfth century found a considerable dissatisfaction with the miscellaneous expeditions that had made up the twelfth-century crusades. While the first crusade had succeeded in achieving its goal, despite the fact that the army was encumbered by thousands of noncombatants of various kinds,[6] later expeditions had not been nearly so successful. The fiasco of the second crusade (1146–48) had already been laid in part to the miscellaneous composition of its forces by such commentators as the annalist of Würzburg (see Introduction). Clearly what was wanted was an army of well-equipped, experienced fighting men, who might be able to achieve the military victories needed to reestablish the Latin states. It was evident as, indeed, Urban II had perceived when he proclaimed the first crusade, that miscellaneous bands of pious enthusiasts could contribute only slightly to this end through their participation in the crusade expeditions. Subsequent experience had served to underscore the need to discourage the participation of the merely pious and to convert their enthusiasm into some form of support which would make a solid contribution to the achievement of the crusade's goal—hence the papacy's policy, reflected in the decretal collections, of converting the crusade vows of those whose military usefulness to the crusade was not apparent into other forms of assistance.

The pontificate of Pope Innocent III seems to have been crucial in this, as in so many other canonistic developments. Until his time the papacy had regularly insisted that those who took the crusade vow should do so cautiously and with some sort of prior ecclesiastical counsel or approval. To what extent this earlier policy had been implemented in practice may be questioned, but its existence is clear, whether it was always enforced or not. During the pontificate of Innocent III, however, the policy itself was abandoned. In a letter of general circulation dispatched in April 1213, Innocent communicated the new policy to the bishops of the Western Church:

6. See especially Walter Porges, "The Clergy, the Poor and the Non-Combatants on the First Crusade," *Speculum*, 21(1946), 1–21.

Since it happens that assistance to the Holy Land is much hindered or delayed if each one must be examined prior to taking the cross as to his fitness and ability to fulfill the vow in person, we allow that (save for regulars), whoever wishes to take the sign of the cross may do so, on the assumption that when dire necessity or plain usefulness may so require, the vow may be commuted, redeemed, or postponed by apostolic command.[7]

While some of the most eminent twelfth-century decretists—notably Rufinus and Huguccio—had denied the possibility of any dispensation from any kind of unconditional vow at all,[8] such a possibility had increasingly been admitted in principle by the writers of the latter part of the century. This development was reinforced by the incorporation in the thirteenth-century decretal collections of relevant papal rulings, and much decretalist commentary upon the titles *De voto* in those collections was concerned with attempts to create a doctrinal system which would rationalize, clarify, and explain the practice of releasing persons from their votive obligations. This line of development was important for later generations, as the practice of dispensing from crusade vows came more and more to play the role of a financial expedient to raise money for objectives quite different from the crusade.

DECRETALIST COMMENTARIES ON COMPILATIO PRIMA.   One of the earliest and most important of the commentaries on *Compilatio prima* was that of its compiler, Bernard of Pavia, whose *Summa decretalium* (written between 1191 and 1198) was both a commentary on his own decretal collection and also an introductory treatment of the canon law in general as it had developed up to his period.

In his *Summa,* Bernard stated that a vow might be voided in two ways:

7. *Po,* 4,725; Innocent III, *Registrum* 16.28 (*PL,* 116:819–20): "Quia vero subsidium terrae sanctae multum impediri vel retardari contingeret si ante susceptionem crucis examinari quemlibet oportet an esset idoneus et sufficiens ad hujusmodi votum personaliter prosequendum, concedimus ut, regularibus personis exceptis, suscipiant quicunque voluerint signum crucis; ita quod cum urgens necessitas aut evidens utilitas postulaverint, votum ipsum de apostolico possit mandato commutari aut redimi vel differri." See also Palmer A. Throop, *Criticism of the Crusade: A Study of Public Opinion and Crusade Propaganda,* pp. 83–94, on the results of the change in policy.

8. As noted by J. de Brys, *De dispensatione in iure canonico,* pp. 129–31; see Rufinus, *Summa* to C. 1 q. 7 d. a. c. 6 (ed. Singer, p. 234); Huguccio, *Summa* to C. 17 d. a. c. 1 in Paris, Bibliothèque Nationale, MS. lat. 3892, fol. 243vb.

through the lack of a necessary condition and through the power of a superior. The lack of a necessary condition he related only to conditional vows, i.e. those in which an express stipulation of an antecedent condition was involved in the votive formulation. When dealing with the power of a superior to quash the vow of a subject, he considered the situations already envisioned by Gratian: the nullification of a monk's vow by his abbot, of a serf's vow by his lord, of a minor's vow by his parent or guardian, of a wife's vow by her husband.[9]

Vows in general Bernard divided into two classes: those which could be fulfilled by nonperformance of an act (such as abstinence from food or from sexual intercourse) and those which could be fulfilled by the performance of an act (such as a pilgrimage vow).[10] Further, he distinguished between redeemable vows, which were fulfilled by performing an act, or were vows of abstinence, and irredeemable vows (the only example cited was the solemn vow of chastity; Bernard held, however, that simple vows of chastity might be redeemed in order to avert an evil greater than the nonobservance of the vow). Redemption of the vow might be prescribed by bishops at their discretion, and taking into account the character of the persons involved and the nature of the acts of redemption—almsgiving, fasting, prayer, and the like.[11] Simple vows, on the other hand, might be revoked even without redemption if the revocation were necessary in order to avert a still more serious evil.[12] In treating the exercise of the dispensing power, Bernard took the position that bishops might dispense only in matters where this power was specifically delegated to them. Otherwise he held that the only power competent to dispense would be that power competent to enact the law to be dispensed from.[13]

An *Apparatus* to *Compilatio prima* (written early in the thirteenth century by one of the school of Petrus Brito) took a much more permissive view of the dispensing power than did Bernard of Pavia. The author held that in all questions of dispensation recourse should be had to the bishop, although he noted that some would go so far as to teach that any person exercising the cure of souls might dispense in matters concerning those subject to him. He thus implied rather clearly that the normal

9. *Summa decretalium* 3.29.5 (ed. E. A. T. Laspeyres, p. 114); also in *Summa de matrimonio* 3.1 (ed. Laspeyres, pp. 287–88).
10. *Summa decretalium* 3.29.2 (ed. Laspeyres, pp. 113–14).
11. Ibid., 3.29.3–4 (ed. Laspeyres, p. 114).
12. Ibid., 3.29.3 (ed. Laspeyres, p. 114).
13. Ibid., 5.2.6 (ed. Laspeyres, pp. 205–6).

power of dispensation was vested in the bishop and that inferior clerics could exercise the dispensing power as his delegates. An exception to this rule was the dispensation from the vow of continence, but it was an exception, he argued, simply because there existed no greater good which could be substituted for continence. This argument makes it clear that in his discussion of dispensation the author really had in mind the redemption of the vow and, further, that he saw no apparent distinction between dispensation and redemption.[14] The author warned that illness was not in itself sufficient reason for allowing a pilgrimage vow, specifically, to be redeemed, but that redemption should be granted only when the illness would make the journey impossible or dangerous. Further, redemption of pilgrimage vows was not a prerogative of the rich, but a privilege which might be granted to those who were poor and infirm.[15]

The question of the dispensability of pilgrimage vows was also discussed by Alanus Anglicus in his *Apparatus* to *Compilatio prima* (written between 1201 and 1210).[16] The commutation of a vow, Alanus held, was neither contrary to the natural law nor an infraction of the original vow and hence might be allowed. As to outright dispensations, he re-

14. On the school of Petrus Brito see especially S. Kuttner, "Bernardus Compostellanus antiquus: A Study in the Glossators of the Canon Law," *Traditio,* 1(1943), 317 n. 54; W. Ullmann, *Medieval Papalism,* pp. 208–10; R. Weigand, "Neue Mitteilungen aus Handschriften," *Traditio,* 21(1965), 487–91. *Apparatus* to *Comp. I* 3.29.1, ad v. *presidet,* in Lambeth Palace Library, MS. 105, fol. 180ʳᵃ: "Patet quod episcopus in uotis dispensare potest; idem uidetur de quolibet prelato per hoc quod dicit 'presidet' quod quidam concedit de quolibet qui habet curam animarum quod potest dispensare circa subditos suos. Sed Petrus Brito [p. Bi *scr.*] dicit quod semper recurrendum est in huiusmodi ad episcopum et est generale quod hic dicitur/in uotis abstinentie; infra de penitentiis et remissionibus, c. ult. [*Comp. I* 5.33.3 = X 5.38.4], ⟨x⟩xxii i Latorem [C. 32 q. 3 c. 15]. In uotis continentie secus, quia iusta compensatione redimi non potest, cum nihil melius continentia; ⟨x⟩xxiii Q. v Circumcelliones [C. 23 q. 5 c. 1], quia incurie [?] preter carnem uiuere non terrena uita est, sed celestis." The Lambeth MS. also contains glosses of Richardus Anglicus, but none on the title *De voto.*

15. Ibid. to 3.29.1, ad v. *infirmitate,* in Lambeth Palace Library, MS. 105, fol. 180ʳᵃ: "Si de tali qua iter impediat, non imputatur et sic non est in redemptione; si non impediat dic de tali intelligens nisi periculum iminet si perficiat." Ibid., ad v. *divitiarum:* Quidam arguunt hic pro diuitibus xl⟨i⟩ d. non cogantur [D. 41 c. 3]; Petrus Brito e contra intelligit qui ita delicati sunt quod nolunt implere uotum suum, cum talibus non est dispensandum, sed cum pauperibus infirmis."

16. See especially A. M. Stickler, "Alanus Anglicus als Verteidiger des monarchischen Papsttums," *Salesianum,* 21(1959), 346–406. I have used two MSS. of Alanus' *Apparatus:* Paris, Bibliothèque Nationale, MS. lat. 3932, and the second stratum of glosses in Munich, Bayerische Staatsbibliothek, Clm. 3879, on which see Kuttner, *Repertorium,* pp. 332–33.

ported the views of certain persons who held that vows might not be dispensed at all, since the vow created an obligation under the natural law, from which dispensations were not permitted. In mitigation of this position, however, he argued that only some of the precepts of the natural law could be considered indispensable, and that since every vow or oath implied certain necessary conditions, among them the condition "unless the pope shall direct otherwise," it followed that the pope might grant dispensations from any vow,[17] including vows of abstinence and continence. (In this last he went further than most of his contemporaries.) Indeed, he declared that any freely made vow might be dispensed from,[18] and that vows made in youth might be dispensed without any sort of compensation whatever,[19] while hastily made vows were not binding at all.[20]

17. B.N. lat. 3932, fol. 39ra, and Munich, Clm. 3879, fol. 55rb: "Hec dispensatio non est contra ius naturale, non enim est uoti fractio. Non enim uotum uel iuramentum frangit qui illud commutat in melius, ut supra de iureiurando, peruenit [*Comp. I* 2.17.10 = X 2.24.3]. Sed an papa possit sine aliqua recompensatio⟨ne⟩ uotum remittere queritur, et dicunt quidam quod non quantum ad deum, quoniam contra ius naturale non potest dispensare. Sed uotum est de iure naturali, id est uoti redemptio. Quantum ad ecclesiam tamen potest omnem penam remittere pro uoti fractione infligendam. Vel dicatur quod possit, nec inuenitur sibi prohibita dispensatio contra ius naturale in aliquo iure. Constitutionem tamen contraria iuri naturali facere non posset nec etiam contra quedam precepta iuris naturalis dispensare, ut est istud: 'diliges dominum deum tuum' [Deut. 6:5; cf. Matt. 22:37, Mark 12:30, Luke 10:27]. Vel dicitur ut prius quod non potest dispensare, si tamen uotum remittat, ualet remissio, quoniam in omni uoto et iuramento quedam tacite conditiones subintelliguntur, inter quas et ista est: 'nisi papa aliter disposuerit'; arg. extra c. ex tenore [*Comp. I* 5.34.15 = X 5.39.10]."

18. Alanus, *Apparatus* to *Comp. I* 3.29.1, ad v. *recompensatio*, in Munich, Clm. 3879, fol. 55rb: "In omni uoto, siue abstinentie siue continentie, siue consistat in faciendo siue in non faciendo, siue sit simplex ⟨siue⟩ solempne, locum habet compensatio, dummodo ante uotum libere fuit uoluntatis. Hoc ideo adicio quia articulos fidei uouet unusquisque in baptismo, ante tamen baptismum illud uotum est necessitatis et non libere uoluntatis. Quidam excipiunt uotum continencie cui eque bonum inueniri non potest, ar. xxxii q. ult. c. i et ideo par eque bono compensari non potest; sed uerius quod possit, ar. infra qui clerici uel uouentes, c. ult. [*Comp. I* 4.6.8. = X 4.6.5]."

19. Ibid. to 3.29.2, ad v. *in puerilitate*, in Munich, Clm. 3879, fol. 55rb: "Ergo pubes factus sine omni recompensatione posset a uoto recedere, ar. xx q. i c. i, supra de regularibus transeuntibus, c. ult. [*Comp. I* 3.27.11 = X 3.31.11]. Quare ergo in fine compensatur. Respondes ad cautelam habendantem, uel quod melius est, ratum fuerit uotum postquam adoleuit."

20. Ibid. to 3.29.2, ad v. *facilitate*, in Munich, Clm. 3879, fol. 55rb: "ar. uotum ex ⟨facilitate⟩ [*ms.*: facultate] emissum non esse obligatorium; supra de regularibus transeuntibus ad ⟨religionem⟩ [*ms.*: maiorem]; xxii q. iiii unusquisque [c. 8]; contra ar. xvii q. iiii sunt qui opes [c. 3]." This gloss was also incorporated, with the

Tancredus (ca.1185–ca.1236), in his *Apparatus* to *Compilatio prima* (1210–15), which became the *glossa ordinaria* to the collection, recognized Alanus' position, which he quoted almost verbatim, but took exception to the notion that vows of continence might be subject to commutation or redemption. A commutation of any other freely made vow might be allowed, but Tancredus held, with the anonymous author of the school of Petrus Brito, that the vow of continence was an exception, because there was no equivalent good which might be substituted for consecrated virginity.[21] Tancredus did not question the fact that pilgrimage vows might be commuted into other observances. Rather, he discussed the authority competent to grant the commutation, concluding that bishops had the power to deal with all pilgrimage vows save for the crusade vow, which was reserved to the jurisdiction of the pope alone.[22] Regarding vows made by minors, Tancredus cited the view of Alanus that they were not binding and required no formal action, unless they had been ratified after reaching adulthood; he added a note, however, on contrary arguments.[23]

THE VOW IN COMPILATIO SECUNDA. The decretal collection known as *Compilatio secunda* (although it was in fact the third of the *Quinque compilationes* in order of appearance), drew its material mainly from the decretals of Alexander III, Clement III (1187–91), and Celestine III (1191–98), covering papal legislation for the period between those dealt with in *Compilationes prima* and *tertia*. *Compilatio secunda* was com-

---

siglum of Richardus, in the *Apparatus* of Tancredus (Cambridge, Gonville and Caius College, MS. 28/17, p. 76ᵇ; Durham, Cathedral Library, MS. C.III.4, fol. 34ʳᵇ).

21. Tancredus, *Apparatus* to *Comp. I* 3.29.1, ad v. *recompensatio,* in Gonville and Caius College, MS. 28/17, p. 76ᵇ: "Mihi uidetur quod circa uotum continencie nullus dispensare potest quod asserit vin⟨centius⟩ ar. xxxii q. i nuptie [c. 12]; xxxii q. v. ille [c. 14] et expressum habetur ut extra iii de statu monachorum, cum ad monasterium [*Comp. III* 3.27.2 = X 3.35.6], infra eodem capitulo ultimo uel ii; et haec est causa, quia in uoto continencie commutacio non admittitur. t."

22. Ibid. to c. 29. 1 pr. in Gonville and Caius College, MS. 28/17, p. 76ᵇ: "De peregrinacionis dependet ergo auctoritate papa, non debet quis redimere uotum, sed superioris. Sed nunquid prelatus qualibet potest auctoritate prestare ad ⟨commutationem⟩ [*ms.:* coniunctionem] uoti? Quidam dicunt quod nullus nisi papa uel qui speciale mandatum ab eo super hoc recepit, ut in eodem titulo, ex multa, liber iii [*Comp. III* 3.26.5 = X 3.34.9]. Ego dico quod omnibus episcopis licet et illud est speciale in his qui crucem acceperunt ierosolimam profecturi. t."

23. Ibid. to 3.29.2, ad v. *veniens in puerili,* Gonville and Caius College, MS. 28/17, p. 76ᵇ.

posed by John of Wales, a master and professor of the University of Bologna, between 1210 and 1212.[24] Under the title *De voto et voti redemptione,* John entered four decretals. The first, a decretal of Alexander III, reiterated the position, already familiar to the decretists, that a mental resolve (*conceptio*) to perform an act did not constitute a binding vow.[25] The remaining three decretals all dealt with the problem of commuting vows which had previously been made. One of them laid down the principle that any vow could be commuted to a vow of religion, which was thus posited as the highest and most perfect type of vow.[26] Another specified that a crusade vow in particular must either be fulfilled in person or else commuted to another pious act and that the penalty for nonfulfillment was excommunication.[27] The final canon of the title specified that a suitable commutation for a crusade vow would be the provision of an adequate subsidy to support other persons who were journeying to the Holy Land themselves.[28]

As a whole, the glosses which I have consulted on the title *De voto* in *Compilatio II* are relatively sparse and add little to the plain sense of the decretals themselves.[29] Among the more interesting is the *notabilia "Nota quod non possumus"* by the Dominican Paulus Hungarus (d. 1242), though even his comments are very brief. In his gloss to the first chapter of the title *De voto,* Paulus interpreted the decretal to mean that no obligation arose from a bare promise—a rather sweeping extension, in fact, of the decretal's text—and added that entertaining a wish does not oblige one to fulfill a vow, a position by this time well founded. In a shot at the more traditional forms of the monastic life, Paulus added the further observation that the contemplative life was not the only one which led to salvation, but that the active life might do so too.[30] In subsequent

24. On John of Wales and *Comp. II,* see especially Franz Gillmann, "Johannes Galensis als Glossator, inbesondere der Compilatio III," *Archiv für katholisches Kirchenrecht,* 105(1925), 488–565. The collection is analyzed by Friedberg, *Quinque compilationes,* pp. 66–104.

25. *Comp. II* 3.21.1 = X 3.34.3.

26. Ibid., 3.21.2 = X 3.34.4.

27. Ibid., 3.21.3 (X ——).

28. Ibid., 3.21.4 (X ——).

29. The brief *Casus "Quesivit Anconitanus"* of the early thirteenth century (on which see Kuttner, *Repertorium,* pp. 402–3), which I have examined in Bodleian, MS. Laud. Misc. 646, certainly added nothing significant to the literal meaning of the text and the glosses of Albertus (see Kuttner, *Repertorium,* p. 345) are scarcely more informative, save for a few short notes which were incorporated by Tancredus into his *glossa ordinaria,* on which see below, p. 76.

30. Paulus Hungarus, *Notabilia* to *Comp. II* 3.21.1 in Bibliotheca Apostolica Vaticana, MS. Borgh. Lat. 261, fol. 78[vb]: "Nota quod bonitas hominis scitur per

glosses, Paulus noted that the commutation of a vow did not involve any breaking of it, and he stressed the notion that a just cause was always required for dispensation.[31] In another pointed observation he stated as a general proposition, based on the text which he was glossing, that the greater one's position, the greater the number of persons who might sin because of his example; this principle, Paulus said, ought to be noted against prelates.[32]

The *glossa ordinaria* to *Compilatio II* was written by Tancredus prior to 1215.[33] Although his glosses to the title *De voto* were brief and generally unremarkable, a gloss to chapter 4, bearing the siglum of Albertus, interpreted a provision of the text calling for the payment of an adequate subsidy to the Holy Land as a condition of commutation to mean that in principle the amount of such a subsidy should be proportional to the wealth of the person requesting the commutation. One pound, he suggested, might be an adequate subsidy from a poor person.[34]

THE VOW IN COMPILATIO TERTIA. The decretal collection known as *Compilatio tertia* was the work of Pietro Collivaccino (otherwise known as Petrus Beneventanus), a notary of the Roman Curia under Pope Innocent III, who authorized its redaction. The collection was completed in the summer of 1209 and was officially transmitted by the pontiff to the University of Bologna by the letter *Devotioni vestri precibus,* which formally sanctioned it for official use in the ecclesiastical courts as well as in the schools. Whereas the *Decretum* and the earlier decretal collections had all been private efforts, even though they were widely used as texts both for scholastic and judicial purposes, *Compilatio tertia* represented the

---

famam. Item ex uoto ad uotum non obligatur quis. Item ex nuda promissione non oritur obligatio. Item non solum contemplativis sed etiam activis saluantur."

31. Ibid. to 3.21.2 in Vat. Borgh. Lat. 261, fol. 78[vb]: "Nota quod non frangit uotum qui in melius illud commutat. Item dispensatio fieri non debet nisi iusta ex causa."

32. Ibid. to 3.21.3 in Vat. Borgh. Lat. 261, fol. 78[vb]: "Nota quod quis compellitur ad uotum implendum, uel commutandum. Item tanto plures eius exemplo peccant quanto quis est maior et est notandum contra prelatos."

33. Kuttner, *Repertorium,* p. 346.

34. Tancredus, *Apparatus* to *Comp. II* 3.21.4 in Durham Cathedral Library, MS. C.III.4, fol. 81[va] (also in Lincoln Cathedral Library, MS. 38, fol. 189[ra]): "Affluencia uouentis inspecta est, supra eodem titulo c. i. £ i hoc tamen forte sufficeret in paupere. a."

initial papal effort to promulgate an official collection of the ecclesiastical law. The decretals contained in this collection were taken from the registers of the first twelve years of the pontificate of Innocent III.[35]

The title *De voto* in *Compilatio III* contains five decretals, all drawn from the first four years of Innocent III's pontificate, each dealing specifically with crusade vows. The first of them enunciated the principle that the pope had the power to grant a delay in the fulfillment of crusade vows if good and sufficient reason for the delay were presented.[36] Another, *Quod super his,* clarified the position by declaring that a delay in fulfilling the vow might be granted where the hindrance was merely a temporary matter—sickness or the like—but that when the existence of a permanent impediment to fulfillment was demonstrated, a redemption of the vow was to be granted. Further, the wives of crusaders were conceded the right to follow their husbands on crusade, although crusade vows made by women were generally to be redeemed, unless the lady in question was wealthy and would be accompanied by a retinue of soldiers who would give military assistance to the beleaguered forces of the Latin states.[37] The principle that wives might follow their husbands on crusade was also enunciated in *Ex multa,* a further canon of this title in *Compilatio III;* but if this permission might be considered a concession to the wives of crusaders, *Ex multa* further provided that men might take the crusade vow and fulfill it without seeking their wives' consent. This provision radically altered the status of the crusader's wife and also, incidentally, marked a notable innovation in canonistic attitudes concerning the vows of married persons. As for the redemption and commutation of crusaders' vows, *Ex multa* further stipulated that the power to grant such exemptions was reserved to the pope alone and to those specially commissioned by him to deal with this matter.[38] Another decretal in this title, *Magne*

35. On Pietro Collivaccino see especially Friedrich Heyer, "Ueber Petrus Collivaccinus von Benevent," *ZRG, KA,* 30(1916), 395–405. The collection is analyzed by Friedberg, *Quinque compilationes,* pp. 105–34.

36. *Comp. III* 3.26.1 = *X* 3.34.5 (*Po,* 14).

37. Ibid., 3.26.4 = *X* 3.34.8 (*Po,* 1137).

38. Ibid., 3.26.5 = *X* 3.34.9 (*Po,* 1,469). This decretal was addressed to Archbishop Hubert Walter of Canterbury, who had experienced a number of problems with the vows of English crusaders. On this matter see also Innocent III, *Registrum* 5.94 (*PL,* 214:1088–90 = *Po,* 1,733); as well as C. R. Cheney, *English Bishops' Chanceries, 1100–1250,* p. 131, "Master Philip the Notary and the Fortieth of 1199," *English Historical Review,* 63(1948), 349, n. 2 and especially his *Hubert Walter,* pp. 124–30. On the status of crusaders' wives, see Brundage, "The Crusader's Wife: A Canonistic Quandary," *Studia Gratiana,* 12(1967), 425–42.

devotionis, laid down the general principles by which to determine the amount to be assessed for commutation of a crusade vow, setting it as equal to the sum which would have been spent had the vow been fulfilled in person. This sum should include the outlay required in order to journey to, remain in, and return from Jerusalem.[39] Finally, the decretal *Licet* made the point that the obligation incurred by an unfulfilled crusade vow might be passed on to an heir of the person making the vow and that the heir's obligation could be enforced, if necessary, by sequestration of the inherited estate.[40]

The decretalists who glossed *Compilatio III* were fuller and considerably more enterprising in their interpretations than the glossators of *Compilatio II*. The *Apparatus* attributed to Laurentius Hispanus and written between 1210 and 1215 (see Chapter II), emphasized that exemption from the vow should be refused those who were capable of giving advice and counsel to the crusade army, as well as to those capable of fighting; this distinction would apply to clerics as well as to laymen.[41] Further, the Laurentius *Apparatus* taught that the commutation of a crusade vow must be tailored to fit the facts of the individual case; thus, for example, a knight of great prowess could not well win reprieve from his obligation to go on crusade by sending in his place a timid knight. The glossator's principle here, though he did not state it explicitly, seems to be that the commutation of an obligation must necessarily involve the substitution of a service fully equivalent to the one originally promised.[42] As for the

39. *Comp. III* 3.26.3 = X 3.34.7 (*Po,* 48).

40. Ibid., 3.26.2 = X 3.34.6 (*Po,* 4). The principle of the heritability of votive obligations, although new to the canon law, was no great novelty. A passage incorporated in Justinian's *Digest* clearly set forth the principle: "Voti enim obligationem ad heredem transire constat" (*Dig.* 50.12.2.2). There is ample evidence from Roman inscriptions that heirs frequently did fulfill the vows of decedents, although whether they did so as a result of specific legal actions to enforce the vows is not evident; see Turlan, "L'Obligation 'ex voto'," pp. 532–33. The great legist, Accursius (d. ca.1260), however, denied that the principle of heritability applied to pilgrimage vows: *glos. ord.* to *Dig.* 50.12.2.2, ad v. *voti enim,* "Quod in dando consistit. . . . § Quid autem, si voueat vt vadat ad sanctum Iacobum? Respon. Non transit ad haeredem, vt C. de cad. tol. 1. j § ne autem [*Cod.* 6.50.1.16] et supra de verb. obli. 1. centesimis § si ita [*Dig.* 45.1.46.2]. Accur."

41. Laurentius, *Apparatus* to *Comp. III* 3.26.3, ad v. *pugnatorum* in Paris, Bibliothèque Nationale, MS. lat. 3932, fol. 168ᵛᵃ: "Satis tamen pugnat qui consilio pugnat, ut C. de aduocatis diuersorum iudiciorum, aduocati [*Cod.* 2.7.14.pr.]. Vnde idem an consilio pollet cui uim natura negauit, infra eodem titulo ex multa [*Comp. III* 3.26.5 = X 3.34.9]; nam licet aliquis propter delibitatem excusetur a muneribus; clerici si talia sunt munera que consilio conpleri possunt non excusantur: ff de uacatione ⟨et excusatione⟩ munerum, 1. ii quem ita senio [*Dig.* 50.5.2]."

42. Ibid. to 3.26.4, ad v. *per alios,* in B.N. lat. 3932, fol. 169ᵛᵃ: "Sed esto quod ille qui uouit ferocissimus miles erat, numquid in hoc casu sufficit mittere pro se

provision that husbands might licitly make and fulfill crusade vows without their wives' consent, the *Apparatus* noted that this was an extraordinary variation of the general rule concerning the vows of married persons, and interpreted it as a special favor granted out of solicitude for the peculiar needs of the Holy Land. Further, the glossator remarked, as others had earlier done, that this privilege would seem to elevate the crusade vow to a higher status than even the vow of continence, since no similar favor was granted to those who wished to take that vow.[43]

The *Apparatus* of Vincentius Hispanus, written before 1215,[44] questioned the adequacy of the norm for estimating the compensation required for commutation of the crusade vow. As Vincentius rightly remarked, the amount to be assessed as compensation for the effort which would have been expended in journeying to the Holy Land might be somewhat difficult to determine. He concluded, however, that the terms of the decretal *Licet* would seem to indicate that the calculation need not be a very fine one.[45] In the matter of the papal dispensing power, he reported that some would accept the pope's power to dispense from pilgrimage vows—on the grounds that a more acceptable substitute might replace the pilgrimage itself—but would deny any power to dispense from the vow of continence, since no practice more acceptable to God could be substituted. His own solution to the problem seems to have been that only those practices which were clearly contrary to the faith and the forms of usury which were prohibited in the Old Testament were not subject to dispensa-

---

mediocrem? Videtur quod non, ut ff de solutionibus, inter artifices [*Dig.* 46.3.31]; quamuis posset dici quod non ita amare istud est exigendum, cum ⟨gratuito⟩ [*ms.:* gratuituo] fuerit ab initio ut infra de censibus, ex parte [*Comp. III* 3.37.3]."

43. Ibid. to 3.36.5, ad v. *uxorum*, in B.N. lat. 3932, fol. 169ᵛᵃ: "Contra xxvii Q. ii scripsit [c. 26]; contra xxxiii Q. v quod deo [c. 4]; sed hoc dic speciale in favorem terre sancte, et satis colligitur hic, hic uotum esset maius uoto continentie cum propter continentiam non liceret hoc, ut capitulis precedentis et xxxiii Q. v c. i et xxvii Q. ii sic ⟨tu⟩ [*ms.:* causa] abstines [c. 24]."

44. On Vincentius, see especially Gaines Post, "'Blessed Lady Spain'—Vincentius Hispanus and Spanish National Imperialism in the Thirteenth Century," *Speculum*, 29(1954), 198–209 (revised version in his Studies in *Medieval Legal Thought*, pp. 482–93, but cf. the argument of Wilhelm Berges, "Kaiserrecht und Kaisertheorie der 'Siete Partidas'," in *Festschrift Percy Ernst Schramm*, 1:142–56); S. Kuttner, "Wo war Vincentius Hispanus Bischof?," *Traditio*, 22(1966), 471–74, and "Notes on Manuscripts," *Traditio*, 17(1961), 537–42; Javier Ochoa Sanz, *Vincentius Hispanus canonista boloñes del siglo XIII.*

45. Vincentius, *Apparatus* to *Comp. III* 3.26.4, ad v. *recompensatio*, in Bibliotheca Apostolica Vaticana, MS. Lat. 1378, fol. 75ʳᵇ: "Numquid tantum mittent pro quanto uellent tantum laborem sustinere, uti quia in multis hoc esset difficile estimare cum pro sola salute anime illud sustinerent, sed forte hec compensatio fiet non cum tanta distinctione, ar. e. t. licet."

tion.[46] The concept of the heritability of the crusade vow and the provision in *Licet* that the fulfillment of this inherited obligation might be enforced by a confiscation of the inherited goods was explained by Vincentius as an extension of existing law in favor of the Holy Land.[47] The provision that a man might take the crusade vow without the consent of his wife was likewise noted as a special favor for the Holy Land.[48]

Two glosses bearing the siglum of Laurentius also dealt with the special character of the crusade vow, in particular with the reservation to the pope of the right of dispensation, although Laurentius held that bishops could grant dispensations from all other vows.[49] Further, he argued that by extension of the rule laid down in *Licet* it might be held that one person

46. Ibid. to 3.26.1, ad v. *voti,* in Vat. Lat. 1378, fol. 74ra: "Cum enim quis uoue⟨t⟩ peregrinari, subintelligitur 'si commode fieri potest [*corr. in ms. ex:* potuit] supra de iureiurando, quanto 1. e. [*Comp. III* 2.15.4 = X 2.24.18]; sicut non frangit uotum qui in melius commutat, supra de iureiurando, peruenit 1. i [*Comp. I* 2.17.10 = X 2.24.3]. Alii dicunt quod circa uotum peregrinationis potest papa dispensare sed ⟨non⟩ circa uotum continencie quia est de maioribus bonis, xxxii Q. i nuptie [c. 12], et nichil acceptabilius deo quam continentia. Tercii dicunt quod etiam in uoto continentie potest, ar. supra qui clerici uel uouentes, super eo [*Comp. I* 4.6.5; X ——] et c. ult. 1 e [*Comp. I* 4.6.8 = X 4.6.5]. Soli autem fidei et ea que prohibita sunt in ueteri testamento usure sunt indispensabilia." This passage, with the siglum of Vincentius appended, occurs also in the gloss apparatus to Tancredus (Gonville and Caius College, MS. 28/17, p. 267^a) and in the mixed gloss apparatus of Munich, Clm. 3879, fol. 227vb; cf. *glos. ord.* to X 3.34.5, ad v. *auctoritatis sede apostolici.*

47. Vincentius, *Apparatus* to *Comp. III* 3.26.2, ad v. *regnum,* in Vat. Lat. 1378, fol. 74rb: "Huius canonis rigor legem uincit in [*ms. add. et cancell.:* auctoritate] asperitate. Lex enim [omni] soli extraneo heredi ⟨totum⟩ [*ms.:* quotum] aufert ⟨cum testatoris⟩ [*ms.:* contestatoris] uoluntatem infra annum non implet, auth. de heredibus et falcidia § ii [*Nov.* 1.4.pr.]. Aliis autem reservat debitum [*corr. ex* delictum] naturale supra iiii, ut C. de fideicommissis [*Cod.* 6.42] aut amplius auth. de heredibus et falcidia § ii. Solutio: hic pena augetur in fauorem sancte terre; hanc tamen penam inposuit omnibus lex antiqua, C. de fideiconmissis, 1. ult. [*Cod.* 6.42.32.2]; uel hoc ideo quia regnum sicut marchia ducatus et comitatus non diuiduntur ut constitutione friderici de feudis § preterea de marchia." This passage also occurs in the gloss apparatus of Clm. 3879, fol. 228rb.

48. Vincentius, *Apparatus* to *Comp. III* 3.26.5, ad v. *uxorem,* in Vat. Lat. 1378, fol. 75vb.

49. Gloss to *Comp. III* 3.26.5, ad v. *incumbit,* in Clm. 3879, fol. 229va: "Ecce hic unum mirabile quod est in ius commune, ubi dispensetur in uoto cum debilibus et huius⟨modi⟩; ar. supra eodem c. i, et tamen eius executio non permittitur alicui nisi cum papa speciale commiserit. quod in tantum restringendum est circa uotum huius⟨modi⟩ quod pro succursu terre sancte emissum est, cum hic sibi specialiter dispensationem papa reseruet; in aliis autem uotis episcopum credo dispensare posse. lau."

could perform a fast for another, since the dead were allowed to fulfill their vows through the actions of their survivors.[50]

The glosses of Joannes Teutonicus carried the argument on the dispensing power still further. In one gloss bearing his siglum, Joannes posited that the pope could dispense from anything save an article of faith and, while his conclusion seemed to favor the view that the vow of continence, too, might not be dispensed from, he did not take a positive stand against the more permissive position which he had earlier voiced.[51] Joannes also noted that the amount of money to be levied as a suitable redemption for a crusade vow should allow for the expenses of transferring funds.[52] Finally he rejected the argument that the special privilege granted by the decretal *Ex multa* implied that the crusade vow was superior to the vow of continence.[53]

THE VOW IN COMPILATIONES QUARTA AND QUINTA. The title *De voto* did not figure at all in *Compilatio quarta*, a brief decretal collection composed in 1215/16 by Joannes Teutonicus, and drawn mainly from the decrees of the Fourth Lateran Council (1215) and the decretals of Inno-

50. Tancredus, *Apparatus* to *Comp. III* 3.26.2, ad v. *commisit* in Durham Cathedral Library, MS. C.III.4, fol. 178ʳᵇ: "Ar. quod alius potest ieuniare pro alio: ⟨uotum⟩ [*corr. in ms. ex:* uoto] alterius adimplere⟨t⟩, quia mortuus soluit uotum suum per super⟨stitem⟩, ut xxxiii Q. ii anime defunctorum [*recte:* C. 13 q. 2 c. 22] et xxvi Q. vi Si ⟨aliquis excommunicatus⟩ [C. 26 q. 6 c. 22; *ms.:* quis fuerit]; infra eodem quod super [*Comp. III* 3.26.4]; supra de sententia excommunicationis, inspectis [*Comp. II* 5.18.2]. lau."

51. Gloss to *Comp. III* 3.26.1, ad v. *sedis apostolice,* in Clm. 3879, fol. 227ᵛᵇ: "Vnde si papa aliud placet per hoc non dispensat sed tantum suum uelle declarat, uel dic quod papa in omnibus dispensat praeterquam in articulos fidei, ut lxxxii di. presbiter [c. 5] et xxxiiii di. lector [c. 18] ubi contra apostolum dispensat; ar. contra predicta et de statu monachorum, cum ad monsterium [*Comp. III* 3.27.2] in fi. Respondeo, alium est in uoto continentie quam in peregrinationis uel abstinentie uel dic ut ibi. Jo."

52. Ibid. to 3.26.3, ad v. *diminutione,* in Clm. 3879, fol. 229ʳᵃ: "Praeter illam diminutionem que fiet in pecunia transferenda, quia ille religiosus suis expensis non militabit, supra de rescriptis, cum ex officii [?] uel C. xii q. ii caritatem [c. 45]; uel intelligo de religioso qui alias esset illuc iturus. Jo."

53. Ibid. to 3.26.5, ad v. *uxorem,* in Clm. 3879, fol. 229ᵛᵇ: "Specialissimus casus est iste quod uir possit facere uotum sine licentia uxoris contra illud ius, xxxiii q. v quod deo [c. 4], xxvii q. ii si tu [c. 24]; et per hoc uidetur quod aliqua uotum sit maius uoto continentie, nam propter continentiam non liceret fieri hoc, ut xxxiii q. v c. i; licet inuito abstinentie secus dicam dum tamen per tale uoti neutrum fiat preiudicium, ut xxxiii q. ⟨v⟩ [ms.: iiii] noluit [c. 16]. Jo."

cent III.[54] That there was no mention in it of the crusade or the crusade vow was an anomaly which requires some explanation, since the formal actions of the Fourth Lateran Council concluded with the promulgation of a long and important constitution, *Ad liberandam,* concerning plans for the forthcoming expedition that Pope Innocent III was then organizing and that finally took shape as the ill-fated fifth crusade of 1217–22.[55] One possible explanation for this omission might be that the constitution was considered a purely temporary document, relating to the organization and arrangements for one expedition alone, and hence of no enduring legal value.[56] This argument, however, is not convincing. For one thing, *Ad liberandam* presented the most extensive and ambitious catalogue of crusader rights and privileges promulgated by the papacy up to that time and, in point of fact, its provisions were repeated verbatim in most papal letters concerning the crusade throughout the rest of the middle ages.[57] The thirteenth-century popes certainly treated *Ad liberandam* as a constitution of permanent importance. For another thing, it is difficult to reconcile the position that Joannes Teutonicus considered this constitution of little juridical value with the fact that he also went on to provide a set of glosses to it in his gloss apparatus to the canons of the Fourth Lateran Council.[58] Further, one section, dealing with the prohibition of commerce with and aid to the Saracens, was later included by St. Raymond of Peñafort in the great decretal collection of Gregory IX, which would seem to indicate that part of the constitution was authoritatively considered to have permanent legislative value.[59] Finally, this constitution was the subject of an extended commentary by Hostiensis when he dealt with the

---

54. See especially Kuttner, *Repertorium,* pp. 372–73, and "Joannes Teutonicus"; and see above, ch. II, n. 129. The collection is analyzed by Friedberg in *Quinque compilationes,* pp. 135–50.

55. *COD,* pp. 243–47. The history of the council and its legislation is discussed and significant new testimony presented by Stephan Kuttner and Antonio García y García, "A New Eyewitness Account of the Fourth Lateran Council," *Traditio,* 20(1964), 115–78.

56. This was the position, for example, of Damasus Hungarus, the author of the *Apparatus "Si persistat in contumacia"* to the constitutions of the Fourth Lateran Council. At the end of his *Apparatus,* speaking of *Ad liberandam,* Damasus noted: "Hec est quedam dispositio temporalis et ideo non curo glossare." —quoted by Antonio García y García, "El concilio IV de Letrán (1215) y sus comentarios," *Traditio,* 14(1958), 498.

57. Villey, *La Croisade,* pp. 183–85.

58. García y García, "El concilio IV de Letrán," p. 487.

59. *X* 5.6.7.

institutions of the crusade in his *Lectura in quinque libros decretalium,* completed in 1270/71.[60] The fact that, writing more than half a century later, Hostiensis could allege that "it is mentioned daily in apostolic letters" and that the material treated in it "is practical, useful, and necessary" is significant testimony that the contents of *Ad liberandam* were of much more than merely temporary importance.[61] Accordingly it is difficult to determine just what principle may have led Joannes Teutonicus to omit the crusade provisions of *Ad liberandam* from his collection— or, for that matter, also to omit the constitution *Sicut volumus* of the same council.[62] Whatever the reason, none of the provisions relating to the crusade vow, to the crusade indulgence, or to the privileges of the crusaders found their way into this collection. *Compilatio IV* was refused papal approval for some reason which is still not clear; perhaps these omissions may be related to the refusal.

The last of the major pre-Gregorian decretal collections, *Compilatio V,* was commissioned by Pope Honorius III (1216–27), who authorized the influential Bolognese professor, Tancredus, to prepare it. With the exception of one imperial constitution of the Emperor Frederick II, *Compilatio V* consisted entirely of decretals of Honorius himself. Its publication and

---

60. The date of the *Lectura* is dealt with by C. Lefebvre, "Hostiensis," *DDC,* 5:1220–21.

61. Hostiensis, *In quinque libros decretalium commentaria* to X 5.6.17 (Venice, 1581, ed., vol. 2, fol. 33[ra]): "In hac decisione continetur pars quedam in quo ponuntur indulgentiae siue priuilegia cruce signatis concessa, de qua etiam fit mentio quotidie in litteris apostolicis. . . . Et immo cum practicatoria sit et utilis, et necessaria, nullatenus debuit removeri. . . . Et ipsam multi quotidie querunt nec inueniunt, eamdem quatenus tangit hunc articulam, duximus hic apponendam." Nevertheless, the notion that *Ad liberandam* was merely a temporary provision was cited by other canonists to account for its omission from the decretal collections; e.g. Jacobus de Albegna, *Apparatus* to *Comp. V,* gloss to 3.20.1, ad v. *vicesimam,* in British Museum, MS. Royal 11.C.VII, fol. 263[vb]: "Isti qui erant crucesignati non tenebantur dare uicesimam suorum prouentuum, sed alii clerici sit, tam subditi quam prelati, et debebant illis qui fueran(t) electi a sede apostolica ad hoc, ut scilicet de succursu terre sancte ad liberandam i. iiii circa medium. Hodie uero locum non habet hec decretalis nec illa constitutio ad liberandam que habuit locum usque ad triennium, ut in [*add. ms.:* ex] textus ipsius constitutionis manifeste perpenditur; unde, salue pace compilatoris, non debuit esse porcionem in hac compilatione nisi pro tanto ut antiquitatis nichil ignoremus, ut in inst. de testamentis [*Inst.* 2.10.1] et ut idem in similibus obseruemus."

62. See the analysis by García y García, "El concilio IV de Letrán," pp. 485–86; for the text of c. 42, which forbade clerics to cite laymen before ecclesiastical courts to the prejudice of secular jurisdictions, see *COD,* p. 229.

official use, both in court and classroom, were sanctioned by the bull *Nove causarum* of 2 May 1226.[63] Only one of the 223 decretals in the collection dealt with vows and that one concerned a pilgrimage vow, rather than a crusade vow proper. The decretal prescribed conditions, identical with those relating to the crusade vow, under which the pilgrimage vow to Compostella might be commuted by devoting the money which would have been spent on the journey to some pious work and by undertaking a regimen of fasting and prayer.[64]

Although this decretal added nothing of significance to the doctrine of the commutation of vows, the *Apparatus* of Jacobus de Albegna to two passages of it raised some interesting points. In one of these passages, Jacobus reviewed again the problem of the dispensation from vows, citing in particular the opinions of Laurentius, Joannes, and Huguccio. One interesting opinion, attributed merely to "*alii*," held that while the pope might dispense against the natural law, he could not make a law contrary to it. To this Jacobus added that we can daily observe the pope granting dispensations against the natural law.[65] In another passage, Jacobus noted that the crusade obligation became binding as soon as the cross had been taken, or when a definite proposal to take the cross had been made, or when a vow to do so had been made.[66] The order of this passage is

---

63. Kuttner, *Repertorium,* p. 382; R. Naz, "Compilationes, Quinque antiquae," *DDC,* 3:1241; Friedberg, *Quinque compilationes,* pp. 151–86.

64. *Comp. V* 3.19.*un.* = *Po,* 25,651 (*X——*).

65. Jacobus de Albegna, *Apparatus* to *Comp. V* 3.19. *un.,* ad v. *commutare,* in British Museum, MS. Royal 11.C.VII, fol. 263ᵛᵃ: "Numquid sua auctoritate posset episcopus commutare et ⟨dicunt⟩ [*ms.:* debent] quidam quod nullus habet potestatem uotum commutandi nisi papa uel qui habet speciale mandatum ab eo, ut supra eodem titulo ex multa [*Comp. III* 3.26.5]. Laurentius contrarium dicit et dicit quod quilibet episcopus habet potestatem uotum commutandi et dicit speciale esse in his qui tenentur ierosolimam proficisci in succursum terre sancte, sed ei uidetur contradicere littera ista que dicit 'auctoritate nostra'. Sed ipse dicit quod nichilominus auctoritate sua hoc posset facere et est simile supra de electione, transmissam, 1. ii [*Comp. II* 1.3.7]. Sed Ioannes dicit hic quod papa ⟨dixit⟩ 'auctoritate nostra' quia plus solet timeri, et cetera, xxiii di. quamquam [c. 6] et xii q. ii augusto [c. 2]. Sed numquid papa ⟨posset⟩ sine aliqua ex compensatione? H⟨uguccio⟩ dicit quod non, quia hoc esset contra ius naturale; alii dicunt contrarium, nec reperitur prohibitum quia papa possit dispensare contra ius naturale, sed constitutionem iuri naturali contrarium facere non posset, supra ius enim dispensare potest papa ut supra de concessione prebende et ecclesie non vacantis c. i 1. iii [*Comp. III* 3.8.1] et quod contra ius naturale dispensare [*ms. add.:* posset] papa cotidie uidemus." Cf. *Comp. I* 3.8.1 = *X.* 3.8.4.

66. Jacobus de Albegna, *Apparatus* to *Comp. V* 3.19. *un.,* ad v. *teneatur,* in British Museum, MS. Royal 11.C.VII, fol. 263ᵛᵇ: "Postquam alter signum crucis arripuerit

somewhat surprising, inasmuch as the usual presumption was that the crusade vow preceded the taking of the cross and, therefore, that the obligation came into being at that point. Possibly Jacobus' meaning was simply that when the cross was taken the obligation became an open, formal one, binding in foro externo, although a moral obligation to go on crusade existed from the time of taking the vow or making a firm proposal to take the cross.

THE VOW IN OTHER DECRETALIST WRITINGS PRIOR TO 1234. In the anonymous collection of notabilia, *"Potius utendum est,"* which summarized the decretals of *Compilationes I, II,* and *III,* there are some minor observations on the matter of the vow.[67] The notabilia emphasized, for one thing, that when for a just cause one individual transferred the obligation of fulfilling his vow to another person, the votive obligation became fully as binding upon the second party as it had originally been upon the first.[68] Further, the obligation of the bishop to scrutinize and review each individual case in which the redemption of a vow was sought was emphasized, as was the power of the Church to compel the fulfillment of a vow by imposing censure upon those who failed to discharge the votive obligation.[69] Further points of comment in these notabilia included the observation that bishops must receive both the permission of their chapter and of the pope before undertaking a lengthy pilgrimage, and that the utterance of a vow was not in itself binding unless there was also the intention of making a binding vow.[70]

---

uel dic quod reliquus firmiter proposuerat signum crucis assumere, quare sine peccato contrauenire non poterat, ut xvii q. ⟨i⟩v, qui bona [c. 4], uel forte uotum emiserat."

67. Kuttner, *Repertorium,* pp. 410–11, misreading *videndum* for *utendum.*

68. *Notabilia "Potius utendum est"* to *Comp. I* 3.29 in Bibliotheca Apostolica Vaticana, MS. Borgh. Lat. 261, fol. 116vb: "Votum factum ab aliquo ex iusta causa ⟨alio⟩ [ms.: alij] potest committi ut impleatur et maxime heredi et tenetur qui illud pro alio suscipit. . . ."

69. Ibid., fol. 116vb: "Votum peregrinationis redemi debet consilio prelati qui debet diligenter discutere personam et causam utrum melior sit peregrinatio uel compensatio. . . ."; and, "Per censuram ecclesiasticam possunt compelli uouentes, ut uotum adimpleant. . . ." The term "censure" was interpreted to mean excommunication, interdict, or suspension: *X* 5.40.20 = *Comp. III* 5.24.4 (*Po,* 3,865).

70. Vat. Borgh. Lat. 261, fol. 116vb: "Prelatus sine licentia sui capituli uotum peregrinationis emittere non debet: uide iii extra magne [*Comp. III* 3.26.3 = *X* 3.34.7; *deleted in ms.:* episcopus sine]. Episcopus sine licentia pape non debet uotum peregrinationis longe emittere, ut iii extra, magne"; and, "Verba prolata ab aliquo sine animo uouendi non obligant quamuis ad uotum pertinere uideantur. . . ."

More significant treatments of the vow are found in the *Questiones* of Damasus Hungarus (written ca.1215) and in his *Summa* (written ca.1215–17).[71] Although apparently original with him, Damasus' definition of the term "vow" in his *Summa* as "a firm promise made to God concerning matters relating to divine worship" does not add a great deal to our understanding of the subject.[72] Of greater importance was his treatment of simple and solemn vows, since his notion of the solemn vow in particular was rather unusual. Damasus distinguished between the two species of vow by declaring that simple vows might involve either a promise to perform actions or a promise not to perform them, while solemn vows involved only promises not to perform actions—a distinction whose basis is difficult to discover. Damasus thereupon concluded that only the vow of continence could be solemnized,[73] and evidently reasoned from that to the premise that only vows not to perform actions could be solemnized at all. It is clear, in any case, that to Damasus' mind the crusade and other pilgrimage vows were not solemn in character at all. This position contrasted sharply with the position of the decretists in general and with that of most of the other decretalists as well.

In his *Questiones* Damasus discussed two further problems involving vows. One of these was the familiar problem of the power to redeem votive obligations. After disposing of the argument that vows could not be dispensed from by invoking the distinction between commutation and dispensation, Damasus concluded that the rule which held that only the pope could determine the redemption of vows was a special case, relating to the crusade vow alone, and that for all other vows the bishop was empowered to decide concerning commutation or redemption.[74] A further

71. See especially S. Kuttner, "Damasus als Glossator," *ZRG, KA,* 23(1934), 380–90.

72. Damasus, *Summa* to *Comp. I* 3.29 in Bibliotheca Apostolica Vaticana, MS. Lat. 261, fol. 6va, and Oxford, Bodleian Library, Laud Misc. 646, fol. 117vb: "Votum est firma mentis pollicitatio facta deo de his que ad cultum diuinum pertinent."

73. Ibid., Vat. Borgh. Lat. 261, fol. 6va, and Bodleian, Laud. Misc. 646, fol. 117vb: "Sunt autem [*om.* autem *ms. Bodl.*]uoti due species: simplex et sollempne. Simplicia uota quedam consistunt in faciendo, ut ire ad sanctum iacobum, quedam in non faciendo, ut non contrahere. Sollempnia autem consistunt in non faciendo tantum, quia sola uota continentie sollempnizatur; et qualiter sollempnizentur notabitur infra qui clerici uel uouentes [*Comp. I* 4.6]."

74. Damasus, *Questiones* to *Comp. III* 3.26.5 in Vat. Borgh. Lat. 261, fol. 38rb, and Bodleian, Laud. Misc. 646, fol. 95ra: "Queritur circa illam decretalem extra iii eodem titulo [*scil.:* De voto et voti redemptione], ex multa, utrum hec sit generale in quolibet uoto quod non [*ms. Vat. corr. ex* nisi]possit redimi nisi auctoritate pape

questio concerned the doctrine of the heritability of vows, as described in the decretal *Licet:* Might a dying father command his son to fulfill the father's pilgrimage vow as a condition of the inheritance of the father's estate? Although he admitted the force of *Licet* in determining this case, Damasus argued that in interpreting the provisions of the decretal one should distinguish between an obligation to satisfy a pilgrimage vow by personal performance of the pilgrimage and the obligation to satisfy such a vow by redemption of the obligation. The former, he concluded, might not be imposed as a condition of inheritance, although the latter could be.[75]

---

uel eius delegati, et uidetur quod ad uoti obseruationem ex precepto diuino tenentur quo dicitur 'uouete et reddite'. Vnde semel obligatus ad observanciam illius precepti non poterit ab illo discedere nisi de auctoritate illius qui uicem dei tenet in terris, scilicet pape. Item probatur hoc per aliam decretalem quia iuramenti obseruatio descendit similiter ex precepto diuino et si quis uelit discedere ab obseruatione iuramenti illiciti, consulere debet papam, ut extra iii de electione, uenerabilem [*Comp. III* 1.6.19 = *X* 1.6.34; *Po,* 1,653]; et ar. ad hoc extra iii qui filii sint legitimi, per uenerabilem [*Comp. III* 4.12.2 = *X* 4.17.13; *Po,* 1,794]. Contra dicit Alexander simpliciter quod redemptio uoti potest fieri auctoritate illius qui presidet. Laboriosum enim esset quemlibet rusticellum et quamlibet mulierculam papam super hoc requirere et ideo sufficit episcoporum auctoritas, ut extra i, eodem titulo c. i [*Comp. I* 3.29.1 = *X* 3.34.1; *JL,* 13,916]. Item uelis nolis probo quod redemptio uoti siue commutatio potest fieri auctoritate episcopi. Ius enim commune est quod non uenit contra sacramentum uel uotum qui commutat illud in melius, ut extra i, de iureiurando, peruenit [*Comp. I* 2.17.10 = *X* 2.24.3]. Si ergo commutet in melius et constet quod melius sit illud quod fecit, non intelligitur transgressor uoti, puta si ⟨uouerit⟩ [*ms.:* uoluerit] uisitare limina sancti iacobi et postmodum ingrediatur religionem, sua auctoritate; sed numquid si sine auctoritate superioris peccabit? Non, et hoc uidetur dici extra eodem titulo, scripture [*Comp. II* 3.21.2 = *X* 3.34.4; *JL,* 13,848]. Si ergo potest auctoritate sua, ut certum est, cum in melius commutare poterit ubi dubium est fiat auctoritate sui episcopi, ut extra iii, de regularibus, licet quibusdam [*Comp. III* 3.24.4 = *X* 3.31.18; *Po,* 2,763], ubi is qui transit ad strictiorem religionem si dubitetur an bono animo faciat, subit iudicium superioris. Solutio: speciale est quod dicitur in illa Ex multa in uoto emisso in succursum terre sancte; in aliis commutationem facere potest episcopus; alias questiones usitatas inuenies in notulis exaratas."

75. Ibid. to 3.26.2 in Vat. Borgh. Lat. 261, fol. 38[rab], and Bodleian, Laud. Misc. 646, fol. 94[vb]–95[ra]: "Queritur de illa extra iii de uoto et uoti redemptione, licet, utrum pater moriens possit iniungere filio ut compleat uotum peregrinationis que pater emiserat et ita sit heres et uidetur hoc expressum extra iii eodem titulo Licet uniuersis. Item uult canon quod satisfactio possit fieri pro animabus defunctorum per elemosinas aut ieiunia cognatorum. Cum igitur licitum sit preceptum huius de satisfaciendo et possit per cognatos expediri ad quos successio deuoluitur. . . . Si precipiat testator et heredes non adimpleant illud amittent id quod habent de iudicio testatoris. . . . Item expressum est quod testator possit iniungere heredibus suis satisfactionem quem sibi incumbat, ut extra ii de sententia excommunicationis, inspectis

In the *Questiones* of Bernardus Compostellanus antiquus there is also a discussion of the pilgrimage vow, specifically of the right of a wife to forbid the fulfillment of a vow made by her husband before marriage. Bernardus upheld the right of the man to fulfill the vow, noting however the distinction that this privilege applied only to the crusade vow, as specified in the decretal *Quod super his*.[76]

THE VOW IN THE WORKS OF ST. RAYMOND. The great Catalan canonist, St. Raymond of Peñafort (d. 1275), whose career marked a major watershed in the development of medieval canonistic thought, dealt with vows in general and the crusade vow in particular at several different points in his writings.[77] In the earliest of his major writings, the *Summa iuris* (written between 1218 and 1221), St. Raymond merely noted in passing that the commutation of the crusade vow was a papal prerogative.[78] It was in his widely-used *Summa de casibus penitentiae* (written between 1222 and 1228/29) that he first dealt with the matter of

---

[*Comp. II* 5.18.2; *X*—— (*JL*, 16,622)]. Contra lex dicit quod ⟨si⟩ aliquis instituerit filium suum sub conditione casuali uel mixta non tenet institutio, C. de institutionibus ⟨uel⟩ [*mss.*: et] substitutionibus, si pater filium [*Cod.* 6.25.4. pr.]. Immo etiam si preceptum testatoris teneret si filii non faciant illud non priuabuntur propter hoc debita bonorum subsidio, ut in illo aut. hoc amplius. Solutio: non potest pater iniungere filio necessitatem peregrinandi, unde in illa Licet [*X* 3.26.2] ideo renuit ⟨iniunctio⟩ [*ms.*: inuencio] quia filius hoc approbauit; pecuniaram uero satisfactionem bene posset iniungere, ut in illa inspectis, sic iura ista uidentur esse distinguenda."

76. G. Fransen, "Deux collections de questiones," *Traditio*, 21(1965), 496. On Bernardus, see especially Kuttner, "Bernardus Compostellanus antiquus"; Geoffrey Barraclough, "Bernard of Compostella," *English Historical Review*, 49(1934), 487–94.

77. On St. Raymond, see especially S. Kuttner, "Zur Entstehungsgeschichte der Summa de casibus poenitentiae des hl. Raymond von Penyafort," *ZRG, KA*, 39(1953), 419–34; A. Teetaert, "La 'Summa de Poenitentia' de Saint Raymond de Penyafort," *Ephemerides theologicae Lovanienses*, 5(1928), 49–72, and "Summa de matrimonio Sancti Raymundi de Penyafort," *Jus pontificium*, 9(1929), 54–61, 218–34, 312–22; A. Walz, "S. Raymundi de Penyafort auctoritas in re paenitentiali," *Angelicum*, 12(1935), 346–96; Pierre M. Quantin, "A propos des premières summae confessorum," pp. 300–5; P. Mandonnet, "La Carrière scolaire de Saint Raymond de Peñafort," *Analecta sacri Ordinis Fratrum Praedicatorum*, 14(1920), 277–80; Fernando Valls-Taberner, *San Ramón de Peñafort*; Antonio García y García, "Valor y proyección histórica de la obra jurídica de San Raimundo de Peñafort," *Revista Española de Derecho Canónico*, 18(1963), 233–51.

78. *Summa iuris* 2.1 (ed. José Rius y Serra, p. 48). On the *Summa*, see Kuttner, *Repertorium*, pp. 438–42.

vows at any length. He began his treatment of the theme by defining a vow as "a promise of any good thing made with deliberation" and, while he admitted the possibility that a vow might be made to perform an evil act, such a vow, he declared, would not be binding.[79] He then proceeded to distinguish the various types of vows. The first distinction was between necessary and voluntary vows, i.e., between those necessary for salvation and those undertaken out of personal piety and devotion.[80] The class of voluntary vows he subdivided into simple and solemn types. While noting that the simple vow was no less binding, so far as God was concerned, than the solemn vow, nonetheless St. Raymond stated that breaking a solemn vow was more serious than breaking a simple vow and that failure to fulfill a solemn vow was an offense both against the public order (*constitutio*) of the Church and against God.[81] St. Raymond then intro-

79. On the *Summa de casibus,* see Kuttner, "Zur Entstehungsgeschichte der Summa de casibus," and *Repertorium,* pp. 443–45. I have used the printed version of the *Summa de casibus* published at Verona in 1744 and also two glossed manuscript texts: Innsbruck, Universitätsbibliothek, MS. 339 (thirteenth-century), and MS. 266 (fourteenth-century). *Summa de casibus* 1.8.1 (Verona ed., p. 54; Innsbruck, MS. 339, fol. 20ᵛᵃ): "Votum est alicuius boni cum deliberatione facta promissio. Si uero fiat de re mala, uel de bona sed sine deliberatione, non obligat: Isidorus, causa 22 quest. 4 c. In malis promissis rescinde fidem [c. 5]."

80. Ibid., 1.8.1 (Verona ed., p. 54; Innsbruck, MS. 339, fol. 20ᵛᵃᵇ): "Votorum alia necessitatis, alia uoluntatis. Vota necessitatis dicuntur ea, ad que implenda omnis homo necessario tenetur, siue uoueat siue non, ut obrenunciare diabolo et omnibus pompis eius, tenere fidem catholicam, seruare decalogum, et breuiter omnia alia, sine quibus non est salus, et ad hec se obligat quilibet in baptismo: unde quotiescumque postea peccat mortaliter, est transgressor huiusmodi uoti; ergo tenetur agere penitentiam pro illo peccato, et pretterea pro transgressione. Sed dic quod non est sibi imponenda penitentia tamquam pro diuersis mortalibus, sed tamquam pro uno, ex circumstantiis transgressionis uoti aggrauato. Require infra, de penitentia et remissione § Item circa idem, vers. Ad tertium quesitum.

"Votum uoluntatis dicitur illud bonum ad quod non tenetur aliquis, quia sine illo potest esse salus et tamen sponte obligat se ad illud et postea tenetur: ut uotum continentie, abstinentie, peregrinationis, et similia. De hoc dicitur in Psalm. 75, 'Vouete et reddite,' id est, si uouetis, reddite. De utroque uoto, scilicet necessitatis et uoluntatis, dicit Augustinus, 'Sunt quedam que et non uouentes debemus; quedam etiam que nisi uouerimus, non debemus, sed postquam ea Deo promittimus, necessario reddere constringitur. . . .'"

81. Ibid., 1.8.1 (Verona ed., p. 54; Innsbruck, MS. 339, fol. 20ᵛᵇ): "Votum autem uoluntatis subdistinguitur, quia aliud priuatum, seu simplex, aliud publicum, seu solemne. Quod dicatur simplex, et quod solemni require in summa de matrimonio, in tractatus de impedimento uoti.

"Hoc tamen notandum est: quantum ad deum uotum simplex non minus obligat quam solemne et utriusque transgressor peccat mortaliter; Extra, Qui clerici uel uouentes matrimonium contrahere possunt, c. rursus [X 4.6.6]. Et inter simplex uerbum et iuramentum deus non facit differentiam. Causa 22 q. 5 iuramenti [c. 12]."

duced another set of distinctions, this time between the pure (or absolute) and the determined (or conditional) vow.[82]

Having defined the vow and distinguished its various forms to his satisfaction, St. Raymond then took up the matter of commutation. Necessary vows (those upon which salvation depended) and the voluntary vow of continence were not subject to commutation, he declared.[83] Other voluntary vows, however, were, as appeared from examples cited in the Old Testament,[84] provided that two conditions were satisfied: there

Grauius tamen peccat qui frangit solemne et grauior penitentia est sibi imponenda, causa 27 q. 2 si uir [c. 23], causa 27 q. 1 c. uirginibus [c. 14]. Quid ergo dicitur 'non minus obligat' simplex quam solemne, id est, non minori turpi, quia utriusque fractio est mortale, sed alterius maius, et est ratio, quia in fractione uoti solemnis et deum offendit et constitutionem ecclesie et scandalem suscitat; in alio non sic."

82. Ibid., 1.8.1 (Verona ed., p. 55; Innsbruck, MS. 339, fol. 20vb–21ra): "Alia diuisio uotorum: aliud purum et absolutum, ut sine omni conditione uel determinatione quis emittit uotum continentie uel peregrinationis, uel simile; aliud determinatum aut conditionale, ut cum dicit uouens sic: 'uoueo peregrinationem si dominus dederit mihi sanitatem, uel usque ad annum,' et similia."

83. Ibid., 1.8.2 (Verona ed., p. 55; Innsbruck, MS. 339, fol. 21^{rab}): "Circa redemptionem uotorum uel commutationem nota quod quedam uota nullo modo possint redimi uel commutari, ut omnia uota necessitatis et de uoluntariis uotum continentie, quia non est commutatio uel dispensatio contra deum, 25 q. 1 sunt quidem [c. 6] et D. 14 sicut [c. 2], 11 q. 3 qui resistit [c. 97]. Potest tamen papa uerbum euangelii interpretari, extra de testibus, licet primo in fi. [Comp. I 2.13.14 = X 2.20.14]; ut uerbum 'In ore duorum uel trium testium stet omne uerbum' [Matt. 18.16] interpretatur sic: id est, non paucorum; sunt enim plures casus in quibus plures testes requiruntur. Item potest dispensare contra apostolum et omnem hominem quantumcumque sanctum et eorum dicta mutare, nisi in his que illi de fidei articulis dixerunt; uerba gratia, in canonem apostolorum precipitur quod presbiter si fuerit fornicator deponatur, D. 81 presbiter [c. 12]. Item uotum continencie immo non potest immutare, quia uix uel numquam possit melius inueniri in quod fieret commutatio et est expressum extra de statu monachorum, cum ad monasterium in fi. [Comp. III 3.27.2 = X 3.34.6; Po, 1,734]; 32 q. 2. Hoc tamen uerum est quod is uotum continentie non est sollempnizatum sed simplex, licet talis qui sic uouit simpliciter mortaliter peccat matrimonium contrahendo; si tamen contrahat et per uerba de presenti, tenet matrimonium et ipse debet agere penitentiam de fractione uoti; extra qui clerici uel uouentes, ueniens [Comp. I 4.6.8 = X 4.6.5; JL, 14,165], rursus [Comp. II 4.4.2 = X 4.6.6; JL, 17,649]. Sicut econtrario soluitur matrimonium per religionis ingressionem ante carnalis copulam, extra de conuersione coniugatorum, uerum [Comp. I 3.28.2 = X 3.32.2; JL, 14,091], ex publico [Comp. I 3.28.7 = X 3.32.7; JL, 13,787]."

84. Ibid., 1.8.2 (Innsbruck, MS. 339, fol. 21rb): "Alia uero uoluntatis uota possunt redimi uel commutari. Cum enim in ueteri legi, in quam non minus preceptum domini obligabat quam uotum hodie in ecclesia, primogenita que domino mandabantur offeri quedam domino redderentur, ut primogenita leuitarum, quedam redimerentur, ut aliarum tributum, quedam commutarentur in aliud, ut asini primogenita, quod oue commutabatur: patet quod uotum etiam commutari possit in opus

must be an adequate cause and the commutation must be allowed by a superior authority. To illustrate this point, he cited the case of a person who had vowed to go on crusade. A proper cause for commutation of such a vow would arise from the situation of the person making the vow, who might be in ill health, or a cleric and hence unable to fight, or a poor woman who could not subsidize a company of warriors to accompany her, or a person who could not support himself by his own labor. Where one of these conditions was temporary, such as a brief bout of illness, only a temporary delay might be authorized, but where there was some permanent condition, then commutation of the vow was allowable.[85] As for the requisite authority for the commutation of a vow, this authority was vested in the bishop for all save the crusade vow, which was reserved to the pope.[86] After noting that any vow might be commuted to a vow of religion,[87] St. Raymond discussed the costs of commutation, citing the norms prescribed in the decretals *Magne* and *Quod super his,* and adding that the absolute sum would vary according to the means of the person

aliud pietatis. Item contra preceptum domini Iosue corporale mortem Gabaonitarum commutauit in morte ciuile, id est in perpetuam servitutem [Josue 9.15–27]."

85. Ibid., 1.8.2 (Verona ed., p. 56; Innsbruck, MS. 339, fol. 21ʳᵇ⁻ᵛᵃ): "Nota ergo quod duo exiguntur ad hoc, ut talium uotorum [*scil.:* uota uoluntaria preter uotum continentie] fiat redemptio uel commutatio: causa et superioris auctoritas. Causa, ut si uouens sit senex, debilis, uel infirmus; uel si ex absentia ipsius guerra uel turbatio timeretur in terra; uel si uerisimiliter redemptio uel commutatio melior uideatur et magis accepta Deo quam peregrinatio uel abstinentia; uerba gratia, emisit aliquis uotum Hierosolymitanum qui non est ibi utilis, cum non possit pugnare propter debilitatem, uel persone conditionem, quia clericus est, nec talis qui suo consilio uel predicatione uideatur ibi utilis, uel mulier, nec potest secum ducere bellatores, quia pauper est, nec est artifex uel agricola qui de laboribus suis possit acquirere necessaria et terre subsidia ministrare, quamuis non multi talium propter breuitatem possessionum et paucitatem inhabitantium ibi sunt opportuni. Item utrum habeant causam temporalem uel perpetuam; ut in primo casu indulgeatur dilatio; in secundo redemptio superioris auctoritate exigitur, quia nemini licet auctoritate propria redimere uel commutare."

86. Ibid., 1.8.2 (Verona ed., p. 56; Innsbruck, MS. 339, fol. 21ᵛᵃ): "Est tamen differentia inter uotum terre sancte et alia uota: quia de uoto terre sancte redimendo, commutando, uel differendo nullus potest se intromittere nisi papa uel alius de suo speciali mandato et hoc sine opinione. In aliis autem redimendis, commutandis, uel differendis licet quidam aliter dixerint et alii dubitauerint, dico quod suus diocesanus episcopus, consideratis causis, potest auctoritatem prestare quia expressa est decretalis, extra de uoto et uoti redemptione c. 1."

87. Ibid., 1.8.2 (Innsbruck, MS. 339, fol. 21ʳᵇ): "Nota etiam circa arbitrium superioris quod omne tale uotum potest commutare in uotum religionis, quia id indubitanter melius, unde Alex. iii [X 3.34.4]. Rei seculari uoti nullatenus habeantur qui temporale obsequium in perpetuam noscuntur religionis obseruantiam commutare."

involved: a vow which a poor man might redeem with a hundred *solidi* or a single penny or even with no payment at all, if he possessed nothing, might not be redeemed by a king or a count for a thousand marks of silver.[88]

Dispensations from vows were treated separately by Raymond, who does not appear to have taken a definite position as to whether vows could be dispensed absolutely; he simply contented himself with reporting the views of three schools of thought on the matter. These were: Huguccio and his school, who held that no vows were dispensable and who distinguished sharply between dispensation and commutation; a second group, who held that only pilgrimage vows might be dispensed, but not vows of continence; and another group who taught that without exception any vow might be dispensed, including the vow of continence, on the grounds that every vow contained the implicit stipulation that it might be vitiated by superior authority.[89] The following sections of the *Summa de casibus*

88. Ibid., 1.8.2 (Verona ed., p. 58; Innsbruck, MS. 339, fol. 21vb–22ra): "Item in redemptione seu commutatione debet superior habere considerationem ad facultatem uouentis et expensas quas posset facere uel facturus esset si uotum impleret in eundo, morando, et redeundo, et etiam ad laborem; ut si uotum erat Hierosolymitanum, uel simile, puta contra hereticos, uel aliud tale, omnia sine diminutione transmutat per aliquem, uel per aliquos uiros religiosos in usus et subsidium terre sancte, seu catholicorum pro fide pugnantium totaliter transferendo: extra eodem c. Magne et Quod super his [X 3.34.7–8]. In uotis aliarum peregrinationum, puta sancti Jacobi uel similium, dico idem, hoc excepto quod in locum peregrinationis mittat oblationem, quam ibi esset facturus et alias expensas cum compensatione laboris in alia, que magis Deo placere debent, credo, saluo meliore iudicio, convertendas: arg. extra eodem c. 1 et c. Scripture [X 3.34.4]. In uoto abstinentie habenda est ratio asperitatis ieiuniorum panis et aque et omnium aliorum que in uoto fuerunt comprehensa; considerari etiam debet affluentia uouentis: Extra eodem c. 1. Nam in eadem specie uoti aliquis pauper posset redimere cum centum solidis, uel etiam uno denario, uel nullo, si nihil haberet uel habere potest, ubi rex uel comes non posset cum mille marchis argenti."

89. Ibid., 1.8.9 (Verona ed., pp. 66–67): "Sequitur uidere, an in uotis ualeat dispensari? Circa quod tres inueniuntur opiniones. Quidam dicunt simpliciter quod nec etiam papa potest in uotis dispensare, quia redditio uoti est de iure naturali siue divino, circa quod non dispensatur: causa 25 q. 1 cap. Sunt quidam [c. 6]. Hoc tenet Hugot. et eius sequaces. Et si opponatur eis de redemptione, uel commutatione uotorum, ut dictum est supra, eodem tit. § Circa redemptionem; respondent quod non est ibi dispensatio, sed iuris declaratio, cum enim quis uouet peregrinari, uel abstinere, subintelligitur 'si commode fieri potest': Extra, de iureiurando cap. Quintauallis [X 2.24.23]. . . . Alii dicunt, quod potest dispensare in uotis peregrinationis, sed non in uoto continentie. Tertii dicunt sine exceptione quod in omni uoto uoluntatis ⟨papa⟩ potest dispensare, siue sit de continentia, siue de alio: in omnibus uotis et iuramentis intelligitur 'excepta eius auctoritate': Extra de rescriptis, c. Constitutus [X 1.3.19] et de iureiurando, c. Venientes [X 2.24.19]."

relating to the vow did little more than to summarize the plain sense of the canonistic texts prescribing that a monk might not undertake a vow without the permission of his abbot, that a wife might not make a vow without her husband's consent, and that by way of exception to the general rule concerning the vows of married persons, a husband might undertake a crusade vow without his wife's permission.[90]

As might be expected from the specialized nature of its subject, St. Raymond's other major commentary, the *Summa de matrimonio* (written ca.1235), dealt only peripherally with the matter of the vow and added nothing of significance to the exposition in the *Summa de casibus*.[91]

The best known of all of St. Raymond's labors was the compilation of the great decretal collection of Gregory IX, at which Raymond worked between 1230 and 1234 and which was promulgated by the pope on 5 September 1234.[92] This extensive collection drew all save one of its decretals on vows from the earlier redactions of the *Quinque compilationes antiquae*. The one exception is canon 10, *Per tuas*, a decretal of Innocent III, which none of the earlier decretal collections had chosen to use. Its provisions were of only minor significance for the discipline of the vow, since it merely reinforced the belief that the fulfillment of votive obligations was a matter of primary concern for ecclesiastical law. In the case ruled upon in *Per tuas*, an individual who had vowed to accept the religious habit within a definite period of time had failed to fulfill his vow, and subsequently was elected bishop; he then, apparently, petitioned the pope for release from his vow. The reply contained in *Per tuas* counseled him that he must first fulfill his vow and then, if the chapter wished to elect him to a bishopric, he might accept the post.

Save for this one marginal addition, however, St. Raymond apparently found the existing decretal legislation on vows, as reflected in the *Quinque compilationes antiquae*, substantially complete and adequate for current needs. At any rate, he did not deem it necessary to extend the previous legislation by petitioning for fresh decretals to cover lacunae in this area, as he did in others.[93]

90. Sections of the *Summa de casibus* dealing with these three matters are, respectively, 1.8.4 (Verona ed., pp. 59–60; Innsbruck, MS. 266, fol. 31ʳ); 1.8.7 (Verona ed., p. 64); 1.8.8 (Verona ed., p. 66; Innsbruck, MS. 339, fol. 24ʳᵃ).

91. Kuttner, *Repertorium*, p. 445.

92. Ibid., pp. 447–48.

93. In *Rex pacificus*, the bull of promulgation which introduced the *Decretales*, Gregory IX explicitly described this practice. After mentioning the difficulties of locating and verifying the decretals incorporated in the earlier collections, the pope

Finally, it may be noted that Guilielmus Redonensis (William of Rennes), in his glosses to the *Summa de casibus* (written between 1241 and 1250) alleged an exception to the general rule that any vow could be commuted by entering the religious life.[94] Great noblemen, he said, could not be freed in this way from the obligation incurred through the crusade vow, although lesser persons might be.[95]

THE VOW IN THE DECRETALIST WRITINGS FROM RAYMOND OF PEÑAFORT TO HOSTIENSIS. The recently discovered mid-thirteenth *Summa "Quid sit symonia"* in the University Library at Innsbruck is closely akin to the *Summa de casibus* in its treatment of vows and types of vows, as in many other matters. The definition of the vow is identical in the two *Summae*.[96] Some of the passages which appear to be taken or adapted from Raymond of Peñafort's work, however, bear the siglum "a."

---

stated: "Ad communem et maxime studentium utilitatem per dilectum filium fratrem Raymundum, cappellanum et penitentiarium nostrum, illas in unum uolumen (resecatis superfluis) prouidimus redigendas, adiicientes constitutiones nostras, et decretales epistolas per quas nonnulla, que in prioribus erant dubia, declarantur." In all, 191 decretals of Gregory IX were included in the *Decretales,* although not all of them were postulated by St. Raymond.

94. The rule was illustrated in the gloss by an example: "Omne etiam uotum terre sancte ⟨commutatur per⟩ uotum religionis. Credo tamen quod si raptor uel usurarius cum multa de alieno habuerat aut multos dampnificauerit et quia nesciebat quibus facienda restitutio uouit quod illa expenderet in succursu terre sancte non potest sine speciali licentia pape; in alios uices illa conuertere licet per ingressum religionis; ipso iure absolutus est a labore peregrinacionis." Gloss to *Summa de casibus* 1.8.1, ad v. *omne,* in Innsbruck, MS. 266, fol. 30ᵛ.

95. Ibid., ad v. *commutare,* in Innsbruck, MS. 266, fol. 30ᵛ: "Hoc de mediocribus personis sine dubio uerum est quod per ingressum religionis liberantur a uoto crucis. Sed numquid idem de rege uel imperatore, duce uel comite, ⟨uel⟩ aliquo prepotente ex quo pendet totus exercitus crucesignatorum et de eius absencia desolabitur? Quid etsi uouit quod toto tempore uite sue uel usque ad triennium uel septennium militabit in terram sanctam et tenebit secum mille uel duo milia militum? Respondeo ubi probabiliter dubitatur utrum terra huius arduas personas preponderare debeat communis utilitas et priuata, credo papam pocius esse consulendum in hoc casu quam ibi aliquid temere difiniendum."

96. *Summa "Quid sit symonia",* tit. *De voto,* in Innsbruck, Universitätsbibliothek, MS. 368, fol. 6ʳᵃ: "Votum est alicuius boni cum deliberatione facta promissio." The definition is later repeated in tit. *De impedimento uoti* at fol. 106ᵛᵇ. The types of vows are distinguished thus (fol. 6ʳᵃ): "De speciebus uotorum: aliud est necessitatis, sine quo non est salus, ut quod uouemus in baptismo; aliud uoluntatis. Votorum ⟨uoluntatis⟩ [*ms.:* uotis] aliud est privatum uel simpliciter, aliud publicum uel sollempne et utrumque obligat quoad deum. Item uotorum aliud purum et absolutum, aliud determinatum et conditionale. a." The *Summa "Quid sit symonia"* is certainly later than the *Summa de casibus penitentiae,* which is probably referred to in a pas-

(Alanus?; Albertus?).[97] Among the additional material in this *Summa* there is an interesting note on three means of solemnizing vows—by receiving holy orders, by entrance into religion, and by publication of the vow.[98]

The treatment of the vow in the *Libellus dispensationum* (written ca.1243) of the Portuguese canonist, Joannes de Deo, centered as one might expect on dispensations. Joannes' treatment is of interest in part because he focused his discussion of the papal dispensing prerogative on the theme of the pope's position as "vicar of Jesus Christ."[99] Although he did not note the crusade vow in the list of cases from which the pope could grant dispensations, he did acknowledge this papal prerogative indirectly when he held that the crusade vow was the only one from which bishops could not dispense.[100]

---

sage at fol. 106[vb]: "Quis uouere possit? Et sciendum quod quilibet sane mentis nisi expresse prohibeatur. Sane ideo dixi quoniam si homo alienate mentis uoueat uel monasterium intret non tenet uotum. Require in summa de pe. e. t."

R. Weigand first announced the discovery of the *Summa "Quid sit symonia"* in "Mitteilungen aus Handschriften," *Traditio,* 16(1960), 562; see also Kuttner, "Notes on Manuscripts," *Traditio,* 17(1961), 541–42.

97. In addition to the example in the note above, this siglum appears, together with t[ancredus?] in several other passages, e.g., fol. 6[rb]–7[rb]: "Nota etiam quod omnia uota indistincte possunt commutari in uotum religionis. a. Etiam terre sancte quod tamen intelligendum est quantum ad laborem peregrinationis tantum, nec quoad pecuniam promissam quam sine speciali mandato pape non licet in alios usus commutare. . . . Nota quod in uoto continencie sunt in omnibus pares uir et mulier sed dicitur quod uotum continencie potest uir facere invita uxore nisi per hoc fieret preiudicium uxori in redden do debito. Votum etiam peregrinationis neuter potest facere inuito altero excepto terre sancte quod uir potest facere inuita uxore; ipsa tamen ut consenciat est attencius commonenda, quod si noluerit sequitur eum. a."

98. *Summa "Quid sit symonia,"* tit. *De voto,* in Innsbruck, MS. 368, fol. 6[ra]: "a. dicit quod secundum quosdam uotum sollempnizatur tribus modis, scilicet per sacri ordinis susceptionem, per religionis ingressum, et pare publici, scilicet episcopi uel abbatis."

99. Joannes de Deo, *Libellus dispensationum,* in Gonville and Caius College, Cambridge, MS. 71/38, fol. 1[rb-va]: "De dispensatione domini pape. Super hoc diuersi doctores diuersa senciunt. Quidam dicunt quod papa possit dispensare in omni causa etiam contra apostolum, cum teneat locum beati Petri et sit uicarius Jesu Christi. . . . Item dicunt quidam alii quod in omni causa possit dispensare, scilicet cum non ligetur legibus. . . . " John did not, however, subscribe to this latter view and instead set forth a list of cases in which the pope might dispense and a list where he might not do so. The dispensation from vows, whether crusade vows or others, appears in neither list.

100. Ibid., tit. *De dispensationibus episcoporum,* in Gonville and Caius, MS. 71/38, fol. 5[rb]: Item potest ⟨episcopus⟩ dispensare in uoto, scilicet quod in melius commutetur . . . nisi in uoto Ierosolimitano. . . . "

Still another mid-thirteenth-century canonistic treatise to take up the matter of dispensations from vows was the *Notabilia "Aliter debet"* which is preserved in a unique manuscript in the library of Gonville and Caius College, Cambridge.[101] There are several points of interest in this short treatise. One is the emphasis on the distinction between the Holy Land vow made for piety's sake (*ex devotione*) and the vow to aid the Holy Land (*pro subsidio*), which was the crusade vow properly speaking.[102] Further, the unknown author of this work insisted, unlike almost all other canonists of his time, that there was no distinction between the grant of a dispensation from a vow and a commutation of votive obligations.[103] Unredeemed vows, he added, might be enforced through punitive sanctions by the ecclesiastical courts. As enforcement was only possible if the culprit confessed that he had made the vow, however, the efficiency of the process as set forth here might have left something to be desired.[104] In another passage the author noted, too, the implication of the decretal *Magne* that, since the pope insisted that bishops must obtain papal permission for lengthy pilgrimages, a pilgrimage of moderate length required no such licence.[105] Again, without noting any argument on the point, *"Aliter debet"* denied the inference commonly drawn from *Ex multa* that the crusade vow was greater than the vow of continence, since the former enjoyed privileges which the latter did not share.[106]

The pilgrimage vows of married persons were discussed at length by

---

101. Kuttner, *Repertorium*, p. 414, n. 1.

102. *Notabilia "Aliter debet"* to X 3.34.6 in Gonville and Caius College, MS. 23/12, fol. 41ra: "Item prosequere differentiam inter illos qui uouent pro subsidio uel ex deuotione." The distinction itself, of course, is based on X 3.34.8.

103. Ibid. to X 3.34.1, in Gonville and Caius, MS. 23/12, fol. 41ra: "Nota quod ex quo scribitur episcopo intelligitur quod quilibet episcopus potest peregrinationis uotum commutar⟨e⟩, excepto ultramarino et omne uotum commutare excepta continencia uel dispensari potest; nec est differentia inter commutare et dispensar⟨e⟩, licet eam aliqui faciant."

104. Ibid. to X 3.34.3 in Gonville and Caius, MS. 23/12, fol. 41ra: "In foro ecclesie ex quo qui expressit uotum tenetur, licet non precesserit deliberatio uel si proposuit aliud licitum facere sed uoce non expressit, tenetur licet ecclesiam non cogat eum nisi confiteatur."

105. Ibid. to X 3.34.7 in Gonville and Caius, MS. 23/12, fol. 41ra: "Item modicum peregrinationem faciet episcopus sine pape licentia."

106. Ibid. to X 3.34.9 in Gonville and Caius, MS. 23/12, fol. 41rb: "Non sequitur quod uotum ultramarinum sit maius continentia, quia uxor ipsum potest emittere inuito uiro et econtra."

Bartholomaeus Brixiensis in his *Questiones dominicales* (written between 1234 and 1241).[107] The question posed for this disputation did not concern the crusade vow directly, but Bartholomaeus took the opportunity to discuss in some detail the workings and the rationale of the rule that married persons might not take a vow save by mutual consent. The obvious and basic reason for the rule, he pointed out, was the preservation of marital chastity. If a husband were to make a vow of continence without his wife's consent, this would have the effect of granting her a license for fornication and the fault would ultimately rest with him. Further, he adduced the theological argument that a married man had no power over his own body, but rather by the marriage contract had transferred his rights to his wife. By analogy, then, the vow to undertake a lengthy pilgrimage would have much the same effect as a vow of abstinence from sexual relations, since it would deprive the nonconsenting partner of licit sexual intercourse for a long time. Hence Bartholomaeus concluded that the general rule prohibiting pilgrimage vows by married persons without mutual consent rested upon a sound basis. He added, without however attempting to justify his position save by citing the decretal *Ex multa,* that the general rule was abrogated when it was a matter of a crusade vow.[108]

---

107. The date has been established by Gérard Fransen, "Tribuneaux ecclésiastiques et langue vulgaire d'après les *Questiones* des canonistes," *Ephemerides theologicae Lovanienses,* 40(1964), 409.

108. Bartholomaeus Brixiensis, *Questiones dominicales,* q. 40, in Lambeth Palace Library, MS. 39, fol. 42rb–vb, and British Museum, MS. Arundel 435, fol. 231vb–232ra: "Quidam fecit uotum eundi ad sanctum iacobum; postea contraxit matrimonium cum aliqua; qui cum uellet peregrinari, uxor eius contradicit se dicens continere non posse. Queri solet an inuita uxore peregrinari possit? PRO. Quod possit probo, nam licet uotum ab inicio sit uoluntarium, postquam tamen factum est debet necessitate adimpleri. . . . Scriptum est enim, 'uouete et reddite domino deo uestro,' ut xxvii q. i c. i. Item est obligatus tamen deo, uxori per matrimonium est obligatus; tandem uxori ergo magis debuit deo quam homini obedire. . . . Item uxor subiecta debet esse marito et nullam habet auctoritatem . . . preterea cum uir sit caput mulieris, contra legem dei uxor ei imperare non potest. . . . Item iste antequam contraheret cum uxore matrimonium deo fuerat prius obligatus, ergo cum eo homine ad uxorem transit, ut extra de decimis, cum non sit in homine [X 3.30.33] et ff de contrahenda emptione et uenditione i. alienacio [*Dig.* 18.1.67 pr.]; preterea in iuramento et uoto excepta intelligitur maior potestas, ut extra de rescriptis, constitutus [X 1.3.19] et xxii q. i beatus [C. 22 q. 2 c. 5]; multo forcius in aliquo contractu intelligitur 'excepta maior potestas.' Item iste lege dei ducitur, ergo lege alia astringi non debet, ut xix q. ii due sunt circa finem [c. 2], nam monachus qui ex toto abbati suo subicitur si uitam cupit ducere arctiorem hoc posset facere contradicente abbate suo,

There are some notes of interest, too, in the discussion of the title *De voto* in the *Apparatus* (finished shortly after 1245) of Pope Innocent IV (1243–54). Innocent concluded that any vow, except the vow of continence, might be subject to dispensation or commutation, and concluded that the effort to distinguish between these two methods of escaping from votive obligations was unrealistic, for no commutation was possible without dispensation from the original terms of the vow which was commuted.[109] Again, in his unusually thorough discussion of the heritability of votive obligations, Innocent dwelt at length upon the distinction between vows made in order to aid the Holy Land and those made for devotional reasons alone. Both created obligations (he bolstered this position with an analogy from the Roman law) whose fulfillment might be required of an heir.[110] Innocent held with the rest of the decretalists that the Holy Land

cum lege priuata ducatur qui publice preiudicat, ut extra de regularibus et transeuntes ad religionem, licet [*X* 3.31.18]. Sequatur ergo hec mulier uirum suum si continere non potest, ut xiii q. ii unaqueque [c. 3]. Item secundum ius ciuile tenetur quis ad uotum complendum, ut ff de pollicitationibus, si quis rem, in primo [*Dig.* 50.12.2 pr.]. Respondeo CONTRA. Contrarium probo, nam si maritus abstinet sine uoluntate uxoris, ei prebet licenciam fornicandi et peccatum illius imputatur marito. . . . Item per continenciam mariti illa non debet fornicaria fieri, cum dicitur cum lucro tali tale dampnum uoluit compensare. . . . Non enim recipitur apud deum conuersio uiri cuius sequitur coniugalis federis prostitucio. . . . Item uir non habet potestatem sui corporis, sed mulier . . . ergo sine licencia eius non potuit uir peregrinari; preterea expresse dicit c. quod uotum ante contractum matrimonium emissum altero inuito adimplere non potest, ut xxxiii q. v noluit [c. 16]; itaque immo uotum ante emissum frangitur per matrimonium, quia forcius uinculum superuenit. . . . Item clericus preter licenciam episcopi peregrinari non potest, quia potestatem habet in ipsum . . . nec monachus inuito suo abbate, immo si iniungendum est uotum quod fecit . . . non licet monachis morari itaque uir domi cum ab uxore non debeat seperare, ut C. communia utriusque iudicii, 1. possessionum [*Cod.* 3.38.11] et ff de fundo instruc. quesitum tercia [possibly *Dig.* 33.7.12]; preterea res peruenit ad eum statim a quo increpare; non potuit ergo irritari debet, ut ff de iudiciis, si a me [*Dig.* 5.1.11] et ff de furtis [*Dig.* 47.17] pro parte. Nec debet mulier priuari iure suo sine culpa sua cum simpliciter nupsit . . . nec debet uagari per orbem. . . . SOLUCIO. Solucio credo quod uotum adimplere non possit uir sine uoluntate uxoris . . . nisi uellet ire in subsidium terre sancte. . . .”

109. Innocent IV, *Apparatus* to *X* 3.34.1 (Lyons ed., 1540, fol. 164ʳ; Frankfurt ed., 1570, fol. 428ᵛ): “In omne uoto siue sit in faciendo, siue in non faciendo, dispensari potest, uel potius compensari, etiam si solenniter uouerit, uel commutari, dummodo iusta subsit causa et superioris authoritas interuenerit, et melior sit compensatio, quia aliter non tenet: infra, eodem, scripture etc. non est. In uoto tamen continentie speciale est, quia in eo nullus dispensare potest. . . . Aliqui tamen dicunt quod in uotis non potest dispensari, sed possunt commutari, sed hanc differentiam non uidimus, cum commutatio non fiat sine dispensatione.”

110. Ibid. to *X* 3.34.6 (Lyons ed., fol. 164ᵛ; Frankfurt ed., fol. 429ᵛ): “Hoc est licitum et debitum ubi per se nullo modo potest exequi, sed si per se exequi posset,

vow might be taken by husband or wife without the consent of the other, in virtue of a special papal privilege, and he subscribed to the somewhat less common view that bishops might undertake the Holy Land pilgrimage without papal consent, even though it was required for all other pilgrimage vows.[111]

THE DOCTRINE OF THE VOW IN THE WRITINGS OF HOSTIENSIS. The doctrine of the vow, and the crusade vow in particular, were treated at length in the *Summa aurea* (written between 1250 and 1253) of Hostiensis (d. 1271).[112] Hostiensis defined the vow as a deliberate promise made to God to do or not to do some permitted act. The terms of his

licet inutiliter, scilicet quia esset claudus uel alias mutilatus, tunc si non ad subsidium sed ad deuotionem tantum, scilicet ut uideret terram sanctam uouisset, ire personaliter deberet, et modo, si propter subsidium uouisset, si est talis, quod suum defectum possit supplere per alios, quia secum ducere potest, sed in utroque casu admittitur compensatio. . . . Hanc tamen assignamus differentiam inter eos qui uouent pro subsidio, et eos qui uouent pro deuotione, quia primi morbo uel alio impedimento detenti, coguntur aliis committere, quod eorum uotum compleant. Argumentum hic imo plus uidetur, quia si aliis non committant, tamen heredes compelli possunt, ut uel ipsi compleant uotum patris, uel expensas et subsidium, quod pater uel testator facturus erat ipsi facient, nam uouisse intelligitur subsidium terre sancte, siue per se, siue per alium faciendum, unde ad illud compellendi sunt heredes, cum ex nudo uoto obligatio nascatur, ff de pollicitationibus i. 2 in prin. [*Dig.* 50.12.2 pr.] et nuda promissio facta ciuitati obligat, ff de pollicitationibus, pactum [*Dig.* 50.12.3 pr.]; multo fortius facto Deo, uel subsidio terre sancte; item ar. hoc infra eodem Quod super [*X* 3.34.8] et c. seq. In secundo autem casu, scilicet quando propter deuotionem uidendi terram, uel alias uouit, non credimus quod mittere teneatur si iusto impedimento personaliter ire impediatur, propter conditionem generalem, que subintelligitur, scilicet, 'si potero,' ut supra dictum est."

111. Innocent IV, *Apparatus* to *X* 3.34.4 (Lyons ed., fol. 164ᵛ): "Excipimus uotum peregrinationis ultramarine, quod uiri uel mulieres, si sunt potentes, possunt facere altero inuito . . . sed non uouens potest alium sequi. . . . Clericus autem secularis potest uouere continentiam, sed non peregrinationem sine licentia prelati, de consecratione di. 5 Non oportet [c. 36] et nota supra de clericis peregrinis c. 1 [*X* 1.22.1]. Episcopus autem sine speciali licentia pape, non potest uotum peregrinationis uel religionis emittere, supra de regularibus [*X* 3.31], licet transmarino forsan excepto, infra eodem, Magne [*X* 3.34.7]."

112. See especially Noël Didier, "Henri de Suse, prieur d'Antibes, prévôt de Grasse (1235?–1245)," *Studia Gratiana,* 2(1953), 595–618, "Henri de Suse en Angleterre (1236?–1244)," *Studi in onore di Vincenzo Arangio-Ruiz,* 2:333–51, and "Henri de Suse, évêque de Sistéron (1244–1250)," *RHDF,* 4th ser., 31(1953), 244–70, 409–29; Gabriel Le Bras, "Théologie et droit romain dans l'oeuvre d'Henri de Suse," *Etudes historiques à la mémoire de Noël Didier,* pp. 195–204; Arturo Rivera Damas, *Pensamiento politico de Hostiensis.*

definition were so constructed as to exclude the possibility of a vow to perform an illicit act, on the ground, it seems, that no votive obligation, in the juristic sense, can arise from a promise to perform an illicit act. In such matters, he added, transgressors are more pleasing to God than observers, even if they have sworn an oath on the matter.[113] Anyone at all, according to Hostiensis, was free to make a vow despite any contrary obligation, for those who were moved by the spirit of God were not subject to the public law—including even the canon law—but to the private law, the final law, written in the heart by the Holy Spirit, and not subject to the regulation of public law: for where the spirit is, there also is the letter of the law.[114] This passage reflects a surprising antinomian streak in Hostiensis' thought—not quite what one would expect from a distinguished canon lawyer, a cardinal, and papal legal adviser. From this splendid, if unexpected, position, however, Hostiensis beat a quick retreat as soon as he came down to cases. He proceeded to qualify what he had just said by adducing certain categories of persons who did not enjoy complete freedom in the matter of making vows: bishops, clerics, monks, minors, married women, and serfs.[115] Hostiensis' discussion of the limitations upon the power of these groups to make vows largely repeated and summarized the positions taken by his predecessors, although his treatment contained a few original points of interest. The limitation upon a bishop's power to make a pilgrimage or other vow Hostiensis linked to the marriage-bond relationship which is established between a bishop and his diocese. Because of this he held that bishops must secure a special or general license from the pope before engaging to undertake a pilgrim-

113. Hostiensis, *Summa aurea,* tit. *De voto* (Venice ed., 1605, col. 1125; Lyons ed., 1537, fol. 176[rb]): "Quid sit uotum? Alicuius rei licite faciende, uel non faciende, cum deliberatione animi Deo facta pollicitatio. Bene dico rei licite, quia si mala uel illicita esset promissio, non esset seruanda, licet rescidenda: nam in malis promissis rescinde fidem, in turpi uoto muta decretum 22 q. 4 in malis [c. 5] et in talibus magis placent Deo transgressores quam obseruatores, etiamsi interuenerit iuramentum, ut in auth. scenicas, mulieres [*Auth.* 5.4 = *Nov.* 51. pr.]."

114. Ibid., Venice ed., col. 1129; Lyons ed., fol. 176[vb]: "Quis uouere possit? Quilibet regulariter nullo iugo obstante: quia qui spiritu Dei ducitur, non est sub lege, scilicet publica, et dicitur lex publica lex canonica, uerbi gratia, decretum est in canone, ne clericus de suo episcopatu ad aliam transeat sine litteris commendaticiis, priuata uero lex est illa que instinctu spiritus sancti in corde scribitur et hec est lex ultima, non est sub prima: quia ubi spiritus, ibi libertas." Cf. *X* 3.31.18.

115. Ibid., Venice ed., col. 1129; Lyons ed., fol. 176[vb]: "Prohibentur autem quedam persone, que, quoad uotum emittendum, non habent liberam uoluntatem, sicut episcopus, clericus, monachus, impubes, uxor, seruus."

age.[116] He did not push this analogy so far as to suggest that a bishop required the permission of his flock in order to make a vow which would separate him from it, although such a suggestion was indicated by the decretal *Magne*.[117]

The disability of clerics Hostiensis based upon the obedience due to their bishops, that of monks both upon obedience and the premise that their departure upon pilgrimage might cause scandal and give occasion for aimless wandering, which was foreign to the monastic vocation.[118] Serfs and minors were excepted from the general rule that vows might be taken freely by all, according to Hostiensis' reasoning, because of the *patria potestas* which their masters and fathers held over them.[119] To all of

116. Ibid., Venice ed., col. 1129; Lyons ed., fol. 176[vb]: "Episcopus non potest aliquod uotum emittere sine licentia pape; intelligas per quod dissolvatur uinculum matrimonii: quod esse intelligitur inter ipsum et ecclesiam, sponsam suam. . . . unde nec potest uotum emittere peregrinationis, per quod ipsum ab ecclesia non oporteat absentare sine licentia speciali, uel generali, infra eodem Magne § verum."

117. Bishops did in practice sometimes seek a ceremonial permission from their clergy and people and also from neighboring prelates before departing on crusade; e.g. Odo Rigaldus, *Register,* s.d. 11 Nov. 1269 and 17 Nov. 1269 (ed. and trans. Sydney M. Brown and Jeremiah F. O'Sullivan, pp. 733, 734).

118. Hostiensis, *Summa aurea,* tit. *De voto* (Venice ed., col. 1129–30; Lyons ed., fol. 177[ra]): "Clericus etiam non potest sine licentia prelati sui uotum peregrinationis emittere: de cons. dist. 5 Non oportet [c. 36] de quo c. fit mentio infra eodem, Magne § uerum, nec aliud, per quod relinquere oporteat ipsum in ecclesiam suam. . . . Item nec uotum abstinentie singularis potest emittere monachus, neque pere-grinationis, neque aliquod regulariter et si hoc fecerit sine licentia abbatis non debet exequi, ne fit fratrum scandalum, quibus se debet conformare: uel ne detur ei occasio uagandi. . . . Quid si uotum emiserit, antequam monasterium intraret? Dicas idem scilicet quod sine licentia abbatis ipsum exequi non debet. . . . Nam et omnia temporalia uota uidentur mutasse in religionis obseruationem . . . nec est necessaria circa peccati satisfactionem: ubi totum uite tempus seruitio impenditur conditoris."

119. Ibid., Venice ed., col. 1131, 1133; Lyons ed., fol. 177[rab]: "Sed nunquid uotum peregrinationis longinque emittere potest [*scil.:* filius familias]? Non uidetur, quia nimis preiudicaret patrie potestati, cui non debet preiudicare, ut dictum est argu-men. in his que no. supra eodem uer. episcopus et uer. clericis; excipe peregrina-tionem uoti transmarini, argumentum infra eodem Ex multa § quod autem [*X* 3.34.7] et necessarium ac ineuitabilem, ut si forte a canone per sedem apostolicam absoluendus, argumentum infra de sententia excommunicationis, Relatum [*X* 5.39.37]. . . . Quid de uoto peregrinationis a seruo facto? Dicas quod inuito do-mino non potest ipsum exequi, nisi quando necessaria est, ut infra de sententia excommunicationis, Relatum in finem [*X* 5.39.37] et iniunge alia que not. in filio familias supra eodem, uer. impubes et seq. et quod ibi dictum est quoad filium familias, ⟨hic⟩ [ed.: hanc] quoque ad seruum intelligatur repetitum, cum fortius quam patri filius et seruus domino sit astrictus."

these cases where the power of assuming votive obligations was limited by status, however, there was an exception: the crusade vow could be taken by anyone without the prior permission of another person. Likewise Hostiensis admitted that married men might take the crusade vow, unconditionally. He was more dubious about married women, and he discussed their situation at some length. His doubts as to the desirability of wives executing the crusade vow arose from the thought that their chastity might be endangered on the journey to the Holy Land. A woman who wished to go on crusade alone was regarded by Hostiensis as a suspicious person whose virtue might be too frail to withstand the rigors and temptations of the crusade enterprise. Accusingly, he cited Ovid's line: "Chaste is she whom no man solicits," and counseled that young women or those whose character was suspect should not attempt to fulfill crusade vows in person; rather they should redeem their vows and devote the redemption money to the needs of the Holy Land. Elderly women and matrons of good reputation might be advised to make the journey in person, so long as they brought with them a company of soldiers whose services would be of value to the Holy Land.[120] With quasi-seriousness

---

120. Ibid., Venice ed., col. 1132; Lyons ed., fol. 177rb: "Nunquid ergo et uxor potest Hierosolymitanum uotum uiro inuito emittere? De hoc nihil dicitur expresse et uidetur quod sic, quia non ad imparia iudicantur, ut nota supra eodem uer. proxi; quid enim dices, si sit nobilis mulier habens magnum comitatum, nec uiro suo in dotem datum, quam multi bellatores sequuntur? Certe necessitati terre sancte subueniendum erit et tunc ea ratio uidetur que in uiro est. . . . Sed contra, quia uir caput est mulieris, ut supra eodem uer. uxorem, et unde et in uita et in morte debet sequi uirum, non uir ipsam. . . . Si enim uult ire sine uiro, suspecta est mihi, quia fragilis est et sic dicit Ouidus: 'Casta est quam nemo rogauit.' [Amores 1.8.43] Subtrahenda est ergo uagandi materia et timendum, ne angelus se transformet, sicut dictum est de monacho, supra, eodem uer. monachos. Nec obstat infra eodem Quod super his in fine [X c.34.8] quod enim dicit ibi de mulieribus, aut intelligas que non uouerunt, et quod sequitur, 'cetere vero,' expone: que non habent uiros, et uouerunt, uel que de consensu maritorum uouerunt. Solutio: Puto quod uotum potest emittere, etiam uiro inuito. Utrum autem ipsum possit exequi, eo inuito, distinguendum uidetur utrum suspecta sit et infamata, uel nimis iuuenis, in quo casu personaliter non exequetur, et sic intellige iura. . . . Absit enim, ut ab ecclesia talis compensatio admittatur, infra de usuris, super eo [X 5.19.4]. Quo ergo faciet, redimat uotum cum ad eundem et ad pugnandum inhabilis iudicetur, infra eodem Quod super his § rursus [X 3.34.8]. Si uero sit uetus que multum profecit in diebus suis, et matrona bone fame, uadat, nec uotum redimat, si secum multos possit ducere bellatores et sic intellige quod not. supra eadem q. respon. I, quia tunc eadem ratio in uxore est, que et in uiro, ergo idem ius statuendum est, C. de liberis preteritis uel exheredatis, 1. 1 [Cod. 6.28.1] et C. ad legem Falcidiam 1. fi. ad finem [Cod. 4.18.3], arg. ad hanc distinctionem supra de conuersatione coniugatorum,

Hostiensis went on to discuss the canonical position of a harlot who had vowed to go on crusade. Should she be allowed to redeem her vow? She would, after all, be followed by a multitude of warriors! Reluctantly, Hostiensis concluded that neither the fulfillment of her vow nor the redemption of it would be licit. The former he ruled out because her warriors would be participating in the expedition for a morally inadmissible reason; the latter was rejected because of the source of the funds which would be employed to redeem the vow.[121]

In his discussion of the nature of vows, Hostiensis followed lines of thought already familiar among the decretists, emphasizing the quality of deliberatio as a necessary precondition of a binding vow.[122] He adhered closely—at times, verbatim—to St. Raymond of Peñafort's scheme of distinctions between the various types of vow: necessary and voluntary, simple and solemn, pure and conditional.[123] As for the commutation of

cum sis preditus et capitulum uxoratus [*X* 3.32.4, 8], et si uis scire utrum unus coniugatorum possit uotum continentie altero inuito emittere et ad quid teneatur is, qui hoc facit, uide quod notatur supra de conuersione coniugatorum § qualiter possit converti."

121. Ibid., Venice ed., col. 1132–33; Lyons ed., fol. 177rb: "Quid si publica meretrix, quam multi sequuntur: quia nihil amore vehementius, in authen., quibus modis naturales efficiuntur legitimi § illud, col. 6 [*Auth.* 6.1.4 = *Nov.* 74.4], uotum emiserit transmarinum, numquid poterit uotum redimere? Non uidetur: quia multi bellatores eam sequuntur, ut arg. infra eodem, quod super his in fi. [*X* 3.34.8], dicas quod nisi corrigatur, nec ipsa nec bellatores sui, qui ex corrupto amore sequuntur ipsam, admittendi sunt, neque uotum suum comprobandum, quia nec oblatio sua recipienda est, ut nota supra de decimis de quibus uer. dicas de parochiis, § in quibus, sub § tamen sciendum, uer. 5 si sit meretrix."

122. Ibid., Lyons ed., fol. 176rb: "Cum deliberatione animi ideo dictum est quia uotum quod ex facilitate anime potius quam ex arbitrio discretionis emissum est non est obligatorium usquequam infra eodem uenientes [*X* 3.34.2], supra de regularibus, ad nostram [*X* 3.31.8], supra de conuersione coniugatorum, carissimus et c. ueniens [*X* 3.32.11, 16]."

123. Ibid., Venice ed., col. 1126; Lyons ed., fol. 176^{rb-vb}: "Quot sint species uotorum? Due, nam aliud necessitatis, aliud uoluntatis. Votum necessitatis dicitur illud, quod quis promittit in baptismo, ut abrenunciare satane et pompis eius, tenere fidem, seruare decalogum, et alia sine quibus salus non est . . . unde cum homo peccat post baptismum, dupliciter reus est: et quia peccat in eo quod comittit, et quia uotum preuaricaretur, non tamen tanquam pro duobus mortalibus penitentiam inducit, sed tanquam pro uno circumstantia transgressionis aggrauato. Votum uero uoluntatis dicitur quod quis uoluntarie emittit, et ad quod quis ante uotum non tenebatur, sed post uotum astringitur, sicut et uotum continentie, abstinentie, peregrinationis, secundum Raynaldum. Gof. de his dicitur in Psal. 'Vouete et reddite' glo. 1, si uoueritis, reddite Deo uestro: ut sic primum ad consilium secundum ad imperium referatur, infra eodem Magne [*X* 3.34.7]. . . . Votorum autem uoluntariorum aliud simplex aliud solemne. Simplex uotum dicitur quia

vows, especially pilgrimage vows, Hostiensis repeated the general norms laid down in the decretal legislation for arriving at the sum to be demanded and the factors—equity, honesty, and utility—which were to be taken into account in dealing with such cases.[124] His treatment of the rules for commuting crusade vows in particular was more ample and clearcut than that of most of his predecessors. He made use of the distinction between the two types of vows to visit the Holy Land—devotional and militant—and drew from them two distinct sets of rules for commutation. In brief, his position was that those who had made the devotional vow were not to be accorded a commutation so long as they were able to make the journey, while commutation was to be granted readily to those who had made the militant vow and who were unable to fight, either in person or through others or by giving advice and exhortation. Likewise he laid some stress upon the probable effects of the absence of the *vovens* from his normal resorts. If his absence on crusade would occasion any danger to his land or province, he should be allowed to postpone or forego the personal fulfillment of the vow.[125]

---

simpliciter et sine aliqua solemnitate emittitur et horum aliud consistit in faciendo, ut ire ad sanctum Jacobum, ieiuniare, orare, offere certis temporibus et horis quibus homo non astringitur; aliud in non faciendo, sicut non contrahere matrimonium, non recipere ordines, hec etiam dicuntur uoluntaria, quia sine his salus est, i. q. i § ecce cum honoris [d. p. c. 43]. . . . Sed etiam uotorum aliud purum, ut cum simpliciter emittitur, aliud conditionale, ut cum conditio apponitur, puta cum dicitur 'uolo ieiuniare uel limina talis sancti uisitare si deus michi prestiterit sanitatem, uel filium uel filiam michi concesserit'."

124. Ibid., Venice ed., col. 1135–36; Lyons ed., fol. 177va: "In uoto etiam peregrinationis sic facienda est redemptio, ut expense que fierent in eundo, morando, et redeundo, ad alias pias causas erogentur, et ut labor itineris, ieiuniorum et vigiliarum, et orationum laboribus compensentur. . . . Sed in redemptione, uel commutatione cuiuslibet uoti, tria sunt precipue attendenda, quid liceat secundum equitatem, quid deceat secundum honestatem, quid expediat secundum utilitatem, seu necessitatem, infra eodem, Magne § 1 ideoque [X 3.34.7]."

125. Ibid., Venice ed., col. 1135–36; Lyons ed., fol. 177va: "Sed et in uoto transmarino est consideranda uouentis intentio, utrum scilicet intenderet peregrinari uel bellare, ut in primo casu habilis ad eundum quamuis inhabilis ad pugnandum non redimat, inhabilis uero ad eundum redimat; in secundo casu inhabilis ad pugnandum quamuis habilis ad eundum redimat, nisi consilio strenuus sit, uel secum forte possit ducere magnum numerum pugnatorum. Talis enim est omnino impotens, cum primus lingua, secundus per alios pugnare possit . . . uel nisi sit agricola, uel artifex, qui ibi sit utilis, quamuis non multi talium propter breuitatem possessionum et paucitatem inhabitantium ibi sunt opportuni. . . . Sed inter illos, qui habent impedimentum temporale, ut his dilatio concedatur, et perpetuum, ut ab his recipiatur redemptio est subtiliter distinguendum. . . . In clericis etiam uouentibus considerare oportet utrum clericus cruce signatus consilio uel officio predicationis, uel

In his comments on jurisdiction over vows and their dispensation, Hostiensis acknowledged the power of the bishop to deal with all voluntary vows save the crusade vow and the vow of chastity, over which the pope possessed exclusive jurisdiction.[126]

The papal dispensing power, he granted, extended to all vows, save possibly the vow of chastity, upon which he merely noted that opinions differed, reporting, however, that certain canonists held that this power could dispense from the vow of chastity under highly unusual conditions.[127]

---

quia seruitio alicuius magnatis deputatus est, uel quia secum multos bellatores potest ducere, sit ibi utilis uel necessarius: et tunc non recipietur redemptio, uel non sit sibi opportunus, et tunc recipietur. . . . Nam quoad pugnam personaliter faciendam inhabilis est . . . nisi forte spiritualiter pugnare uelit armis suis, que sunt orationes et lachryme, 23 q. 8 1, et censura ecclesiastica, nam spiritualia arma propria sunt clericorum, ut in auth. d. n. [*Nov.* 5.8?], extra de sententia excommunicationis, dudum responsionem 1, quod dic ut nota supra de treuga et pace § quid iustum bellum uer. 5 ratione persone et seq. Sed et aliquoties possunt uotum redimere, etiamsi bellatores ducere possit: puta si sit nimis senex, fragilis, et confractus. . . . Item oportet considerari, utrum ex facilitate animi iuuenis uotum emissum est, et sic est remittendum redemptione competenti recepta. . . . Nec pretermitti debet, quod licet uotum Hierosolimitanum magni favoris sit. . . . Si tamen propter absentiam unius persone totius terre, siue provincie unius periculum immineret, uotum remittitur, uel differetur, nec est uoti transgressor, qui authoritate Sedis Apostolice illud distulit adimplere. . . ."

126. *Ibid.*, Venice ed., col. 1136–37; Lyons ed., fol. 177[vab]: "Sic patet, quod authoritate episcopi potest quodlibet uotum uoluntarium commutari, uel redimi, excepto transmarino, quod soli Pape reservatur, ut nota supra eodem § 1 respon. 1 et uers. quamuis autem. . . . Item in omni uoto uoluntatis redimendo, uel commutando authoritas Pape sufficit, nullo casu excepto. Episcopi etiam authoritas in omnibus sufficit, exceptis duobus scilicet uoto crucis, ut nota supra eo. uer. quamuis, et continentie, quod soli Pape relinquendum est, ut patet in his que nota supra eodem uer. proxi. . . . Quamuis autem instructus sit predicta, qualiter uotum transmarinum redimi, uel differi possit, non tamen est tutum redemptionem recipere uel differe, uel de ipso aliquo alio modo intromittere sine mandato Sedis Apostolice, speciali ad quam solam hoc noscitur pertinere . . . et ideo de mandato pape remittitur, uel differtur, uel redimitur et ipse de hoc interpretatur . . . et idem puto in uoto crucis cuiuslibet, quia ad ipsum pertinet de talibus iudicare. . . ."

127. *Ibid.*, Venice ed., col. 1136–37; Lyons ed., fol. 177[vb]: "Ideoque nec summus Pontifex potest contra hoc [*scil.:* uotum continentie et castitatis] dispensare: ut expressum legitur, infra titu. § I cum ad monasterium in fine; alii contra, intra quos est do. Hug. Card. Sancte Sabine, et dicunt quod dominus Papa posset ex magna causa dispensare in hoc, puta, si aliquis rex Sarracenorum cum tota terra sua offeret conuersionem suam, si aliqua sancti monialis daretur sibi in uxorem, et hi probabilius dicunt." The same question was discussed by Gérard of Abbéville (fl. 1254–71) in a quodlibetal disputation summarized by Gaines Post, *Studies in Medieval Legal Thought*, pp. 266–68. Gérard held that the pope could dispense from the vow of chastity under these circumstances, since it would be useful, indeed

Finally, in his great *Lectura* on the *Decretals* of Gregory IX, a work upon which he was engaged until the very end of his life, Hostiensis further pursued his doctrine of vows. In the *Lectura* he was more certain than he had been in the *Summa* about the power of dispensing from vows, and held flatly that any voluntary vow was dispensable.[128] The ordinary minister of dispensation was the bishop. Only the vows of continence and the crusade lay outside his authority; they fell under the exclusive jurisdiction of the pope, who might dispense from any voluntary vow, given sufficient cause.[129] Accepting the tripartite scheme of the steps by which a vow was made, Hostiensis held to the doctrine, usual by his time, that a propositum created an obligation which was binding quantum ad Deum, although not quantum ad ecclesiam. A propositum became binding as far as the Church was concerned only when it was openly expressed as a vow, since the Church did not judge hidden matters.[130] The binding power of any vow and the obligation created by it were morally grave in his eyes and he appeared not to distinguish

necessary, for the good of the Church. Thus the notion of a *ratio utilitatis vel necessitatis* was in Gérard's view the controlling factor in determining the case.

128. *Lectura* [*In quinque libros decretalium commentaria*] to X 3.34.1, vol. 1, fol. 124ᵛᵃ: "De peregrinatione uotis uel ieiuniorum, uel alterius speciei cuiuscunque, dummodo uoluntarium fuerit ab initio, sicut est in omnibus illis, que ante emissionem uoti possunt fieri, uel non fieri sine peccato. Talia enim ex causa compensationem recipiunt, arg. i q. vii § nisi rigor et c. seq. [d. p. c. 5 and c. 6] et § utilitatis intuitu et c. seq. [d. p. c. 12 and c. 13]. Secus in necessario, sicut est illud, quod emittitur in baptismo: puta, tenere fidem, seruare Decalogum, et alia, sine quibus salus non est; de consecr. dist. iiii q. i § ecce cum honoris [?]. Tale enim uotum nullam compensationem admittat, infra de usur. super eo et nota supra ti. i. c. i. respon. i in fi. et patet infra eodem Magne § cum igitur et nota infra eodem licet in principio, quod dic, ut nota in summa eodem tit. § quot sunt species uotorum."

129. *Lectura* to X 3.34.1, ad v. *Qui presidet,* vol. 1, fol. 124ᵛᵃ: "Is enim, scilicet episcopus, in omni uoto uoluntario dispensare potest, excepto uoto crucis siue transmarino, infra eodem Ex multa, et excepto uoto continentie, arg. xxxii q. i. nuptie [c. 12] et q. v illic et q. vi c. i et exceptis aliis substantialibus regule. . . . Papa uero in omni uoto uoluntario dispensare potest, etiam in uoto continentie, ex magna tamen causa, licet aliqui contradicant, ut nota infra eodem titulo in fine et in d. c. Cum ad monasterium [X 3.35.6], et hoc teneas, licet super redemptione uotorum quatuor sint opiniones, ut nota in summa, eodem titulo, § utrum et per quem."

130. Ibid. to X 3.34.3, ad v. *Si plus,* vol. 1, fol. 125ʳᵇ: "Hoc ideo dicit, quia quantum ad ecclesiam non obligatur, nisi uotum emittat, quia non iudicat de occultis, infra de simo. Sicut tuis in fi. et capitulum sequentem in fi. [X 5.3.33, 34], uel quia, propositum non deliberatum non obligat, ut supra nota. Alioquin, quasi omnes scholares ad minus tenerentur intrare religionem, quia pauci sunt, qui uitam aliquando mutare non proponant."

between the binding power of simple vows and solemn vows, at least in foro interno.[131] Once the crusade vow had been made, the crusader's cross was imposed as an external sign of the votive obligation created.[132] But in dealing with vows, Hostiensis emphasized, it was the intention, not the form of words used, that was significant.[133]

THE DOCTRINE OF THE VOW IN DECRETALIST WRITINGS FROM HOSTIENSIS TO THE COUNCIL OF TRENT. The work of Hostiensis may for most purposes be taken to mark the culmination of the substantial development of the canonistic doctrine of vows, especially of the crusade vow, as Villey has suggested.[134] There were, however, some additions to the basic theories which are worth remarking in a few works of the later middle ages.

One work of some interest is the *Summa* (written ca.1254–74) of the

131. Ibid. to X 3.34.6, ad v. *Fidei tue,* vol. 1, fol. 126ra: "Ex nudo autem uoto obligatio oritur, ff de policit. 1. ii in prin. [*Dig.* 50.12.2 pr.] et nudo promissio obligat, si facta sit ciuitati, ff de pollicita. 1. pactum [*Dig.* 50.12.3], multo fortius facta Deo, uel subsidio Terre Sancte, quia Deus inter simplicem loquelam et iuramentum non facit differentiam, xxii q. v. iuramenti [c. 12], unde et ecclesia ex pacto nudo dat actionem, ut patet in eo, quod le. et nota supra de pact. c. i. et iii."

132. Ibid. to X 3.34.7, ad v. *Crucem dominicam,* vol. 1, fol. 126vb: "Est igitur crucis delatio signum peregrinationis, siue uoti emissi, ut hic."

133. Ibid. to X 3.34.8, ad v. *Intentionem uouentis,* vol. 1, fol. 129ra: "Nota quod in toto attendenda est intentio uouentis quantum ad Deum plusquam uerba."

134. Villey, "L'Idée de la croisade," p. 567. Among the later decretalists whose writings I have consulted without finding any significant additions to the existing theories on the subject of the crusade vow are: the *Tractatus de dispensationibus* (written ca.1250–53) of Bonaguida de Aretio, in Lambeth Palace Library, MS. 49; the *Summa* (written ca.1241–43) of Goffredus de Trano (d. 1245) in the Fitzwilliam Museum, Cambridge, MS. McClean 137; the *glossa ordinaria* to X by Bernardus Parmensis de Botone (d. 1266); the *Apparatus "In hoc quatuor causas"* in MS. Royal 11.A.II of the British Museum; the *Casus summarii* of Joannes Andreae (d. 1348), the *Notabilia "Prompte volentibus,"* and the *Casus in quibus solus papa dispensare potest,* all three in the same MS, Corpus Christi College, MS. 38; the *Summa summarum* (written ca.1325–27) of William of Pagula (d. ca.1332) in Pembroke College MS. 201 and Christ's College MS. Dd.1.2; the *Dictionarium iuris* (Venice, 1581) of Albericus de Rosate (d. 1354); the fourteenth-century *Apparatus* to the *Summa* of Heinrich von Merseburg (d. after 1276) in Innsbruck, Universitätsbibliothek, MS. 590, and Munich, Bayerische Staatsbibliothek, Clm. 17562; the *Commentaria* (Venice, 1571) of Panormitanus (1386–1453?); the *Repertorium* (written before 1408) of Arnoldus de Gheyloven (d. 1442) in Kloster Neustift-bei-Brixen, Stiftsbibliothek, MS. 4; the fifteenth century *Opusculum tripartitum* in MS. lat. 5664 of the Bayerische Staatsbibliothek; and the *Commentaria* (Venice, 1699) of Manuel Gonzalez Tellez (d. 1649).

Franciscan canonist, Monaldus (d. 1288/89). Monaldus considered, for one thing, the problem of a woman who, in great difficulties or anxiety, had made a vow. Was such a vow binding? According to Monaldus it was, a position for which he cited as a proof Ps. 65.13–14: "I will pay thee my vows, Which my lips have uttered, and my mouth has spoken, When I was in trouble." Juridically, Monaldus followed Hostiensis in taking the position that any vow which was uttered with the intention of creating an obligation to God was *ipso facto* valid and tenable, despite any mitigating circumstances. The absolute terms in which Monaldus expressed his position, however, appeared to dismiss the elaborate analyses of the validity of vows and the obligations they created by earlier (and later) canonists.[135] Further, in his lengthy discussion of the crusade vow, Monaldus distinguished more clearly and precisely than most other canonists between the commutation of the labor involved in the crusade vow, which might be redeemed by entering religion, and the persisting obligation to aid the Holy Land, which required further subsidies for its redemption.[136]

135. Monaldus, *Summa,* tit. *De voto,* in Lambeth Palace Library, MS. 39, fol. 221[rb]: "Votum est alicuius boni cum deliberatione deo facta promissio; si enim fiat de re mala uel etiam de re bona sed sine deliberatione, scilicet cum impetu quodam et perfectionem, non obligat. . . . Sed numquid uota mulierum que faciunt in partu uel infirmitatibus uel angustis suis uel suorum et etiam que uiri fuerunt moti ex aliqua angustia uel perturbatione tenenda sunt? Respondeo, si habeant intentionem obligandi se deo cogitantes et de causa que mouebat eos ad uouendum, scilicet infirmitate et alio periculo et de fine, scilicet de euasione periculi propter quod euitandum uouebant, tenenda sunt, licet in tribulatione et perturbatione sicut emissa secundum illud psalmum 'reddam tibi uota mea etc. in tribulatione mea' [Ps. 65.13–14], xvii q. iiii sunt qui opes [c. 3], nec fiunt huius modi uota sine deliberatione ex quo uouentes sunt in sua mente. In causa uero illius decreti eodem titulo, litteraturam, dicenda quod non fuit ius uotum, sed tantum proponitur solo uerbo expressum sine intentione obligandi."

136. Ibid., Lambeth Palace, MS. 39, fol. 225[rb-va]: *"De uoto Ierosolimitano respondeo.* Votum ierosolimitanum a pauperibus uel debilibus factum uel redimi potest auctoritate domini pape . . . et nullus alius potest se intromittere de uoto terre sancte redimendo, commutando uel differendo, nisi papa uel alius de speciali mandato ipsius. In hiis autem uotis redimendis commutandis uel differendis dyocesanus episcopus consideratis causis potest auctoritatem prorogare secundum quosdam. . . . Item si qui uouit expendere C marchas uel mittere in subsidium terre sancte et postea intrat monasterium licet quantum ad laborem peregrinationis absoluatur per ingressum religionis tamen quoad pecuniam predictam quia nec episcopus nec abbas nec alius a(bsque) papa potest irritare uel commutare uota terre sancte nec ipso uidetur irritari per ingressum religionis nisi quoad laborem peregrinationis. . . . Item licet mediocres persone liberentur a uoto crucis per ingressum religionis numquid idem de imperatore, rege, comite, duce, uel aliquo prepotente, ex quo pendet totus exercitus crucesignatorum et de cuius absentia desolabitur quod etiam si uouit quod toto tempore uite sue uel nisi ad terminum uel septennium militabit in terram sanctam et tenebit secum duo uel tria milia militum? Respondeo,

In the *Lectura* (written between 1259 and 1266) of Bernardus de Montemirato (usually called Abbas antiquus; d. 1296) we find an interesting treatment of the problem of dispensations from crusade vows that were obtained by misrepresentation.[137] Bernardus concluded that such dispensations were worthless and constituted a grave danger to the soul.[138] His analysis of the process of creating a valid votive obligation is also not without interest. Harking back to the earlier decretist treatments of this theme, but altering the terminology slightly, Bernardus distinguished three steps in making a vow: a commencement, a confirmation, and a consummation. The initial stage he referred to as a propositum, when the notion of making the vow was planted in the soul. At this stage there existed no obligation either to God or to the Church to carry the matter further. The second stage, deliberation, created an obligation toward God, though not toward the Church, and defections at this stage were a proper subject of penance in the forum internum. The third stage, consummation, occurred, according to Bernardus, when the vow was expressed verbally and at that point the Church might begin to require its execution.[139]

The *Speculum iuris* (written ca.1271–72; revised ca.1287) of the great

---

nisi prohabiliter dubitatur an circa huius arduas personas preponderare debet communis utilitas uel priuata papa esset pocius consulendum in hac causa quam aliqui timere in diffinendum. Item uotum Ierosolimitanum potest uir sine licencia uxoris facere et adimplere et uxor si uult sequatur eum. . . ."

137. See S. Kuttner, "Wer war der Dekretalist 'Abbas antiquus'?" *ZRG, KA,* 26(1937), 471–89.

138. Bernardus de Montemirato, *Lectura* to X 2.22.7 (Strassburg, 1511 ed., fol. 117ʳ): "Licet etiam essent habiles ad pugnandum et hoc expressissent, tacuerunt tamen qui essent diuites et potentes et qui secum possent ducere bellatores uel tacuerunt qui essent armorum concilio strenui et cum talibus non de facili dispensatur quin debeant uotum adimplere . . . uel expresserunt falsitatem dicendo se inhabiles ad pugnandum uel dicendo se pauperes uel aliquid huiusmodi et ideo de his mandatur inquiri. Casus: per falsitatem obtenta dispensatio nulli prodest, uel per falsam litteram non obstat huic de clericis peregrinis c. i [X 1.22.1], quia ibi dignitas erat incerta an si erant episcopi qui episcopi ibi dicebantur, sed hic non dubitabatur de dignitate cardinalatus, uel ibi maius periculum, quia sibi et aliis hic uero tantum uouenti glo. innuit que incipit Cum uero etc. [*glos. ord.* to X 2.22.7, ad v. *ignota*]."

139. Ibid. to X 3.34.3 (Strassburg ed., fol. 171ʳ): "Ad euidentiam huius nota quod votum dicitur initiari confirmari et consummari. Votum est inchoatum tantum cum propositum in animo seminatur et ex tali quoad deum uel ecclesiam nullus remanet obligatus. Confirmatum dicitur quando super proposito deliberatur et ex tali quis quoad deum est obligatus et ex foro penitentiali est ad executionem omnibus modis inducendus. . . . Est autem consummatum cum propositum deliberatum ore exprimitur et tunc ecclesia cogit . . . et facit bene ad hoc quod nota infra eodem, c. ultima in ultima glosa [*glos. ord.* to X 3.34.11, ad v. *tenemini*]."

French canonist and bishop, Guilielmus Durantis the elder (1231–96) is disappointingly conventional on the matter of the vow and associated topics. Possibly the most interesting contribution of the Speculator to the subject was his attempt (which became a commonplace in later canonistic literature) to define the notion of dispensation as a "relaxation" of the rigor of the law and, alternatively, a "wounding" of the law by duly constituted authority.[140]

In addition to the strictly canonistic discussions of the crusade vow in the late thirteenth and early fourteenth centuries, the topic was also discussed frequently and at length by theologians, whose most common point of inquiry was dispensation. At least a dozen theological *questiones disputate* on this topic have been preserved.[141] Among other matters, they discussed such questions as "Does a vow to enter a religious house still bind after the house has burned down?", "May one fulfill a vow with the intention of negating its effects?", "Must a conditional vow incorporating dishonest conditions be fulfilled if those conditions are fulfilled?", and "May one break a pilgrimage vow in order to save a life?"[142] One theological discussion of the crusade vow is of special interest. This is St. Thomas Aquinas' disputation on the question "Whether a man may take the cross against his wife's wishes if there is reason to fear that she will be unchaste?" Discussing this knotty problem in his quodlibetal disputations of Easter 1271, the Angelic Doctor concluded that such a vow was morally inadmissible. The conclusion was startling; it was directly at odds with the relevant decretal legislation and it also contradicted the position that St. Thomas himself had taken a few years earlier. His grounds were ethical and moral, rather than legal. St. Thomas argued that moral necessities must take precedence over moral acts which are voluntary. Since participation in a crusade was a voluntary act on the husband's part, he had no right to commit himself if this would endanger his necessary obligation to preserve his wife's chastity. He was free to go only if his wife could remain chaste of her own volition during his absence or if he were to take her with him. Thus St. Thomas rejected the legal right guaranteed

---

140. Gulielmus Durantis, *Speculum iuris,* lib. 1, partic. 1, tit. *De dispensatione* § 1 *Dispensatio,* 1/1, fol. 25ʳ: "Dispensatio est prouida iuris communis relaxatio utilitate siue necessitate pensata. Vel sic: Dispensatio est rigoris iuris, per eum, ad quem spectat, canonice facta relaxatio. . . . Vocatur autem dispensatio uulnus, que ius uulnerat."

141. P. Glorieux, *La Littérature quodlibetique de 1260 à 1320,* 1:108, 114, 116, 155; 2:156, 171, 175, 184, 235, 246, 254, 290.

142. Ibid., 1:155, 181; 2:167, 169, 170, 175, 217, 234, 235, 242, 246, 292.

to husbands by the decretal *Magne* by invoking the higher moral obligation of husband to wife.[143]

For the most part, the commentaries of the fourteenth- and fifteenth-cen-
tury authors simply reproduced, with a few minor variations, earlier
viewpoints regarding vows. Even so talented and influential a canonist as
Joannes Andreae (ca.1270–1348) found little new to add to what had
already been written on the matter.[144] He did not, however, classify the
pilgrimage vow (which implicitly included the crusade vow) as a solemn
vow *a iure,* although he held that specific performance of the obligation
resulting from such a vow might be demanded even from laymen and
enforced, if necessary, by penal measures, including excommunication and
deprivation of goods.[145]

The standard canonistic doctrine which held, following the provisions
of *Licet,* that unfulfilled votive obligations of a decedent might be passed
on to his heirs was challenged by another major fourteenth-century legal
writer, the great Civilian, Bartolus of Sassoferrato.[146] In his commentary

143. Thomas Aquinas, *Quodlibetum* 4.11. To the question "Utrum vir possit
accipere crucem uxore nolente, si de ejus incontinentia timeatur?" St. Thomas
replied: "Respondeo dicendum, quod ea quae sunt necessitatis, non sunt praetermit-
tenda propter ea quae sunt propriae voluntatis; unde etiam Dominus, Matth. 15,
Pharisaeos, qui docebant praetermittere mandatum de honoratione parentum, ut
aliqua voluntariae oblationes Deo offerentur. Ex necessitate autem viro imminet ut
gerat curam uxoris, quia *caput mulieris* est *vir,* ut dicitur 1 ad Corinth. 11, 3: Sed
quod accipiat crucem ad transfretandum, subjacet propriae voluntati. Unde si uxor
est talis quae sequi non possit propter aliquod legitimum impedimentum, et de ejus
incontinentia timeatur, non est ei consulendum ut accipiat crucem, et dimittat
uxorem. Secus autem est, si uxor continere voluntarie proponal vel velit, et possit
sequi virum suum." St. Thomas had taken the opposite position in the earliest of
his major works, the *Commentarium in quattuor libros Sententiarum Petri Lombardi*
(written ca.1254–57): 4 *In Sent.* 32.1.4 *ad* 1 in his *Opera omnia,* 7/2:965. I am
grateful to Professor John T. Noonan, Jr., who first drew my attention to this
development in St. Thomas' thought; see also Brundage, "The Crusader's Wife,"
pp. 438–41.

144. On Joannes Andreae see especially S. Kuttner, "Joannes Andreae and His
Novella," *The Jurist,* 24(1964), 393–408; Guido Rossi, "Contributi alla biografia
del canonista Giovanni d'Andrea," *Rivista trimestrale di diritto e procedure civile,*
11(1957), 1451–1502.

145. Joannes Andreae, *Novella commentaria* to X 3.34.10 (fol. 174[rb]): "Nam
uotum peregrinationis non dicitur a iure solenne, sicut tamen uouens peregrinationem
cogitur illam perficere, supra capitulis proximis, sic uouens monasterium etiam per
uerba de futuro, ut hic, et infra 1. quod dei timorem [X 3.35.5]." Ibid. to X 3.34.6
(fol. 169[v]): "Ecclesia compellit laicum ad executionem uoti ultramarini per excommunicationem, et bonorum subtractionem."

146. On Bartolus see especially C. N. S. Woolf, *Bartolus of Sassoferrato: His
Position in the History of Medieval Political Thought.*

to the *Authenticum "Ut omnes obediant"* (*Nov.* 69), Bartolus attacked the decretalist position, noting that men were made poor and beggarly by pilgrimages. Since no one should be obliged to suffer for the faults of another, heirs should not be impoverished because of the failure of a decedent to discharge a votive obligation to make a pilgrimage.[147]

Another late medieval canonistic work of great interest, the *Provinciale* of William Lyndwood (ca.1375–1446), shows considerable concern about frivolous and hasty vows.[148] Commenting on a decree attributed to Archbishop Edmund, warning priests to counsel their flocks not to make vows hastily and to do so only with their pastor's consent, the gloss noted that women were especially given to making hasty vows, particularly in times of trouble and distress. They should do so, however, only with the consent of their husbands and, although not strictly obliged to, should also consult their priests before undertaking votive obligations.[149]

The problem of vows and the commutation of votive obligations continued to be reflected in the canonistic literature of the sixteenth century. A set of proposals for Church reform in 1573, for example, listed as one of the requisite changes in discipline a tightening up of the machinery for the commutation of vows, so that commutations would be granted less freely and so that there would be greater strictness in assessing equivalent

---

147. Bartolus to *Auth. "Ut omnes obediant"* in his *Opera omnia*, 11:77: "Quinto nota . . . quod ex peregrinatione quis efficitur mendicus et pauper . . . et videtur quod filius pro delicto patris non teneatur, nam lex dicit quod unus pro delicto alterius puniri non debet, C. de poenis l. sancimus [*Cod.* 9.27.22 pr.] et ff de poenis et l. crimen [*Dig.* 48.19.26 pr.] cum si gl. hic dicit quod hic loquitur de poena divina, quae dicit in contrariis loquitur de poena humana, ad quod facit supra de conse. distinc. j c. iustam." Cf. *glos. ord.* to *Auth.* Coll. 5 tit. 8 pr. (= *Nov.* 53 pr.), ad v. *arguntur:* "Id est deducuntur que miseria ex inopia contigit: et inopia ex peregrinatione."

148. On Lyndwood, see Emden, *Biographical Register of the University of Oxford,* 2:1191–93; C. R. Cheney, "William Lyndwood's *Provinciale,*" *The Jurist,* 21(1961), 405–34; F. W. Maitland, *Roman Canon Law in the Church of England,* ch. 1.

149. Lyndwood, *Provinciale* 3.18.2 (Oxford, 1679, ed., p. 204): "Precipimus, ut sacerdotes sepe moneant populum, et maxime mulieres, ne faciant uota sua nisi cum deliberatione, et de consensu uirorum suorum, et consilio sacerdotum." Ibid., gloss ad v. *Mulieres:* "Quae facilius solent uota emittere quam uiri, maxime cum sunt in aliqua tribulatione, et angustia positae." Ibid., gloss ad v. *consilio Sacerdotum:* "Istud non est necessitatis, sed potius securitatis. Sed hic quero, nunquid mulier in periculo, in infirmitate, uel aliqua angustia posita, uouens forsan de consensu uiri teneatur reddere uotum? Dic quod sic, si habuit intentionem obligandi se Deo, cogitans etiam de causa movente ad uouendum, scilicet infirmitate, periculo, et huiusmodi; etiam de fine, scilicet euasione illius periculi, uel angustie."

tasks to be accepted in lieu of specific performance of votive obligations.[150]
One of the last references to the canonistic machinery of the crusade vow
occurs in the *Partitiones* (published 1594) of Pierre Grégoire (1540–1617),
who still found it worth while to expound the doctrine that a husband
might take the crusade vow without the consent of his wife.[151] By this
time, however, the canonical institutions of the crusade had fallen into
utter desuetude and the passage reflects merely an antiquarian concern.

CONCLUSIONS. The development of the canonistic theory of the vow,
as the foregoing discussion has shown, began in a systematic way at
almost precisely the same time as the crusade movement itself—at the end
of the eleventh and the beginning of the twelfth centuries. Although the
vow had a long history as an ecclesiastical institution before the time of
Ivo of Chartres, there is no evidence to show that a well defined theory of
votive obligations or any significant analysis of the vow had yet been
worked out in the Western Church. In the work of Ivo, however, we find
the commencement of an effort to gather together and to try to make
sense out of the earlier references to vows in the works of the fathers and
of earlier popes and councils. What Ivo and, somewhat later, Gratian,
contributed to the development of this doctrine was essentially the revival
of the Roman law concept of votive obligations, the beginning of an effort
to analyze the vow-making process, in order to determine the degrees of
moral and legal obligation which were assumed at successive stages, and
the rudimentary elements of a system whereby votive obligations might
be forgiven through dispensation or modified through redemption and
commutation. Gratian's principal contribution to this development was
his distinction between various types of vows.

The process of legal analysis and development of a doctrine of vows
was left at a relatively rudimentary stage in Gratian's *Decretum*. During

150. *Consilium delectorum cardinalium et aliorum praelatorum de emendanda
ecclesia* 4.9, in *Concilium Tridentinum diariorum, actorum, epistolarum, tractatuum,
nova collectio*, ed. Görres Gesellschaft, 12/1:143: "Commutatio etiam votorum neque
ita facile facienda neque commutanda praeterquam in aequivalens bonam."

151. On Pierre Grégoire see F. X. Wernz, *Ius decretalium* 1:435; Van Hove,
Prolegomena, pp. 541, 544. See Grégoire, *Partitiones* 3.2.3 (Lyons, 1594, ed., p. 191):
"Quemadmodum eodem fauore ratum habetur uotum, quod maritus facit inuita
uxore peregrinationis ad subsidium terrae sanctae, si ea commonita non possit
inducere consentire, uxoris porro uotum quodcumque, si displicuerit marito, sine
eius consensu factum ratum non est: si placuerit, contra."

the following century, the theory of the vow expanded rapidly, both in the canonistic commentaries of the decretists (especially Rufinus, Huguccio, and Joannes Faventinus) and in the spate of new papal legislation which began in the pontificate of Alexander III and which effectively ended, as far as the law of vows was concerned, with the pontificate of Gregory IX. Of the important changes and developments in the doctrine of vows in the decretals and the decretalist literature, four matters were especially significant: (1) the revival by Innocent III of the Roman law concept of the heritability of votive obligations; (2) the differentiation of the crusade vow from other pilgrimage vows as the subject of special privileges and distinctive rules; (3) the spelling out of an ordered system for modifying votive obligations or even for escaping from them entirely; and (4) the clarification of the means for legal enforcement of votive obligations in foro externo.

Lastly, it should be noted that the development of the doctrine of vows in general and of the crusade vow in particular was a more slow and gradual growth than has previously been thought. Without denying that the work of St. Raymond of Peñafort, Innocent IV, and Hostiensis in this area was important, it is scarcely justifiable, in view of the evidence here, to conclude that the juridical theory of the crusade vow came almost instantaneously into being as a result of the work of Innocent IV and Hostiensis.[152] Rather, the canonistic doctrine of the crusade vow was part and parcel of the growth over a period of some two centuries of a set of doctrinal theories concerning vows of all kinds. Only rather late in the development of the doctrinal structure was it marked off from other vows, especially from other pilgrimage vows; even then, the differentiation was confined to a relatively small number of specific details.

152. As Villey suggested, in "L'Idée de la croisade," p. 567: "Mais c'est avec l'*apparatus* d'Innocent IV, en 1245, la somme *d'Hostiensis* et son grand commentaire littéral ou *Lectura* (1253 et 1268), les trois oeuvres sans doute les plus marquantes de la littérature canonique médiévale, que la théorie juridique de la croisade apparaît soudain constituée." Villey was even more emphatic in his appreciation of the role of Hostiensis as "the father of the juridical theory of the crusade" in his earlier book, *La Croisade,* pp. 256–57. For his treatment of the crusade vow in particular, see "L'Idée," pp. 581–86, and *La Croisade,* pp. 124–27. My own views and some of the evidence presented in this and the foregoing chapter are also explained in "The Votive Obligations of Crusaders: The Development of a Canonistic Doctrine," *Traditio,* 24(1968), 77–118, as well as in my paper *"Vovete et reddite:* The Canonists and the Crusader's Vow."

CHAPTER IV

Crusader Status and the
Obligations of Crusaders

Cum attendas ad quid tendo,
Crucem tollas, et vovendo
Dicas: 'illi me commendo
Qui corpus èt animam
Expendit in victimam
Pro me moriendo.'

> Berter of Orleans, *Call to*
> *Crusaders*

Vous ki ameis de vraie amor,
esveilliez vos, ne dormeis mais!
l'alüete nos trait lou jor
et si nos dist an ses refrais
ke venus est li jors de pais,
ke Deus, par sa tresgrant dousor,
promet a ceaz ki por s'amor
panront la creus et por lour fais
sofferont poinne nuit et jor!
dont vairait il ses amans vrais.

> Anon., *Chanson de croisade*

CRUSADER STATUS. The canonistic status of the crusader, as all of the canonists who dealt with the matter agreed, resulted from the act of making a crusade vow. From this act flowed a series of juristic consequences: the vow created a set of obligations; it conferred a set of privileges; it invested the person who made the vow with a new juridical status. The act of making the vow itself was followed by the ceremony of taking the cross, which was an outward and visible sign of the new juridical status which the vow had conferred on the vovens. At least to some canonists, the taking of the cross solemnized and made public the intangible change in status which resulted from the act of making the crusade vow (see ch. III).

THE FORM OF THE CRUSADE VOW. In view of the serious and important consequences which resulted from the making of a crusade vow, it is surprising to find that so little evidence has been preserved concerning the nature and substance of the vow itself, despite the fact that hundreds of thousands of intending crusaders unquestionably made such vows in Western Europe over a period of nearly half a millennium. Granted that the vow was essentially a personal matter between the individual vovens and God; granted, too, that the vow might easily be made privately without ceremony or witnesses; and granted further that the taking and wearing of the sign of the cross would in most cases have sufficed to attest to the crusader's status, obligations, and privileges; still it is somewhat disconcerting to find so little in the way of public record of the form, character, and terms of crusaders' vows. Thus far only a handful of texts or substantial attestations of crusade vows have been discovered and published, and unless or until some further documents come to light, it is upon these texts that we must principally rely for our knowledge of exactly what was promised when a crusader made a vow.[1]

From the known texts, plus the marginal information which can be gleaned from letters testimonial issued to crusaders and from hints in the narrative sources, it is apparent that the vow was in form a promise made to God to perform two acts: to journey to and visit the Holy Sepulchre in Jerusalem and to do so in the ranks of a general expedition to the Holy Land.[2] The form makes it clear that the vow was in essence a pilgrimage

1. Three previously known texts and one newly discovered one from the *Formularium Indersdorfense* are discussed in my "Note on the Attestation of Crusaders' Vows," *Catholic Historical Review,* 52(1966), 234–39. Professor Richard Kay has subsequently drawn my attention to the attestation of the crusade vow of Louis VIII in the campaign against the Albigenses, published in the *Layettes du trésor des chartes,* ed. A. Teulet et al., 2:69–70 (no. 1745); it is also to be found in Claude de Vic and I. Vaisette, *Histoire générale de Languedoc.* . . . , 2d ed., 16 vols. (Toulouse: E. Privat, 1872–1905,) 8:817–19 (Preuves, no. 244 [162]).

2. In the words of the Indersdorf text (Brundage, "Note on Attestation," p. 238): ". . . vovit sanctum dominicum sepulchrum in Ierusalem pergere et visitare et . . . iuramento promisit devote huiusmodi quidem votum suum ultramarinum . . .

vow, but that it was differentiated from the more usual type of pilgrimage vow by the additional qualification that the pilgrimage must be made in the ranks of an organized, armed expedition ("passagium generale") proclaimed by the Holy See.

To these essential ingredients some reservations and conditions were apparently added as a matter of common practice. Although all of them are late and hence may very well not reflect early practice in this regard, every one of the known records of a crusade vow includes some sort of qualification of the basic promises. In some cases the qualification was a simple statement that the vow would be fulfilled if no legitimate obstacle arose;[3] sometimes the promises were qualified by a phrase which provided for fulfillment of the obligations by a substitute if the vovens was unable or unwilling to perform them himself;[4] sometimes, too, they were hedged about with an elaborate battery of escape clauses which attempted to foresee and provide for a variety of contingencies.[5] Beyond this, however,

---

debite adimplere saltem cum proximum generale ad terram sanctam passagium per sacrosanctam Romanam ecclesiam fuerit ordinatum."

3. Thus in the formula published by A. Franz, *Die kirchlichen Benedictionen,* 2:304, there is the simple qualification: "Impedimento legitimo semoto."

4. Both in the Indersdorf text published in my "Note of Attestation" and in the Paris text, first published by Charles Kohler, "Documents inédits concernant l'Orient Latin et les croisés (XIIᵉ–XIVᵉ siècles)," *Revue de l'Orient Latin,* 7(1899), 33–34, there is explicit provision for the performance of the votive obligations by another person.

5. This is true of most of the vows for a crusade against the Turks found in Olivier de la Marche's account of the so-called "Banquet of Vows" in February 1453. Thus, for example, the vow of Philip the Bold, as reported by Olivier, *Mémoires* 1.30 (ed. Henri Beaune and J. d'Arbaumont, 2:381–82) stipulates a considerable variety of contingencies: "Je voue tout premierement à Dieu, mon créateur, et à la glorieuse vierge Marie, sa mere, en après aux dames et au faisant, que se le plaisir du très chrestien et très victorieux prince monseigneur le Roy est de prendre croisée et exposer son corps pour la deffence de la foy chrestienne . . . et se lors je n'ay loyal ensoigne de mon corps, je le serviray en ma personne et de ma puissance audit sainct voyage, le mieulx que Dieu m'en donnera la grace; et se les affaires de mondit seigneur le Roy estoient telz qu'il n'y peust aller en sa personne, et son plaisir est d'y commetre aucun prince de son sang ou autre seigneur chief de son armée, je à son dit commis obeiray et serviray audit sainct voyaige, le mieulx que je pourray, et ainsi que se luy mesme y estoit en personne. Et se, pour ses grans affaires, il n'estoit disposé d'y aller me d'y envoyer, et que aultres princes Chrestiens à puissance convenable empreignent le sainct voyage, je les y accompaigneray, et me employeray avecques eux à la deffence de la foy Chrestienne le plus avant que je pourray, pourveu que ce soit du bon plaisir et congé de monseigneur le Roy, et que les pays que Dieu m'a commis à gouverner soyent en paix et sehureté. . . . [e]t se durant le sainct voyage je puis, par quelque voye ou maniere que ce soit, savoir ou congnoistre que ledit Grand Turc ait voulenté d'avoir à faire à moy corps

the extant records of crusade vow texts yield little information about the character of crusade obligations. Not much more is to be learned, either from the letters testimonial issued to crusaders, although these documents frequently specified in some detail the privileges to which their bearers were entitled.[6]

TAKING THE CROSS. The crusade vow was solemnized and externally attested by the wearing of the crusader's cross, just as religious vows might be symbolized and externalized by the wearing of a religious habit.[7] The use of the insignia of the cross was coeval with the beginning of the crusade movement, for the accounts of Pope Urban II's speech at

---

à corps, je, pour ladicte foy Chrestienne, le combattray, à l'aide de Dieu tout puissant et de sa très doulce Vierge mere, lesquelz j'appelle tousjours en mon ayde. Faicte à l'Isle le dix septiesme jour de fevrier l'an de l'incarnation Nostre Seigneur mille quatre cens cinquante trois signé de ma main. PHILIPPE."

6. Letters testimonial for crusaders have survived in sizable numbers and many of them may be found in episcopal and papal registers of the fourteenth and fifteenth centuries. Formulas for these letters also occur in some abundance, e.g., in the *Summa prosarum dictaminis* and the *Summa dictaminum* of Ludolph von Hildesheim, both of which are published in *Briefsteller und Formelbücher des elften bis vierzehnten Jahrhunderts,* ed. L. Rockinger. Among the unpublished manuscript formularies which I have consulted, I have also noted formulas for similar letters in the thirteenth-century *Formularium* attributed—incorrectly—to Marinus of Eboli in Vat. Lat. 3976 (analyzed by Fritz Schillmann, *Die Formularsammlung des Marinus von Eboli;* also in the fourteenth-century *Formularium litterarum audientie contradictarum,* of which I have used the text in MS. 142 (F. 5) of St. John's College, Cambridge. On the authorship of Marinus of Eboli, see especially Carl Erdmann, "Zur Entstehung der Formelsammlung des Marinus von Eboli," *Quellen und Forschungen aus italienischen Archiven und Bibliotheken,* 21(1929-30), 176–208. These letters testimonial for crusaders were issued routinely by the papal chancery without consulting the pope himself. See Peter Herde, "Papal Formularies for Letters of Justice (13th–16th Centuries)," in *Proceedings of the Second International Congress of Medieval Canon Law,* pp. 321–45.

7. Thus in the so-called Laurentius *Apparatus* to *Comp. III* 3.26.2 (Paris, B.N. lat. 3932, fol. 167[vb]): "Sollempnitatem uocat impressionem signaculi sancte crucis; sed pone quod proponat in animo suo quod ibit ultra mare, numquid teneatur? Videtur quod sic, ut xxvii Q. i proposito [c. 21]; sed non est uerum, ut Extra ii de uo. et uo., litteraturam [*Comp. II* 3.21.1 = *X* 3.34.3], nam ibi positam accipitur iam assumptam, ut patet ex littera. c⟨ardinalis⟩." Also the gloss to Raymond of Peñafort, *Summa de casibus* 1.8, ad v. *privatum sive simplex* (Innsbruck, Universitätsbibliothek, MS. 266, fol. 28[v]–29[r]): "Nota quod uotum simplex est cui nulla adhibetur sollempnitas. Sollempne uotum dicitur cui certa notificatio uel expressio de iure aut de consuetudine introducta adhibetur. In uoto peregrinationis adhibetur sollempnitas per susceptionem pere et baculi benedicti a sacerdote et per susceptionem crucis in uoto terre sancte."

Clermont in 1095 agree that he there instructed those who vowed to participate in the crusade that they were to sew crosses to their clothing as a symbol of their commitment.[8] In the first crusade the assumption of the cross seems to have been rather an informal procedure: the sources speak of Bohemund, for example, cutting a garment into crosses to be affixed to the clothing of those who joined his crusade expedition[9] and there seems to have been no particular uniformity of color or manner of wearing the insignia,[10] although in the third crusade we are told that the French wore red crosses, the English white, and the Flemings green.[11] There is no evidence of any formal rite for taking the cross during the first crusade, and it is not until the mid-twelfth century at the earliest that any evidence occurs for the development of such a liturgical rite. One might perhaps infer from the description of Louis VII's reception of the cross at Vézelay in 1146 that some more or less formal ceremony was in use at that time,[12] and the accounts of the preaching of the third crusade convey this impression even more strongly.[13]

The liturgical texts of the period bear out the impression gleaned from

8. Thus Fulcher of Chartres, *Historia* 1.4.4 (ed. Hagenmeyer, pp. 140–42); Robert the Monk, *Historia* 1.2 (*RHC, Occ,* 3:729–30).

9. *Gesta Francorum* 1.4 (ed. Hill, p. 7): "Mox Sancto commotus Spiritu, iussit preciosissimum pallium quod apud se habebat incidi, totumque statim in cruces expendit."

10. Robert the Monk, *Historia* 1.2 (*RHC, Occ,* 3:730), reports that the pope commanded the cross to be worn on the breast by those journeying toward Jerusalem and between the shoulders by those returning from the Holy City. This detail is not confirmed by any of the other accounts of the Council of Clermont, and other sources speak of different customs. According to the *Gesta Francorum* 1.1 (ed. Hill, p. 2), the cross was to be worn on the right shoulder. Fulcher speaks both of the variety of colors employed (*Historia* 1.4.4, ed. Hagenmeyer, p. 140), and of the custom of wearing the cross on the shoulders. A century later, Villehardouin, *La Conquête de Constantinople* 44 (ed. Edmond Faral, 1:44), referred to the custom of wearing the cross on the shoulders during the fourth crusade. Pissard, *La Guerre sainte en pays chrétien,* p. 43, declares that the cross was worn on the shoulder in crusades against the Saracens and on the breast in crusades against heretics.

11. Matthew Paris, *Chronica majora,* s.a. 1188 (ed. H. R. Luard, 2:330).

12. Odo of Deuil, *La Croisade de Louis VII, roi de France* I, ed. Henri Waquet, Documents relatifs à l'histoire des croisades, 3, pp. 20–22.

13. E.g., the account by Gerald of Wales in his *Itinerarium Cambriae* 1.1, 5, of the preaching of the crusade in Wales, ed. in Gerald's *Opera* by J. S. Brewer et al., 6:14, 55. An entry in the *Annales Marbacenses,* s.a. 1195 (*MGH, SS,* 17:166) relates as an exceptional circumstance the reception of the cross by Henry VI in a private ceremony at which only the bishop of Sutri and three of the emperor's chaplains were present. The taking of the cross by Count Henry of Champagne in a solemn public ceremony is reported in an undated letter by Cardinal Henri de Marcy (d. 1188) to Pope Alexander III: *PL,* 204:216.

the narrative texts, that a ceremony for taking the cross developed only in the later twelfth century.[14] The earliest text thus far noted of a rite for conferring the crusader's cross occurs in a pontifical of Ely, which may be dated to the third quarter of the twelfth century, and the circumstances of its appearance there suggest strongly that the rite was a comparatively recent innovation at the time this text was copied.[15] From this point onward, some form of the rite—and it was far from uniform—appears commonly in English and French pontificals, and presumably is also represented in the liturgical texts of other areas as well.[16] Its occurrence in pontifical texts, where it is almost always found in close proximity to the rites for bestowing the scrip and staff, the customary insignia of pilgrims, further emphasizes the pilgrimage character of the crusade. Indeed it is probable that the crusader rites were derived directly from the pilgrim rites[17] and that crusaders were commonly invested with the scrip and staff, as well as with the cross—the added insignia of their particular pilgrimage.[18]

Presumably at least one purpose served by the ceremony of taking the cross was to distinguish the genuine crusader from other travellers of all kinds and to assure to the crusader a proper observance of his privileged position at law. On the other hand, complaints were frequent that the

14. For a more detailed treatment of the development of this rite in England and an analysis of some of the relevant texts, see my article "Cruce signari;" see also the treatment of the subject by Adolf Franz, *Die kirchlichen Benediktionen*, 2:302–7.

15. Briefly, there are two late twelfth-century MSS. of the Ely pontifical, both of them now in Cambridge (University Library, MS. Li.2.10, and Trinity College, MS. B.XI.10). The Trinity MS. contains a rite for taking the cross, while the University Library MS., probably slightly older, does not. This fact, combined with the placement of the rite in the Trinity MS., particularly in its relation to the rite for bestowing the scrip and staff upon pilgrims, would seem to support a theory of recent adoption. For a more detailed discussion and an edition of the text, see my "Cruce signari."

16. For the French pontificals, see the inventory of V. Leroquais, *Les Pontificaux Manuscrits des bibliothèques publiques de France*. Preliminary examination of Leroquais' inventories shows at least 27 pontifical MSS. which contain forms of this rite.

17. On this matter my conclusions agree with those of Garrisson, "A propos des pèlerins," pp. 1168–77, as against those of Franz, *Die kirchlichen Benediktionen*, 2:273.

18. A very early hint of such a practice occurs in an apocryphal speech which was put into the mouth of the Egyptian emir al-Afdal after the first battle of Ascalon (1099): "Superatus sum a gente mendica, inermi et pauperrima; quae non habet nisi saccum et peram." (*Gesta Francorum* 10.39, ed. Hill, p. 96.) See also the suggestive statement in the gloss to the *Summa de casibus* cited above, n. 7. The frontispiece to this book shows the investing of a crusader with his insignia.

insignia of the cross was often used by "crusaders," who can only be labeled bogus, to secure for themselves numerous privileges to which they were not legally entitled. These gentry must frequently have constituted a public nuisance.[19] In 1198 Innocent III complained in a letter that was later incorporated into the decretal collections and ultimately found its way into the *Decretales Gregorii IX* about the use of bogus crusaders by the Knights Hospitalers for the collection of alms. The pope directed that this practice should cease forthwith and that those responsible should be punished.[20] As the privileges and exemptions of crusaders were multiplied in the canonistic legislation of the later twelfth and thirteenth centuries the number of complaints about abuses of their status by crusaders, both real and bogus, increased correspondingly.[21]

These developments led, in turn, to an increased attention to defining the obligations of crusaders and to attempts to systematize and enforce their fulfillment.

CRUSADERS' OBLIGATIONS. The notion that the making of a vow involved the assumption of an obligation to carry out the action therein promised was, of course, basic to the whole system of vows.[22] Without this understanding, the vow would become altogether meaningless. In the Roman law of votive obligations, on which the canon law discussion was, at least implicitly, based, the person who made a vow became *voti reus,* or *voti debitor,* and remained in this condition until the vow had been discharged (*solutus*). If the vow was conditional, then the binding obligation did not come into being until the fulfillment of that condition—at which point the vovens immediately and automatically became both *voti*

19. Bridrey, *La Condition juridique,* pp. 22–25.

20. *Comp. III* 5.16.1 = X 5.33.11 (*Po,* 468).

21. As early as 1188 or '89, Peter of Blois in his *De Hierosolymitana peregrinatione* (*PL,* 207:1064) was moved to complain of the abuses which arose on the eve of the third crusade. For some further complaints, see Innocent III, *Registrum* 15.199 (*PL,* 216:729–30); Gregory IX, *Registres* 1,760, 3,308, 3,927 (ed. Lucien Auvray, 1:968–69; 2:471–72, 799–800); Gerard J. Campbell, "Clerical Immunities in France during the Reign of Philip III," *Speculum,* 39(1964), 416–17; Charles-Victor Langlois, *Le Règne de Philippe III le hardi,* p. 271.

22. In Roman law, an obligation was defined as a "iuris vinculum, quo necessitate adstringimur alicuius solvendae rei secundum nostrae civitatis iura" (*Inst.* 3.13.pr.). In essence, the person under obligation must give something, do something, or perform some act to discharge the obligation or otherwise suffer punitive sanctions (*Dig.* 44.7.3.pr.). On this whole complex subject see Kaser, *Das römische Privatrecht,* 1:397–434, 2:236–62.

compos (i.e., possessed of the good desired) and *voti damnatus* (i.e., absolutely and rigorously required to fulfill the promise made in his vow).[23] Furthermore, the failure to discharge a votive obligation entailed legal penalties which although essentially religious were nonetheless real and effective. The violation of a vow was an *impietas;* by it the violator was deemed to have broken the *pax deorum* and was forthwith excluded from all religious rites whatever. Moreover, since the state had an interest in preserving the pax deorum, the violator of a vow was subject to civil penalties for his impietas. He lost thereby his civil status and his legal personality; accordingly, he might risk death for his offense.[24]

The canon law carried over from the Roman law the essential idea of an enforceable obligation arising from the vow (see above, ch. II). With respect to the crusade vow in particular, then, four questions arise: (1) What specific actions were necessary to discharge the obligation it created? (2) How was the discharge of the obligation to be proved? (3) What methods of enforcement were employed to secure the discharge of the obligation? (4) How might release from undischarged obligations be secured?

DISCHARGE OF CRUSADE OBLIGATIONS. As we have seen above, the few surviving texts of crusaders' vows specified the obligation to visit the shrine of the Holy Sepulchre in Jerusalem in the ranks of a passagium generale. This visit to the Holy Sepulchre was the crucial nexus of the crusade obligation, as contemporary accounts of crusade expeditions clearly imply. The discharge of this obligation was most dramatically accomplished on the first crusade when, after the capture of Jerusalem and the slaughter of the city's population, the army repaired to the Holy Sepulchre. There, "rejoicing and weeping from their overwhelming gladness," they adored the Holy Sepulchre, prayed, offered gifts, clapped their hands, and sang songs of thanksgiving to God.[25] Those members of the

23. Turlan, "L'Obligation 'ex voto'," pp. 522–24; *Dig.* 50.12.2.pr. is the basic text; others are cited by Turlan.

24. Ibid., pp. 524–25.

25. *Gesta Francorum* 10.38 (ed. Hill, p. 92): "Venerunt autem omnes nostri gaudentes et prae nimium gaudio plorantes ad nostri Saluatoris Iesu sepulchrum adorandum, et 'reddiderunt ei capitale' debitum." Other details are furnished by Fulcher of Chartres, *Historia* 1.29.2 (ed. Hagenmeyer, pp. 304–5); Raymond d'Aguilers, *Historia Francorum* 20 (*RHC, Occ,* 3:300); Robert the Monk, *Historia* 9.9 (*RHC, Occ,* 3:868–69).

expedition who had not accompanied the victorious army to Jerusalem, even though they had fought in its ranks during the earlier part of the crusade, clearly felt constrained to discharge their vows by travelling to Jerusalem after the city's capture and making the ceremonial visit to the Holy Sepulchre and other shrines. Only in this way could they be freed of the obligation they had incurred.[26] That the critical character of the visit to the Holy Sepulchre at Jerusalem was not confined to the first crusade is amply indicated by the reported actions of participants in later expeditions. To cite but a few random examples, we are told that the survivors of the ill-fated expedition of 1101 continued their journey to Jerusalem, where they fortunately happened to arrive in time to visit the holy places and discharge their vows at Easter.[27] In 1108 most of Bohemund's soldiers, after their unsuccessful attack upon the Byzantines, continued to Jerusalem by sea in order to fulfill their vows as crusaders.[28] Toward the end of the twelfth century, Richard of Devizes acidly related how the archbishop of Rouen, after seeing Jerusalem from afar, considered himself acquitted of his crusade vow and returned home—obviously a minimal performance, in Richard's eyes.[29] Shortly after the turn of the thirteenth century, the Emperor Baldwin I of Constantinople, in a letter to Archbishop Adolf of Cologne, made it clear that the vows of those participating in the fourth crusade had not been discharged by their capture of Constantinople.[30] This was also the impression of Innocent III.[31] While examples of this sort could easily be multiplied, these few will perhaps suffice to illustrate the unanimous testimony of the crusade narratives to the technical necessity of visiting the Holy Sepulchre and praying there in order to discharge the obligation resulting from the crusade vow.

It is interesting to note this testimony for the first crusade in particular, in view of the thesis, advanced by Erdmann and supported by Villey and others, that military aid to Constantinople, not the deliverance of Jerusalem, was the real goal of the crusade in the thinking of Urban II at

---

26. The best-known examples are those of Bohemund I, Baldwin I of Edessa, and Stephen of Blois. On Bohemund and Baldwin, see Fulcher of Chartres, *Historia* 1.33.5, 15–18 (ed. Hagenmeyer, pp. 325, 331–32). For Stephen, see my article, "An Errant Crusader."

27. Fulcher of Chartres, *Historia* 2.18.1 (ed. Hagenmeyer, p. 436).

28. Ibid., 2.39.3 (ed. Hagenmeyer, pp. 524–25).

29. Richard of Devizes, *Chronicle*, s.a. 1191 (ed. and trans. John T. Appleby, pp. 27–28).

30. *Annales Colonienses maximi*, s.a. 1203 (*MGH, SS*, 17:818).

31. *Registrum* 6.136 (*PL*, 215:699–702; trans. in *CDS*, pp. 208–9).

Clermont.[32] In Erdmann's reconstruction of the pope's intentions, Constantinople was to be the *Kampfziel* of the expedition, although Jerusalem, he concedes, may have been its *Marschziel*.[33] This ingenious distinction raises a fundamental doubt about the role of Urban in the whole affair. If the Erdmann thesis be accepted, we are required to believe, as Frederic Duncalf pointed out, either that Pope Urban "was guilty of deliberately deceiving all those who went, or that he was misunderstood."[34] Further, we must also postulate either a conspiracy or else a very remarkable coincidence of misunderstanding among the chroniclers of the first crusade and those participants whose letters and other documents happen to have survived. If there was any truth at all to the chronicle accounts of the fulfillment of votive obligations on the first crusade, then the clear obligation to worship at the Holy Sepulchre should be given due weight. It seems scarcely credible that so widespread and consistent a misunderstanding as Erdmann implicitly postulates could have been incorporated into the basic canonistic device upon which the whole juridical structure of the crusade depended. Even if this were so, it must also be noted that the obligation remained unaltered during subsequent expeditions. In other words, the visitation of the Holy Sepulchre was an integral part of the structure of the crusade throughout its history, whether Pope Urban II was confused or not.

PROOF OF THE DISCHARGE OF CRUSADE OBLIGATIONS. Granted that a crusader in virtue of his vow incurred an obligation and satisfied it as set forth above, how should proof of the discharge of the obligation be furnished should questions arise? One time-honored symbol of the returned pilgrim from the Holy Land was apparently used, at least during the first century of the crusades, in this fashion. This was the custom of bearing home palms gathered at a spot near Jericho which was known as the Garden of Abraham. Fulcher of Chartres, at any rate, testified that Count Robert of Flanders and Robert Curthose, Duke of Normandy, returned from the first crusade bearing palms gathered from Abraham's Garden,[35] and that when Bohemund and Baldwin of Edessa journeyed to Jerusalem in 1100 they, too, were careful to gather palms to take back to

32. Erdmann, *Die Entstehung des Kreuzzugsgedankens,* pp. 363–77; Villey, *La Croisade,* pp. 83–85.

33. Erdmann, *Die Entstehung des Kreuzzugsgedankens,* p. 374.

34. Frederic Duncalf, "The Councils of Piacenza and Clermont," in *Crusades,* ed. Setton, 1:244.

35. Fulcher of Chartres, *Historia* 1.32.1 (ed. Hagenmeyer, pp. 318–20).

their new domains. The custom continued to flourish: by the late twelfth century the shops of merchants who specialized in selling palms to returning pilgrims were clustered in one street in Jerusalem, hard by the Church of St. Mary of the Latins.[36] William of Tyre, writing ca.1180, said that the Jericho palms "are for us the symbol of a pilgrimage fulfilled,"[37] while the use of the term "palmer" for the returned pilgrim is amply attested in the literature of the later middle ages.[38]

Obviously the bearing of palms as a proof of the fulfillment of the crusade obligation was a usage open to abuses of many kinds, and it is not surprising to find that Innocent III moved early in his pontificate to tighten up the procedures of proof. In a letter of 31 December 1199, Innocent laid down the rule that those who returned from the Holy Land should produce letters from the king or the patriarch of Jerusalem, the Master of the Knights Hospitalers or the Templars, or a papal legate, testifying to their actual fulfillment of the crusade obligation.[39] Although this letter referred specifically to crusaders who had been assisted by a subsidy from the offerings of the faithful, it is unlikely that they were the only group from whom testimonial proof of this sort was required. A census list of crusaders from Lincolnshire, dated ca.1197, for example, noted skeptically the names of several individuals who claimed, but were unable to prove, that they had fulfilled their crusade vows by going to

---

36. Jean Richard, "Sur un passage du 'Pèlerinage de Charlemagne': Le Marché de Jérusalem," *Revue Belge de philologie et d'histoire*, 43(1965), 553. Other late twelfth-century references to the custom of bearing home palms may be found in Ekkehard of Aura, *Chronicon universale*, s.a. 1104 (*MGH, SS*, 6:225) and in his *Hierosolimitana* (*MGH, SS*, 6:266).

37. William of Tyre, *Historia rerum in partibus transmarinis gestarum* 21.17 (*PL*, 201:831): "His ita gestis, dominus comes, cum Hierosolymis quasi per quindecim dies fuisset, completur orationibus et sumpta palma, quod est apud nos consumatae peregrinationis signum, quasi omnino recessurus Neapolim abiit." On William's career and the chronology of his work, see A. C. Krey, "William of Tyre," *Speculum*, 16(1941), 149–66; R. B. C. Huygens, "Guillaume de Tyr étudiant," *Latomus*, 21(1962), 811–29; Hans Eberhard Mayer, "Zum Tode Wilhelms von Tyrus," *Archiv für Diplomatik*, 5–6(1959–60), 182–201.

38. Thus, Dante, *Purgatorio* 33.76: ". . . per quello / che si recca il bordon di palma cinto"; Chaucer, *Canterbury Tales*, A prol. 1. 13; and cf. *Oxford English Dictionary*, s.v. "Palmer."

39. Innocent III, *Registrum* 2.270 (*PL*, 214:828–32; *Po*, 922): ". . . qui etiam cum redierint, non prius absolvantur a praestita cautione quam litteras regis vel patriarchae aut Hierosolimitani Hospitalis aut militiae Templi magistri aut etiam legati nostri vobis exhibuerint de mora ipsorum testimonium perhibentes." Bridrey, *La Condition juridique*, p. 28, n. 1, is mistaken, however, in holding that Innocent required letters from all returning crusaders. Bridrey based his statement upon *X* 2.22.7 (*Po*, 2,350), which dealt only with letters issued by the Holy See to certify dispensation from crusade obligations.

Jerusalem, "nullum tamen habens testimonium."[40] By the middle of the thirteenth century those who were required to make any pilgrimage as a penance were expected to prove their fulfillment of the obligation with letters testimonial,[41] and it may safely be assumed that at the very least this practice included those who were required as part of their penance to go on crusade.[42]

When a crusader died while on his journey proof of discharge of crusade obligations was especially important. Although it was quite generally held that a crusader who died while fulfilling his vow was fully acquitted of his obligations,[43] adequate proof of his death was necessary, in the first place, lest the heirs to his estate be forced to redeem his vow. Second, proof of the husband's death was required before a widow could remarry.[44] Third, the whole apparatus of crusade privileges became inoperative as soon as certain news of the crusader's death was received.[45]

40. Historical Manuscripts Commission, *Reports, Various Collections,* 1(1901), 235–36, prints this list as item 227 of its census of the Christ Church Letters in the muniments of the dean and chapter of Canterbury Cathedral.

41. See, e.g., the entries in the *Registrum visitationum* of Bishop Odo Rigaldus of Rouen, s.d. 5 October 1259 and 13 May 1266; ed. Th. Bonin.

42. Participation in a crusade was enjoined as a penance or punishment for a variety of offenses by both spiritual and secular courts. Among others, arsonists were required to serve for one year in the Holy Land (Canon 18 of the Second Lateran Council, 1139, in *COD,* p. 177; C. 23 q. 8 c. 32); murderers might likewise be sentenced to the service of the cross: e.g., *Curia Regis Rolls* 48, Trinity Term, 10 John (5:157); *The Earliest Lincolnshire Assize Rolls,* A.D. *1202–1209,* ed. D. M. Stenton, p. 166, no. 1008; Philippe de Beaumanoir, *Coutumes de Beauvaisis,* ch. 41, § 1296–97 (ed. A. Salmon, 2:168–70); Emil Göller, *Die päpstliche Pönitentiarie von ihrem Ursprung bis zu ihrer Umgestaltung unter Pius V,* 3–4:7–8; Bishop Haymo de Hethe, *Registrum,* ed. Charles Johnson (Canterbury and York Society Publications, 48), 1:387–89. Reconciled heretics were frequently required to serve in the crusade, too, as part of the reparation for their sins; e.g., Gregory IX, *Registres* 3,811, 4,783 (ed. Auvray, 2:771–73, 1267–74); Innocent IV, *Registres* 3,677 (ed. Elie Berger, 1:556); Mansi, *Concilia,* 23:356–57. Oliver Sutton, Bishop of Lincoln 1280–99, even imposed the crusade as a penance on one Henry Vintner, who had struck Adam the Chaplain on the nose, making it bleed. *The Rolls and Register of Bishop Oliver Sutton,* ed. Rosalind M. T. Hill (Lincoln Record Society Publications, 39, 43, 38, 52), 3:20. See also Throop, *Criticism of the Crusade,* pp. 96–100, for further examples.

43. E.g., in *Ad liberandam:* Constitution 71 of the Fourth Lateran Council, *COD,* pp. 243–47.

44. X 4.1.19; see also my paper, "The Crusader's Wife Revisited," *Studia Gratiana,* 4(1967), 241–52.

45. This is the usual provision in grants of privilege; see especially *Ad liberandam* (*COD,* pp. 243–47), whose provisions were copied in almost all subsequent grants of crusade privileges, e.g., *Afflicti corde* (First Council of Lyons, c. 5, in *COD,* pp. 273–77).

Thus the dead man's executors, administrators, feudal lords, and creditors all had a keen interest in establishing securely the fact of his death. In all of these situations, the normal method of certifying the death of an individual crusader was to secure a letter or other testimony from the commander of the army or the expedition in which he served, a procedure which was copied by the canonists from the Roman law provisions for certification of the death of soldiers in the imperial armies.[46] Failing this, the best advice which the canonists could offer was that the interested parties should direct inquiries to the area where the crusader was last known to be alive in order to secure the certain news which the law (at least in theory) required.[47]

METHODS OF ENFORCING THE DISCHARGE OF CRUSADE OBLIGA-
TIONS. What happened if a man who had taken the crusade vow should in fact fail to fulfill the resulting votive obligation? In principle, there were two licit answers: either the reluctant crusader might be coerced into fulfilling his obligation, or else he might be allowed, under appropriate circumstances, to commute or redeem his vow. Neither of these answers, however, appears to have been quite so simple in practice as it seemed to be in theory.

First of all, what sorts of action were taken (or were supposed to be taken) to coerce the reluctant crusader? It is evident that from the beginning of the crusades there were many who vowed to go on crusade and then regretted their rash promise. If Fulcher of Chartres is to be believed, the actual armies on the first crusade numbered only one-tenth of those who at one point or another had joined the crusade's ranks. While many of those who fell by the wayside did so more or less literally

46. *Glos. ord.* to *X* 4.1.19, ad v. *donec certum nuncium*. For the Roman law provisions, see *Cod.* 5.17.7; *Nov.* 117.11; cf. *Dig.* 24.2.6.

47. Tancredus, *Apparatus* to *Comp. I* 4.22.3 (= *X* 4.22.2; *JL*, 15,211), ad v. *vita*, in Gonville and Caius College, MS. 28/17, p. 107ᵇ: "Sed quid faciet si nunc per magistrum militum ut ibidem dicitur certificari ⟨non⟩ poterit de morte uiri, sicut sepe accidit in magnis preliis et precipue sarracenorum et christianorum, ubi multi pereunt de quibus nichil nouerunt hii qui ducebant exercitum? Mittat ad uicinas ciuitates si possit; alias contrahat [*scil.:* uxor]. la⟨urentius⟩." Much the same advice, but a rather different conclusion, is given in the *glos. ord.* to *X* 4.1.19, ad v. *donec certum nuncium*: "Sed pone quod fuit aliquis in exercitu Sarracenorum, uel etiam in aliis, nec est reuersus, nec potest certificari mulier de morte per magistrum militum, uel per alium? Tunc mittat ad locum si potest, uel ad uicina loca, ut inquirat, si potest; alias expectet quamdiu certificata fuerit de morte, un paret hic, et per iura predicta. B⟨ernardus⟩."

—they died en route, either of sickness, as a result of enemy action, or from accident or exhaustion—this still left a large number of persons who simply gave up the idea and returned to their homes.[48] Fulcher is not very explicit about what happened to these deserters, save that in a general way he tells us "they became vile before men and were utterly disgraced."[49]

More than this, however, the Church was prepared from early in the history of the crusade movement to take action against those who failed to fulfill their obligations. While Guibert of Nogent may possibly be guilty of some slight anachronism when he relates that Pope Urban II at the Council of Clermont had declared that those who abandoned their crusading purpose were to become perpetual outlaws, at least until they resumed the cross, the anachronism is probably rather slight.[50] At any rate, the papal legate, Adhémar of Le Puy, writing from Antioch about 18 October 1097, assumed that it was common knowledge in the West that those who had put aside the cross were excommunicated and were placed in the class of apostates. Moreover, Adhémar called upon the bishops to see to it that such laggard crusaders were struck with the sword of anathema unless they hurried to join the crusading army in Syria.[51] Similar messages were sent in January 1098 by the patriarch of Jerusalem, in July of the same year by Anselm of Ribemont, and late in 1099 by Archbishop Manasses of Reims.[52] In December 1099, Pope Paschal II in a letter to the archbishops, bishops, and abbots of France expressly decreed excommunication for

48. Fulcher's figures (*Historia* 1.10.5, ed. Hagenmeyer, pp. 184–85) do credit to his imagination, for he estimated that when the crusade armies finally assembled before the walls of Nicaea they numbered 600,000 able-bodied warriors, in addition to clerics, monks, women, children, and the poor. He goes on to declare that if everyone who had gone on crusade had stayed with the expedition, there would have been 6,000,000 warriors, in addition, one must assume, to proportionally increased numbers of noncombatants. While one fully sympathizes with Hagenmeyer's statements about these numbers—"selbstverständlich ebenfalls ungeheuerliche und einer 'kraftvoll schopferischen Phantasie' entsprungene"—one can also properly give some attention to the approximate proportions which Fulcher reports, even if one balks at the absolute numbers. On the problem of such numerical estimates generally see R. C. Smail, *Crusading Warfare (1097–1193)*, pp. 109–10, 171–72.

49. Fulcher, *Historia* 1.7.5 (ed. Hagenmeyer, p. 165).

50. Guibert of Nogent, *Gesta Dei per Francos* 2.5 (*RHC, Occ,* 4:140).

51. On Adhémar's role in the direction of the first crusade and the efforts which he made to control its members, see John H. Hill and Laurita L. Hill, "Contemporary Accounts and the Later Reputation of Adhémar, Bishop of Puy," *Medievalia et humanistica,* 9(1955), 30–38; James A. Brundage, "Adhémar of Puy: The Bishop and His Critics," *Speculum,* 34(1959), 201–12. For the letter of October 1097, see *Epistulae et chartae,* ed. Hagenmeyer, p. 142.

52. *Epistulae et chartae,* ed. Hagenmeyer, pp. 148–49, 160, 176, respectively.

those crusaders who had fled from the siege of Antioch, unless and until they returned to the Holy Land, presumably in order to fulfill their still undischarged votive obligations at the Holy Sepulchre and other shrines there.[53] There is ample evidence that these sanctions were sufficiently effective to encourage many laggard crusaders, of whom Count Stephen of Blois was perhaps the best known, to participate in the ill-fated expedition of 1101 to Jerusalem.[54] Even more formal enactments followed in subsequent years. In 1123 the First Lateran Council took note of the problem and in canon 10, *Eis qui Hierosolymam,* the council formally enacted penalties against those who had taken the cross but had not discharged their votive obligations. If such persons failed to do so before the following Easter they should be forbidden thenceforth to enter the churches and an interdict was to be placed upon their lands.[55] While this canon was not incorporated into Gratian's *Decretum,* a decretal of Alexander III on this subject found its way into *Compilatio II,*[56] though not into the great collection of Gregory IX. In addition, numerous further admonitions on the matter occur in the papal registers of the thirteenth century.[57] Warnings to individual crusaders were sufficiently common to warrant the inclusion of form letters for this purpose in some formularies as well, and the *Speculum* of Gulielmus Durantis (first redaction ca.1271–72; second redaction ca.1287) contained a form for a bill of complaint to initiate judicial action against one who had failed to discharge the obligation arising from a pilgrimage vow.[58] The ecclesiastical censures which are mentioned as penalties to be inflicted upon recalcitrant crusad-

53. Ibid., p. 175; *JL*, 5,812.

54. Ordericus Vitalis, *Historia ecclesiastica* 10.11, 19 (ed. Le Prévost, 4:67–68, 118–19); Albert of Aachen, *Historia Hierosolimitana* 8.6 (*RHC, Occ,* 4:563); Paschal II, *Epist.* 9, in *RHGF,* 15:20 (*JL*, 5,812); Fulcher of Chartres, *Historia* 2.16.1 (ed. Hagenmeyer, pp. 428–30); Guibert of Nogent, *Gesta Dei per Francos* 2.5 (*RHC, Occ,* 4:140); Hugh of Flavigny, *Chronicon II,* s.a. 1100 (*MGH, SS,* 8:487); see also Duncalf, "Councils of Piacenza and Clermont," in *Crusades,* ed. Setton, 1:247; James L. Cate, "Crusade of 1101," ibid., 1:345; E. Bridrey, *La Condition juridique,* p. 27.

55. *COD*, pp. 167–68; Bridrey, *La Condition juridique,* p. 27; Karl J. Hefele and H. Leclercq, *Histoire des conciles,* 5/1:635.

56. *Comp. II* 3.21.3 (*JL*, 14,077).

57. *Po,* 1,346; Gregory IX, *Registres* 1, 1,957 (ed. Auvray, 1:1–3, 1063); Innocent IV, *Registres* 2,054, 4,926, 5,979 (ed. Berger, 1:305; 2:160–61; 3:111); Clement IV, *Registres* 1,675 (ed. Edouard Jordan, 1:488); Nicholas III, *Registres* 172 (ed. Jules Gay, p. 52); Martin IV, *Registres* 74 (ed. F. Olivier-Martin et al., p. 29).

58. *Summa prosarum dictaminis,* no. 103, in *Briefsteller und Formelbücher,* ed. Rockinger; the *Formularium* attributed to Marinus of Eboli, in Vat. Lat. 3976, fol. 206ᵛ; Durantis, *Speculum iuris,* lib. 3, partic. 3, tit. *De voto,* vol. 2/3, fol. 173ᵛᵃ.

ers were defined in a decretal of Innocent III as excommunication, interdict, and suspension, although the judge of a particular case might, of course, modify the penalties to suit the circumstances.[59] In addition, the decretal *Licet* (X 3.34.6) was interpreted as authorizing the disinheritance of those heirs who failed to discharge the unsatisfied votive obligations of a deceased crusader.[60]

In order to translate into practice the theory that the Church could compel crusaders to fulfill their vows, it was obviously necessary that the officers of the Church know which of their subjects were bound by the crusade obligation, and it is no surprise to discover that by the late twelfth century attempts were being made to survey and list the crusaders dwelling in various areas. Thus in the *Christ Church Letters* among the muniments of the dean and chapter of Canterbury there appears a list of crusaders from Lincolnshire which was compiled about 1197. Mostly this schedule is just a list of names, but there are occasional notes attached to entries, usually stating particulars which might support an appeal for release from the votive obligation. Thus we are told that Robert, son of Brummann, at Skirbeck near Boston, had attempted to make the journey to Jerusalem, but had returned without completing it. It was further noted that he was married, that he had a son, and that his means were scarcely sufficient for the completion of his journey. John Buchard of Wyberton had also tried, but failed to complete his journey. John had had the foresight to bring back a papal rescript authorizing him to defer the completion of his voyage until such time as it might more expeditiously be resumed. That he would do so seemed unlikely, as the document added that he was middle-aged, married, had many children, and was very poor. Richard, son of Turstin, at Algarkirk, and William, son of Swift, at Sutterton, both alleged that they had been to Jerusalem, but neither could produce evidence to support his assertion. At Pinchbeck, to cite one final case, Ulf Poucer was said to have taken the cross eight years previously. Although Ulf denied that he had ever become a crusader, his neighbors testified to it and so did the priest who had conferred the cross upon him. Ulf was young, married, had seven children, and was very poor. He was obviously an unpromising candidate for service in the Holy

---

59. *Comp. III* 5.23.4 = X 5.40.20 (*Po*, 3,865).

60. This interpretation was succinctly stated by Joannes Andreae in his *Casus summarii* to X 3.34.6 (Cambridge, Corpus Christi College, MS. 38, fol. 25ᵛ): "Ecclesia compellit laycum ad executionem per excommunicationem et paterni successionis privationem." See also the *glos. ord.* to *Licet*.

Land.[61] Another such list, not so detailed, in the muniments of the Canterbury dean and chapter gives the names of a further forty-three crusaders from the archdeaconry of Cornwall, identifying some individuals by occupation. Their ranks included a tailor, a smith, a shoemaker, two chaplains, a gamekeeper, a merchant, a miller, and two tanners, as well as two women.[62] Obviously the crusade in twelfth-century Lancashire and Cornwall was a far from aristocratic affair.

Further evidence of continuing attempts to keep track of crusaders and to make sure that votive obligations did not go undischarged is furnished by some thirteenth-century lists of questions to be asked concerning crusaders by bishops making their visitations. In the articles of interrogation detailed in the *Register* of Bishop Oliver Sutton, for example, we find questions about the numbers and conditions of those in each parish who have taken the cross, whether any of them have attempted to make the journey to Jerusalem but have returned before completing it, and questions about the estates of crusaders who had died without discharging the obligation, subsidies and gifts made by crusaders to the Holy Land, persons who had been appointed to deputize for crusaders, dispensations and commutations of the crusade vow, and a host of related matters.[63]

The purpose of these lists of crusaders and the systematic inquiries about their status was twofold: first and foremost, to identify those who had taken the cross and to discover which of them had satisfied the obligations arising therefrom; second, to pinpoint those who had failed to discharge these obligations, so that they might either be coerced into personally fulfilling their vows or cajoled into securing a formal release by redemption or commutation of their obligations.

RELEASE FROM CRUSADE VOWS. Various methods of securing release from the discharge of crusade and pilgrimage obligations were in use in the medieval Church. As early as the tenth century, the substitution of a pilgrimage by one person for that by another who was prevented by some serious reason from fulfilling his vow was accepted as an adequate

61. Historical Manuscripts Commission, *Reports: Various Collections*, 1(1901), 235–36.
62. Ibid., *Fifth Report* (1876), 1:462.
63. Sutton, *Rolls and Register*, ed. Hill, 3:157–59. A similar but shorter list occurs in the *Registrum Ricardi de Swinfield, episcopi Herefordensis*, ed. William W. Capes (Canterbury and York Society Publications, 6), pp. 78–79; also in Register I of the dean and chapter of Canterbury: Historical Manuscripts Commission, *Eighth Report* (1881), Appendix, 1:345.

discharge of the votive obligation;[64] this release by substitution was practiced with some frequency throughout the history of the crusades. The substitution might be voluntary or it might be paid for.[65]

Another method of securing release was through the commutation of the votive obligation into some other form of pious work. One method of release, rather infrequently used, involved the performance of some other penitential or religious observance in place of participation in the crusade. Much more common was the form of release which was secured by making a donation of money, either as a subsidy for the crusade army, for defence of the Holy Land, i.e., by hiring mercenaries, or as a contribution made to some other approved religious cause.[66] Money contributed for the

64. *AASS,* 17 January (Jan., 2:516–17).

65. Thus, to take a handful of examples, Otto of Freising relates that Louis VII went on the second crusade in order to discharge the votive obligation of his deceased brother, Philip: *Gest Frederici* 1.37 (ed. Schmale, pp. 200–6). William Marshall served on crusade as a substitute for Henry the Young King: Sidney Painter, *William Marshall,* p. 54; the place of Geoffrey, Count of Perche, who was taken on the fourth crusade by his brother, Stephen: Villehardouin, *La conquête de Constantinople,* 46 (ed. Faral, 1:46–48); *Annales Herbipolenses,* s.a. 1202 (*MGH, SS,* 16:10); in 1268 Pope Clement IV authorized Henry III of England to send his son, Prince Edward, on crusade as a substitute: Clement IV, *Registres* 609 (ed. Jordan, 1:212).

Examples of a hired substitute are numerous. Notable is the case discussed by Innocent III in the decretal *Magne* (*X* 3.34.7). Other sample cases are reported in Honorius III, *Regesta* 176, 1,120 (ed. P. Pressutti, 1:33, 188); Innocent IV, *Registres* 3,727 (ed. Berger, 1:563); Nicholas IV, *Registres* 4,490 (ed. Ernest Langlois, 1:650); *Curia Regis Rolls* 33, Michaelmas Term, 6 John (3:193). A contract dated 20 July 1270, providing for the services of a paid substitute on crusade is printed as Appendix VI of H. G. Richardson and G. O. Sayles, *The Governance of Mediaeval England,* pp. 463–65.

66. For some examples of payments in aid of the Holy Land see *Po,* 1,660, 1,931, 3,002, 5,208, 5,471, 10,522. Examples of the payment of subsidies to crusading forces in return for redemption of crusade vows may be found in *Po,* 10,666, 10,670, 10,676; Innocent IV, *Registres* 2,785, 2,843 (ed. Berger, 1:411, 425); Clement IV, *Registres* 1,501 (ed. Jordan, 1:460); *Close Rolls* 35 Henry III (8:522, 528), 36 Henry III (9:219), 44 Henry III (13:269–70). A few examples of the redemption of crusade vows by performing other pious works are: *JL,* 5,674; *Po,* 1,603, 9,134. Henry II of England took the crusade vow as part of his penance for his role in the murder of Becket, but after three years as a nominal crusader, he redeemed his vow upon promising to found three monasteries: John T. Appleby, "The Ecclesiastical Foundations of Henry II," *The Catholic Historical Review,* 48(1962), 205–6. One of the more peculiar cases of the redemption of a crusade vow is recorded in the *Calendar of Inquisitions Post Mortem* 118 (14:117), where an inquiry at Cambridge on 17 June 1376 (49 Edward III) revealed that Joan, widow of Gilbert de la Chaumbre, as part of a complicated scheme to convey property to her fiance, John Fitz John, stipulated that within seven years after their marriage John must find a man to go to the Holy Land in order to fulfill a vow made by Joan's first husband before his death.

redemption of the crusade vow, however, seems to have been used in actual practice for a variety of purposes, many of them quite unrelated to the defense of the Holy Land.[67] A third, not uncommon, method of redemption was the stipulation that an obligation arising from a vow to go on crusade in the Holy Land might be redeemed by participating in crusade expeditions to other areas—to Livonia, Poland, Constantinople, Provence, etc.[68]

The privilege of commuting and redeeming crusade vows was closely controlled by the papacy. The popes repeatedly asserted their exclusive right to deal with this type of settlement, an assertion assiduously echoed by the canonists,[69] and numerous mandates delegating this power to crusade preachers and others testify to the continuing effort to restrict this right to papal appointees alone.[70] The difficulty of obtaining release from or relaxation of the crusade vow obligation seems to have varied considerably from one period to another. In general, the surviving documents seem to indicate that relaxations were relatively infrequent during the twelfth century, became much more common and easy to obtain from the time of Innocent III (1198–1216) to the time of Nicholas IV (1288–92), and then diminished in number and ease of attainment from that point to the close of the pontificate of Boniface VIII (1294–1303). After Boniface's pontificate, however, the difficulty of securing release from or relaxation of the obligation became increasingly slight, as the papacy found the granting of redemption and commutation a welcome source of revenue during the Avignonese period and afterward.[71] Up to 1240, moreover, each individual application for relaxation of the vow was supposed to be examined on its merits and, at least for important crusaders, this seems to

67. Thus in 1233, Gregory IX directed that a sum of money from this source be used to pay the Dominicans of Worms as part of the settlement for a house owned by them: Gregory IX, *Registres* 1,209 (ed. Auvray, 1:687); *Po,* 9,134. Further examples are cited below, p. 137; see also Throop, *Criticism of the Crusade,* pp. 87–90.

68. E.g., *Po,* 5,433, 5,459; Benedict XI, *Registres* 1,007 (ed. Ch. Grandjean, col. 607–8); Gervais of Prémontré, *Epist.* 2, in *Sacrae antiquitatis monumenta historica, dogmatica, diplomatica,* ed. C. L. Hugo, 1:3–5. On the crusades in Eastern Europe against the Slavs see Helmut Beumann, ed., *Heidenmission und Kreuzzugsgedanke.*

69. *X* 3.34.9; see above, pp. 80–81, 95, 105–6.

70. E.g., *Po,* 1,532, 1,552; Honorius III, *Regesta* 359 (ed. Pressutti, 1:63–64); Gregory IX, *Registres* 3,965 (ed. Auvray, 2:818–19); Innocent IV, *Registres* 6,285 (ed. Berger, 3:168); Urban IV, *Registres* 2,912 (ed. J. Guiraud, 4:45); Clement IV, *Registres* 291 (ed. Jordan, 1:77); Honorius IV, *Registres* 117 (ed. Maurice Prou, col. 101–2).

71. Paulus, *Geschichte des Ablasses,* 2:33–39.

have been done in practice.[72] The substitutes who were provided to take the place of crusaders exempted from personal service were also supposed to be examined to make sure of their capacity to carry out their tasks.[73]

The reasons most commonly cited for commutation of the crusade vow were illness, poverty, old age, and public necessity; these were the causes, also, which were alleged in the standard form letters employed in the formularies of the papal chancery.[74] Interesting and peculiar variations on these basic themes were sometimes alleged in the petitions for relaxation of the crusade obligation, as, for example, in the case of Walter of Avesnes, who sought to be excused from his crusade vow in 1211 because he feared that his brother, a subdeacon who had thrown off the clerical habit, might devastate, burn, and lay waste his lands,[75] or in the case of Bishop John of Norwich, who sought release from his vow because he had been set upon by robbers while on his way to join the third crusade and, as a result, was reduced to such penury that he could not continue his journey.[76]

72. X 3.34.7, 9. For a commission to examine the basis of a request for redemption, see Gregory IX, *Registres* 132 (ed. Auvray, 1:69–70); see also c. 88 of the *Constitutiones cuiusdam episcopi* of 1225–30 in *Councils and Synods*, ed. Sir F. M. Powicke and C. R. Cheney, 2:196: ". . . nec parcatur alicui aut votum relaxetur cuiuslibet sexus aut cuiuslibet conditionis existat, nisi tanta et tam manifesta infirmitate laboret vel adeo valetudinarius quod nulli dubium esse debet ipsum non posse exequi votum suum."

73. Innocent IV, *Registres* 2,963 (ed. Berger, 1:444).

74. Thomas of Capua, *A Formulary of the Papal Penitentiary in the Thirteenth Century*, nos. 175 (1, 4), 176 (1) (ed. Henry Charles Lea, pp. 166–68). This formulary is dated between 1216 and 1223 and the author was identified by C. H. Haskins; see E. Göller, *Die päpstliche Pönitentiarie*, 1/1:20–23. The so-called formulary of Marinus of Eboli also contains several form letters of this type. Schillmann's attribution of this formulary to Marinus has clearly been disproved; see especially Carl Erdmann, "Zur Entstehung der Formulelsammlung des Marinus von Eboli"; Geoffrey Barraclough, "The Chancery Ordinance of Nicholas III: A Study of the Sources," *Quellen und Forschungen aus italienischen Archiven und Bibliotheken*, 25(1933–34), 192–250; Peter Herde, *Marinus von Eboli: 'Super revocatoriis' und 'De confirmationibus.'* A. Vetulani has recently described in some detail a further manuscript of this formularium in the library of the Metropolitan Chapter of Gniezno: "Gnieźnieński Rękopis Formularza Marina de Ebulo," *Prawo Kanoniczne*, 4(1961), 211–22. I have used the version of the *Formularium* in Vat. Lat. 3976, where the relevant letters may be found at fol. 205ʳ–206ᵛ. Other similar formulas may be found in the penitential *Summa* of Walther of Strassburg, Vat. Lat. 2663, fol. 236ᵛ, 239ᵛ. Securing the commutation or redemption of a crusade vow was often a costly business. In addition to the sums paid for the commutation itself, the fee for issuing a letter of commutation, according to the fourteenth-century *Formularium penitentiariorum*, was four *livres tournois* (Vat. Lat. 3994, fol. 14ᵛ).

75. *Po*, 4,345; Innocent III, *Registrum* 14.133 (*PL*, 216:493).

76. *The Chronicle of Richard of Devizes*, s.a. 1190 (ed. Appleby, pp. 10–11).

Whatever the reasons alleged in individual cases, the relaxation of the obligations flowing from the crusade vow was already common practice by the time of the third crusade, when, for example, only two of the bishops of England fulfilled in person the crusade vows they had made.[77] By the mid-thirteenth century the practice had become so usual that Gregory IX found it necessary to remind the dean of Paris that crusaders who proposed to fulfill their vows in person could not also be required to pay the fees for redemption of their vows.[78] By 1240 the decision as to whether the crusader should fulfill his vow or seek a relaxation of it, after paying the appropriate fees, was to be left up to the individual to decide. No longer was it necessary to allege or prove a reason for the relaxation: it was granted as a matter of course to all who asked or paid for it.[79] At this point, in other words, the crusade vow was being converted into a money-raising device for the support of crusade activities. Persons who took the crusade vow found it convenient to avail themselves of the privileges enjoyed by crusaders without committing themselves to the hazards and inconveniences of actually participating in an expedition, while the papacy found the redemption of crusade vows a lucrative source of revenue.[80] The papal registers and other records of the thirteenth century abound in commissions to collect the revenues derived from this source and directions for handling, forwarding, and accounting for the monies thus received.[81]

Predictably, scandals quickly arose from this situation and, indeed, there were those who looked upon the whole system as a sordid enough scandal in its own right.[82] In 1247 Innocent IV ordered a halt to the sale of commutations and redemptions of crusade vows;[83] he later explained that

77. Ibid., ed. Appleby, p. 15.

78. Gregory IX, *Registres* 4,222 (ed. Auvray, 2:958).

79. Gregory IX, *Registres* 5,296 (ed. Auvray, 3:317–18); Paulus, *Geschichte des Ablasses*, 2:35. *The Register of Walter Giffard, Lord Archbishop of York, 1266–1279*, s.a. 1275 (ed. W. Brown [Surtees Society Publications, 109], pp. 279–86), contains a series of entries showing the amounts paid by crusaders in the archdeaconries of Richmond, the East Riding, Cleveland, York, and Nottingham in return for commutation and redemption of their vows. The commonest payment by far was 5 s. W. E. Lunt, *Papal Revenues in the Middle Ages*, 2:517, prints a translation of a standard form of receipt for redemption of the crusade vow.

80. Lunt, *Papal Revenues*, 1:115–21; Ferdinand Remy, *Les Grandes Indulgences pontificales aux Pays-Bas à la fin du moyen-âge (1300–1531)*; J. Heers, "La Vente des indulgences pour la croisade à Gênes et en Lunigiana en 1456," *Miscellanea storica Ligure*, 3(1963), 69–101.

81. E.g., *Po*, 48, 1,603, 1,660, 1,931, 3,002, 5,208, 5,209, 9,134, 10,522, 10,666, 10,670, 10,676, 13,966, 15,272, 15,867, 17,123, 19,908, 20,429, 20,610, 22,312, etc.

82. Matthew Paris, *Chronica majora*, s.a. 1250 (ed. Luard, 5:196).

83. Innocent IV, *Registres* 3,054, 3,384 (ed. Berger, 1:459, 509).

the practice was bringing the preaching of the cross into disrepute and that many were sorry that they had ever responded to the call for a crusade.[84] Although the practice was resumed, difficulties continued to arise. In 1273, Gregory X complained to the abbot of St. Denis about the sharp practices of some who had taken the cross in France. As crusaders they were exempt from the taxes levied in support of the crusade, and, once the tax collectors had left their neighborhoods, they then paid appropriate sums of money for release from their vows. The problem, according to the pope, was that the cost of commutation and redemption of the vow was lower than the taxes they had avoided by taking the cross in the first place. Such unscrupulous rascals, he directed, were to be dealt with sternly; they must at least make up the difference between the crusade tax—a levy of a twentieth, in this case—and the sum which they had paid for commutation of their vows, or face excommunication.[85]

Thus during the thirteenth century the crusade was transformed into an internal European institution. At the beginning of the century the crusades had still been aimed and organized primarily for the purpose of conquering the Holy Land and enlarging the Latin States there; during its course they became very largely a means of raising revenues in Europe to support papal policy, not only in the Holy Land, but elsewhere, especially in Western Europe. From holy wars, spurred on by religious enthusiasm to oust the infidel from the sacred shrines of the Near East, the crusades slowly developed, as is well known, into multi-purpose institutions for the raising of money and the prosecution of any and all of the objectives of papal policy. Under the technical guise of crusades, we find wars of aggression against the European rivals of the papacy, against the Hohenstaufen in southern Italy and Sicily, against rebellious barons in England and rebellious peasants in Germany, against heretics in Provence, pagans in Livonia, Moors in Spain, and domestic enemies in the Papal States—in the fifteenth century there was even a crusade against an antipope.[86] The amounts—ultimately quite large—raised by redemption

84. Ibid., 3,708 (ed. Berger, 1:560–61); for further examples of abuses, see Throop, *Criticism of the Crusade,* pp. 85–94.

85. Gregory X, *Registres* 322 (ed. Jean Guiraud, p. 125).

86. A fundamental short account of the expeditions in southern Italy and the Mediterranean is Joseph R. Strayer, "The Political Crusades of the Thirteenth Century," in *Crusades,* ed. Setton, 2:343–75; see also Pierre Toubert, "Les Déviations de la croisade au milieu du XIII° siècle: Alexandre IV contre Manfred," *Le Moyen Age,* 69(1963), 391–99. For the war against the English barons, see Clement IV, *Registres* 56 (ed. Jordan, 1:16), and *Po,* 19,124; for that against the

and commutation of crusade vows, and the even greater sums raised by taxes to support crusade ventures, were funnelled into the papal privy purse,[87] from which they were disbursed for a marvellous variety of purposes: to subsidize the papacy's allies in Europe[88] and to undermine its enemies, to repair St. Peter's Basilica when the popes returned to Rome from Avignon.[89] It was the technical character of the crusade as an institution which accounted for its long survival through the later middle ages and into the sixteenth century, when, in its technical form, it even played a part in providing an ideological basis for the Spanish conquest and colonization of the New World.[90] In its most debased form, the crusader's status lingered on into the twentieth century in the guise of the *cruzada*—an ecclesiastical tax, in return for which grants of indulgences

---

rebellious peasants who had refused to pay a tithe to the archbishop of Bremen, see *Po,* 9,236; *Annales Stadenses,* s.a. 1233–34 (*MGH, SS,* 16:361–62); *Annales Coloniensis maximi,* s.a. 1234 (*MGH, SS,* 17:843–44). Fortified by the crusade indulgence, the expedition was entirely successful in annihilating the stiff-necked peasantry.

There are numerous studies of the Albigensian crusade; the chapter "The Albigensian Crusade" by Austin P. Evans in *Crusades,* ed. Setton, 2:277–324, is a brief, reliable treatment.

The crusade in the Baltic against the Livs, Letts, and Esths has yet to be given a full-scale study. An excellent recent treatment of some phases of it, however, may be found in Friedrich Benninghoven, *Der Orden der Schwertbrüder.* See also my *Chronicle of Henry of Livonia,* and Gisela Gnegel-Waitsches, *Bischof Albert von Riga.* On the Slavic crusades see especially Beumann, ed., *Heidenmission und Kreuzzugsgedanke.*

The Spanish *reconquista* operated as a theatre of crusade activity from at least 1100 onward. On the *reconquista* perhaps the most useful current book is the cooperative history, *La reconquista española y la repoblación del país* (1951), published by the Consejo Superior de Investigaciones Científicas.

Daniel Waley, *The Papal State in the Thirteenth Century,* pp. 293–94, comments on the "crusade" in the papal territories, and Paulus, *Geschichte des Ablasses,* 3:196, notes that Gregory XII granted a crusade indulgence in 1411 to those who aided the King of Naples in his war against John XXIII (1410–15).

87. Lunt, *Papal Revenues,* 1.28.

88. Thirteenth-century papal documents abound in schemes to use crusade funds from various sources in order to subsidize, e.g., Henry III of England or Charles of Anjou, at the expense of the papacy's political enemies: *Po,* 13,966, 14,704, 15,382, 15,383, 15,863, 16,415, 16,539, 16,540, 17,123, 17,134 (Henry III); *Po,* 19,057, 19,082, 19,500, 21,082 (Charles of Anjou).

89. Göller, *Die päpstliche Pönitentiarie,* 1/1:112; 1/2:22.

90. See Mario Góngora, *El estado en el derecho indiano, época de fundacion* (*1492–1570*); J. H. Parry, *The Spanish Theory of Empire in the Sixteenth Century,* esp. ch. 1–2; D. Carro Venancio, *La teología y los teólogos-juristas españoles ante la conquista de América,* esp. 1:329–45, 381–89, 397–408; Silvio A. Zavala, *Las instituciones jurídicas en la conquista de América,* ch. 1–2.

and minor ecclesiastical privileges continued to be made in Spain and Latin America within living memory.[91]

The transformation of the crusade into an institution of European life in the later middle ages depended upon the working of two legal mechanisms. One of these was the legal status of the crusader with the inherent obligations, flowing from the crusade vow, that made possible the development of a system of coercion which could effectively raise men for armies and money to support their efforts. The other was the crusade privilege, which made it possible to continue to attract men into the ranks of the crusade long after the veneer of religious enthusiasm and millenarian fervor for the possession of Jerusalem had worn thin.

91. See especially José Goñi Gaztambide, *Historia de la bula de la cruzada en España*. See also E. Bernardet, "Croisade (Bulle de la)," *DDC*, 4:773–99; H. C. Lea, *A History of Auricular Confession and Indulgences in the Latin Church*, 3:160–61, 412–14. The cruzada was collected in the Spanish colonies of the New World at least as early as 1535: C. H. Haring, *The Spanish Empire in America* (New York: Harcourt, Brace, and World, 1963), pp. 267–68. As recently as 1945, the bishop of Pueblo, Colorado, found it necessary to abrogate privileges flowing from the cruzada within his diocese: *The Jurist*, 5(1945), 292–93.

CHAPTER V

The Privilege of the Cross:
The Spiritual Privileges

Ha, rois de France, rois de France,
La loi, la foi et la creance
Va presque toute chancelant.
Que vous iroie plus celant?
Secourez la, qu'or est mestiers,
Et vous et le cuens de Poitiers
Et li autre baron ensamble:
N'attendez pas tant que vous emble
La morz l'ame, pour Dieu, seigneur;
Mais qui voudre avoir honeur
En paradis, si la deserve,
Quar je n'y voi nule autre verve.
Jhesu-Criz dist en l'Evangile
Qui n'est de trufe ne de guile:
'Ne doit pas paradis avoir
Qui fame et enfanz et avoir
Ne laist pour l'amour de Celui
Qu'en la fin est juges de lui.

Rutebeuf, *La   Complainte*
d'Outremer

One of the perennial puzzles of the history of the crusades is why men went on them. A part of the answer, beyond much doubt, must lie in the privileges which crusaders enjoyed, and which were granted in ever increasing quantity and variety by successive pontiffs from Pope Urban II onward.

St. Bonaventura, in one of his sermons for Low Sunday, tried to dissect

139

the motivations of crusaders and came up with four acceptable reasons for taking the cross. The first, as one might expect, was a spiritual reason: men took the cross in order to follow Christ's example. Next, was the assurance of divine help which crusaders would surely enjoy. Third, there was the attraction of the crusader's privilege, and last came the temporal reward which participation might bring.[1] While St. Bonaventura's list was far from exhaustive, it may in fairness be said that he hit upon at least some of the main motives which were at work with a good many crusaders. Although twentieth-century observers might quarrel with his order of priority, it was probably one which thirteenth-century crusaders would have agreed to be right and proper, at least in theory. But, whatever the order of emphasis in analysis of the reasons which impelled so many thousands over so many hundreds of years to take the crusader's cross, the privileges which this status conferred will inevitably rank fairly high on the list.

THE CANONISTIC DOCTRINE OF PRIVILEGE. The notion of privilege in canon law was, like the notion of the vow, slow to crystallize. The term "privilege," as it ultimately developed, was used by the canonists to cover positive enactments concerning particular individuals and groups, variances of the general law in favor of special individuals or groups (*ius singulare*), and also special status or variance in the general positive law which was established by custom.

The justification of grants of privilege was rooted in the notion that the public welfare could be promoted in certain circumstances by granting special rights to groups who served the general interests of the community in some specialized way. Thus those who defended the community, who advanced society's intellectual interests, or who served as religious functionaries might be granted privileges which would enhance the performance of their particular functions.[2] Privileges extended to such groups

---

1. St. Bonaventura, *Sermo III pro dominica in octava Pasche,* in his *Opera omnia,* ed. A. C. Peltier, 13:235–36. Bonaventura's purpose in this sermon was to contrast these reasons with the reasons for taking the more meritorious way of the cross, i.e., the religious life. Still, his analysis of the motives involved is of interest, even if it was subordinate to his basic homiletic purpose.

2. Privileges for soldiers abound in Roman law: e.g., *Inst.* 1.25.14; 2.11; 2.19.6; *Dig.* 12.1.26; 26.1.1–44; 49.16.1; 49.17.1–20, etc. The privileges of medieval scholars have recently been the subject of a special study by Pearl Kibre, *Scholarly Privileges in the Middle Ages.* Religious affairs were in general considered matters of public

were normally thought to be proper and justified so long as there was no injury therefrom to the public interest.[3]

Among the canonists, the foundations for the discussion of privileges must be sought in Gratian's *Decretum*. Gratian, borrowing from Isidore of Seville, defined a privilege simply as a law affecting only a private person—a private law, as it were.[4] He later dealt with some of the problems of interpreting and applying privileges in particular cases, and, in the process, pointed out a basic rule for the interpretation of this sort of law: that later privileges may not invalidate prior ones, unless they emanate from the same authority which granted the earlier privilege.[5] Further, Gratian adduced a respectable body of precedents and argument for the right of the Holy See in particular to grant iura singularia for particular persons or groups.[6]

The earlier commentators on the *Decretum* did little to advance this analysis, save by way of spelling out in slightly greater detail the basic notions involved in Gratian's position.[7] The earliest well-developed definition of the canonistic notion of privilege seems to have been the one found in the *Summa Monacensis,* written a generation after the appearance of the *Decretum*.[8] This definition brought into play the notion of a privilege as a variance of the general law in favor of a specific person or group and

---

welfare and clerical privileges were accordingly granted on this account, as the *glos. ord.* to *Dig.* 1.1.1.2, ad v. *in sacris,* explains: "Consistit ius publicum in sacris: ut sint ecclesie in quibus petimus ueniam peccatorum. . . . Item in sacerdotibus: quia interest ut sint sacerdotes, a quibus ueniam petimus peccatorum . . . et propter iniuriam eis factam quilibet agit. . . ."

3. When the public interest required it, however, such privileges might be abrogated *ratione publicae utilitatis*: Gaines Post, *Studies in Medieval Legal Thought,* pp. 18, 241–309.

4. D. 3 c. 3: "Privilegia sunt leges privatorum, quasi privatae leges"; Isidore of Seville, *Etymologiae* 5.18.

5. C. 25 q. 2.

6. C. 25 q. 1 d. p. c. 16.

7. Thus, Stephen of Tournai, *Summa* to D. 3 c. 3 (ed. Schulte, p. 13): "*Privilegia.* vel inde privilegium dicitur, quod aliquem privat a iure commune, vel in aliquo commune ius privat officio suo." *Summa Parisiensis* to D. 3 c. 3 (ed. McLaughlin, p. 4): "Privilegium est quo a commune lege privato beneficio aliqua persona eximitur." Cambridge, Corpus Christi College, MS. 10, fol. 156va: "Priuilegium est quod alique aut iure commune priuat seu immune faciat."

8. On the *Summa Monacensis,* see Kuttner, *Repertorium,* pp. 179–80. The definition, "Privilegium est constitutio preter legem communem aliquid ex dispensatione indulgens, vel ita: Privilegium est iuris publici derogatio per dispensationem aliqua causa subnixa," is given by Dominikus Lindner, *Die Lehre vom Privileg nach Gratian und den Glossatoren des Corpus iuris canonici,* pp. 14–15.

allied it to the notion of dispensation as well. From this time onward, the canonistic doctrine of privilege quickly grew into a full-fledged legal theory concerning the means by which the general law of the Church might be modified with respect to its effects upon particular persons or groups through grants of special rights and status to individuals, classes, and corporate bodies. In the decretal legislation of the late twelfth and thirteenth centuries there was an extensive treatment of some especially significant types of privileges, as well as of general principles applicable to the interpretation of canonical privileges of all kinds.[9] Although the special privileges of crusaders did not enter into the decretals included in the major collections,[10] there nonetheless was a large battery of papal documents upon which these privileges were based.

THE LEGAL BASIS OF CRUSADERS' PRIVILEGES. The legal basis of the privileges enjoyed by crusaders was twofold: in part they enjoyed the privileges, customary and otherwise, common to all pilgrims (see above, ch. I); in addition, they enjoyed the privileges granted specifically to them by successive popes.

The privileges of pilgrims, as already mentioned,[11] consisted principally in the right of protection from personal attack, and a few related rights, particularly the recovery of land and possessions illicitly appropriated during their absence,[12] delay in judicial proceedings against them pending their return,[13] and minor canonical privileges.[14]

9. In addition to treatments of some special privileges, such as those of exempt religious (X 5.33.3), exemption from tithes on noval lands (X 5.33.31), and the like, these decretals were concerned mainly with the basic rules of interpretation and with the limits of privileges in general—e.g., the effect of infringement of another's privileges (X 5.33.4), or the rules for prescription against ecclesiastical privileges (X 5.33.6, 15). On this whole subject see esp. Lindner, *Die Lehre vom Privileg;* also W. Plöchl, *Geschichte,* 2:45–50; C. Lefebvre, "Privilège," *DDC,* 7:225–29; Le Bras, Lefebvre, and Rambaud, *L'Age classique,* pp. 487–513; Van Hove, *De privilegiis,* tit. 5, esp. pp. 1–17, 22–27, 33–42, 54–55, 69–71, 135–38, 171–88, 283–85, and "La notion du privilège," *Nouvelle revue théologique,* 49(1922), 5–18, 74–85.

10. The only one of these decretals to deal with crusaders concerned the fraudulent use of counterfeit crusaders by the Knights Hospitalers, who employed them to collect alms: X 5.33.11.

11. See especially C. 24 q. 3 c. 23–25.

12. X 2.29.1.

13. C. 3 q. 3 d. p. c. 4.

14. A list of these is enumerated in the *Distinctiones decretorum* of Richardus Anglicus, British Museum, MS. Royal 10.C.III, fol. 7[r]: "Nota ratione peregrinationis licet tabernas ingredi, ut hic [D. 44 c. 4]; licet fouere capillos, di. xxiii c. penult.

Specific grants of privileges to crusaders can be found in a series of papal letters and conciliar decrees, commencing with the proclamation of the first crusade in 1095. From that crusade itself, we have little in the way of official papal documentation. Essentially all of the information which we have is contained in a single terse sentence of the decrees of the Council of Clermont, in Pope Urban II's two letters to the Flemings and the Bolognese, and in the more diffuse and considerably less reliable accounts of the chroniclers of the expedition. The conciliar decree relating to the crusade and the two letters dealt only with the crusade indulgence.[15] Other aspects of the crusade privilege were mentioned by the narrative writers, but it is difficult to be sure that they were not anachronistically ascribing to the first crusade privileges that were inaugurated later. If any other significant privileges had been granted by the pope at the Council of Clermont, he would most likely have mentioned them in his two subsequent letters to the Flemings and the Bolognese, especially since these letters were primarily concerned with recruiting men for the expedition. The argument from silence is always treacherous, and nowhere more so than in dealing with medieval evidence, but here it nonetheless seems to bring in doubt the veracity of the chroniclers' allusions to crusade privileges in the first crusade. A quarter of a century later, however, canon 10 of the First Lateran Council (1123) added to the privilege of the crusade indulgence a definite statement that crusaders' goods and possessions lay under the protection of the Holy See, a protection which the decree alleged had been extended to them by Pope Urban II.[16]

Not until the proclamation of the second crusade by Pope Eugene III in 1145 do we find an extensive official notice of the privileges of crusaders.[17] Thereafter these privileges were enumerated, extended, and clarified in successive papal letters and conciliar decrees, notably in documents of Alexander III, Gregory VIII, and Innocent III,[18] as well as in conciliar

---

[c. 32]; licet mutare habitum, xxi q. iiii episcopi [c. 3]; licet cum excommunicatis in cybis communicare, xi q. iii quoniam [c. 103]; licet a quolibet missam audire ⟨ix⟩ [MS.: X̶I̶] q. ii nullus [c. 5]; licet a qualibet ecclesia baptismum accipere, x q. iii nec numerus [c. 5]; non restituitur spoliatus ante reditum adversarii, ut extra de officio et de consultationibus [?]."

15. Mansi, *Concilia*, 20:816; *Epistulae et chartae*, ed. Hagenmeyer, pp. 136–38.

16. *COD*, pp. 167–68.

17. Text in Otto of Freising, *Gesta Frederici* 1.37 (ed. Franz-Josef Schmale, pp. 200–6).

18. See especially Alexander III, *Epist.* 1,504 (*PL*, 200:1294–96; *JL*, 14,360); Gregory VIII, *Epist.* 4 (*PL*, 202:1539–42; *JL*, 16,019); Innocent III, *Registrum* 1.336

constitutions and decrees, especially those of the Fourth Lateran Council and the First Council of Lyons.[19] These grants of privilege continued to be republished and modified in minor details throughout the rest of the medieval period and into the sixteenth century.

For purposes of analysis and discussion here, we may divide the privileges granted to crusaders into two basic categories: the spiritual privileges, i.e., those which pertained principally or solely to the crusader's *status animae;* and the temporal privileges, i.e., those which pertained largely or solely to the crusader's condition in this world. To the first of these categories the remainder of this chapter will be devoted; the second category will be examined in chapter VI.

THE SPIRITUAL PRIVILEGES OF CRUSADERS. The spiritual privileges of crusaders quite naturally took precedence over the temporal privileges, in part because the greatest of them, the crusade indulgence, was a notable innovation with far-flung canonical and theological implications, and in part because to medieval men the spiritual privileges were the more valuable part of the whole roster of privileges which crusaders enjoyed. It is well to keep this in mind, because twentieth-century writers commonly tend to devalue the spiritual motives which inspired so much of what their ancestors did and to overemphasize correspondingly the force of economic, social (or antisocial), and other temporal factors in terms which for the middle ages may be more than a trifle anachronistic. Although it would be foolish to deny the force of secular motives, it would be even more foolish to write off the force of a genuine, if at times grotesque, spirituality. It may be doubted if anyone ever went on crusade as the result of a calculated balancing of the reasons for and against the venture. The atmosphere of the crusade movement is rather a fervent, emotional, and intuitive one, not that of a firm of accountants or a strategic intelligence analysis group. It is furthermore very doubtful that anyone ever set off on one of these expeditions without giving some thought to the spiritual rewards which were promised to crusaders.

These privileges may be classified as (1) the crusade indulgence, (2)

(*PL*, 214:308–12; and ed. O. Hageneder and A. Haidacher, *Die Register Innozenz' III.*, 1:498–505), 11.158 (*PL*, 215:1469–70), 16.28 (*PL*, 216:817–22). For further grants of crusade privileges by Innocent III and other pontiffs, see the lists of crusade proclamations in Ursula Schwerin, *Die Aufrufe der Päpste zur Befreiung des Heiligen Landes von den Anfängen bis zum Ausgang Innozenz IV.*

19. *COD*, pp. 243–47, 272–77.

release from spiritual censures *auctoritate crucis*, (3) the privilege of dealing with excommunicates while on crusade without incurring censure, (4) enjoyment of ecclesiastical ministrations during interdict, (5) absolution from various types of canonical irregularities, (6) the privilege of choosing a personal confessor, (7) release from other vows by virtue of taking the cross, and (8) the spiritual benefits accruing from the prayers offered for crusaders by the medieval Church.

THE CRUSADE INDULGENCE. Of all of these spiritual privileges, by far the most important by any standard of measurement was the crusade indulgence. Indeed, the granting of this indulgence for any expedition may well be considered to define it as a crusade; expeditions for which it was not given can scarcely be considered crusades at all.

Much has been written about the crusade indulgence—including not a little that is plainly mistaken. To understand what was involved, it is well to clarify at the outset what an indulgence is. The term is, of course, a theological one, and may be defined as a remission of the temporal penalties resulting from sin, granted after the eternal penalties for the sinful act have already been forgiven in sacramental confession; it is, further, a remission which draws its effectiveness from the treasury of spiritual merits of the Church, of which the pope is understood to be the principal custodian.[20]

It is quite certain that the word *indulgentia* in the eleventh, twelfth, and thirteenth centuries did not carry this clear and precise meaning; hence arises much of the confusion in what is sometimes written about early crusade indulgences. To speak of the ninth-century letters of Pope Leo IV and Pope John VIII (see above, pp. 22–23), for example, as granting indulgences is to speak nonsense, if the term "indulgence" is understood in the sense in which the word is used by modern theologians. The earliest known papal grant of anything approaching an indulgence proper was that given by Pope Alexander II in 1063 to the participants in a campaign against the Moors in Spain. In this letter the pope for the first

20. Thus in *CIC*, can. 911: "Omnes magni faciant indulgentias seu remissionem coram Deo poenae temporalis debitae pro peccatis, ad culpam quod attinet iam deletis, quam ecclesiastica auctoritas ex thesauro Ecclesiae concedit pro vivis per modum absolutionis, pro defunctis per modum suffragii." See also the definition of Cardinal Bellarmine, *De indulgentiis* 1.1 (quoted in Gottlob, *Kreuzablass*, p. 2, n.1); also E. Jombart, "Indulgences," *DDC*, 5:1331–52; *A Dictionary of Moral Theology*, s.v. "Indulgences," pp. 621–23.

time claimed to relieve the participants in a military expedition of the penance which they had merited for their sins.[21]

It must be admitted, however, that the pope's meaning is not quite clear. If his words are interpreted in any literal sense, then this was clearly a commutation of penance and not, technically, an indulgence. The distinction between these two concepts, although subtle, is significant. A commutation of penance is a privilege by which the penance enjoined for a given sinful act is remitted in return for the performance of another penitential act. An indulgence, on the other hand, is a remission of the temporal punishment merited by a sin. Now the terms "penance" and "temporal punishment" are not interchangeable, for it is far from certain just what amount of temporal punishment may be required by God in satisfaction for a given sin, and therefore the penance enjoined upon the sinner for his transgression may not necessarily satisfy fully for all of the temporal punishment required to atone for his act. Thus there is a real theological distinction between the remission of enjoined penance for a sin (which may be more than, less than, or equal to the sum of temporal punishment required for the specific act) and the remission of the temporal punishment itself.[22]

The much better known "indulgence" granted by Pope Urban II at Clermont to the participants in the first crusade seems also to have been a commutation of penance, if the words of the most authentic documents describing it are taken literally. In the *textus receptus* of the canons of the Council of Clermont, there is no mention of a remission of the temporal punishment for the sins of those participating in the crusade expedition. Rather, the canon stipulated that participation would satisfy for all of the penance owed by those who took part in the expedition and who did so for the proper reasons.[23] Pope Urban's letter to the Bolognese also spoke of the "indulgence" in terms of a remission of the penance owed for all of

<hr>

21. *JL,* 4,530; text in *Epistolae pontificum Romanorum ineditae,* ed. Löwenfeld, no. 82, p. 43 (see ch. I): "Nos vero auctoritate sanctorum apostolorum Petri et Pauli et penitentiam eis levamus et remissionem peccatorum facimus, oratione prosequentes."

22. This distinction and its application to the history of the crusade indulgence was first brought to my attention by Dr. Hans Eberhard Mayer, to whom I am much indebted.

23. Council of Clermont, can. 2 (Mansi, *Concilia,* 20:816): "Quicumque pro sola devotione, non pro honoris vel pecuniae adeptione, ad liberandam ecclesiam Dei Jerusalem profectus fuerit, iter illud pro omni poenitentia reputetur." See also Schafer Williams, "Concilium Claromontanum, 1095: A New Text," *Studia Gratiana,* 13(1967), 27–43.

the confessed sins of the crusaders,[24] while his letter to the Flemings spoke in more vague and general terms of a "remission of all of the sins" of those who took part in the expedition.[25] The letters of Pope Urban's successor, Pope Paschal II (1099–1118), dealing with the crusade likewise specified a "remission or forgiveness of the sins" of the crusaders, rather than an indulgence in a proper technical sense.[26] The same phraseology reappeared in canon 10 of the First Lateran Council (1123)[27] and still later in the bull *Quantum praedecessores* (1145) of Pope Eugenius III (1145–53).[28] The matter was rather more carefully defined in a letter of Pope Alexander III on 29 July 1169, but here again the pope described not an indulgence but a commutation of penance.[29] Although Pope Alexander used the term *indulgentia peccatorum* in referring to this grant, what he seems to have had in mind was a remission of the penance which had been enjoined upon participants in the proposed crusade as satisfaction for their confessed sins; much the same terminology was employed in another crusade bull of the same pontiff in 1181,[30] as well as in the proclamation of the third crusade by Gregory VIII.[31] Still later, in the great crusade proclamations of the thirteenth century, the same vagueness of description reappeared. In the constitution *Ad liberandam* of the Fourth Lateran Council (1215) and the constitution *Afflicti corde* of the First Council of

24. *Epistulae et chartae,* ed. Hagenmeyer, p. 137: "Sciatis autem eis omnibus, qui illuc non terreni commodi cupiditate sed pro sola animae suae salute et ecclesiae liberatione profecti fuerint, paenitentiam totam peccatorum, de quibus ueram et perfectam confessionem fecerint, per omnipotentis Dei misericordiam et ecclesiae catholicae preces tam nostra quam omnium paene archiepiscoporum et episcoporum qui in Gallis sunt auctoritate dimittimus. . . ."

25. Ibid., p. 136: ". . . huiusmodi procinctum pro remissione omnium peccatorum suorum in Aruernensi concilio celebriter eis iniunximus. . . ."

26. Ibid., p. 175: "Omnes ergo regionum uestrarum milites in peccatorum suorum remissionem uel ueniam cohortamini, ut ad illam matrem nostram Orientalem ecclesiam studeant festinare. . . ."

27. *COD*, p. 167.

28. Otto of Freising, *Gesta Frederici* 1.37 (ed. Schmale, p. 206).

29. *JL*, 11,637; text in *PL*, 200:599–600: "Nos autem . . . illis qui pro divinitatis amore laborem hujus profectionis assumere, et quantum in se fuerit implere studerint, de indulta nobis a Domino auctoritatis officio, illam remissionem imposite penitentie per sacerdotale ministerium facimus, quam felicis memorie Urbanus et Eugenius patres et antecessores nostri temporibus suis statuisse noscuntur, ut videlicet . . . remissionem injuncte penitentie se letetur adeptum, et cum contritione cordis et satisfactione oris profectionem istam satisfactionis loco ad suorum hanc indulgentiam peccatorum. . . ."

30. *JL*, 14,360; text in *PL*, 200:1294–96.

31. *JL*, 16,019; text in *PL*, 202:1539–42.

Lyons (1245)—in both of which the indulgence formula was the same[32]—
there was a carefully phrased statement concerning the crusade indulgence which, while not referring explicitly to a remission of temporal
punishment, came closer than earlier statements to expressing the privilege in terms of a sweeping forgiveness of sin. The words of the privilege in these two documents referred to "a complete pardon of the sins
for which they [the crusaders] have been thoroughly sorry at heart and
which they have confessed orally" and further promised "an increase
of eternal life as a reward for the just."[33]

All of this left open, however, a considerable area of doubt. Did
Alexander II, Urban II, and the rest mean what they said in a literal,
technical sense—i.e., were they granting a commutation of penance only?
Or did they rather intend to grant an indulgence in something like the
modern sense of the term and were they simply using the term "penance"
loosely to mean the temporal punishment of sins? Is it really possible now
to perceive their intent? There are two important considerations in
interpreting their words.

First, it is unlikely in the extreme that the popes themselves had an
absolutely clear notion of the sort of remission they were granting when
they issued the spiritual crusade privileges we have just examined. The
theoretical structure which we now use in defining the indulgence had in
their day not yet been developed by the theologians of the Western
Church. Probably the only way in which we can approach an answer is to
postulate that they intended the participants in the crusade to gain as
complete a remission as possible of the consequences of sin. They must
have had some inkling of the distinction between the guilt (*culpa*)
resulting from sin and the punishment (*poena*) merited by sin—notions
distinguished briefly by Gratian, at greater length by the twelfth-century
decretists.[34] But the distinction between penance and punishment was not
fully or clearly grasped by pontiffs, theologians, or canonists in the twelfth
and early thirteenth centuries, nor had they yet developed the theory of
the treasury of merits to account for the pope's power to remit the

32. *COD*, pp. 246–47, 277.

33. Ibid.: "Nos igitur omnipotentis Dei misericordia, et beatorum apostolorum
Petri et Pauli auctoritate confisi, ex illa quam nobis, licet indigne, Deus ligandi
atque solvendi contulis potestate, omnibus qui laborem propriis personis subierint
et expensis, plenam suorum peccaminum, de quibus liberaliter fuerint corde con-
triti et ore confessi, veniam indulgemus, et in retributione iustorum salutis aeternae
pollicemur augmentum. . . ."

34. C. 15 q. 1 d. p. c. 2 § 1; see also Kuttner, *Kanonistische Schuldlehre*, pp.
86–95. The opinions of the major decretists are cited in ibid., p. 86, n. 3.

punishment due for sin.[35] Perhaps it is significant that neither Gratian nor Peter Lombard felt it necessary to deal with indulgences in their influential works.[36] Rather, it was the work of the great scholastic theologians of the mid- and later thirteenth century—in particular of Alexander of Hales (ca.1186–1245), St. Bonaventura (1221–74), and St. Thomas Aquinas (1225–74)—which first clarified these matters.[37]

A second clue to the meaning of the early grants of indulgence to crusaders is the way in which the papal promises were understood by the crusaders themselves and by those who preached and chronicled the crusades. It is obvious enough that these people for the most part were neither expert theologians nor learned canonists; nonetheless the popular understanding of what the crusade indulgence involved gives some insight into why it was so persuasive an inducement to don the cross.

All the chroniclers of the first crusade were in complete agreement in describing the scope of the indulgence: it granted a "remission of sins" for those who took part in the expedition.[38] What was understood by this "remission of sins" was quite clearly a complete and total wiping out of past misdeeds—an expunging of the record, so to speak—so that the crusader who died was believed to enter immediately, without qualification or post mortem penance, into eternal bliss with the saints in paradise. This theme was repeated over and over in the narratives: "Take up this journey, therefore, for the remission of your sins, secure in the unfading glory of the Kingdom of Heaven," one eyewitness reported Pope Urban

35. Interestingly, Pope Innocent IV seems at one point to link the pope's right to grant indulgences for the reconquest of the Holy Land with his property rights there in virtue of the Donation of Constantine: *Apparatus* to *X* 3.34.8 (Frankfurt ed., fol. 430ʳ), "Quod autem papa facit indulgentias illis, qui occupant terram sanctam, licet eam possideant Sarraceni, et etiam indicere bellum, et dare indulgentias illis, qui occupant terram sanctam, quam infideles illicite possident, hoc totum est causa, nam iuste motus est papa, si intendit terram sanctam, que consecrata est natiuitate habitatione, et morte Iesu Christi, et in qua non colitur Christus, sed Machometus, reuocare ut incolatur a Christianis. Item terra sancta iusto bello uicta fuit ab Imperatore Romano post mortem Christi, unde licitum est pape ratione Imperii Romani, quod obtinet illud ad suam iurisdictionem reuocare, quia iniuste expoliatus est. . . ."

36. Paulus, *Geschichte des Ablasses*, 1:213.

37. For their contributions to the analysis, see Gottlob, *Kreuzablass*, pp. 270–88; see also the treatment of the commutation of penance by Robert Courçon (fl. 1204–10) in his *Summa*, partially ed. by V. L. Kennedy, "Robert Courson on Penance," *Mediaeval Studies*, 7(1945), 331–32.

38. Robert the Monk, *Historia* 1.2 (*RHC, Occ*, 3:729); Bernold of Constance, *Chronicon*, s.a. 1096 (*MGH, SS*, 5:464); Ekkehard, *Chronicon universale*, s.a. 1099 (*MGH, SS*, 6:213); Fulcher of Chartres, *Historia* 1.3.5 (ed. Hagenmeyer, p. 135).

II to have said at Clermont.[39] The crusaders' recompense would be an eternal prize, said another,[40] while yet another writer explained that crusaders would surely save their souls.[41] In the same vein, the chroniclers regularly referred to slain crusaders as martyrs[42] and depicted their souls as marching triumphantly from the dust of battle to the bliss of heaven.[43]

The same themes reappeared in chronicles and sermons dealing with the later crusade expeditions. A justly famous description of the privilege of the indulgence was that used by St. Bernard while preaching the second crusade. Bernard compared the crusader to a prudent merchant, who by taking the cross gained a supreme bargain: he exchanged his service on crusade for the certainty of eternal salvation. "Take the sign of the cross," he urged his audience; "if placed on the devout shoulder, it is without doubt worth the Kingdom of God."[44] At the beginning of the thirteenth century, Villehardouin, writing about the fourth crusade, was equally certain of the supreme value of the crusade indulgence:

> All those who took the cross and did God's service for a year in the army will be quit of all the sins which they have committed, if they confessed them. Because this pardon was so great, it greatly stirred the people's hearts and many took the cross because the pardon was so great.[45]

39. Robert the Monk, *Historia* 1.2 (*RHC, Occ,* 3:729): "Arripite igitur viam hanc in remissionem peccatorum vestrorum, securi de immarescibili gloria [1 Peter 5.4] regni coelorum."

40. Fulcher of Chartres, *Historia* 1.3.7 (ed. Hagenmeyer, p. 136): "nunc aeterna praemia nanciscantur, qui dudum pro solidis paucis mercenarii fuerunt."

41. *Gesta Francorum* 1.1 (ed. Hill, p. 1): "si quis animam suam saluam facere uellet, non dubitaret humiliter uiam incipere Domini. . . ."

42. E.g., ibid., 1.2 (ed. Hill, p. 4): "Isti primo felix acceperunt martirium pro nomine Domini Iesu." and cf. ibid., 1.25 (ed. Hill, p. 85). Fulcher of Chartres, *Historia* prol. 4 (ed. Hagenmeyer, p. 117): "o quot milia martyrum in hac expeditione beata morte finierunt!" and cf. ibid., 1.16.4 (ed. Hagenmeyer, pp. 226–27).

43. E.g., *Gesta Francorum* 7.18 (ed. Hill, p. 40): "Fueruntique in illa die martyrizati ex nostris militibus seu peditibus plus quam mille, qui ut credimus in caelum ascenderunt, et candidati stolam martyrii receperunt." Cf. ibid., 2.8 (ed. Hill, p. 17).

44. St. Bernard, *Epist.* 363 (*PL,* 182:567): "Si prudens mercator es, si conquistor huius seculi magnas quasdam tibi nundinas indicio; uide ne pereant. Suscipe crucis signum, et omnium pariter, de quibus corde contrito confessionem feceris, indulgentiam obtinebis. Materia ipsa se emitur, parvi constat: si devoto assumitur humero, valet sine dubio regnum Dei."

45. Villehardouin, *La Conquête de Constantinople* 1.1 (ed. Faral, 1.4): "tuit cil qui se croisseroient et feroient le servise Deu un an en l'ost servient quite de toz les pechiez que il avoient faitz, dont il seroient confés. Porce que cil pardons fu issi granz, si s'en esmurent mult li cuer des gens, et mult s'encroisierent porce que li pardons ere si granz."

As these examples indicate, there was little popular confusion about what the crusade indulgence involved: it was accepted as a complete quittance of all former sins. Without any quibbling over *poena et culpa,* the common understanding was that the crusade indulgence wiped away the blot of sin altogether and that the crusader was automatically restored to a state of spiritual innocence.

Understandably, the canonists and theologians were more cautious in their assessment. St. Bonaventura, in particular, was concerned lest the crusade indulgence be taken as a flat guarantee of eternal salvation. "Rather," he taught, "it is greatly to be feared that not everyone who dies on the cross will follow Christ to rest." Instancing the example of the bad thief who died on the cross with Christ and yet was not saved, Bonaventura warned his hearers that crusaders who failed to live righteously would risk eternal damnation.[46]

Other theologians debated the conditions under which the crusade indulgence was granted. Did it automatically become effective when one took the cross, or was it only imparted upon the completion of the crusader's task? What of the spiritual state of a crusader who died before completing or even before commencing his journey? These questions reappeared with considerable frequency in the theological disputations of the late thirteenth century.[47] The best known treatment of them was that of St. Thomas Aquinas, who held a quodlibetal disputation on the question, "Does a crusader who dies before commencing his journey receive an indulgence for his sins?"[48] After proposing four objections to the thesis, St. Thomas argued that there were three things necessary to merit an indulgence: that the matter pertain to the honor of God or the needs of the Church; that the indulgence be proclaimed by a person empowered to grant it; and that the person who hoped to receive the

46. St. Bonaventura, *Sermo I, Feria III Pentecostes,* in his *Opera omnia,* ed. Peltier, 13:311.

47. Glorieux, *La Littérature quodlibétique,* 1:114 (Gérard d'Abbéville, *Quodlibeta* 3.1–2, 1264), 1:189 (Henry of Ghent, *Quodlibeta* 8.17, 1284); 2:248 (Raymond Rigaud, *Quodlibeta* 7.13, ca.1287); 1:281 (Thomas Aquinas, *Quodlibeta* 5.14, Christmas, 1271). These questions were also discussed by Augustinus Triumphus de Ancona (ca.1243–1328), *Summa de potestate ecclesiastica* 1.33.2, fol. 128ᵛ–129ʳ; by William of Pagula (fl. 1314–32) in his *Summa summarum* 5.56 (Cambridge, Pembroke College, MS. 201, fol. 291ᵛᵇ); by Ludovicus Bologninus de Bologna (1447–1508), *Tractatus solennis et quotidianus de indulgentiis,* in *Tractatus universi iuris,* 3:101ʳ⁻ᵛ, and by Hieronymus de Zanetinis (d. 1493), *Tractatus de foro conscientie et contentioso,* in *Tractatus universi iuris* 1:88ᵛ.

48. *Quodlibetum* 2.16, in his *Opera omnia,* 9:484.

indulgence be in "the condition of love."[49] Given these three requisites, the validity of an indulgence in a particular case depended upon the wording of the grant itself: if it were for those who took the cross in order to aid the Holy Land, then its effectiveness would date from the taking of the cross and it would be valid even if the crusader should die before commencing his journey, since the reason for granting the indulgence was the making of the crusade vow. If, on the other hand, the grant of indulgence specified that it was to be given to those who crossed the sea in order to aid the Holy Land, then the crusader who died before commencing his journey was out of luck: "He does not receive the indulgence because he has not fulfilled the condition for the indulgence."[50] In another quodlibet, St. Thomas discussed the related question, "Whether a crusader dies in a better state while going overseas or while returning thence?"[51] To this he replied that, other things being equal, the returning crusader ought to be in a better spiritual state, for he should have both the merit of intending to go on crusade and the additional merit of his performance on crusade to stand him in good stead at the throne of judgment.[52]

49. Ibid.: "Ad hoc ergo quod indulgentia alicui valeat, tria requiruntur. Primo causa pertinens ad honorem Dei, vel ad necessitatem aut utilitatem ecclesie. Secundo auctoritas in eo qui facit: Papa enim potest principaliter, alii vero in quantum potestatem ab eo accipiunt vel ordinariam vel commissam, seu delegatam. Tertio requiritur ut sit in statu caritatis ille qui indulgentiam percipere vult. Et hec tria designantur in littera papali. . . ."

50. Ibid.: "Est ergo dicendum in questione proposita, quod si secundum formam papalis littere indulgentia concedatur accipientibus crucem in subsidium terre sancte, crucesignatus statim habet indulgentiam, etiamsi decedat antequam iter arripiat; quia sic causa indulgentie erit non iter, sed votum itineris. Si autem in forma littere contineatur quod indulgentia detur his qui transierint ultra mare, ille qui decedit antequam transeat, non habet indulgentiam, quia non habet indulgentie causam." Cf. the discussion of this matter in the *Summa "Quid sit symonia,"* tit. *De generalibus remissionibus,* in Innsbruck, Universitätsbibliothek, MS. 368, fol. 98vb–99ra: "Sed numquid ex sola crucis susceptione uel proposito proficiscendi consequitur quis plenam omnium peccatorum suorum indulgentiam quam facit papa proficiscentibus in subsidium terre sancte uel contra hereticos et huiusmodi si statim decesserit? Responsum: credo sine preiudicio quod non, nisi hoc quantitas contritionis et deuotionis ad negocium habite mereatur. Recurrendum tamen est ad formam indulgentie et intentionem pape, qui multum potest in talibus et latissime interpretanda est hic indulgentia generalis, precipue cum ex magnitudine fidei et caritate assumpto tanti periculi procedere uidetur."

51. *Quodlibetum* 5.14, in his *Opera omnia,* 9:554.

52. Ibid., "Respondeo dicendum quod quanto aliquis cum pluribus meritis moritur, tanto melius moritur. Merita autem manent homini, non solum illa que actu agit, sed etiam illa que jam fecit, quasi apud Deum deposita, secundum illud II ad

In three questiones in the Supplement to the *Summa theologica* we can see the doctrine of indulgences assuming something very like its modern Catholic shape.[53] The first of these questiones is devoted to the character and nature of indulgences in general. Here St. Thomas clearly stated the notion of the indulgence as a means whereby the whole of the punishment due to sin might be satisfied by drawing upon the superabundant merits of Christ and His Church.[54] He made the point that the remissive power of the indulgence was defined by the terms of its proclamation, not by the merits or internal dispositions of those who performed the works prescribed to gain the indulgence.[55] In addition, St. Thomas held that the indulgence might properly be granted in return for a valuable consideration (*pro temporali subsidio*), but not for that alone, since otherwise there would be danger of falling into simony.[56] A second question concerned the power to grant indulgences—this was a function of jurisdictional powers and not of the sacrament of orders within the Church. Hence a priest might not be able to grant an indulgence while a deacon or a bishop, or others who were not priests, might be able to, provided they enjoyed the appropriate jurisdictional rights.[57] A third question concerned those who received the indulgence and dealt with such matters as the spiritual disposition necessary to receive a valid indulgence, whether the actual performance of the conditions stipulated for the indulgence was required for its receipt, or whether the mere desire to perform them was adequate, and so forth.[58]

CRUSADE INDULGENCES AND NON-CRUSADERS. For very nearly the first century of their existence, crusade indulgences were granted exclu-

---

Timoth. I, 12: 'Scio cui credidi; et certus sum quia potens est depositum meum servare.' Manifestum est autem, quod ille qui moritur in redeundo de ultra mare, ceteris paribus, cum pluribus meritis moritur quam ille qui moritur in eundo: habet enim meritum ex assumptione itineris, et ulterius ex prosecutione, in qua forte multa gravia est passus: et ideo, ceteris paribus, melius moritur redeundo; quamvis ire sit magis meritorium quam redire, genus operis considerando."

53. The *Supplement* was put together from other works of St. Thomas, particularly from his writings on the *Sentences* of Peter Lombard. The compiler may have been Reginald of Piperno, one of St. Thomas's secretaries. See Etienne Gilson, *The Christian Philosophy of St. Thomas Aquinas,* trans. L. K. Shook, p. 388.

54. *Summa theologica, supplementum,* q. 25 a. 1.

55. Ibid., q. 25 a. 2.

56. Ibid., q. 25 a. 3.

57. Ibid., q. 26 a. 1-3.

58. Ibid., q. 27 a. 1-3.

sively to persons who took the cross and who presumably intended to participate personally in a crusade. Commencing with the pontificate of Pope Gregory VIII (1187), however, these indulgences were granted also to those who simply assisted a crusade without personally taking an active part in it.[59] This development was no doubt due in large part to the desire to raise crusading armies composed of trained, well-equipped troops and in part to the increasing cost of the crusade effort itself.[60] It paralleled, too, the increasing ease with which monetary commutations could be obtained.

The process of increasing the numbers of persons who might secure the indulgence proceeded rapidly and relentlessly. In 1188 the bishops of England and France were permitted to grant one-half of a full crusade indulgence to those who paid up their share of the tithe collected for the third crusade,[61] while in 1213, Pope Innocent III directed that those who attended the sermons of crusade preachers should likewise be granted a fractional indulgence—a grant frequently reiterated by his successors.[62] The conditions for the grant of the crusade indulgence and other privileges to non-crusaders were stated in classic form in *Ad liberandam* (1215),[63] and continually broadened by later popes. In 1252, Innocent IV decreed that the wives of crusaders were to receive the same indulgence that their husbands earned on crusade.[64] In 1263, Urban IV explicitly granted the crusade preachers themselves the full indulgence as a reward for their labors on behalf of the Holy Land.[65] The indulgence was

59. *JL*, 16,019; Paulus, *Geschichte des Ablasses*, 1:203–4.

60. See above, ch. IV, and Gottlob, *Kreuzablass*, p. 167.

61. *Acta pontificum*, ed. Pflugk-Harttung, 3:363–64; *JL*, 16,252; Paulus, *Geschichte des Ablasses*, 1:205–6.

62. Especially by Clement IV (1265–68): see *Po*, 19,070, 19,859, and his *Registres* 58 (ed. Jordan, 1:17); Paulus, *Geschichte des Ablasses*, 2:44–45. Innocent's grant of 1213 is in *Po*, 4,711.

63. *COD*, pp. 246–47. The provisions of *Ad liberandam* relating to crusade privileges, spiritual as well as temporal, were several times republished during the thirteenth century. They were also reiterated, with those of the constitution *Afflicti corde*, by Urban IV in 1263 (*Registres* 467, ed. Guiraud, 2:226–28) and by Nicholas IV in 1291 (*Po*, 23,609; *Bullarum, diplomatum, et privilegiorum sanctorum Romanorum pontificum*, 4:111–15); see also Paulus, *Geschichte des Ablasses*, 1:207, and Georg Schreiber, *Kurie und Kloster im 12. Jahrhundert*, 2:229.

64. Innocent IV, *Registres* 2,665, 5,980 (ed. Berger, 1:397, 3:111); also Nicholas IV, *Registres* 1,941 (ed. Langlois, 1:347); Paulus, *Geschichte des Ablasses*, 2:41–42.

65. Urban IV, *Registres* 2,973 (ed. Guiraud, 4:67); also Clement IV, *Registres* 1,627 (ed. Jordan, 1:481); Paulus, *Geschichte des Ablasses*, 2:42–43.

extended to those who collected money and alms in aid of the Holy Land,[66] to missionaries working on Europe's frontiers,[67] to colonists who settled in the Holy Land,[68] to an advance party of scouts sent to spy out conditions there in preparation for a new crusade,[69] to the regents for a crusading king,[70] and ultimately to inquisitors and their helpers, on the theory that they, too, were performing an heroic Christian labor by combatting the inroads of heresy.[71]

OTHER SPIRITUAL PRIVILEGES OF CRUSADERS. There were other crusade privileges whose operation was entirely or principally in foro interno and which may, therefore, be classed as spiritual privileges. These included release from the spiritual penalty of excommunication, a release which began in the early part of the thirteenth century as a favor granted in particular instances to individual crusaders, but had been converted by the time of the pontificate of Gregory IX into a normal part of the bundle of privileges which crusaders regularly received auctoritate crucis.[72] During the last third of the century, this privilege, like the indulgence, was routinely granted to anyone who made the crusade vow in return for a monetary and comparatively casual commutation of the vow.[73]

The privilege of dealing voluntarily with excommunicates, without incurring the automatic ban decreed in such instances by the general law of the Western Church, was inaugurated by Innocent III in a decretal of 20 June 1203, incorporated in *Compilatio III* and later in the *Decretals* of Gregory IX.[74] Such dealings might become necessary in the course of carrying out the crusader's obligation; analogous privileges existed in the

66. Paulus, *Geschichte des Ablasses,* 2:43–44.

67. *Po,* 10,525, 16,163; Boniface VIII, *Registres* 1,306 (ed. Georges Digard et al., 1:470); Paulus, *Geschichte des Ablasses,* 2:45.

68. *Po,* 16,805.

69. *Po,* 20,755; Paulus, *Geschichte des Ablasses,* 2:41.

70. John XXII, *Lettres communes* 61,202 (ed. G. Mollat and G. Lesquen, 12:214).

71. Paulus, *Geschichte des Ablasses,* 2:43–44.

72. E.g., Honorius III, *Regesta* 1,364, 1,723 (ed. Pressutti, 1:226, 287); Gregory IX, *Registres* 2,820, 2,805, 3,236 (ed. Auvray, 2:184, 190–91, 442); Innocent IV, *Registres* 6,414 (ed. Berger, 3:193).

73. E.g., Walter Giffard, *Register,* ed. William Brown, pp. 277–79; *Historical Papers and Letters from the Northern Registers,* ed. James Raine, pp. 46–47; Sutton, *Rolls and Register,* ed. Hill, 3:22, 160; 4:13.

74. *Comp. III* 5.21.7 = X 5.39.34 (*Po,* 1,947). For the ban, see C. 11 q. 3 c. 102–5.

general law for travellers and for members of the household of an excommunicate.[75]

Crusaders were freed from some of the most serious effects of another major ecclesiastical penalty, the interdict.[76] The basis for this privilege was also laid down by a decretal of Innocent III providing that crusaders and other pilgrims might be allowed to receive the sacrament of penance during a period of interdict.[77] Joannes Teutonicus in his *Apparatus* to *Comp. IV* was inclined to interpret this privilege very strictly—it should apply, he believed, only to those crusaders who were actually travelling on their journey to the Holy Land, and should not be extended to cover the performance or participation in other rites or services by crusaders, since so general a mitigation of the severity of the interdict might tend to undermine the disciplinary power of the Church.[78] More generous views were current, for example, the glosses to the *Summa de casibus* of St. Raymond of Peñafort and the interpretation of Tancredus, reported in the *glossa ordinaria* to this decretal in the *Decretales Gregorii IX.*[79] Ulti-

---

75. C. 11 q. 3 c. 103; see also the *Distinctiones decretorum* of Richardus Anglicus, cited above, ch. II, n. 112. The rationale for the situation was discussed by Guido in his *Casus "Scribit dominus papa"* to *Comp. III* 5.21.7 (Oxford, Bodleian Library, MS. Laud. Misc. 646, fol. 49ʳᵃ).

76. The nature and effects of the interdict, an ecclesiastical adaptation of the interdictal procedure of the Roman law, were succinctly described by Hostiensis, *Summa aurea*, lib. 2, tit. *De causa proprietatis* 3–6 (Lyons ed., fol. 86ᵛ–87ʳ). There is abundant secondary literature on the subject, for which see E. Jombart, "Interdit," *DDC*, 5:1464–75; Plöchl, *Geschichte*, 2:349–54.

77. *Comp. IV* 5.14.3 = X 5.38.11.

78. Joannes Teutonicus, *Apparatus* to *Comp. IV* 5.14.3, in Cambridge, Gonville and Caius College, MS. 44/150, fol. 150ʳᵃ: "*penitentia.* Hoc est in eis speciale, ut periculo mortis admittantur penitentiam. Sed certe ibi necessitas quod hoc intelligo ubi cum proficiscantur, idem dico si aliqui profici⟨s⟩cantur ad iustum bellum, quia ibi est causa timoris. Idem dico si aliqui essent excommunicati a papa, ut in iusto bello possunt absolui a quocunque, ar. Extra i de sen. excommunicationis c. ult. [*Comp. I* 5.34.16 = X 5.39.11] et xxxiii Q. ii In adolescencia [c. 14]. Sed quid si interdicta ciuitate aliqui uellent satisfacere? Numquid in eis relaxandum esset interdictum? Non, quia alius sine culpa sua interdici potest, ut Extra i de sponsal., non est uerum [*Comp. I* 4.1.13 = X 4.1.11], et quia sic rigor ecclesie dissolueretur, ut supra de priuilegiis, Vt priuilegia [*Comp. IV* 5.12.7 = X 5.33.24; IV Lat. Council, c. 57, in *COD*, p. 237]."

79. Gloss to Raymond of Peñafort, *Summa de casibus*, ad v. *aliis peregrinis*, in Innsbruck, Universitätsbibliothek, MS. 266, fol. 237ʳ⁻ᵛ: "*Aliis peregrinis* interdictis pro culpa aliena. Secus si pro propria et intelligo hoc ⟨tam⟩ de illis qui iam sunt in uia sue peregrinacionis quam de illis qui adhuc sunt in preparatione ad eundum, licet quidam restringant hoc ad illos solos qui iam sunt in uia ut dictum est. Sed numquit benedicet eis sacerdos peram et baculum? Item numquit in uia poterunt audire diuina in ecclesia aut poterunt cum uenerint ad locum destinatum intrare

mately the less rigorous interpretation was explicitly confirmed in the decretals of the later thirteenth-century pontiffs.[80]

The confessors of crusaders were commonly allowed to dispense those who had taken the cross from a wide selection of irregularities and to grant pardon for many classes of offences that were normally reserved to the jurisdiction of the pope—among them homicide, matrimonial consanguinity, bastardy, irregular ordination, perjury, and pluralism.[81] Fulfillment of the crusade vow was considered, from the thirteenth century onward, to satisfy the obligations incurred by any other vows which the crusader might have made, even including such weighty matters, apparently, as the vow to enter the religious life and the vow of chastity.[82]

PRAYERS FOR CRUSADERS. Finally, crusaders enjoyed the further spiritual benefit—not, technically speaking, a privilege—of the prayers and suffrages which were offered at various times for the safekeeping of the Holy Land and the welfare of those who fought in its defense. A curious twelfth-century Anglo-Norman gloss to the *Decretum* raised the interesting moral question of whether one ought to pray for all crusaders or only

ecclesiam et ibi offere? Respondeo ad primum: Quod cum benediccio pere et ⟨baculi⟩ [*ms.:* baculum] non reperiatur talibus interdicta uidetur esse concessa. Ad secundum dic quod non debent audire diuina in uia in ecclesia; possunt tamen orare priuata oratione et offere nisi sint interdicti ab ingressu ecclesie pro culpa aliena. Queritur tamen illa decere cum uite uidelicet approbare peregrinacionem huius dans eis beneficium speciale, uidetur concedere ea que sunt quasi de substantia peregrinacionis, scilicet intrare ad loca destinata et ibi offere sicut eo ipso quod filius familias licenciatus est a patre quod eat ad scolas."

Glos. ord. to X 5.38.11, ad v. *penitentia,* reported the opinions of both Joannes and Tancredus: "T. dixit quod si aliqui vellent iurare stare mandato ecclesie, quod essent admittendi. Sed finis iste uidetur contradicere: quia hic specialiter hoc concedit recipientibus signum crucis et peregrinis, ergo aliis intelligitur prohibere, sicut quod de uno negatur, de alio conceditur, 25 dist. qualis [c. 4], quod uerius puto, licet inuenias contrarium dictum."

80. E.g., Clement IV, *Registres* 1,571–72 (ed. Jordan, 1:472).

81. Paulus, *Geschichte des Ablasses,* 3:501. Examples are: homicide: Nicholas IV, *Registres* 2,099 (ed. Langlois, 1:370); consanguinity: Innocent IV, *Registres* 1,833, 4,168, 4,177 (ed. Berger, 1:273; 2:11, 13); Nicholas III, *Registres* 493 (ed. Gay, p. 188); bastardy: Clement IV, *Registres* 1,580 (ed. Jordan, 1:473); irregular ordination: Walter Giffard, *Register,* ed. Brown, p. 278; perjury: Nicholas IV, *Registres* 1,710 (ed. Langlois, 1:321); pluralism: ibid., 1,726, 6,649 (ed. Langlois, 1:323; 2:885); Benedict XI, *Registres* 1,013 (ed. Grandjean, col. 612–13).

82. Gregory IX, *Registres* 2,757 (ed. Auvray, 2:159; *Po,* 10,011); John XXII, *Lettres communes* 63,881 (ed. Mollat and Lesquen, 13:192); Paulus, *Geschichte des Ablasses,* 3:506–7.

for some of them, and determined that it would be proper to pray only for certain crusaders, or, alternatively, for all of them, but with the intention that one's prayers be applied only to certain ones.[83]

More commonly, the authorities ordained that prayers be offered generally for the whole crusading effort. Thus in England in 1188 there were to be daily prayers, offered at all masses, for the deliverance of Jerusalem and the Holy Land.[84] Again, in 1213, Innocent III decreed that there was to be in each parish a monthly procession to beg divine intervention for the crusaders and for the protection of the Holy Land, and special prayers daily in all masses.[85] Still further directions for prayers and services of intercession were laid down by local ecclesiastical assemblies—witness the decree in the Statutes of Worcester II (1230) and the instructions of the legatine council of 1268 at London.[86] Toward the end of the thirteenth century, Archbishop Winchelsey commanded the observance in the province of Canterbury of an even more elaborate regime of prayers for crusaders and for the Holy Land. There were to be special sermons and special masses of intercession on Wednesdays and Fridays of each week, while further prayers were to be inserted into the daily masses and a weekly penitential procession was to be held.[87]

It is thus obvious that the twelfth- and thirteenth-century Church showed a considerable solicitude for the spiritual wellbeing of crusaders; but its care for their temporal interests was almost equally great.

---

83. Gonville and Caius College, MS. 283/676, fol. 151ᵛᵃ, gloss to C. 23 q. 1 c. 3, ad v. *non facere:* "Queritur num pro omnibus crucesignatis se orasse debent? Respondeo etiam si pro omnibus noluit exaudiri, immo pro quibusdam; uel sic, alius pro quibusdam orauit et pro illis facit exauditus."
84. *Gesta regis Henrici II,* s.a. 1188 (ed. William Stubbs, 2:53–54).
85. Innocent III, *Registrum* 16.28 (*PL,* 216:817–22); *Po,* 4,725.
86. Statutes of Worcester II, c. 30, in *Councils and Synods,* ed. Powicke and Cheney, 2.175; also ibid., 2:781–82; Lyndwood, *Provinciale,* pp. 137–40.
87. *Councils,* ed. Haddan and Stubbs, 1:614–16.

CHAPTER VI

The Privilege of the Cross:
The Temporal Privileges

Se vous servez Dieu a l'eglise
Dieu vous resert en autre guise
Qu'il vous pait en vostre maison.

Rutebeuf, *La   Complainte*
d'Outremer

While man may not live by bread alone, he cannot well live without it. The spiritual privileges of crusaders may have drawn many men to take the cross; but more was required to make the crusades a widely attractive and practical proposition. In order to fulfill his votive obligations, after all, the crusader must confront a great number of practical problems. He must leave his landed possessions and often also his wife and family behind when he left; hence provision for their welfare was well-nigh a necessity. While some might have enlisted without such safeguards, the numbers of participants in the crusades would obviously have been far smaller than they actually were had there been no machinery to deal with these elemental but not elementary problems. Further, the crusader who was preparing to depart from home, lands, family, and possessions for an indeterminate but probably lengthy campaign could not well afford to do so without first settling whatever legal claims might be outstanding against him; this, in turn, demanded some method for speeding up the time-consuming machinery of justice. The crusader required some assurance that further legal claims might not be raised against him during his absence and that he might not lose property, rights, and possessions by default while engaged in his pious purpose. And he required money, lots of it, to buy food and shelter for himself and his entourage, to replace horses, weapons, and equipment en route, and to care for the thousand and one contingencies which might arise during his journey. Since most feudal warriors had relatively little ready cash, even though they might be wealthy in terms of landed possessions and other frozen capital investments, some provision had to be made to enable them to borrow the money they needed and to hypothecate property. Many crusaders required outright subsidies, in addition to whatever money they might be able to raise from their own resources, if they were to play an effective role in the crusade enterprise. Clerical crusaders had special problems of their own. They needed ready money too, and for this purpose had to be able to pledge the income from their benefices, sometimes for years in advance. They also had to secure a waiver of the general rule which, for good reason, forbade clerics to collect the income of their clerical livings while not personally serving in the offices committed to their care. For practical reasons, clerics on crusade needed dispensations from a number of disciplinary regulations which (at least in theory) guided the conduct of those who remained at home. Finally, all crusaders, clerical or lay, required some form of effective redress against those who might have violated their privileges, while society at large, *e converso,* required some safeguard against abuses of crusade privileges, either by genuine or counterfeit crusaders.

It was this complex of practical needs which dictated the form and character of the temporal privileges of the cross and which gave a special legal status and character to the crusader in medieval society. For purposes of analysis and description, the temporal privileges of crusaders fall readily into four categories: (1) protected status for crusaders, their possessions and families; (2) jurisdictional privileges and special legal favors; (3) financial privileges; (4) special disciplinary privileges. To round out a discussion of these four categories of temporal privileges, we should also discuss the problems which arose over crusader status and privileges as a result of violation or abuse of crusaders' special rights, as well as the means of terminating an individual's claim to the special status and privileges of a crusader through renunciation or revocation of the privilege of the cross, either in whole or in part.

THE PRIVILEGE OF PROTECTED STATUS. Possibly the most basic and certainly one of the earliest of the temporal privileges granted to crusaders was the guarantee of personal protection. This was an obvious outgrowth of the privilege of personal protection which the Church had sought to guarantee for pilgrims and travellers of all kinds for generations before the first crusade;[1] the great problem arising from it was effective enforcement. Here the Church seems to have had greater success than it had achieved in earlier attempts to assure protection for other travellers. Again, this privilege was in its early years only vaguely outlined; it was subsequently defined with greater precision as a result both of practical experience and also of the increasing elaboration and definition of ecclesiastical law during the twelfth and thirteenth centuries.

The canons of the Council of Clermont in the received form of the text did not touch upon the problem of protecting crusaders from attack. One variant version of the Council's decrees, however, did contain a specific declaration that both the persons and belongings of crusaders were to be protected by the Truce of God.[2] Fulcher of Chartres in his report likewise indicated that ecclesiastical protection was decreed for pilgrims and others, and that violators were threatened with anathema. Fulcher did not, however, link this protection specifically to crusaders.[3] About all that can be concluded from the references to the personal protection of crusaders during the first crusade is that they were considered in the same class and subject to the same general ecclesiastical protection as other types of pilgrims—the distinction between the two in this area was at that time very vague indeed.

Further pledges of protection for pilgrims of all types occurred in a number of documents of the early twelfth century. The Byzantine emperor, Alexius Comnenus, for example, as a part of the settlement involved in the Treaty of Devol (1108) between him and Bohemund of Antioch, promised protection of the persons of pilgrims passing through his domains.[4] The First Lateran Council (1123) took notice of the problem with special reference to pilgrims visiting Rome, and decreed that those who seized the persons of pilgrims, despoiled their goods, or dared to impose unaccustomed taxes upon them were to be excommunicated.[5] Fulcher of Chartres, again, commented on the fate of some

---

1. See above, ch. 1; Villey, *La Croisade*, pp. 151–52, exaggerates the originality of Urban II in extending ecclesiastical protection to crusaders.

2. *Acta pontificum,* ed. Pflugk-Harttung, 2:161–62: "Ammoneri populum de itinere Hierosolimitano et, quicumque ibit per nomen penitentie, tam ipse quam res eius semper sint in treuga domini."

3. Fulcher of Chartres, *Historia* 1.2.11 (ed. Hagenmeyer, p. 128).

4. Ibid., 3.29.2 (ed. Hagenmeyer, p. 524).

5. Can. 14 (*COD,* p. 169).

unprincipled pirates who in 1125 had attacked pilgrims bound for Jerusalem. For this act they were condemned and excommunicated; dying impenitent, they were lost. They descended, living, into Hell, for by their act they had disobeyed the pope, had scorned the patriarch, and had despised the decisions of the holy fathers.[6]

Gratian in the *Decretum* and other collections of the mid-twelfth century, such as the *Penitentiale* of Bartholomew of Exeter, did touch upon the personal inviolability of pilgrims of all classes but they made no distinction between the general protection of pilgrims and travellers and a special protection for crusaders.[7]

It was during and after the second crusade that the crusader seems first to have been set apart as a pilgrim who was entitled in a special way and with special force to the personal protection of the Church. This attitude was reflected strongly in a letter of St. Bernard of Clairvaux dealing with the second crusade. Writing in 1147 to the archbishops, bishops, and all the faithful of God, Bernard called especially upon the prelates of the Church to take particular pains to see that the protection guaranteed to crusaders was diligently enforced.[8] At the time of the third crusade, the matter was dealt with in a number of ways. Provincial councils, such as the one held by Archbishop Walter of Rouen in 1189, instructed their clergy to take special care of these matters and to enforce the guarantees made to crusaders.[9] Individual crusaders sometimes sought papal letters of protection in testimony of their status and these letters spelled out in some detail the types and varieties of protection to which their bearers were entitled.[10] This practice increased in frequency during the pontificates of Innocent III and his immediate successors. At the same time, the types of guarantees of personal protection became progressively more specific and detailed. In a letter of 1208 to Duke Leopold of Austria, for example, Innocent III, after accepting the duke under papal protection in virtue of his status as a crusader, specified what this involved. He called upon the archbishops and other prelates through whose jurisdictions the duke

6. Fulcher, *Historia* 3.41.4 (ed. Hagenmeyer, p. 761).

7. *Decretum* C. 24 q. 3 c. 23–25. Bartholomew of Exeter, *Penitentiale* c. 127–28 (ed. Morey, pp. 286–87; also, Cambridge, Gonville and Caius College, MS. 151/201, fol. 184ra).

8. St. Bernard of Clairvaux, *Epist.* 457 (*PL*, 182:651–52).

9. Mansi, *Concilia*, 22:584, c. 17.

10. E.g., *JL*, 16,087, 16,472, 16,670. Individual bishops might also grant letters of protection for crusaders; e.g., the request for such a letter from the bishop of Paris by Gervase of Prémontré, *Epist.* 75, in *Sacrae antiquitatis monumenta*, ed. Hugo, 1:69.

might pass to honor and enforce the papal guarantees and to preserve the duke against the attacks of his enemies, either until such time as he might return from the Holy Land or until certain news of his death might be received.[11] In the thirteenth century such letters of protection were freely granted by the chancery without consulting the pope; they were therefore included in the *Formularium audientie.*[12] Only those letters which were granted to kings and bishops required the pope's personal approval, obviously because of their possible political implications.[13] Sometimes, indeed, this protection might, under some extraordinary circumstances, be extended to crusaders after their return, as was done, for example, for Walter de Lacy in 1221, after he had lost more than half of his men in the fifth crusade.[14]

At the end of the twelfth century, Bernard of Pavia testified to the efficacy of the personal protection of crusaders. The crusader's cross, he reported, was used by those who desired to travel unmolested through dangerous territories. Travellers put it on to secure safe passage, even if they had no intention of going on crusade.[15] There are a number of notices in the papal registers concerning actions taken against those who attacked crusaders. Thus in 1217 Pope Honorius III mentioned the imposition of excommunication upon those who had allegedly seized a crusader, and in 1233 Gregory IX instructed the archbishop of Milan and two other bishops to renew the excommunication pronounced by the bishop of Piacenza against the civic officials of Milan, who were held responsible for the restitution of 1,500 marks stolen by some Milanese citizens from two

11. Innocent III, *Registrum* 11.2 (*PL,* 115:1341); *Po,* 3,303. Form letters of protection for crusaders were included in the formulary ascribed to Marinus of Eboli (Vat. Lat. 3976, fol. 205ᵛ–206ᵛ) and examples of other letters of protection may be found in the thirteenth-century papal registers, e.g., Gregory IX, *Registres* 1,785 (*Po,* 9,399), 1,787–91, 2,121–22 (*Po,* 9,733–34), 2,511 (*Po,* 9,878), 2,823 (*Po,* 10,041), 3,074 (*Po,* 10,136), 4,010, 4,112–13 (ed. Auvray, 1:981, 1142; 2:33, 193, 344–45, 839–40, 904); Innocent IV, *Registres* 6,147 (*Po,* 14,803; ed. Berger, 3:142); Clement IV, *Registres* 1,562 (ed. Jordan, 1:470); *The Register of William Wickwane, Lord Archbishop of York, 1279–1285,* ed. William Brown (Surtees Society Publications, 114), pp. 121–22.

12. *Formularium audientie,* ed. Peter Herde in *Audientia litterarun contradictarum,* vol. 2 Q. 13.

13. See the Chancery Constitution of Nicholas III, ed. by G. Barraclough in "The Chancery Ordinance of Nicholas III," § 34. On the constitution, see also P. Herde, *Beiträge zum päpstlichen Kanzlei- und Urkundenwesen im 13. Jahrhundert,* 2d ed. (1967), pp. 62, 223, and *passim.*

14. *Curia Regis Rolls* 78, Michaelmas Term, 5/6 Henry III (10:240).

15. Bernard of Pavia, *Summa de matrimonio* 3.3 (ed. Laseyres p. 290).

distressed crusaders.[16] The same pope in 1236 felt called upon to warn the king of France and the queen mother that they must see to it that crusaders in their domains were not attacked. It was the business of the king, the pope added, to keep peace in his kingdom and thereby to further the cause of the crusade.[17]

The First Council of Lyons was concerned—as well it might have been, in view of the events of the immediately preceding years[18]—with the problem of piracy, specifically with piratical attacks upon crusaders making their way to the Holy Land. The Council invoked especially severe sanctions: not only were the pirates themselves to be excommunicated—in view of their calling, perhaps a comparatively ineffectual remedy—but also all doing business with them or communicating with them in any way were subject to the supreme ecclesiastical penalty.[19]

Still, it cannot be said that there was any radical distinction, even by the end of the thirteenth century, between the personal protection guaranteed by the Church to crusaders and that guaranteed to other pilgrims. This was reflected in the fourteenth century by a well-known writer on the law of war, Honoré Bonet (ca.1340–ca.1405), who considered both pilgrims and crusaders under the single rubric of "peregrini" when discussing their rights of personal protection from attack and molestation.[20]

While the primary responsibility for protecting the persons of crusaders was assumed by the Church, secular and royal governments also sought to reinforce the ecclesiastical guarantees with measures of their own. The English monarchs of the thirteenth century issued dozens of royal letters of protection for individual crusaders.[21] These letters generally com-

16. Honorius III, Epist. 296 in *Regesta,* ed. Pressutti, 1:53; Gregory IX, *Registres* 1,501 (ed. Auvray, 1:828–29).

17. Gregory IX, *Registres* 3,195 (ed. Auvray, 2:413–14); *Po,* 10,194.

18. One of the most celebrated naval actions of the thirteenth century had occurred in May 1241, when a Sicilian and Pisan fleet in the service of Frederick II captured two cardinals and a hundred other prelates who were sailing from Genoa to attend a Church council that Gregory IX had summoned to meet that year in Rome. From the viewpoint of the papacy, at any rate, this was a lawless, piratical attack.

19. First Council of Lyons, c. 5 (*COD,* p. 276).

20. Honoré Bonet, *The Tree of Battles* 4.99 (ed. and trans. G. W. Coopland, pp. 187–88).

21. *Patent Rolls* 1 Henry III (2:21, 57), 11 Henry III (3:126, 129), 12 Henry III (3:196), 14 Henry III (3:323, 390), 17 Henry III (4:6, 17), 19 Henry III (4:109), 32 Henry III (5:18), 33 Henry III (5:43, 51), 45 Henry III (6:154), 54 Henry III (17:411, 424, 425, 440, 464–65, 479–80), 9 Edward I (8:437), 10 Edward I (9:39), 33 Edward I (11:304, 306–7). *Close Rolls* 11 Henry III (2:204), 38 Henry III (10:114).

mended the bearer to the good graces and help of royal officials and of foreign governments and forbade, under pain of the royal displeasure, any attack on or molestation of them, their companions, servants, and goods. The customary law of France, as reflected by Beaumanoir, likewise was cognizant of royal guarantees of immunity for pilgrims and made provisions for punishing those who disregarded these immunities.[22] Similar guarantees appeared in the *Siete partidas* of Alfonso *el Sabio* in Spain.[23]

PROTECTION OF CRUSADERS' FAMILIES AND PROPERTY. Hand in hand with the ecclesiastical and royal protection of crusaders went a similar protection for their wives, families, property, and possessions. Exactly when this protection was granted is not easy to determine. There was no mention of the matter in the decrees of the Council of Clermont or in the letters of Pope Urban II concerning the crusade; neither did any of the accounts of the pope's speech at Clermont deal with this theme. Either during or very shortly after the first crusade, however, the Church assumed the task of safeguarding the property of those who were involved in the expedition, as is clear from a letter of Pope Paschal II, probably of December 1099, to the archbishops, bishops, and abbots of France. At the close of his letter the pope instructed these prelates to see to it that all of the possessions of crusaders were restored to them "as was ordained, you may recall, by our predecessor, Urban of blessed memory, in a synodal decree."[24] Urban died on 29 July 1099. The protection must therefore have been decreed before that date, and there is a possibility that the synod mentioned by Paschal was the Council of Clermont.

Some details of an actual case from the early twelfth century (around 1106 or '07) can be recovered from the correspondence of the canonist Bishop Ivo of Chartres.[25] Hugh, Viscount of Chartres, a crusader, claimed

22. Beaumanoir, ch. 25 § 742 (ed. Salmon, 1:382); ch. 59 § 1689 (ed. Salmon, 2:364–65). Mistakes might nonetheless occur, as Beaumanoir showed in a moral tale about a pilgrim who fell in with evil companions and was hanged in error, despite his guarantees of protection.

23. *Las Siete partidas* 1.24.1–2 (Madrid; 1807, ed., 1:714–15).

24. *Epistulae et chartae,* ed. Hagenmeyer, pp. 174–75; "porro fratribus, qui post perpetratam diuinitus uictoriam reuertuntur, iubemus sua omnia restitui, sicut a beatae memoriae Urbano praedecessore nostro reminiscimini synodali definitione sancitum."

25. Ivo of Chartres, *Epist.* 168–70, 173 (*PL,* 162:170–74, 176–77). On the dates of these letters and the events to which they refer, see Jean Baptiste Souchet, *In Ivonis epistolas novae observationes* (*PL,* 162:474); Hoffman, *Gottesfriede und Treuga Dei,* pp. 200–2; Sprandel, *Ivo von Chartres,* pp. 140–41.

that his rights had been infringed when Rotrou II, Count of Perche, had built fortifications upon a site which Hugh claimed was legally his. A hearing in the court of the countess of Chartres was decided in favor of Rotrou, and the matter was ultimately referred to the pope, who appointed judges delegate to inquire into the matter. The judges found it difficult to agree, especially because they considered the ecclesiastical protection of crusaders' property an unaccustomed novelty, and were accordingly unsure of the extent of the protection offered. Did it extend only to the personal property directly held by crusaders, or did it also include property that crusaders were obliged to defend? It was proposed that an appeal on this point of law be carried to Rome. In reporting these developments to the pope, Ivo confessed his inability to settle the question and still more his inability to preserve peace among the powerful men involved.[26] This case is crucial in that it involves the earliest direct invocation known of the crusader's right to preserve and protect his property during his absence on crusade.[27] That it should have been raised within Ivo's jurisdiction was ironic, for Ivo's enthusiasm for the crusade was limited.[28] The case clearly pointed to a recognition of this privilege of crusaders, even if the exact boundaries of the privilege were not agreed upon. It also demonstrated that within the first decade of the twelfth century local prelates might intervene on demand to vindicate the crusader's privilege, although in this case at least Ivo was clearly not sanguine about their ability to enforce their findings.

This matter was clarified by the formal written guarantees of the Church's protection of the lands, families, and possessions of crusaders which were commonly found in later concessions of crusade privileges. The First Lateran Council specifically spelled out this guarantee,[29] and it was repeated in greater or lesser detail in all of the subsequent major grants of crusade privileges—*Quantum praedecessores*,[30] *Ad liberandam*,[31] *Afflicti corde*,[32] and the rest.

As with the privilege of personal protection, powerful and wealthy crusaders sometimes sought from the pope personal letters of guarantee,

26. Ivo, *Epist.* 173 (*PL*, 162:177).
27. This was made clear, e.g., in *Epist.* 173 (*PL*, 162:177); cf. Hoffman, *Gottesfriede und Treuga Dei*, pp. 200–2.
28. Sprandel, *Ivo von Chartres*, p. 141, n. 14.
29. First Lateran Council, c. 10, *COD*, p. 167.
30. Otto of Freising, *Gesta Frederici* 1.37, ed. Schmale, pp. 200–6.
31. *COD*, p. 245.
32. *COD*, p. 275.

which spelled out in advance the immunity from attack of their property and possessions during their absence, and took them under papal protection.[33] *Littere executorie* of this type were usually addressed to a bishop or other prelate living close to the lands in question and commissioned him to supervise the enforcement of the privilege. Other letters of protection were issued directly to the crusader himself.

Other authorities, notably monarchs, might also extend protection to the property of crusaders. A number of cases of alleged infringement of such royal guarantees are docketed in the English close rolls for the thirteenth century.[34] Such protection might be made by arranging agreements between monarchs, as was done at the time of the third crusade.[35]

A famous twelfth-century case which involved the protection of the property and possessions of a crusader—that of Richard I—is discussed in the nearly contemporary *Quaestiones Londinenses,* two questiones disputatae which were held, apparently, in the canon law schools at Oxford during the last decade of the twelfth century. One of these disputations turned on the right of a papal legate to enter the lands of an absent crusader—a question having reference to the attempt of two papal legates, Cardinal Octavian, Bishop of Ostia, and Cardinal Jordan of Fossanova, to enter the duchy of Normandy during Richard's absence on the third crusade. Forbidden by Richard's seneschal to set foot in Normandy, Cardinal Octavian had laid the duchy under interdict and had excommunicated the seneschal. Nicholas de l'Aigle, who disputed the question at Oxford, upheld the crusader's right, under his privilege of protection from molestation, to bar even a papal legate from his domains. In this conclusion Pope Celestine III apparently concurred, as he finally lifted the interdict and forbade the legates to enter Normandy.[36]

The second disputation dealt with the same question, this time with specific reference to the harassment of Richard I's lands during his absence by the men of Bishop Philip of Beauvais. Master Nicholas de l'Aigle, who disputed this question also, developed the argument that

33. There are many such letters in papal registers and other documents of the twelfth and thirteenth centuries, e.g., *JL,* 10,514, 12,028, 14,445, 16,765; *Po,* 2,017, 3,302, 3,514, 5,489, 5,569, 5,827, etc. See above, n. 12–13.

34. E.g., *Close Rolls* 7 Henry III (1:553b), 34 Henry III (8:368), 56 Henry III (16:571–72); *Curia Regis Rolls* 26, Easter Term, 4 John (2:203).

35. Matthew Paris, *Chronica majora,* s.a. 1188 (ed. Luard, 2:330–31). Matthew's account here relies, as usual, upon Roger of Wendover: Richard Vaughan, *Matthew Paris,* pp. 21–34.

36. J. A. Brundage, "The Crusade of Richard III: Two Canonical *Quaestiones,*" *Speculum,* 38(1963), 444–45, 451–52.

since King Richard enjoyed papal protection while on crusade, he also enjoyed the right, if his possessions were attacked during his absence, to recover the lands and property of which he had been despoiled by such an unjust attack. This was true even when the attacker was, as in this case, a bishop; in such circumstances a bishop could not invoke papal protection to save himself from the consequences of his own folly. Rather, Nicholas argued, under such conditions the pope neither could nor should lend the bishop assistance, for the bishop, having broken the law, could not subsequently claim its aid to mitigate the consequences of his earlier action.[37]

The discussions in the *Quaestiones Londinenses* were apparently the most detailed and extensive treatments of the crusader's privilege of immunity from attack upon his possessions which the canonistic literature produced, but other aspects of the privilege found an occasional place in the disputations of the schools. One of them, which appeared in varied forms in different collections of questiones disputatae, dealt with the right of a crusading cleric to preserve his possession of an ecclesiastical benefice during his absence.[38] Other canonistic mentions of this privilege are few and add little to our knowledge of its scope or effectiveness.[39] The common *locus* of canonistic discussions of the problem was the decretal *Conquerente* of Celestine III, which was included both in *Compilatio II* and in the *Decretals* of Gregory IX. This decretal, however, was primarily concerned, not with crusaders, but with pilgrims, especially pilgrims to Rome. In it the pope specifically guaranteed the property rights of pilgrims during their absence upon pilgrimage and also forbade the initiation of legal actions against them during their absence.[40] It would seem that we have here an instance of a privilege originally granted to crusaders which was then extended to the whole class of pilgrims of which the crusaders constituted a part.

For the actual supervision of crusaders' estates and other possessions, various arrangements might be made. While the crusader's wife or next of kin might ordinarily be expected to assume the actual management of his affairs during his absence, additional safeguards were frequently em-

37. Ibid., pp. 445–50.
38. G. Fransen, "Les 'Questiones' des canonistes," *Traditio*, 12(1956), 569, 573; 13(1957), 483.
39. E.g., Paulus Hungarus, *Notabilia "Nota quod non possumus"* to *Comp. II* 2.20.un. (= X 2.29 un.) in Vat. Borgh. Lat. 261, fol. 77^{ve}: "Nota quod res ascendencium ad curiam romanam, item peregrinorum, nullus inuadere uel occupare debet."
40. *Comp. II* 2.20.un. = X 2.29.un. (*JL*, 17,604).

ployed. Diocesan bishops commonly assumed a general responsibility for the protection of the property of crusaders from their dioceses, as was stipulated in *Quantum praedecessores* and other crusade bulls (see above, n.27–31). For particularly important crusaders and especially for monarchs, it was customary to appoint a special officer charged with this specific task as a *conservator crucesignatorum*. This was done, for example, when Louis VII left on the second crusade.[41] The conservator was commonly an ecclesiastic, inasmuch as the guardianship of crusaders' interests was primarily a matter of ecclesiastical law. As has been pointed out, Suger of St.-Denis, while serving as conservator during the absence of Louis VII, functioned as a papal vicar in actual fact.[42] In the thirteenth century, *conservatores* were frequently appointed for lesser men as well. These guardians of crusaders' interests were also normally churchmen,[43] although laymen might be appointed, as for example when Gregory IX authorized two crusaders as guardians for the lands of the count of Champagne in 1238.[44] In England it was common for crusaders to secure from the crown the right to appoint attorneys, usually laymen, to defend their interests before the royal courts.[45] The duration of the attorney's commission was limited to a crusader's term (see below, p. 173–74). Crusaders whose attorneys died while their principals were on crusade or who had no attorneys to represent them might be granted a stay of hearing until their return.[46]

41. A. Grabois, "Le Privilège de croisade et la régence de Suger," *RHDF*, 4th ser., 42(1964), 458–59.

42. Ibid., p. 464.

43. For some examples see Jacques de Vitry, *Lettres*. . . . (1160/70–1240) 1:72–80 (ed. R. B. C. Huygens [Leiden: E. J. Brill, 1960], p. 74); Odo Rigaldus, *Registrum visitationum*, s.d. 23 July 1248 (ed. Bonin, p. 5); *Acta Stephani Langton Cantuariensis archiepiscopi A. D. 1207–1228* 45 (ed. Kathleen Major [Canterbury and York Society Publications, 50], p. 61); *Rotuli Hugonis de Welles, episcopi Lincolnniensis A. D. MCCIX–MCCXXXV*, ed. W. P. W. Phillimore, F. N. Davis, et al. (Canterbury and York Society Publications, 1, 3–4), 2:196, 224–25; Gregory IX, *Registres* 850, 1,153, 2,745 (ed. Auvray, 1:523–24, 656; 2:150); Innocent IV, *Registres* 2,962, 4,664, 6,420, 7,348 (ed. Berger, 1:444; 2:109–10; 3:194–95, 382–83); Urban IV, *Registres* 2,913 (ed. Guiraud, 4:45) and his *Registre caméral* 320 (ibid., 1:88); *Les Olim, ou registres des arrêts rendus par la cour du roi*, ed. A. Beugnot, 2:323. A form letter for the appointment of a conservator crucesignatorum is contained in the formulary attributed to Marinus of Eboli (Vat. Lat. 3976, fol. 206ʳ).

44. *Po*, 10,655.

45. *Close Rolls* 3 Henry III (1:393); 54 Henry III (16:260, 278, 281–84, 288–90); 55 Henry III (16:392). *Patent Rolls* 54 Henry III (7:484–85); 55 Henry III (7:587); 33 Edward I (11:368).

46. *Fleta, seu commentarius juris anglicani* 6.9.11, p. 383.

THE PLEA OF CRUSADER'S STATUS. The crusader who wished to avail himself of this or of any other of the crusaders' privileges had the obligation to lay claim to his privileges at a proper stage in any legal proceedings in which he was involved. The plea took the form of entering an exception to the demands made against him: "I will not reply, because I am a crusader" is the form given in one procedural manual.[47] The plea must be timely: the crusader could not first enter his defense to his opponent's case and then attempt to secure recognition of his privileged status. Rather, he must enter his exception at the first opportunity and refuse to proceed with the case on the grounds of his privileged position if he hoped to make good his claim. Against this claim, if it was properly entered, it was difficult to proceed; pleading against it, one manual noted, was a perilous business.[48] How perilous it was will appear if we examine the jurisdictional privileges conferred upon crusaders.

THE JURISDICTIONAL PRIVILEGES OF CRUSADERS. Fundamental to the whole sphere of crusaders' jurisdictional privileges was their claim to the privilegium fori: the right to be judged by the ecclesiastical courts, rather than by the secular courts to which laymen were ordinarily answerable. Here we have once again the application to crusaders of the general law of the Church governing the status of pilgrims. Pilgrims, crusaders, penitents, widows and orphans, were protected by the Church, which asserted its right to jurisdiction over their actions similar to that it exercised over clerics.[49] While the early papal documents concerning the crusades did not specify this privilege, it may reasonably be assumed to have been a part of the general papal protection extended to crusaders' persons and possessions. That it was claimed and recognized during the twelfth century is evidenced by a number of documents and particularly by two letters of Pope Eugene III. In one, a decretal widely used in several different contexts, the pope ruled that a case which had arisen before the

47. "Le Livre des constitucions demenées el chastelet de Paris," ed. Charles Mortet, *Mémoires de la Société de l'histoire de Paris et de l'Ile de France*, 10(1883), 84: "et cil die 'je n'i vueil pas respondre, quar je sui croisiez'." See also on this subject Bridrey, *La Condition juridique*, pp. 151–52.

48. "Constitucions del chastelet de Paris," 69 (ed. Mortet, p. 78).

49. R. Génestal, *Le Privilegium fori en France*, 1:57–59; Walter Koch, *Die klerikalen Standesprivilegien nach Kirchen- und Staatsrecht unter besonderer Berücksichtigung der Verhältnisse in der Schweiz*, pp. 60–65.

crusader involved had taken the cross did not fall under the crusader's privilegium fori.[50] In the other, the pope dealt with a case brought against a crusader in the ecclesiastical courts over a vexed and complicated question of property rights.[51] The decretal implicitly recognized the crusader's right to the privilegium fori, in that the suit was before the ecclesiastical courts under the governing rule that the plaintiff must sue in the jurisdiction proper to the defendant.[52] The advantages of the privilegium fori to defendants are obvious; equally obvious is the interest of the secular courts in limiting as far as possible this extension of the jurisdiction of the canon law courts.

The first significant limitation came late in the twelfth century, when a decretal of Alexander III directed that the ecclesiastical courts were not to deal with cases in which feudal tenures and other purely secular affairs were at issue, even when such cases involved crusaders.[53] Further limitations followed. By the terms of a French ordinance of 1214, royal officers were allowed to imprison crusaders who were seriously suspect of grave crimes, although the Church might still intervene to rescue them after their arrest. In the same ordinance, the royal courts successfully asserted their jurisdiction over major crimes involving a sentence of death or mutilation even in the case of crusaders, while the Church retained its exclusive jurisdiction only over civil litigation involving crusaders and over lesser crimes—a compromise ratified by papal letters of the thirteenth century.[54] Beaumanoir outlined the law as it was recognized in his time.

50. *JL*, 8,959 = X 3.6.2; 3.50.2; 5.9.1.

51. S. Löwenfeld, "Documents relatifs à la croisade de Guillaume comte de Ponthieu," *Archives de l'Orient Latin*, 2(1884), 253.

52. C. 11 q. 1 c. 15. Formulas for mandates concerning crusaders appear in the late thirteenth- and fourteenth-century *Formulare audientie contradictarum*, ed. P. Herde, vol. 2, no. QV.359 and especially Q13, 1, Q13, 4b. Cf. no. 47 (ed. Herde, 2:55).

53. *Comp. I* 2.1.7 = X 2.1.8 (*JL*, 14,349); *Comp. I* 4.18.7 = X 4.17.7 (*JL*, 14,002). See also the gloss to these decretals in Gonville and Caius College, MS. 44/150, fol. 19[rb]: "Hic habes quod semper sub domino feudi questio feudi tractanda est si agatur de iure feotali, et extra e.t. ex transmissis et c. uerum [*Comp. II* 2.2.2 = X 2.2.6 (*JL*, 14,099); *Comp. II* 2.2.3 = X 2.2.7 (*JL*, 14,324)]." See also Bridrey, *La Condition juridique*, pp. 143–45.

54. Bridrey, *La Condition juridique*, pp. 178–86; Ferdinand Lot and Robert Fawtier, *Histoire des institutions françaises au moyen âge*, 3:275; Gregory IX, *Registres* 1,243, 3,731, 4,126, 4,163 (ed. Auvray, 1:704–5; 2:678, 911–12, 921); Innocent IV, *Registres* 3,592, 4,623, 4,641 (ed. Berger, 1:540; 2:100, 103–4); Nicholas III, *Registres* 171 (ed. Gay, p. 52); Matthew Paris, *Chronica majora*, s.a. 1246 (= *Po*, 11,776). See also Bridrey, *La Condition juridique*, p. 189–90.

Whoever has crossed himself with the cross of Outremer is not required to answer to any secular court if he so chooses in any matter concerning movable property or dwellings. Nonetheless, if the crusader is wanted in a criminal case or an inheritance case, the cognizance of the matter belongs to the secular court. In lesser affairs, the crusader may answer in the secular court if he so chooses.[55]

The thirteenth-century Norman customal also prescribed procedures for dealing with crusaders suspected of crimes, but provided that those who were of good character might be released until they had fulfilled their crusade obligation, on condition that they provided adequate security for their subsequent appearance. Otherwise they were to be held in custody until the proclamation of the next general passage to the Holy Land.[56]

In general, crusaders' jurisdictional privileges remained relatively intact through the latter part of the thirteenth century. The considerable agitation against these privileges in France during the reign of Philip III (1270–85) resulted in no fundamental changes, although the existing regulations seem to have been applied thereafter more rigorously than they had been before.[57]

THE PRIVILEGE OF ESSOIN. The crusader was entitled to other jurisdictional privileges, notably the right to essoin, or delay of juridical proceedings to which he was a party. Although the principle was mentioned by Vacarius in his *Liber pauperum* as early as 1149,[58] this privilege made its first explicit appearance in ecclesiastical law in the decretal *Consultationibus,* issued between 1173 and 1176 by Alexander III.[59] The decretal provided that judgment ought not be given against those who were absent by reason of study or pilgrimage from the proceedings to which they were party, save where they had absented themselves contumaciously.[60] Richardus Anglicus in commenting upon dilatory exceptions

55. Beaumanoir, ch. 11 § 318 (ed. Salmon, 1:156). Also, ch. 43 § 1322 (ed. Salmon, 2:180): "Veves fames et croisié se pueent bien obligier en deterie ou en plegerie, ou en quel que plet qu'il leur plera, par devant la justice laie; ou, s'il leur plest, il ne respondront fors par devant leur ordinaire."

56. *L'Ancienne Coutume de Normandie* 1.2.24 (ed. W. L. de Gruchy, pp. 63–64).

57. Campbell, "Clerical Immunities," pp. 416–17.

58. Vacarius, *The Liber Pauperum* 1.6, gloss to c. 13 (ed. F. de Zulueta, p. 12).

59. *Comp. I* 1.21.5 = X 1.29.10 (JL, 12,636).

60. *Comp. II* 2.8.1 = X——(JL, 13,734).

in general gave the term of delay as nine months only, but when the principle was confirmed with explicit reference to crusaders by Innocent III in *Ad liberandam,* the term of essoin was set at one year.[61]

The crusader's essoin seems to have been readily accepted by the secular courts. In England, Ranulf Glanvill, who died in 1190 while on crusade with Richard I, dealt briefly with the pilgrimage essoin in his *Tractatus* (completed in 1189) and set the term of essoin for the Jerusalem pilgrimage at one year.[62] In the great common law manual written between 1250 and 1258, Bracton discussed in detail the varieties of crusader essoin and the term allotted for it, which varied according to whether the crusader was participating in a general passage or in a plain pilgrimage to the Holy Land. For a simple pilgrimage, the term was a full year and a day, with an additional essoin *de malo veniendi* of a further fifteen days after return before the pilgrim was responsible for answering in the courts. For a general passage, however, Bracton allotted an essoin without fixed term, lasting until the return of the crusader or the receipt of definite news of his death.[63] The crusader's essoin, as Bracton explained it, applied not only to stays of judicial processes against him, but also to other services which he might owe to the king.[64] *Fleta* (ca.1290) wrote of the essoin in similar terms, and also gave the form for entering notice on the court rolls.[65]

Among thirteenth-century French legal writers who treated the crusader's essoin, Beaumanoir was more liberal in his interpretation than Bracton, allowing the crusader up to a year and a day after his return to make his response to charges brought during his absence.[66] The Anglo-Norman *Miroir des justices* noted that the essoin was never allowed to the plaintiff and that the defendant might not claim the privilege if he were summoned a reasonable time before his departure on crusade. Like Bracton, the *Miroir* distinguished between the essoin allowed for a simple passage (one year) and for a general passage (without fixed term).[67] The *Ancienne Coutume de Normandie* similarly allowed an essoin of one year

61. Richardus Anglicus, *Summa de ordine iudicario* 22, in *Quellen,* ed. Wahrmund, 2/3:28; *COD,* p. 245.

62. Glanvill, *Tractatus de legibus et consuetudinibus regni Anglie* 2.29 (ed. and trans. G. D. G. Hall, pp. 16–17).

63. Bracton, *De legibus et consuetudinibus Angliae* 5/2.1 (ed. Sir Travers Twiss, 5:158–60).

64. Ibid., 5/2.3 (ed. Twiss, 5:164).

65. *Fleta* 6.7.2, 6.8.1–2, 5–6, pp. 381–83.

66. Beaumanoir, ch. 8 § 265 (ed. Salmon 1:135).

67. *Le Miroir des justices* 2.30, in *Traités sur les coutumes Anglo-Normandes,* ed. David Houard, 4:484–85.

and a day to crusaders (presumably for a simple passage) and set a maximum limit of seven years for the essoin for a general passage.[68]

There is ample evidence from the thirteenth-century judicial and administrative records of the English kingdom that the crusader's essoin was frequently pled and was almost always respected in the royal courts.[69] The few cases where it was questioned were ones in which there was an apparent abuse of the privilege: in one case the crusader admitted that he had taken the cross four years before and had seemingly done nothing about preparing for his journey, in another it was charged that he had assumed the cross only after the charges were made against him.[70]

THE PRIVILEGE OF SPEEDY JUSTICE. To facilitate the work of the crusade and to assure maximum participation by those who had vowed to go, the crusader was entitled to a speedy settlement of outstanding litigation in which he was involved. Processes in the ecclesiastical courts were notoriously slow-moving and the secular courts were frequently not much better. Accordingly, there was occasional intervention, both from popes and from secular authorities, to hasten the disposition of matters in which crusaders were involved.[71] *Fleta* noted, as an example of special cases in which a short summons was allowed, those brought by merchants against crusaders.[72]

Another device to cut down the delay involved in settling disputes was the imposition of a rule against citing crusaders to answer in courts

---

68. *L'Ancienne Coutume de Normandie* 1.4.45 (ed. de Gruchy, p. 124). An attenuated remnant of the crusader's essoin was in later French law was the privilege, still alive in the seventeenth century, by which gentlemen serving in the army were allowed a one-year stay in the processing of judicial actions against them: Olivier Martin, *Histoire de la coutume de la prévôté et vicomté de Paris,* 2:588, n. 2.

69. *Curia Regis Rolls* 25, Michaelmas Term, 3 John (2:58); 26, Easter Term, 4 John (2:196); 31, Trinity Term, 5 John (2:275–76); 30, Trinity Term, 5 John (2:294); 33, Michaelmas Term, 6 John (3:193, 205); 60 B, Hilary Term, 10 John (7:314); 71, Michaelmas Term, 3–4 Henry III (8:23–24, 58, 71–72); 72, Easter Term, 4 Henry III (9:24); 79, Hilary Term, 5 Henry III (9:18); 89, Hilary Term, 9 Henry III (12:47–48); 97, Trinity Term, 11 Henry III (13:69); 109, Trinity Term, 15 Henry III (14:422). *Close Rolls* 4 Henry III (1:413), 6 Henry III (1:515b), 25 Henry III (6:287–88), 37 Henry III (9:512), 38 Henry III (10:108).

70. *Curia Regis Rolls,* 41, Hilary Term, 7 John (4:71–72); 59, Hilary Term, 15 John (7:107).

71. E.g., *Close Rolls* 36 Henry III (9:231); see also the formulas for letters on this matter in the *Formulare audientie contradictarum,* Cambridge, St. John's College, MS. 142, fol. 6ᵛ–7ʳ.

72. *Fleta* 6.6.11 (1647 ed., pp. 378–79).

outside their own dioceses as long as they were prepared to state their cases before the court of their ordinaries.[73] This seems to have been a special amplification of the general law, enacted by the Fourth Lateran Council, forbidding the ecclesiastical courts to compel defendants to make more than a two-day journey outside their dioceses in order to answer papal rescripts affecting their interests, unless this were agreeable to the parties involved.[74]

THE PRIVILEGE OF PAPAL COMPOSITION. This privilege, in effect, substituted the devotion of goods or services to the crusade in place of the restitution normally required in cases involving stolen property. The general law of the Church required that property stolen from its rightful owner must be restored before absolution could be granted.[75] When the article could not be found or recovered, however, restitution of its value or the devotion of its value to pious causes was demanded, a settlement which was known as papal composition. In 1237 Gregory IX declared that the crusade was a pious cause in this sense; thereafter papal composition became a common feature of crusade privileges throughout the later middle ages.[76]

THE FINANCIAL PRIVILEGES OF CRUSADERS. Among the most valuable and coveted privileges to which crusaders were entitled were economic and financial advantages.

First among them we may consider the crusader's right to dispose of property, much of which was in the ordinary way of things inalienable. Under this heading might be included the right to sell lands outright, and to mortgage or hypothecate them, even including fiefs. Allied to this privilege was the right of clerical crusaders to mortgage the income of their benefices in order to raise money to defray crusade expenses, and to make direct use of a fraction of the total income of their benefices during their absence on crusade.

73. *Po*, 18,366, 18,666, 19,163; Richard of Swinfield, *Registrum*, ed. Capes, pp. 61–62.
74. Fourth Lateran Council, c. 37 (*COD*, pp. 227–28); *Comp. IV* 1.2.5 = X 1.3.28. The *glos. ord.* to this decretal argues that the two days shall be understood in the ordinary sense of a day's journey, not in the technical sense, in which twenty miles was held to constitute a legal day's journey.
75. C. 14 q. 6 c. 1.
76. Paulus, *Geschichte des Ablasses*, 3:501–6.

THE PRIVILEGE OF ALIENATING AND HYPOTHECATING SECULAR PROPERTY. From the very beginning crusaders usually found it necessary to finance their expeditions by turning to account their landed property in some fashion. The mortgaging of the Norman duchy by Robert Curthose to his brother, William Rufus, for 10,000 silver marks was a well-known instance of such an arrangement during the first crusade, but the first explicit official notice of such a privilege occurred in the great crusade bull of Eugene III, *Quantum praedecessores,* in 1145. Here the pope provided:

> It shall be allowed to them also that when, after their relatives or the lords to whom their fiefs belong, have been warned, if these people either cannot or do not wish to lend them money, then they may freely and without contradiction pledge their lands or other possessions to churches, to churchmen, or to any other of the faithful.[77]

The meaning of the privilege was quite clear. The provision allowed the use of land as a security for loans of money (commodatio) and plainly envisioned that feudal holdings as well as land held in fee simple might stand as a pledge for the repayment of the loan. It also established a procedure for negotiating loans of this kind. The prospective borrower was expected to approach his family or his proper feudal lord first, to warn them of his intention and to give them the first opportunity to make the required loan so that they might receive the fief as a pledge in return. If these sources failed, then the crusader had the right to approach other parties, without reference to any residual rights of his lord and family— rights which under ordinary circumstances often would have made it impossible to place such lands in pledge at all. Although not subsequently reaffirmed in the great crusade decrees of the thirteenth century, this privilege was regularly used,[78] was recognized by the secular courts of the thirteenth century,[79] and frequently granted by royal licence in England.[80]

Ultimately this privilege contributed to the destruction of feudal land-

---

77. *Gesta Frederici* 1.37 (ed. Schmale, p. 206, trans. in *CDS,* p. 88).

78. Bridrey, *La Condition juridique,* pp. 43–44.

79. Bracton 2.6.4 (ed. Twiss, 1:156–58). Forms for such transactions are given by Joannes Anglicus, *De arte prosayca* 8, in *Briefsteller und Formelbücher,* ed. Rockinger, 1:507–8.

80. E.g., *Curia Regis Rolls* 25, Michaelmas Term, 3 John (2:13–14); *Close Rolls* 3 Henry III (1:383b); *Patent Rolls* 1 Henry III (2:25), 6 Henry III (2:320), 11 Henry III (3:120, 122), 12 Henry III (3:169, 188), 18 Henry III (4:74), 19 Henry III (4:93, 98, 99, 101), 22 Henry III (4:231), 54 Henry III (7:425, 441, 443).

holding patterns in Western Europe during the thirteenth century—a development of fundamental importance in shaping the future economic and social contours of Europe, for it made possible the spread of landholding among larger and more diverse sections of the population. As Gibbon put it, "The conflagration which destroyed the tall and barren trees of the forest gave air and scope to the vegetation of the smaller and nutritive plants of the soil."[81] In this instance the crusade privilege provided a useful technique to accomplish what was often desired for other ends.[82]

THE PRIVILEGE OF HYPOTHECATING ECCLESIASTICAL BENEFICES. This privilege was granted only tardily. Its antecedents went back to Henry II's Ordinance of Le Mans in 1188,[83] but it was not confirmed by the papacy until the beginning of the thirteenth century. In 1208, Pope Innocent III allowed clerics serving in the armies of the Albigensian crusade to mortgage the revenues of their benefices for a term of two years.[84] In a letter of 1213, Innocent further provided that clerics might pledge the income of their benefices for up to a three-year period in order to contribute to the support of warriors for the defense of the Holy Land.[85] Two years later *Ad liberandam* granted leave to clerics, where necessary, to hypothecate their benefices for three years in order to underwrite the expenses of their own participation in the crusade,[86] a provision which, like most of those granted in *Ad liberandam,* was reenacted verbatim in the constitution *Afflicti corde* of the First Council of Lyons in 1245.[87] Usual practice forbade laymen to receive the income of ecclesiastical benefices, but in these provisions there was no such limitation.[88] Furthermore, since the income could be pledged for a fixed period, the right of a clerk to the income of his benefice might survive his own death and accrue to his creditors, despite the fact that this right was a

81. *The Decline and Fall of the Roman Empire,* ed. J. B. Bury, 12 vols. (New York: F. De Fau, 1906–7), 6:446.
82. On this phenomenon and some of the other factors involved see Edward Miller, "The State and Landed Interests in Thirteenth Century France and England," in *Change in Medieval Society,* ed. Sylvia Thrupp, pp. 116–32.
83. Bridrey, *La Condition juridique,* p. 55.
84. *Po,* 3,510.
85. *Po,* 4,725.
86. *COD,* p. 243.
87. *COD,* p. 274.
88. *Charters and Documents . . . of Salisbury,* ed. W. Rich Jones and W. Dunn Macray, p. 151.

personal one which in law was extinguished with the death of the benefice holder.[89] This was, in fact, the only way in which the term of a benefice could be extended beyond the lifetime of a given beneficiary—a somewhat ironic legal anomaly.

THE PRIVILEGE OF NONRESIDENCE WITH FULL INCOME. Closely allied with the privilege of mortgaging a benefice was that of enjoying its full income, even though the cleric was nonresident while on crusade. The general law of the Church, of course, held that residence in a benefice was necessary for the enjoyment of its income, under pain of deprivation for notorious neglect of this requirement.[90] Granted that there were numerous exceptions to the rule and that it was often flouted, still the importance of this privilege for clerical crusaders was not negligible. If nothing else, it protected their legal rights and rendered their position more secure amid the perils of their crusade expeditions than it might otherwise have been. Certainly it made it more difficult for the clerical crusader's enemies to take advantage of his absence to call into question his title to his benefice.

This privilege is another which was not mentioned in the records of the early crusades and which first found a place in ecclesiastical law with the constitution *Ad liberandam*.[91] It was reaffirmed by the First Council of

---

89. Thus the question was posed in the *Quaestiones Borghesianae* 23, Vat. Borgh. Lat. 261, fol. 109[vab]: "Capitulum Bononiensis habet priuilegium quod mortuo aliquo canonico redditus prebende illius percipiebat per annum. Quidam de canonicis assumpsit crucem in subsidium terre sancte, uendidit redditus cuidam mercatori usque ad triempnium; iuit et mortus est ante triempnium; capitulum uult habere fructus, ratione sui priuilegii; mercator uult habere, quia emit et licite. Queritur quid iuris sit?" To this puzzle the solution was proposed: "Credo mercator est preferendus, quia priuilegium, scilicet ad liberandum, non est contrarium primo priuilegio, scilicet ciuili." William of Pagula, however, thought differently. In his *Summa summarum* 3.17 in Cambridge, Pembroke College, MS. 201, fol. 150[vb], he posed a similar case with a contrary solution: "Quid si prelatus crucesignatus alienauerit fructus ecclesie sue usque ad quinquennium, prout in priuilegio crucesignatis dato continetur, et idem prelatus moritur infra mensem in uia, arrepto itinere, nec pecunia dicti rectoris inuenitur, numquid firmus erit contractus usque ad predictum temporem? Dic quod non, quia ultra tempore uite locare non potuit." A sample letter authorizing a crusading cleric to obligate his income for an unspecified period may be found in the *Formularium* attributed to Marinus of Eboli in Vat. Lat. 3976, fol. 206[r].

90. See especially *X* 3.4.

91. *COD*, p. 243.

Lyons and confirmed by papal letters in numerous individual cases.[92] Hostiensis asserted that the right to the enjoyment of full income should be interpreted in the widest sense, so as to include daily distributions and all other forms of income for which personal residence was normally required.[93]

THE PRIVILEGE OF USING ECCLESIASTICAL INCOME ON CRUSADE. A final financial privilege granted to clerical crusaders was an authorization by Pope Honorius III allowing them to make use of one-twentieth of the gross revenues of their churches in order to finance their crusade expeditions.[94] Thus the clerical crusader could draw not only upon his personal income from his benefice, but also upon the total revenues of the churches entrusted to him. This, as the *glossa ordinaria* to the *Decretals* noted, was in effect a grant of subsidy to clerical crusaders. Crusading clerics were not liable to the crusade subsidy of one-twentieth, as non-crusaders were,[95] but were allowed to retain this fraction and to apply one-twentieth of their church's revenues to their needs while on crusade.[96]

THE PRIVILEGE OF MORATORIUM ON DEBTS AND EXEMPTION FROM INTEREST. One more important and amply documented privilege enjoyed by crusaders was that which granted them a moratorium on the

92. *COD*, p. 274; Gregory IX, *Registres* 18, 19 (ed. Auvray, 1:12); Innocent IV, *Registres* 2,304, 4,443 (ed. Berger, 1:341; 2:63); Urban IV, *Registres cameral* 313 (ed. Guiraud, 1:87), and *Registres* 1,986 (ibid., 3:318–19); Nicholas IV, *Registres* 5,229, 6,016 (ed. Langlois, 2:727, 807); John XXII, *Lettres communes* 60,796 (ed. Mollat, 12:184). Similar notices occasionally appeared in episcopal registers as well; e.g., Walter Giffard, *Register* 238 (ed. Brown, pp. 64–65); Thomas de Cantilupe, *Registrum*, ed. R. G. Griffiths (Canterbury and York Society Publications, 2), pp. 6–7, 290; Hugh of Wells, *Rotuli*, ed. Phillimore, 1:100. See also Bridrey, *La Condition juridique*, p. 53.

93. Hostiensis, *Lectura* to X 5.6.17, ad v. *Integre* (Venice, 1581, ed., 2: fol. 33rb–va^).

94. *Comp. V* 3.20.1 = X 3.34.11 (*Po*, 7,814).

95. Thus *COD*, pp. 244–45.

96. *Glos. ord.* to X 3.34.11, ad v. *Vigesimam:* "Quam soluere tenebantur omnes tam clerici seculares quam regulares ad subsidium terre sancte secundum quod fuerat constitutum in concilio generali in decre. illa, Ad liberandam, que non est in hac compilatione; sed qui erant cruce signati, uel qui etiam uellent signari, non tenebantur ad hoc: immo sibi poterant retinere, ut hic dicit."

repayment of debts and freedom from the payment of interest on loans from the day on which they took the cross.[97]

The basis for this privilege was laid down by the bull *Quantum praedecessores,* which provided that:

> Those who are laden with debt to another and who shall, with pure heart, begin the holy journey, shall not pay interest for time past. If they, or others for them, are bound by their word or by an oath for the payment of interest, we absolve them by the apostolic authority.[98]

This privilege was, it is true, a special application of a general policy which forbade the taking of interest by Christians at all, a policy which was in part an outcome of papal concern to protect noble debtors who were bound for the crusade.[99] Although the provisions of *Quantum praedecessores* on this matter did not find their way into any of the twelfth-century decretal collections, the very similar provisions of a later decretal of Pope Gregory VIII were incorporated into *Compilatio II* and later into the *Decretals* of Gregory IX.[100]

97. See Bridrey, *La Condition juridique,* pp. 199–233.
98. *Gesta Frederici* 1.37 (ed. Schmale, p. 206).
99. John T. Noonan, Jr., *The Scholastic Analysis of Usury,* p. 13.
100. *Comp. II* 2.16.4 = X 2.24.1 (*JL,* 16,078). The governing rule was interpreted to mean that no Christian was obliged to pay interest unless he had sworn an oath so to do. Thus in the *Collectio Lincolniensis,* tit. *De usuris,* in Lincoln Cathedral, MS. 121, fol. 26^r: "Super eo quod nos consulere uoluisti utrum clericus sit cogendus usuras creditori suo soluere preterea. Respondemus quod cum periculosum sit omnibus dei fidelibus usuras accipere, ad eorum solutione nullus Christianus sit cogendus nisi iuramento eas solvere uel fide teneatur, sed pocius creditores ab usurarum exactione ecclesiastica sententia prohiberi" (*JL,* 14,151; on the *Collectio Lincolniensis* see Kuttner, *Repertorium,* p. 291, and Duggan, *Twelfth-Century Decretal Collections,* pp. 138–39). The *Casus "Quesivit Anconitanus"* to *Comp. II* 2.16.4 in Oxford, Bodleian Library, MS. Laud. Misc. 646, fol. 24va assigned to the bishop the power of enforcing the provisions of this decretal: "Usurarii debitores astringuntur iuramento ad soluendas usuras, queritur quid sit faciendum? Resp. quod quilibet episcopus potest compellere creditores ut eis remittant iuramenta omnibus et maxime illis qui ad succursum terre sante proficiscuntur et ipse uel etiam quilibet suus heredes." Cf. the *glos. ord.* to X 2.23.1, ad v. *iuramenta:* "Recepta a debitoribus pro persoluendis usuris creditoribus que in preiudicium animarum quoad creditores seruari non possunt, et ideo ratione peccati compelluntur creditores relaxare huiusmodi iuramenta: supra de iudiciis, nouit [X 2.1.13]. Sed quantum ad iurantes non est peccatum, infra de debitoribus unde soluere tenentur; sed si iurauit non repetere, potest illud denunciare ecclesie et sic compelleretur creditor restituere usuras quasi indirecte officio iudicis, infra eodem ad nostram ii [X 2.24.20]; arg. infra de cognatione spirituale, tua [X 4.11.7] et ii q. i si peccauerit [c. 19]. Vel compellitur relaxare iuramentum ut hic. Vel si nondum sunt solute, compelluntur desistere ab exactione, infra de usuris, tuas [X 5.19.17]."

With the proclamation by Philip Augustus in 1188 of a lengthy and detailed statute concerning crusaders' debts as a part of the preparation for the imminent departure of his own expedition on the third crusade, the privilege was extended, to provide also for a moratorium on the repayment of the loan principal. Debts owed by crusaders, whether to Christians or to Jews, were to be repaid in three equal annual installments, with the first payment to fall due on the feast of All Saints (1 November) two years next following the king's departure on crusade.[101] The statute contained detailed regulations limiting its applicability, and sanctioned the use of excommunication by the ecclesiastical authorities to compel obedience to it. No crusader, moreover, might be held to answer in the courts for debts contracted under the provisions of this statute until his return from the crusade.[102]

The statute of Philip Augustus provided the framework for the provisions concerning crusaders' debts which were written into *Ad liberandam*, and republished in *Afflicti corde*. Crusaders were to be immune from the payment of any interest on debts owed by them; if interest were collected the guilty creditor might be forced to make restitution. Secular rulers were to make adequate provision for postponement of the repayment of

---

101. Rigordus, *De gestis Philippi Augusti Francorum regis,* in the *Recueil des historiens des Gaules et de la France,* vol. 17 (Paris: Académie des Inscriptions et Belles Lettres, 1878), p. 25: "Usura autem non currit super aliquem a die qua ipse crucem assumpsit, de debitis prius contractis. . . . Constitutum est a domino Philippo Francorum rege, consilio archiepiscoporum, episcoporum et baronum terrae suae, quod episcopi et praelati et clerici conventualium ecclesiarum, et milites qui signum crucis assumpserint, de debitis suis reddendis, quae debantur tam Judaeis quam Christianis antequam crucem Rex assumpsisset, respectum habebunt a proximo festo omnium Sanctorum post diem motionis domini Regis in duos annos, ita videlicet quod primo festo omnium Sanctorum creditores habebunt tertium debiti, et sequenti festo omnium Sanctorum alium tertium debiti, et tertio festo omnium Sanctorum ultimum tertium."

102. Ibid., p. 26: "Si quis dominorum vel principum in quorum jurisdictionibus dicti creditores vel debitores fuerint, quod ordinatum est de respectu debitorum dando vel assignamentis faciendis, tenere noluerint vel teneri non fecerit, et a metropolitano vel episcopo suo commonitus, id infra quadraginta dies non emandaverit, ab eodem excommunicationis sententiae supponi poterit. Verumtamen, quamdiu dominus vel princeps monstrare voluerit in praesentia metropolitani vel episcopi sui, se super hoc creditori vel etiam debitori non deesse, et paratum quod inde ordinatum est tenere, metropolitanus vel episcopus non poterit eum excommunicare. . . . Nullus crucem habentium, sive clericus sive miles, sive alius quilibet, alicui respondebit super hoc unde tenens erat ea die qua crucem assumpsit, donec ab itinere suscepto redierit, nisi super eo tantum unde in causam tractus erat antequam crucem assumpsisset."

principal on debts owed to Jews until after the crusader's return from his mission.[103]

Serious difficulties arose over these privileges in the French kingdom during the 1230's. Although Pope Gregory IX in 1235 reiterated the principle of the three-year moratorium for crusader debts, he soon found it expedient to modify the privilege as a favor to Florentine merchants who had complained to him of their difficulties in recovering sums owed to them by French crusaders. But the Florentines, it also appeared, had insisted on the prior condition that the crusaders to whom they loaned money must renounce their privileged status. This, the pope complained, had not been his intention.[104] In consequence, he ordered royal officials not to cooperate with the Florentines in forcing crusaders to pay their debts, although he also directed that clerical crusaders be compelled by ecclesiastical censures to make arrangements for the repayment of the sums owed by them. To complicate matters further, the papal *scriptor* charged with dealing with this affair exceeded his instructions by also bringing ecclesiastical penalties to bear upon lay crusaders who were reluctant to discharge their debts.[105] Finally, in 1238, when the three-year moratorium announced in 1235 had expired, the pope summarily directed that laggard crusaders must pay up within four months and requested the French king to assist the Florentine moneylenders in collecting the sums still outstanding.[106] It was the memory of this muddled affair which led St. Louis in 1245 to proclaim further regulations on the whole matter in his instructions to his *baillis*. Reaffirming the principle of a three-year moratorium on the repayment of crusaders' debts, the king forbade the excommunication of crusaders for non-repayment and ordered that, if any crusaders had been excommunicated for this reason, their creditors were to be forced to secure their absolution.[107]

On a more theoretical level, the *Ordo judiciarius "Scientiam"* (written between 1235 and 1240) upheld the validity of a moratorium on the repayment of crusaders' debts, basing the conclusion upon the Roman

103. *COD*, pp. 245, 275.

104. Gregory IX, *Registres* 2,512–17, 2,766 (ed. Auvray, 2:34, 165–66).

105. Ibid., 3,723, 3,882 (ed. Auvray, 2:675–76, 771–73); *Po*, 10,381.

106. Gregory IX, *Registres* 4,180, 4,264, 4,198 (ed. Auvray, 2:932–34, 972–73, 949–51).

107. *Recueil des historiens des Gaules et de la France*, vol. 24 (Paris: Académie des Inscriptions et Belles Lettres, 1904), p. 303; Gerard J. Campbell, "The Attitude of the Monarchy toward the Use of Ecclesiastical Censures in the Reign of St. Louis," *Speculum*, 35(1960), 404–24.

law,[108] while Cardinal Robert de Courçon warned crusaders on moral grounds against raising money for their expeditions by usurious bargains.[109] It seems doubtful, however, that the cardinal's warnings had much real effect. Practically speaking, the risks involved were so great and the difficulties of securing repayment were so common that moneylenders of all kinds were inevitably chary of making loans to crusaders at all. It was, after all, much too easy for a dishonest debtor to shield himself behind the privileges of the crusader's status and to postpone for a long time or even indefinitely the repayment of his obligations. As a result, the credit of crusaders was virtually nil everywhere. Increasingly the only way in which they could raise loans to defray their expenses was by renouncing the privileges which had been granted to enable them to secure loans on easy terms.[110] After the mid-thirteenth century, a clause renouncing the crusade privilege became a common feature of contracts and agreements of many kinds.[111] Pierre Dubois, writing ca.1306, voiced the sentiments of his age and the lessons of experience when he urged, as one of his proposed social reforms, that crusaders should settle up their affairs with their creditors and shield themselves no longer behind privileges designed to make it easy for them to evade the financial obligations incurred as a result of their vows.[112]

THE CRUSADER'S EXEMPTION FROM TOLLS AND TAXES. The origins of this privilege of exemption from certain types of taxes appear to go back to the general exemption from new and unaccustomed forms of tolls extended by the First Lateran Council to pilgrims and merchants.[113] The next step in its evolution was the crusader's exemption from the general levy of 1188, the "Saladin tithe" whose purpose was to provide subsidies for participants in the third crusade. Those who had taken the cross were,

108. *Ordo judiciarius "Scientiam"* 9, in *Quellen*, ed. Wahrmund, 2/1:24–25.
109. Robert de Courçon, *De usura*, ed. G. Lefèvre, p. 77.
110. Bridrey, *La Condition juridique*, pp. 233–36.
111. Ibid., pp. 237–63; for some additional examples see *Patent Rolls* 33 Henry III (5:43); *Durham Annals and Documents of the Thirteenth Century*, ed. Frank Barlow, p. 181; Historical Manuscripts Commission, *Sixth Report* (1877), Appendix, p. 486. The renunciation of the crusader's privilege continued to be a normal feature of many French contracts and other legal documents until its final suppression as a useless relic by an ordinance of 1667; see Bridrey, *La Condition juridique*, pp. 265–66.
112. Pierre Dubois, *The Recovery of the Holy Land* 2.138 (trans. Walther I. Brandt, p. 195).
113. C. 14 in *COD*, p. 169.

for obvious reasons, exempted entirely from payment.[114] A more general exemption from tallage and census was accorded to French crusaders by the *Stabilimentum crucesignatorum* of Philip Augustus in 1214.[115] Finally, in 1215 the constitution *Ad liberandam* in this respect as in so many others set forth the mature canonical position regarding the crusader's exemption from tolls, taxes, and other exactions during the period of his service—a provision again repeated in 1245 by the First Council of Lyons.[116] There is evidence in the thirteenth-century close rolls that in England an exemption from tallage was sometimes granted as a royal favor to individual crusaders. In 1235 Henry III granted a general exemption from tallage in favor of London crusaders who were prepared to set out on their journey.[117] In France the evidence shows that while crusaders generally were immune from royal tallage and other forms of taxation, those crusaders who were citizens of towns were usually required to pay local municipal taxes, despite any immunity which they might claim.[118]

FINANCIAL SUBSIDIES FOR CRUSADERS. All of the privileges previously discussed may be viewed as forms of indirect financial subsidy to the individual crusader. The late twelfth century saw in addition the gradual introduction of schemes for direct money subsidies to him.

Once again we have here a crusade privilege for which there was precedent in the earlier law concerning pilgrims and pilgrimages. Although as a general rule the canon law strictly forbade the alienation of ecclesiastical property,[119] one of the very few exceptions allowed the use of ecclesiastical property in order to succor poor clerics or pilgrims.[120] On this

114. Mansi, *Concilia,* 22:577–80.

115. *PL,* 217:239–41.

116. *COD,* pp. 245, 275.

117. *Close Rolls* 5 Henry III (1:457), 11 Henry III (2:188b), 18 Henry III (2:408), 19 Henry III (3:82).

118. Bridrey, *La Condition juridique,* pp. 64–65. Hostiensis' remarks in his *Lectura* to X 5.6.17, ad v. *Gravaminibus* (Venice, 1581, ed., 2: fol. 33[vb]) indicate that the privilege was commonly ignored in his day: "Hoc autem sciendum, quod omnes tallie et collecte, non obstante abusu contrario hodie, generaliter sunt damnate. . . ."

119. C. 12 q. 2 deals with the matter at length.

120. C. 16 q. 1 c. 61; also Rufinus, *Summa* to C. 12 q. 2 pr. (ed. Singer, p. 323). The *Summa "De multiplici iuris diuisione"* to C. 12 q. 2 in Cambridge, Pembroke College, MS. 72, fol. 73[ra], follows Rufinus closely on this point: "Si quis fuerit etiam inopes clerici uel peregrini, illis de redditibus ecclesie ad tempus potest consului; uide infra c. xvi q. i ca. possessiones [c. 1] et infra eodem questio ca. sepe [C. 12 q. 2 c. 72]."

basis the granting of ecclesiastical subsidies to crusaders, who were, after all, peregrini and who were frequently *inopes* as well, was clearly in order. How frequently this may have been done in the early history of the crusades is difficult to tell, but at any event from the mid-twelfth century the Church began to experiment with methods of raising extraordinary sums of money for the express purpose of subsidizing crusaders and crusade expeditions.

The earliest of these schemes dates from 1166; further experiments of the same type followed in 1185 and 1188. The 1188 subsidies were derived from the Saladin tithe—a tax which, incidentally, the Scots characteristically refused to pay.[121] The scheme in all three of these early experiments with crusade subsidies was quite simple: to impose a direct tax upon the whole population in order to raise funds for the use of crusaders and the defense of the Holy Land. Obviously such schemes could not be and were not in fact conducted without reference to the secular rulers involved. In the three twelfth-century instances, the collection of the crusade subsidies was in fact carried out as a result of the agreement of the kings of England and France to levy a graduated direct tax, based upon income and the value of movable property, for a three-year period upon everyone, cleric and layman, in the two kingdoms. Exempted from computation in determining the tax base were some specific categories: the horses, arms, and clothing of knights, for example, and the utensils, gems, vestments, vases, horses, books, treasure, and ornaments of the clergy and the churches. The tax was to be assessed and collected in each diocese by a Templar and an Hospitaler especially deputed to this task and they were to join with them the priest and two parishioners in each parish.[122]

Pope Innocent III from the beginning of his pontificate was active in extending and regularizing this aspect of the Church's crusade activity. The topic recurred time and time again in the registers of Innocent and his immediate successors. Subsidies were directed to be paid to individual crusaders, either from general funds, from special taxation, or from the revenues of a specific diocese or religious house.[123] In 1213, Innocent directed that hollow chests were to be set up in all churches in order to receive alms for use as crusade subsidies. The keys to these trunks, which

---

121. *Councils,* ed. Haddan and Stubbs, 2:272–73.

122. Fred A. Cazel, Jr., "The Tax of 1185 in Aid of the Holy Land," *Speculum,* 30(1955), 385–92.

123. E.g., *Po,* 347, 3,787, 4,725, 5,652, 5,858, 10,469, 12,760, 12,761, 19,742, 19,769, 21,226.

were to be closed with three locks, were to be confided to the care respectively of an honest priest, a devoted layman, and a member of a religious order, who were to have charge of the collection and disbursement of the funds for subsidies to local crusaders.[124] Still further devices were originated by Innocent's successors. Clement IV allowed Portuguese crusaders, for example, to seize the illicit profits of usurers for a three-year period in order to finance their expeditions.[125] When the Second Council of Lyons decreed the suppression of superfluous religious orders, Honorius IV was quick to divert the proceeds from the disposition of their property into subsidies for the prosecution of the crusade.[126] On occasion, the income of vacant benefices might be channeled into crusade subsidies pending the appointment of new benefice holders, or tithes held without sufficient title by secular rulers might be required to be paid out to deserving crusaders.[127] The clergy were also requested by the First Council of Lyons to urge the faithful in their sermons and while administering the sacrament of penance to provide in their wills for legacies in aid of crusaders and for the defense of the Holy Land.[128]

Nor was the Church by any means the only agency to grant subsidies to crusaders, although the major part of the subsidies granted by twelfth- and thirteenth-century monarchs may reasonably be considered to have come ultimately from ecclesiastical sources. The thirteenth-century records of the English monarchy showed numerous grants of money for various crusade ventures,[129] and a considerable royal control over the collection and disbursement of money subsidies, even where they were ostensibly handled by the Church. Thus in 1252 both the bishop of Chichester and the abbot of St. Edmund's were forbidden to distribute to crusaders the

124. *Po*, 4,725.
125. *Po*, 20,427.
126. Second Council of Lyons (1274), c. 23 (*COD*, p. 302); also Honorius IV, *Registres* 77, 81, 84, 353, 456 (ed. Prou, col. 64–65, 66, 67, 261, 320–21); Nicholas IV, *Registres* 278, 461, 2,731 (ed. Langlois, 1:49–50, 88, 455).
127. Nicholas IV, *Registres* 2,025 (ed. Langlois, 1:360); Innocent IV, *Registres* 2,068 (ed. Berger, 1:308).
128. C. 3 (*COD*, p. 272); also Innocent IV, *Registres* 3,793 (ed. Berger, 1:574), and Clement IV, *Registres* 1,508 (ed. Jordan, 1:461).
129. E.g., *Close Rolls* 3 Henry III (1:391), 5 Henry III (1:449b), 6 Henry III (1:515), 32 Henry III (8:49), 39 Henry III (11:207), 43 Henry III (12:485), 54 Henry III (16:195–96). *Patent Rolls* 32 Henry III (5:19), 34 Henry III (5:58), 37 Henry III (5:168, 188). Historical Manuscripts Commission, *Reports, Various Collections*, 1(1901), 253–54. Form letters to authorize the payment of subsidies to crusaders are given in the *Formularium* attributed to Marinus of Eboli, Vat. Lat. 3976, fol. 206ᵛ.

moneys collected as crusade subsidies without the prior approval of the monarch.[130] Likewise, the king might prohibit the export from the kingdom of sums which had been collected as subsidies for the defence of the Holy Land, as Edward I did in 1282.[131] There was, obviously, ample opportunity for the monarch to apply to his own purposes and interests much of the subsidy money nominally raised for the crusade; that this was often done in practice cannot be doubted. The Würzburg chronicler put it succinctly: "Although the [crusade] tithe was carefully demanded and collected, it is nevertheless not apparent what advantage was thereby secured for the Holy Land."[132]

DISCIPLINARY PRIVILEGES OF CRUSADERS. There were some miscellaneous privileges to which crusaders were entitled by way of exemption from a few of the minor disciplinary regulations of the Church. Earlier noted were the release of clerics from the rules governing residence and those concerning the entering of taverns while travelling.[133] In the later middle ages other minor privileges were allowed—dispensation from some of the ritual requirements for celebrating mass, dispensation in part from the obligation of reciting the office, and the like. For the rest, however, clerics on crusade were at least technically obliged to abide by the usual regulations governing their state in life. For lay crusaders, perhaps the principal disciplinary privilege was the relaxation of the laws of fast and abstinence, so as to allow them to consume milk, cheese, and dairy products during fasting season.[134]

PROBLEMS ARISING FROM CRUSADE PRIVILEGES. On the whole, complaints about violations of the privileges of crusaders were comparatively few in number and minor in extent. The papal protection extended to them was, as St. Bonaventura noted, violated frequently.[135] In 1281, for

---

130. *Close Rolls* 37 Henry III (9:272).

131. Ibid., 10 Edward I (18:157).

132. *Annales Altahenses*, s.a. 1274 (*MGH, SS*, 17:410).

133. Stephen of Tournai, *Summa* to D. 44 c. 2, ad v. *Tabernas* (ed. Schulte, p. 63); Rufinus, *Summa* to D. 45 c. 1 (ed. Singer, pp. 89–90); Raymond of Peñafort, *Summa iuris* 2.7 (ed. Rius y Serra, p. 66); Mansi, *Concilia*, 23:481.

134. Paulus, *Geschichte des Ablasses* 3:511–12, 514–15.

135. St. Bonaventura, *Sermo III pro dominica in octava Paschae*, in his *Opera omnia*, ed. Peltier, 13:236.

example, the suffragan bishops of Bordeaux complained to the French king that royal officials in their dioceses were seizing crusaders in violation of their privilege and were refusing to allow them access to the ecclesiastical courts.[136] Other instances of such violations were reported, such as the seizure of the ships of intending crusaders in Sicily in 1186,[137] or the attack upon a royal crusader of which Innocent IV took notice in 1252.[138] There were instances of petty harassment, such as was reported in Lombardy in 1202,[139] and occasional cases of serious personal violence, such as the murder of a crusade preacher in 1234.[140]

|Rather more common are complaints arising from the abuse of these privileges by crusaders themselves—the bulk of them concerning abuses of financial privileges or suspicions that money collected for aid to the Holy Land was being embezzled by the collectors or their aides.| Gervase of Prémontré complained at length to Pope Honorius III of crusaders who had used their financial privileges to escape from their just obligations and to defraud their creditors; of embezzlement and plain larceny of the money in the hollow chests that Innocent III had ordered to be placed in the churches; of misuse of the subsidies actually paid to crusaders; and in general of the need for close and regular supervision of the financial provisions for crusade subsidies.[141]

Typical of other types of complaint was a protest made by Philip III of France to Pope Gregory X, centering on the abuses of the crusaders' privilege of ecclesiastical jurisdiction. Hiding behind their immunity from the secular courts, he alleged, crusaders were committing the most enormous crimes—theft, murder, rape—with impunity. This charge was answered by subsequent papal action to deprive crusaders of the benefit of ecclesiastical proceedings in criminal cases of a serious nature.[142]

In cases of notorious abuse of crusade privileges, the ecclesiastical

---

136. The letter is edited by H. Beauchet-Filleau in the *Revue des sociétés savantes*, 4th ser., 4(1866), 451–55; see also *Les Olim*, ed. Beugnot, 2:231–32, and Campbell, "Clerical Immunities," p. 415.

137. *Annales Colonienses maximi*, s.a. 1186 (*MGH, SS*, 17:792).

138. Innocent IV, *Registres* 6,150 (ed. Berger, 3:143); *Po*, 14,807.

139. *Annales Herbipolenses*, s.a. 1202 (*MGH, SS*, 16:10).

140. *Annales Marbacenses*, s.a. 1233 (*MGH, SS*, 17:177).

141. Gervase of Prémontré, *Epist.* 4, in *Monumenta*, ed. Hugo, 1:6–8.

142. Campbell, "Clerical Immunities," pp. 416–17; Langlois, *Le Règne de Philippe III*, p. 271. For an earlier protest against similar abuses, see Léopold Delisle, *Catalogue des actes de Philippe-Auguste* . . . (Paris: A. Durand, 1856), pp. 217, 509–10. I am grateful to Professor John C. Moore for drawing my attention to this and to other interesting episodes.

authorities were prepared to revoke the privileges earlier granted to crusaders. The general law of the Church already provided this avenue of remedy for complaints against the abuse of privileges of all kinds.[143] As early as 1216, Honorius III acted to strip of their privileged position those who had taken the cross while detained in secular prisons, hoping to avoid the punishment deserved by their past deeds,[144] and in 1231 and 1236 provincial councils at Tours decreed the loss of priviledge position for all crusaders who were guilty of murder and other enormous crimes —actions subsequently ratified by similar rulings of the Holy See.[145] Late in the thirteenth century the papacy acted to strip crusade privileges from those crusaders who unreasonably postponed departure for the Holy Land, thus striking at another common abuse.[146] Abuses persisted, however, as long as there were crusades. Even as late as 1478, Pope Sixtus IV found it necessary to revoke the indulgences of crusaders who were guilty of notorious crimes.[147]

It is remarkable how little of the papal legislation regarding the privileges and the practical problems of crusaders found its way into the canonistic collections of the middle ages and into the commentaries of the canonistic writers. Although the canonists recognized the crusader's status, obligations, and privileges, they never really came to grips in a systematic way with the problem of clarifying his role in medieval society. While canonists treated the problems of numerous other groups and institutions of their society specifically and coherently in special treatises and commen-

143. Richardus Anglicus enumerated reasons which might lead to deprivation of privileges in his *Distinctiones decretorum* to C. 11 q. 3 in London, British Museum, MS. Royal 10.C.III, fol. 22ʳ: "Hoc faciunt ut suo quis priuetur priuilegio: Scandalum, iii q. vi Quippe [c. 10].—Potestatis abusio, lxxiiii ubi ista [c. 7].—Fauor alicuius alterius di. xxii Renouantes [c. 6].—Atrocitas criminis, xxv q. ii ita nos [c. 25].—Auctoritas romane ecclesie, ix q. iii Conquestus [c. 8]—Renunciatio: expressa, vii q. i Quantum periculosum [c. 8]; tacita, extra de priuilegiis, si de terra [*Comp. I* 5.28.9 = X 5.33.6; *JL*, 13,739]." See also Le Bras, Lefebvre, and Rambaud, *L'Age classique*, p. 512; Van Hove, *De privilegiis*, pp. 283–85.

144. Paul Fournier, "Les Conflits de juridiction entre l'eglise et le pouvoir séculier de 1180 à 1228," *Revue des questions historiques*, 27(1880), 463.

145. Mansi, *Concilia*, 23:237–38, 411. Gregory IX, *Registres* 3,279, 3,502 (ed. Auvray, 2:459–60, 560–61); Innocent IV, *Registres* 2,230 (ed. Berger, 1:331); Gregory X, *Registres* 1,017 (ed. Guiraud, p. 391).

146. John XXII, *Registres* 68 (ed. L. Cadier, p. 25); Honorius IV, *Registres* 398 (ed. Prou, col. 285–86); Peter of Blois, *De Hierosolymitana peregrinatione* (PL, 207:1064) complained strongly about abuses of this kind in his day; see also Bridrey, *La Condition juridique*, p. 63.

147. *Extravagantes communes* 5.9.5.

taries, no treatise *De crucesignatis* has yet been discovered throughout the vast literature of the medieval canon law.

An adequate reason for this apparent anomaly cannot readily be assigned. As *miserabiles personae*, crusaders fell into a peculiar class. Although most of them were laymen, they had legitimate rights to ecclesiastical protection and thus were subject to secular courts in some matters and to ecclesiastical courts in many others. Given these facts, it is difficult to understand why the compilers of papal legislation in the thirteenth century found it preferable to omit from their collections almost all of the decretals dealing with crusading matters, save for the material on vows. Because of these omissions, the commentators had some excuse for restricting their treatment of the crusade primarily to the problem of vows. The apparent reluctance of the compilers of decretal collections to incorporate in them any substantial part of the legislation on crusade privileges apparently puzzled some medieval canonists also; Hostiensis in particular expressed his wonder that such practical information which was in daily demand could not be found in the decretal collections.[148]

148. *Lectura* to *X* 5.6.17: "Et immo practicatoria sit, et utilis, et necessaria nullatenus debuit remoueri . . . quia ipsam multi quotidie querunt, nec inueniunt. . . ."

CHAPTER VII

Conclusions

Take away from History Why, How, and to What End, Things have been done, and Whether the thing done hath succeeded according to Reason; and all that remains will be an idle Sport and Foolery, than a profitable Instruction; and though for the present it may delight, for the future it cannot profit.

William Camden, Preface to *The History of the Re-nowned Princess Elisabeth*

Intertwined throughout the history of the crusades and the canonistic regulations which governed them were the twin themes of pilgrimage and holy war—the former unquestionably dominant throughout most of the early period. The concept of pilgrimage and the juristic notions with which pilgrim status was garbed before the crusades began were of paramount importance to the development of crusader law. Both in the vocabulary used to describe the crusader and in the canon law which regulated his relationship to the Church, to his monarch, and to society at large, the pilgrim theme was repeated with numerous, sometimes subtle, variations.

In the eyes of the canonists, the crusader was and remained basically a pilgrim, albeit a pilgrim of a specific and favored kind, a pilgrim with a special goal. In the writings of the twelfth-century canonists, indeed, the crusade was somewhat difficult to separate from other pilgrimages. Gratian, the most influential and in many ways the greatest of them, did not, as we have seen, consider the crusader *in specie* at all. The obvious implication, in the work of a canonist who undertook so wide-ranging an attempt to describe the whole juridical panorama of his age, is that Gratian did not consider that the crusader had any status, situation, or

191

privilege which was sharply distinct from those shared by all pilgrims, of whatever kind or destination. Gratian's attitude was apparently shared by his disciples and commentators in the latter part of the twelfth century. Not until the great decretal collections of the very end of that century and the beginning of the next does a special vocabulary and a special treatment of crusaders in the canon law begin to emerge with any clarity at all.

But if the fundamental canonistic institutions which governed the crusader—the vow which made him one, the obligations which flowed from that vow, and the privileges which graced his new status—were derived, more or less directly, from his canonistic position as a pilgrim, it is nonetheless true that several of the leading ideas and institutions involved—most notably the vow itself—took sharp outline only under pressure of the need to refine them for the purposes of the crusade.

Thus when Bridrey and Villey spoke of the law governing the crusade as a spontaneous creation of the customary law, they misconstrued the process which was taking place.[1] Rather than the creation of a new, particular law for crusaders as a result of the *ad hoc* efforts of courts and legislators, there was a continuing effort to reshape the existing, but vaguely defined, institutions governing pilgrims along lines more suited to the particular needs of the crusader.

If the crusade was a pilgrimage and the crusader a pilgrim, it was at the same time, paradoxically, a holy war, and the crusader a much blessed warrior. In the legislation of the popes, it was this latter theme which became increasingly dominant in the century which began with the pontificate of Alexander III and ended with that of Innocent IV. Throughout this period the crusader was endowed with ever greater and more extensive privileges. His status was more closely defined, his privileges enumerated, the process of fulfilling or legally commuting his obligations clarified, his relationship to the rest of society spelled out in greater detail.[2]

Even more striking, however, was the way in which the crusade

1. Bridrey, *La Condition juridique,* p. 9; Villey, *La Croisade,* pp. 263–64.
2. This clarification and elaboration were, in a sense, symptoms of the declining vitality of the movement. The popular enthusiasm which had fired the participants in the early crusades no longer burned so bright and required constantly increasing infusions of privilege and regulation to keep it alive. John Henry Newman once remarked, in connection with quite another type of institution, that the history of society begins in the poet and ends in the policeman. The history of the crusades reflects precisely this course of institutional development.

gradually changed in nature. The pilgrimage motif, though still present, faded into the background, and the crusade, from being a specific type of holy war, directed against a particular group of non-Christians in a particular area, was transformed into an all-purpose holy war, an instrument to serve the politico-religious policy of the papacy in its combats with all sorts of enemies in all corners of the known world. Crusades against the Balts and Slavs, against the Hohenstaufen and the Ghibellines —these represented a thoroughgoing transformation of the earlier crusade idea. The crusade was clearly becoming the secular arm of the spiritual power.[3] In this metamorphosis, the legal status of crusaders played a major role, but in the process the canonistic obligations of crusaders had to be modified drastically. A crusade against Manfred of Sicily, for example, could only with grave difficulty be regarded as a pilgrimage. It could, however, be explained with some facility as a holy war of a special type—a holy war in which the participants were rewarded with the privileged status of the pilgrim-crusader in return for the services which they performed in other theatres of action. The crusade against the Turks, which occupied so prominent a place in the polemical literature of the late middle ages, was not in any real sense a pilgrimage either, although it might very plausibly be represented as a holy war against the Muslims. Thus the pilgrim motif of the early crusades became a convenient legal fiction, which served to justify the rewarding of knights and others with a privileged status that might attract them to fight for the objectives proposed by papal policy. Similarly, the use of crusade status as a legal fiction to reward those who gave financial support, above and beyond what was demanded of right, to the papacy in the thirteenth century and after may be regarded as another aspect of its transformation into a convenient institution for the achievement of ends rather different from those animating the first crusade.

The holy war concept of the crusade was certainly dominant during the later middle ages—say from the pontificate of Clement VI (1342–52) to that of Pius II (1458–64). The pontificate of Clement was a turning point in that he undertook a serious effort to use the crusade as a major weapon in a projected Eastern policy. Checked by the rising power of the

---

3. This is not to say that earlier crusade expeditions had been wholly innocent of involvement in the papacy's international policy. Some of them, such as the Albigensian crusade, were clearly at least as much concerned with implementing political policy as they were with any spiritual objectives. The late thirteenth-century changes in crusade policy, however, involved a sizable shift in emphasis and in style.

Western monarchies and prevented by them from achieving a freedom of political maneuver in Europe, Clement and his successors turned their sights to the Orient.[4] None of Clement's plans ever materialized, but at least as a vision and as a projected goal, the crusade in the East loomed large. Pius II's Eastern plans and projects—the last full-scale attempt undertaken by the papacy to launch a crusade in the East—died with him at Ancona in 1464.[5] Thereafter, although never formally abolished—witness the fact that the rite for blessing the crusader's cross lingers on in the *Roman Pontifical* to our own day—the institution fell gradually into desuetude.[6]

The developments traced in the foregoing chapters should be seen as part of the larger fabric of medieval social and religious history. The canonists whose opinions have been explored here and the popes whose legislation they interpreted were obviously not writing in a vacuum. The canonistic regulation of the crusades represented a continuing effort to adapt the institutions of the crusades to the changing conditions of medieval society and to the fluid political realities of the European scene.

The early crusades were in part a product of the eleventh-century reform movement in the Western Church and could recruit massive, if somewhat inefficient, armies on the basis of popular enthusiasm for pilgrimages and the strong currents of religious fervor of their period.[7] By the late twelfth and thirteenth centuries, new possibilities of alleviating land hunger in Europe itself had opened up, and the organization of economic life was changing in many areas. The growth of cities, new developments in agricultural technology leading to higher productivity, the in-

4. See especially Jules Gay, *Le Pape Clément VI et les affaires d'Orient (1342–1352)*, p. 163. Before his election as pope, Clement (then known as Pierre Roger) had been a notable preacher of anti-Turkish crusades; see G. Mollat, "L'Oeuvre oratoire de Clément VI," *Archives d'histoire doctrinal et littéraire du moyen-âge,* 3(1928), 239–72, and Philibert Schmitz, "Les Sermons et discours de Clément VI, O.S.B.," *Revue bénédictine,* 4(1929), 15–34.

5. Pius described his crusade project at length in the last two books of his journals: *The Memoirs of a Renaissance Pope: The Commentaries of Pius II,* ed. and trans. Florence A. Bragg and Leona C. Gabel, pp. 341–76; cf. the account of Rosamond J. Mitchell, *The Laurels and the Tiara,* pp. 227–37.

6. For a treatment of some sixteenth-century crusade ideas and of Luther's reaction against the crusades, see Kenneth M. Setton, "Lutheranism and the Turkish Peril," *Balkan Studies,* 3(1962), 133–68.

7. Some aspects of this background have recently been studied by Jeffrey B. Russell, *Dissent and Reform in the Early Middle Ages.*

creasing stability and power of Western European monarchies—all of these factors affected the recruitment and operation of crusade armies.

These changes were reflected in the changing methods that the popes of the thirteenth century and later employed to raise and direct their crusade armies, and in the canon law and its commentators. As the importance of money transactions in the economy increased, so too grew the need to raise large sums of cash to finance crusade expeditions. As new agricultural land became more readily available in Europe because of land clearance, reclamation of previously unusable soil, and the eastward expansion of Christendom itself, the attractiveness of settlement and colonization in the Near East decreased and, correspondingly, more ample and attractive privileges had to be devised to recruit crusaders. As monarchical power grew in the West, its development affected both the objectives and also the operational modes of the later crusade expeditions.

The canonistic glossators and commentators were, moreover, far from being mere passive interpreters of legislation. They played an active, creative role in the development of canonical jurisprudence, in the first place, by developing a theoretical framework within which legislation was interpreted. The development of the canonistic doctrine of the vow furnishes an example, for the whole elaborate analysis of the process of making a vow, of types of vows, and the more important elements of the doctrine of dispensation was their work, not the work of the legislators on whose texts they commented.

Another form that the creative role of the canonists might take was in ignoring or limiting aspects of the substantive legislation that they found useless, uninteresting, or unpalatable; thus they might effectively abrogate (or virtually so) the effects of positive legislation. This happened, for example, with the elaborate forms for letters dimissory which were incorporated in the *Decretum* of Gratian and which were rejected by the canonists.[8] I have shown elsewhere how the provisions of the decretal *Ex multa* concerning the right of husbands to make and fulfill crusade vows without the consent of their wives were restrictively interpreted by the canonists, so as to limit the possible implications of the decretal.[9]

8. D. 73 c. 1–2. The *glos. ord.* to D. 73 d. a. c. 1 dismisses these canons: "Hic intitulatur 73 dist. quae in scholis non legitur . . . et ideo quia in ea nulla uel modica utilitas continetur, ideo membranas occupare non debet. . . ."

9. "The Crusader's Wife." The influence of academic legal doctrine upon substantive law is a common feature of civil law jurisdictions down to the present time. Thus, for example, M. Cappelletti, J. H. Merryman, and J. M. Perillo, *The Italian Legal System: An Introduction* (Stanford: Stanford University Press, 1967), p. 243,

The legal institutions of the crusade, as the present study has demonstrated, were not static. Rather their history is a history of change, adaptation, and development, closely tied to the changes which were taking place in other areas of medieval life. The virtual limit of the development of the legal institutions of the crusade was reached by Hostiensis. From his generation onward, crusade institutions were in a state of stasis; predictably, their subsequent history was one of desuetude and gradual decay.[10]

---

remark that, "the work of legal scholars dominates the Italian legal process. Realistically speaking, the law in Italy is to a large extent what the scholars say it is. . . . Their formal authority is nil; their real authority is great."

10. A related point is made by Throop, *Criticism of the Crusade,* p. 289: "The decay of the crusading movement indicated by the criticism offered during the pontificate of Gregory X convinces one that the real crisis of the papal monarchy came before the dramatic debacle of Boniface VIII. Contemporary objections to the crusade prove that the papacy had lost one of its most powerful weapons against the rising national state."

REFERENCE
MATTER

SELECTED BIBLIOGRAPHY

The following bibliography contains information about the canonistic collections and commentaries, important other sources, and modern works frequently cited in the foregoing pages. There are several types of sources which are not individually listed or analyzed here, notably (1) the collections of papal registers published or analyzed in the *Bibliothèque des Ecoles françaises d Athènes et de Rome,* ser. 2 and 3, (2) English episcopal registers in the Publications of the Canterbury and York Society, the Lincoln Record Society, and the Surtees Society, and (3) English royal documents in the Publications of the Public Record Office and the Record Commissioners. For documents in these series the reader is referred to the listings in the *Repertorium fontium historiae medii aevi,* vol. 1, *Series collectionum* (Rome: Istituto Storico Italiano per Il Medio Evo, 1962). For source collections frequently cited in the notes, see the List of Abbreviations, Section IV.

1. *Canonistic Collections and Commentaries*

Abbas antiquus. *See* Bernardus de Montemirato.

Abbas modernus; Abbas Siculus. *See* Panormitanus.

Alanus. *Apparatus* to *Compilatio I.* Munich, Bayerische Staatsbibliothek, Clm. 3879, fol. 1ʳ–97ᵛ; Paris, Bibliothèque Nationale, MS. lat. 3932, fol. 1ʳ–69ᵛ.

Albericus de Rosate. *Dictionarium iuris tam civilis quam canonici.* Venice, 1581.

Albertus. *Apparatus* to *Compilatio II.* Paris, Bibliothèque Nationale, MS. lat. 3932, fol. 70ʳ–102ᵛ.

Alexander III. *See* Bandinelli, Rolandus.

Andreae, Joannes. *Casus summarii* to the *Decretales Gregorii IX.* Cambridge, Corpus Christi College, MS. 38, fol. 9ʳ–32ʳ.

——. *Glossa ordinaria* to the *Liber sextus decretalium.* In *Corpus iuris canonici,* vol. 4.

——. *Glossa ordinaria* to the *Constitutiones Clementis Papae V.* In *Corpus iuris canonici,* vol. 4.

——. *Novella commentaria in libros decretalium.* 4 vols. Venice: apud

Franciscum Franciscium, Senensen., 1581; r.p. Turin: Bottega d'Erasmo, 1963.

Apparatus "Ecce vicit leo." Cambridge, Trinity College, MS. O.V. 17; Paris, Bibliothèque Nationale, nouvelles acquisitions latins, 1576; St. Florian, Stiftsbibliothek, MS. XI.605.

Apparatus "In hoc quatuor causas." London, British Museum, MS. Royal 11.A.II, fol. 118ʳ–194ᵛ.

Apparatus "Labia sacerdotis" to the *Summa* of Heinrich von Merseburg. Innsbruck, Universitätsbibliothek, MS. 590; Munich, Bayerische Staatsbibliothek, Clm. 17562.

Arnoldus de Gheyloven. *Repertorium iuris.* Neustift-bei-Brixen, Stiftsbibliothek, MS. 4.

Augustinus Triumphus de Ancona. *Summa de potestate ecclesiastica.* Cologne: Arnoldus ther Hurn, 1475.

Baldus de Ubaldis. *Margarita Baldi de Eubaldis loco repertorii Innocentii super decretalibus.* Lyons: in aedibus Ioannis Moylin, 1540.

Bandinelli, Rolandus [Alexander III]. *Die Summa magistri Rolandi, nachmals Papstes Alexander III.,* ed. Friedrich Thaner. Innsbruck: Wagner, 1874.

Bartholomaeus Brixiensis. *Glossa ordinaria* to the *Decretum Gratiani.* In *Corpus iuris canonici,* vols. 1–2.

———. *Questiones dominicales.* London, British Museum, MS. Arundel 435; Lambeth Palace Library, MS. 39, fol. 31ʳ–66ᵛ.

Bartholomew of Exeter. *Penitentiale.* Cambridge, Gonville and Caius College, MS. 151/201, fol. 162ʳ–186ᵛ; ed. A. Morey, in *Bartholomew of Exeter, Bishop and Canonist,* pp. 175–300.

Benencasus. *Casus.* London, British Museum, MS. Royal 9.E.VII, fol. 161ʳ–190ʳ.

Bernard of Pavia [Bernardus Papiensis]. *Summa decretalium,* ed. E. A. T. Laspeyres. Regensburg: Josef Manz, 1860; r.p. Graz: Akademische Druck- und Verlagsanstalt, 1956.

Bernardus de Montemirato [Abbas antiquus]. *Lectura aurea domini abbatis antiqui super quinque libros decretalium.* Strassburg: Johannes Schottus, 1511.

Bernardus Parmensis de Botone. *Glossa ordinaria* to the *Decretales Gregorii IX.* In *Corpus iuris canonici,* vol. 3.

Bonaguida de Aretio. *De dispensationibus.* London, Lambeth Palace Library, MS. 49, fol. 116ʳ–118ʳ.

Burchard of Worms. *Decretorum libri viginti.* PL, 140:537–1058.

Casus in quibus solus papa dispensare potest. Cambridge, Corpus Christi College, MS. 38, fol. 63ᵛ–67ᵛ.

Casus "Quesivit Anconitanus." Oxford, Bodleian Library, MS. Laud. Misc. 646, fol. 22ʳ–29ᵛ.

Collectio canonum Hibernensis. Medieval Handbooks of Penance, trans. McNeill and Gamer, pp. 139–42.

Collectio canonum Lipsiensis. Quinque compilationes antiquae, ed. E. Friedberg, pp. 189–208.

Collectio Lincolniensis. Lincoln, Cathedral Library, MS. 121, fol. 1ʳ–61ʳ.

Collectio Tanner. Oxford, Bodleian Library, MS. Tanner 8, pp. 591–720.

Constitutiones Clementis Papae V. In *Corpus iuris canonici,* vol. 4.

Corpus iuris canonici una cum glossis. 4 vols. Venice: apud Iuntas, 1605; also ed. E. Friedberg. 2 vols. Leipzig: B. Tauchnitz, 1879; r.p. Graz: Akademische Druck- und Verlagsanstalt, 1959.

Courçon, Robert de. *De usura,* ed. G. Lefèvre. Travaux et mémoires de l'Université de Lille. Lille: Université de Lille, 1902.

Damasus. *Questiones.* Vatican City, Bibliotheca Apostolica Vaticana, MS. Borgh. Lat. 261, fol. 19ʳ–44ᵛ; Oxford, Bodleian Library, MS. Laud. Misc. 646, fol. 82ʳ–99ᵛ.

———. *Summa.* Vatican City, Bibliotheca Apostolica Vaticana, MS. Borgh. Lat. 261, fol. 1ʳ–18ᵛ; Oxford, Bodleian Library, MS. Laud. Misc. 646, fol. 107ʳ–128ʳ.

Decretales D. Gregorii papae IX suae integritati una cum glossis. In *Corpus iuris canonici,* vol. 3.

Durantis, Gulielmus, the Speculator. *Speculum iuris.* 4 vols. in 2. Turin: apud heredes Nicolae Bevilaque, 1578.

Extravagantes communes. In *Corpus iuris canonici,* vol. 4.

Extravagantes D. Ioannis papae XXII. In *Corpus iuris canonici,* vol. 4.

Formulare audientie contradictarum. Cambridge, St. John's College, MS. 142 (F.5).

Formularium (attributed to Marinus of Eboli). Vatican City, Bibliotheca Apostolica Vaticana, MS. Vat. Lat. 3976, fol. 25ʳ–380ᵛ.

Formularium Indersdorfense. Munich, Bayerische Staatsbibliothek, Clm. 7536, fol. 298ᵛ–374ᵛ.

Formularium penitentiariorum. Vatican City, Bibliotheca Apostolica Vaticana, MS. Vat. Lat. 3994.

Frédol, Bérenger. *Le 'Liber de excommunicacione' du Cardinal Bérenger Frédol,* ed. Eugène Vernay. Paris: Arthur Rousseau, 1912.

Glossa Palatina. Cambridge, Trinity College, MS. O.X.2; Vatican City, Bibliotheca Apostolica Vaticana, MS. Pal. Lat. 658; Durham, Cathedral Library, MS. C.III.8.

Goffredus de Trano. *Summa.* Cambridge, Fitzwilliam Museum, MS. McClean 137.

Gonzalez Tellez, Manuel. *Commentaria perpetua in singulo textus quinque librorum decretalium Gregorii IX.* 5 vols. in 4. Venice: N. Pezzana, 1699.

Gratian. *Decretum.* In *Corpus iuris canonici,* vols. 1–2.

Grégoire, Pierre. *Partitiones iuris canonici seu pontificii in quinque libros digestae.* Lyons: apud Ioannem Pillehotte, 1594.

Guido. *Casus "Scribit dominus papa."* Oxford, Bodleian Library, MS. Laud. Misc. 646, fol. 30ʳ–49ᵛ.

Guido de Baysio. *Rosarium, seu in decretorum volumen commentaria.* Venice: apud Iuntas, 1577.

Hieronymus de Zanetinis. *Tractatus de foro conscientie et contentioso.* In *Tractatus universi iuris* (Venice, 1584), 1:80ʳ–88ᵛ.

Hostiensis [Henricus de Segusio]. *In quinque libros decretalium commentaria.* 6 pts. in 2 vols. Venice: apud Iuntas, 1581; r.p. Turin: Bottega D'Erasmo, 1965.

————. *Summa aurea.* Lyons: Joannes de Lambray, 1537; r.p. Aalen: Scientia Verlag, 1962.

Huguccio. *Summa.* Cambridge, Pembroke College, MS. 72, fol. 116ʳ–159ʳ; Vatican City, Bibliotheca Apostolica Vaticana, MS. Vat. Lat. 2280; Lincoln, Cathedral Library, MS. 2; Paris, Bibliothèque Nationale, MS. lat. 3892.

Innocent IV [Sinibaldo dei Fieschi]. *Apparatus toto orbe celebrandus super V libris decretalium et super decretalibus per eum editis.* Lyons: in aedibus Ioannis Moylin alias de Cambray, 1540.

Ivo of Chartres. *Decretum. PL,* 161:59–1036.

————. *Panormia. PL,* 161:1045–1344.

Jacobus de Albegna. *Apparatus* to *Compilatio V.* London, British Museum, MS. Royal 11.C.VII, fol. 246ʳ–271ᵛ.

Joannes de Deo. *Libellus dispensationum.* Cambridge, Gonville and Caius College, MS. 71/38, fol. 1ʳ–11ᵛ.

Joannes Faventinus. *Summa.* Arras, Bibliothèque Municipale, MS. 1064 (271), fol. 1ʳ–148ᵛ; London, British Museum, MS. Add. 18369, fol. 1ʳ–166ʳ, and MS. Royal 9.E.VII, fol. 1ʳ–160ʳ; Oxford, Bodleian Library, MS. Tanner 8, pp. 301–586.

Joannes Hispanus. *Flores totius decreti.* In *Corpus iuris canonici,* vol. 2.

Joannes Teutonicus [Johann Zemeke]. *Apparatus* to *Compilatio III.* Munich, Bayerische Staatsbibliothek, Clm. 3879, fol. 150ʳ–266ᵛ.

————. *Apparatus* to *Compilatio IV.* Cambridge, Gonville and Caius College, MS. 28/17, pp. 329–81, and MS. 44/150, fol. 120ʳ–151ᵛ; Durham, Cathedral Library, MS. C.III.4, fol. 202ʳ–231ᵛ.

————. *Glossa ordinaria* to the *Decretum Gratiani.* In *Corpus iuris canonici,* vols. 1–2.

Die Kanones der wichtigsten altkirchlichen Concilien nebst den apostolischen Kanones, ed. Friedrich Lauchert. Sammlung ausgewahlter kirchen- und dogmengeschichtlicher Quellenschriften, 12. Frankfurt a/M.: Minerva, 1961.

Laurentius Hispanus. *Apparatus* to *Compilatio III*. Paris, Bibliothèque Nationale, MS. lat. 3932, fol. 103^r–201^v.

Lemoine, Jean. *Apparatus* to the *Extravagantes communes*. In *Corpus iuris canonici*, vol. 4.

Libellus de dispensationibus. London, British Museum, MS. Arundel 435, fol. 300^r–304^r.

Liber sextus decretalium D. Bonifacii papae VII. In *Corpus iuris canonici*, vol. 4.

Ludovicus Bologninus de Bologna. *Tabula*. In *Corpus iuris canonici*, vol. 3.

————. *Tractatus solennis et quotidianus de indulgentiis*. In *Tractatus universi iuris* (Venice, 1584), 3:87^v–104^r.

Lyndwood, William. *Provinciale, seu constitutiones Angliae*. Oxford: R. Davis, 1679.

Martinus Polonus. *Margarita Decreti*. In *Corpus iuris canonici*, vol. 2.

Medieval Handbooks of Penance, ed. and trans. John T. McNeill and Helena M. Gamer. Records of Civilization, Sources and Studies, 29. New York: Columbia University Press, 1938.

Monaldus. *Summa in iure canonico*. London, Lambeth Palace Library, MS. 39, fol. 67^r–232^r.

Notabilia "Aliter debet." Cambridge, Gonville and Caius College, MS. 23/12.

Notabilia "Potius utendum est." Vatican City, Bibliotheca Apostolica Vaticana, MS. Borgh. Lat. 261, fol. 111^r–121^v.

Notabilia "Prompte volentibus." Cambridge, Corpus Christi College, MS. 38, fol. 127^r–161^r.

Opusculum tripartitum de decimis, de voto et redemptione votorum, et de septem sacramentis. Munich, Bayerische Staatsbibliothek, Clm. 5664, fol. 175^r–221^v.

Ordo judiciarius "Scientiam." In *Quellen zur Geschichte des römisch-canonischen Processes im Mittelalter*, ed. Ludwig Wahrmund (Innsbruck: Wagner, 1913), 2/1.

Panormitanus [Niccolo Tedeschi; Abbas Siculus; Abbas modernus]. *Commentaria*. 7 pts. in 3 vols. Venice, 1571.

Paucapalea. *Die Summa des Paucapalea über das Decretum Gratiani*, ed. Johann Friedrich von Schulte. Giessen: Emil Roth, 1890.

Paulus Hungarus. *Notabilia "Nota quod non possumus."* Vatican City, Bibliotheca Apostolica Vaticana, MS. Borgh. Lat. 261, fol. 76^r–80^r; Oxford, Bodleian Library, MS. Laud. Misc. 646, fol. 65^v–74^r.

Peter of Blois. *Summa*. London, British Museum, MS. Royal 10.B.IV, fol. 9^v–32^v.

Petrus Salinensis. *Lectura super Decreta*. Durham, Cathedral Library, MS. C.II.6; London, British Museum, MS. Arundel 435.

Pseudo-Isidore. *Decretales Pseudo-Isidorianae et Capitula Angilramni,* ed.
Paul Hinschius. Leipzig, 1863; r.p. Aalen: Scientia Verlag, 1963.

Quaestiones Borghesianae. Vatican City, Bibliotheca Apostolica Vaticana, MS.
Borgh. Lat. 261, fol. 103ʳ–110ᵛ.

Quaestiones Londinenses. London, British Museum, MS. Royal 9.E.VII, fol.
191ʳ–198ᵛ.

Quinque compilationes antiquae necnon Collectio canonum Lipsiensis, ed. E.
Friedberg. Leipzig: B. Tauchnitz, 1882; r.p. Graz: Akademische Druck-
und Verlagsanstalt, 1956.

Raymond of Peñafort, St. *Summa de casibus penitentiae.* Verona: ex typographia Seminarii, 1744; Innsbruck, Universitätsbibliothek, MSS. 266 and
339.

——. *Summa iuris. Sancti Raymundi de Penyafort opera omnia,* ed. José
Rius y Serra, 1. Barcelona: Universidad de Barcelona, 1945; Vatican City,
Bibliotheca Apostolica Vaticana, MS. Borgh. Lat. 261, fol. 91ʳ–102ᵛ.

——. *Summa de matrimonio.* Innsbruck, Universitätsbibliothek, MS. 266.

Richardus Anglicus. *Apparatus* to *Compilatio I.* London, Lambeth Palace
Library, MS. 105, fol. 137ʳ–213ᵛ; Munich, Bayerische Staatsbibliothek, Clm.
6352, fol. 1ʳ–80ʳ.

——. *Distinctiones decretorum.* London, British Museum, MS. Royal
10.C.III, fol. 4ʳ–48ᵛ.

——. *Summa de ordine iudiciario.* In *Quellen zur Geschichte des römisch-
kanonischen Processes im Mittelalter,* ed. Ludwig Wahrmund (Innsbruck:
Wagner, 1915), 2/3.

Robert of Flamborough. *Penitentiale.* Cambridge, Corpus Christi College, MS.
441; University Library, MS. Ii.6.18, fol. 3ʳ–129ᵛ, and MS. Kk.6.1, fol. 1ʳ–
97ᵛ.

Rufinus. *Die Summa magistri Rufini zum Decretum Gratiani,* ed. Heinrich
Singer. Paderborn: Ferdinand Schöningh, 1902; r.p. Aalen: Scientia Verlag,
1963.

Sicardus of Cremona. *Summa.* London, British Museum, MS. Add. 18367.

Simon of Bisignano. *Summa.* London, British Museum, MS. Royal 10.A.III.

Sinibaldo dei Fieschi. *See* Innocent IV.

Les Statuta ecclesiae antiqua, ed. Charles Munier. Bibliothèque de l'Institut de
droit canonique de l'Université de Strasbourg, 5. Paris: Presses Universitaires
de France, 1960.

Stephen of Tournai. *Die Summa des Stephanus Tornacensis über das Decretum Gratiani,* ed. Johann Friedrich von Schulte. Giessen: Emil Roth, 1891;
r.p. Aalen: Scientia Verlag, 1965.

Summa "De iure naturali." Durham, University Library, MS. Cosin V.III.3,
fol. 30ʳ–77ᵛ.

Summa "De multiplici iuris divisione." Cambridge, Pembroke College, MS. 72, fol. 68^r–75^v.

The Summa Parisiensis on the Decretum Gratiani, ed. Terence P. McLaughlin. Toronto: Pontifical Institute of Mediaeval Studies, 1952.

Summa "Prima primi uxor Ade." London, British Museum, MS. Royal 11.D. II, fol. 321^r–332^r.

Summa "Quid sit symonia." Innsbruck, Universitätsbibliothek, MS. 368.

Summa Reginensis. Vatican City, Bibliotheca Apostolica Vaticana, MS. Reg. Lat. 1061, fol. 1^r–48^v.

Tancredus. *Apparatus* to *Compilatio I.* Cambridge, Gonville and Caius College, MS. 28/17, pp. 1–134; Durham, Cathedral Library, MS. C.III.4, fol. 3^r–61^r.

——. *Apparatus* to *Compilatio II.* Durham, Cathedral Library, MS. C.III.4, fol. 62^r–94^v.

——. *Apparatus* to *Compilatio III.* Cambridge, Gonville and Caius College, MS. 28/17, pp. 135–328; Durham, Cathedral Library, MS. C.III.4, fol. 95^r–201^v.

Tedeschi, Niccolo. *See* Panormitanus.

Thomas of Capua. *A Formulary of the Papal Penitentiary in the Thirteenth Century,* ed. Henry Charles Lea. Philadelphia: Lea Brothers, 1892.

Vincentius Hispanus. *Apparatus* to *Compilatio III.* Vatican City, Bibliotheca Apostolica Vaticana, Vat. Lat. 1378.

Walther of Strassburg. *Summa de penitentia.* Vatican City, Bibliotheca Apostolica Vaticana, MS. Vat. Lat. 2663.

William of Pagula. *Summa summarum.* Cambridge, Christ's College, MS. Dd.1.2; Pembroke College, MS. 201.

Zemeke, Johann. *See* Joannes Teutonicus.

Zenzelinus de Cassanis. *Apparatus* to the *Constitutiones XX D. Joannis Papae XXII.* In *Corpus iuris canonici,* vol. 4.

II. *Other Sources*

Acta pontificum romanorum inedita: Urkunden der Päpste, 748–1198, ed. Julius von Pflugk-Harttung. Tübingen: Franz Fues, 1881; r.p. Graz: Akademische Druck- und Verlagsanstalt, 1958.

Acta sanctorum Ordinis s. Benedicti . . . , ed. Jean Mabillon et al. 3d ed., 3 vols. Autun: Protat Freres, 1935.

Adamnan. *De locis sanctis,* ed. and trans. Denis Meehan. Scriptores Latini Hiberniae, 3. Dublin: Institute for Advanced Studies, 1958.

L'Ancienne Coutume de Normandie, ed. William Laurence de Gruchy. Jersey: Charles Le Feuvre, 1881.

Augustine, St. *De civitate Dei,* ed. B. Dombart and A. Kalb. Corpus Christianorum, series Latina, 47. Turnhout: Brepols, 1955.

The Babylonian Talmud, ed. and trans. Isidore Epstein et al. 18 vols. London: Soncino Press, 1948–52.

Bartolus of Sassoferrato. *Opera quae nunc extant omnia.* 11 pts. in 4 vols. Basel: ex officina Episcopiana, 1588–89.

Beauchet-Filleau, H., ed. "Lettre," *Revue des sociétés savantes,* 4th ser., 4(1866), 451–55.

Beaumanoir, Philippe de. *Coutumes de Beauvaisis,* ed. A. Salmon. 2 vols. Collection de textes pour servir à l'étude et l'en–seignement de l'histoire, 24, 30. Paris: Alphonse Picard, 1899.

Bede. *Opera,* ed. Charles Plummer. 2 vols. in 1. Oxford: Clarendon Press, 1896; r.p. 1961.

Benedict, St. *Regula monachorum,* ed. Rudolf Hanslik. Vienna: Hoelder-Pichler-Tempsky, 1960.

Bonaventura, St. *Opera omnia,* ed. A. C. Peltier. 15 vols. Paris: L. Vives, 1864–71.

Bonet, Honoré. *The Tree of Battles,* ed. and trans. G. W. Coopland. Cambridge: Harvard University Press, 1949.

Bracton, Henry de. *De legibus et consuetudinibus Angliae,* ed. Sir Travers Twiss. 6 vols. Rolls Series, 70. London: Longmans, 1878–83.

Briefsteller und Formelbücher des elften bis vierzehnten Jahrhunderts, ed. Ludwig Rockinger. 2 vols. Quellen und Eröteringen zur bayerischen und deutschen Geschichte, 9. Munich: Kommission zur Herausgabe bayerischer und deutscher Quellenschriften, 1863–64 r.p. New York: Burt Franklin, 1961.

Bullarum, diplomatum, et privilegiorum sanctorum Romanorum pontificum. . . . 25 vols. Turin: S. Franco and H. Dalmazzo, 1857–72.

Die Bussordnungen der abendlandischen Kirche, ed. F. W. H. Wasserschleben. Halle: Graeger, 1851; r.p. Graz: Akademische Druck- und Verlagsanstalt, 1958.

Charters and Documents Illustrating the History of the Cathedral, City, and Diocese of Salisbury in the Twelfth and Thirteenth Centuries, ed. W. Rich Jones and W. Dunn Macray. Rolls Series, 97. London: Longmans, 1891.

Chartularium Universitatis Parisiensis, ed. H. Denifle and E. Chatelain. 4 vols. Paris, 1891–99; r.p. Brussels: Culture et Civilisation, 1964.

Concilia Magnae Britanniae et Hiberniae, ed. David Wilkins. 4 vols. London: R. Gosling et al., 1737; r.p. Brussels: Culture et Civilisation, 1964.

Concilium Tridentinum diariorum, actorum, epistolarum, tractatuum nova collectio, ed. Görres Gesellschaft. Freiburg i/Br.: Herder, 1901——.

Corpus iuris civilis, ed. Paul Krueger et al. 3 vols. Berlin: Weidmann, 1963.

——, with the *glossa ordinaria* of Accursius. 5 vols. Lyons: [Vincentius?], 1584.

Councils and Ecclesiastical Documents Relating to Great Britain and Ireland, ed. Arthur W. Haddan and William Stubbs. 3 vols. Oxford: Clarendon Press, 1869; r.p. 1964.

Councils and Synods with Other Documents Relating to the English Church, ed. Sir Frederick Maurice Powicke and Christopher R. Cheney. 2 vols. Oxford: Clarendon Press, 1964——.

Documents relatifs à l'histoire des croisades. 6 vols. Paris: P. Guenther, 1946——.

DuBois, Pierre. *The Recovery of the Holy Land,* trans. Walther I. Brandt. Records of Civilization, Sources and Studies, 51. New York: Columbia University Press, 1956.

Durham Annals and Documents of the Thirteenth Century, ed. Frank Barlow. Surtees Society Publications, 155. Durham: Surtees Society, 1955.

The Earliest Lincolnshire Assize Rolls, A.D. 1202–1209, ed. Doris M. Stenton. Lincoln Record Society Publications, 22. Lincoln: Lincoln Record Society, 1926.

Epistola ad Diognetum, ed. and trans. Henri I. Marrou. Sources chrétiennes, 33. Paris: Editions du Cerf, 1951.

Epistolae pontificum Romanorum ineditae, ed. S. Löwenfeld. Leipzig: Veit, 1885; r.p. Graz: Akademische Druck- und Verlagsanstalt, 1959.

Epistulae et chartae ad historiam primi belli sacri spectantes, ed. Heinrich Hagenmeyer. Innsbruck: Wagner, 1901.

Eusebius. *The Ecclesiastical History,* ed. and trans. Kirsop Lake et al. 2 vols. Loeb Classical Library. New York: Putnam, 1926–32.

Fleta, seu commentarius juris anglicani. London: Guil. Lee and Dan. Pakeman, 1647.

Fulcher of Chartres. *Historia Hierosolymitana (1095–1127),* ed. Heinrich Hagenmeyer. Heidelberg: Carl Winter, 1913.

——, trans. Martha E. McGinty [Book 1 only]. Translations and Reprints from the Original Sources of History, 3d ser., 1. Philadelphia: University of Pennsylvania Press, 1941.

Gerald of Wales. *Opera,* ed. J. S. Brewer et al. 8 vols. Rolls Series, 21. London: Longmans, 1861–91.

Gesta Dei per Francos . . . , ed. Jacques Bongars. 2 vols. Hanover: Wechelianis apud heredes I. Aubrii, 1611.

Gesta Francorum et aliorum Hierosolimitanorum, ed. and trans. Rosalind M. T. Hill and Sir Roger Mynors. London: Nelson, 1962.

Gesta regis Henrici II, ed. William Stubbs. 2 vols. Rolls Series, 49. London: Longmans, 1867.

Glanvill, Ranulf. *Tractatus de legibus et consuetudinibus regni Anglie . . . ,* ed. and trans. G. D. G. Hall. London: Nelson, 1965.

Henry of Livonia [Henricus de Lettis]. *The Chronicle of Henry of Livonia,* ed.

and trans. James A. Brundage. Madison: University of Wisconsin Press, 1961.

Honorius III. *Regesta* . . . , ed. Pietro Pressutti. Rome: ex typographia Vaticana, 1888–95.

Innocent III. *Die Register Innozenz' III.,* ed. Othmar Hageneder and Anton Haidacher. Oesterreichischen Kulturinstitut in Rom, Abteilung für historische Studien, Publikationen, 2. Abt., 1. Reihe, Bd. 1———. Graz, Cologne: H. Böhlau, 1964———.

The Irish Penitentials, ed. Ludwig Bieler. Scriptores Latini Hiberniae, 5. Dublin: Institute for Advanced Studies, 1963.

Isidore of Seville. *Etymologiarum sive originum libri XX,* ed. W. M. Lindsay. 2 vols. Oxford: Clarendon Press, 1957.

Itinera Hierosolymitana et descriptiones terrae sanctae bellis sacris anteriora, ed. Titus Tobler and Augustin Molinier. Société de l'Orient Latin, Publications, série géographique, 1–2. Paris: Société de l'Orient Latin, 1879–85; r.p. Osnabrück: Otto Zeller, 1966.

Itinera Hierosolymitana saeculi III–VIII, ed. Paul Geyer. Corpus scriptorum ecclesiasticorum Latinorum, 39. Vienna: F. Tempsky, 1898.

Kohler, Charles. "Documents inédits concernant l'Orient Latin et les croisés (XIIe–XIVe siècles)," *Revue de l'Orient Latin,* 7(1899), 1–37.

Lair, J. "Encyclique de Sergius IV relative à une projet de croisade," *Bibliothèque de l'Ecole des Chartes,* 18(1856–57), 246–53.

Layettes du trésor des chartes, ed. A. Teulet et al. 5 vols. Inventaires et documents publiés par la direction des Archives. Paris: H. Plon, 1863–1909.

Li Livres de jostice et de plet, ed. P. N. Rapetti. Paris: Firmin Didot, 1850.

Löwenfeld, S. "Documents relatifs à la croisade de Guillaume comte de Ponthieu," *Archives de l'Orient Latin,* 2(1884), 251–55.

Marche, Olivier de la. *Mémoires,* ed. Henri Beaune and J. d'Arbaumont. 4 vols. Paris: Renouard, 1883–88.

Matthew Paris. *Chronica majora,* ed. H. R. Luard. 7 vols. Rolls Series, 57. London, Longmans: 1873–83.

Mortet, Charles, ed. "Le Livre des constitucions demenées el chastelet de Paris," *Mémoires de la Société de l'histoire de Paris et de l'Ile de France,* 10(1883), 1–99.

Odo Rigaldus. *Registrum visitationum archiepiscopi Rothomagensis,* ed. T. Bonin. Rouen: August Le Brument, 1852.

———. *Register,* ed. and trans. Sydney M. Brown and Jeremiah F. O'Sullivan. Records of Civilization, Sources and Studies, 72. New York: Columbia University Press, 1964.

Otto of Freising. *Gesta Frederici seu rectius chronica,* ed. Franz-Josef Schmale, trans. Adolf Schmidt. Berlin: Deutscher Verlag der Wissenschaften, 1965.

Les Olim, ou registres des arrêts rendus par la cour du roi, ed. A. Beugnot. 3 vols. in 4. Paris: Imprimerie Royale, 1838–48.

Ordericus Vitalis. *Historiae ecclesiasticae libri tredecim,* ed. Auguste le Prévost. 5 vols. Paris: J. Renouard, 1838–55.

Pius II [Aeneas Silvius Piccolomini]. *Memoirs of a Renaissance Pope: The Memoirs of Pius II,* ed. and trans. Florence A. Bragg and Leona C. Gabel. New York: Capricorn, 1962.

Publications of the Palestine Pilgrims' Text Society. 13 vols. London: Committee of the Palestine Exploration Fund, 1890–97.

A Rabbinic Anthology, ed. and trans. C. J. G. Montefiore and H. M. J. Loewe. Philadelphia: Jewish Publication Society, 1963.

The Registrum antiquissimum of the Cathedral Church of Lincoln, ed. Kathleen Major. 8 vols. Lincoln Record Society Publications, 27–29, 32, 34, 41, 46, 51. Lincoln: Lincoln Record Society, 1931–58.

Richard of Devizes. *The Chronicle of Richard of Devizes of the Time of King Richard I,* ed. and trans. John T. Appleby. London: Nelson, 1963.

Sacrae antiquitatis monumenta historica, dogmatica, diplomatica, ed. Charles L. Hugo. 2 vols. Evital: J. M. Heller, 1725; St.-Deodat: J. Charlot, 1731.

Las Siete Partidas. 3 vols. Madrid: Real Academia de la Historia, 1807.

Thomas Aquinas, St. *Opera omnia.* 25 vols. Parma: P. Fiaccadori, 1852–73; r.p. New York: Musurgia, 1948–49.

————. *Summa theologiae.* 5 vols. Ottawa: Commissio Piana, 1953.

Traités sur les coutumes Anglo-Normandes . . . , ed. David Houard. 4 vols. Rouen: Le Boucher le jeune, 1776.

University Records and Life in the Middle Ages, ed. and trans. Lynn Thorndike. Records of Civilization, Sources and Studies, 38. New York: Columbia University Press, 1944.

Vacarius. *The Liber pauperum,* ed. F. de Zulueta. Selden Society Publications, 44. London: B. Quaritch, 1927.

Villehardouin, Geoffroi de. *La Conquête de Constantinople,* ed. Edmond Faral. 2 vols. Paris: Les Belles Lettres, 1961.

III. *Modern Works*

It is not the purpose of this book to treat in any detail the lives and careers of the various canonistic authors whose works have been dealt with here. For such information the reader should consult the appropriate entries in the *DDC* and the major secondary manuals, such as Schulte, *Geschichte der Quellen und Literatur des canonischen Rechts,* Van Hove, *Prolegomena,* Kuttner, *Repertorium der Kanonistik,* Plöchl, *Geschichte des Kirchenrechts,* M. Sarti and M. Fattorini, *De claris archigymnasii Bononiensis professoribus.* The best source of information in English on the major canonistic writers is generally the *New Catholic Encyclopedia,* which carries articles on most of the major figures referred to above. Current work is reflected in the listings of the "Select Bibliography" of the *Bulletin* of the Institute of Medieval Canon Law, published annually since 1955 in *Traditio.*

Abry, Alexandre. *Yves de Chartres, sa vie et ses oeuvrages.* Strassburg: G. L. Schuler, 1841.

Appleby, John T. "The Ecclesiastical Foundations of Henry II," *Catholic Historical Review,* 48(1962), 205–15.

Archives de l'Orient Latin. 2 vols. Paris: Ernst Leroux, 1881–84.

Argnani, Giovanni. "Ioannes Faventinus glossator: brevis commentatio de vita et operibus eius," *Apollinaris,* 9(1936), 418–43, 640–58.

Atiya, Aziz S. *The Crusade: Historiography and Bibliography.* Bloomington: Indiana University Press, 1962.

Balon, Joseph. *Ius medii aevi.* Namur: Les anciennes établissements Godenne, 1959——.

Bardi, Francesco. *Bulla cruciatae explicata et illustrata.* Palermo: J. Bisagni, 1656.

Barraclough, Geoffrey. "Bernard of Compostella," *English Historical Review,* 49(1934), 487–94.

———. "The Chancery Ordinance of Nicholas III: A Study of the Sources," *Quellen und Forschungen aus italienischen Archiven und Bibliotheken,* 25(1933–34), 192–250.

Belkin, Samuel. "Dissolution of Vows and the Problem of Anti-Social Oaths in the Gospels and Contemporary Jewish Literature," *Journal of Biblical Literature,* 55(1936), 227–34.

Benninghoven, Friedrich. *Der Orden der Schwertbruder: Fratres Milicie Christi de Livonia.* Ostmitteleuropa in Vergangenheit und Gegenwart, 9. Cologne: H. Böhlau, 1965.

Benson, R. L. "Plenitudo Potestatis: Evolution of a Formula from Gregory IV to Gratian," *Studia Gratiana,* 14(1967), 193–217.

Berger, Adolf. *Encyclopedic Dictionary of Roman Law.* Transactions of the American Philosophical Society, new. ser., vol. 43, pt. 2. Philadelphia: American Philosophical Society, 1953.

Berges, Wilhelm. "Kaiserrecht und Kaisertheorie der 'Siete Partidas'," in *Festschrift Percy Ernest Schramm,* 1:142–56. 2 vols. Weisbaden: Franz Schreiner, 1964.

Berlière, Ursmer. "Anciens pèlerinages bénédictins au moyen-âge," *Revue liturgique et monastique,* 11(1925–26), 205–13, 247–53.

———. "Les Pèlerinages judiciaires au moyen âge," *Revue bénédictine,* 7(1890), 520–26.

Beumann, Helmut, ed. *Heidenmission und Kreuzzugsgedanke in der deutschen Ostpolitik des Mittelalters.* Darmstadt: Wissenschaftliche Buchgesellschaft, 1963.

Bierzanek, P. "Sur les origines de la guerre et de la paix," *RHDF,* 4th ser., 38(1960), 83–123.

Bloch, Marc. *Feudal Society,* trans. L. A. Manyon. Chicago: University of Chicago Press, 1961.

Bonnaud-Delamare, R. "La Paix en Flandre pendant la première croisade," *Revue du Nord,* 39(1957), 147–52.

Boyle, Leonard E. "The *Oculus sacerdotis* and Some Other Works of William of Pagula," *Transactions of the Royal Historical Society,* 5th ser., 5(1955), 81–110.

Bréhier, Louis. *L'Eglise et l'Orient au moyen-âge: les croisades.* 2d ed. Paris: J. Gabalda, 1907.

Bridrey, Emile. *La Condition juridique des croisés et le privilège de croix: étude d'histoire du droit français.* Paris: V. Giard et E. Brière, 1900.

Brundage, James A. "Adhémar of Puy: The Bishop and His Critics," *Speculum,* 34(1959), 201–12.

———. "Cruce signari: The Rite for Taking the Cross in England," *Traditio,* 22(1966), 289–310.

———. "The Crusade of Richard I: Two Canonical *Quaestiones,*" *Speculum,* 38(1963), 443–53.

———. "The Crusader's Wife: A Canonistic Quandary," *Studia Gratiana,* 12(1967). *Collectanea Stephan Kuttner* (spec. issue), 2:425–41.

———. "The Crusader's Wife Revisited," *Studia Gratiana,* 14(1967). *Collectanea Stephan Kuttner* (spec. issue), 4:241–52.

———. "An Errant Crusader: Stephen of Blois," *Traditio,* 16(1960), 380–95.

———. "A Note on the Attestation of Crusaders' Vows," *Catholic Historical Review,* 52(1966), 234–39.

———. "Recent Crusade Historiography: Some Observations and Suggestions," *Catholic Historical Review,* 49(1964), 493–507.

———. "The Votive Obligations of Crusaders: The Development of a Canonistic Doctrine," *Traditio,* 24(1968), 77–118.

———. "*Vovete et reddite:* The Canonists and the Crusader's Vow." Paper delivered at the third Biennial Conference on Medieval Studies, Western Michigan University, Kalamazoo, Mich., 18 March 1966.

Brys, J. de. *De dispensatione in iure canonico praesertim apud decretistas et decretalistas usque ad medium saeculum decimum quartum.* Universitas Catholica Lovaniensis, Dissertationes ad gradum doctoris in facultate theologica consequendum conscriptae, ser. 2, 14. Bruges: C. Beyaert; Wetteren: J. de Meester, 1925.

Buchanan, George Wesley. "Some Vow and Oath Formulas in the New Testament," *Harvard Theological Review*, 58(1965), 319–26.

Buckland, W. W. *A Text-book of Roman Law from Augustus to Justinian.* 2d ed. Cambridge: at the University Press, 1932.

Campbell, Gerard J. "The Attitude of the Monarchy toward the Use of Ecclesiastical Censures in the Reign of St. Louis," *Speculum*, 35(1960), 535–55.

——. "Clerical Immunities in France during the Reign of Philip III," *Speculum*, 39(1964), 404–24.

Campenhausen, Hans von. *Die asketische Heimatslosigkeit im altkirchlichen und frühmittelalterlichen Mönchtum.* Sammlung gemeinstandlicher Vorträge und Schriften aus dem Gebiet der Theologie und Religionsgeschichte. Tübingen: J. C. B. Mohr, 1930.

Capelle, Germaine Catherine. *Le Voeu d'obéissance dès origines au XIIe siècle: étude juridique.* Bibliothèque d'histoire du droit et droit romain, 2. Paris: R. Pinchon et R. Durand-Auzias, 1959.

Capobianco, Pacificus. "De ambitu fori interni in iure ante Codicem," *Apollinaris*, 8(1935), 591–605.

——. "De notione fori interni in iure canonico," *Apollinaris*, 9(1936), 364–74.

Carro Venancio, D. *La teología y los teólogos-juristas españoles ante la conquista de América.* 2 vols. Universidad de Sevilla, Escuela de Estudios Hispano-Americanos, Publicaciones, sec. 6, ser. 2, no. 2. Madrid: Consejo Superior de Investigaciones Científicas, 1944.

Cazel, Fred A., Jr. "The Tax of 1185 in Aid of the Holy Land," *Speculum*, 30(1955), 385–92.

Change in Medieval Society: Europe North of the Alps, 1050–1500, ed. Sylvia L. Thrupp. New York: Appleton-Century-Crofts, 1964.

Cheney, Christopher R. *English Bishops' Chanceries, 1100–1250.* University of Manchester, Publications of the Faculty of Arts, 3. Manchester: Manchester University Press, 1950.

——. *Hubert Walter.* London: Nelson, 1967.

——. "Master Philip the Notary and the Fortieth of 1199," *English Historical Review*, 63(1948), 342–50.

——. "William Lyndwood's *Provinciale*," *The Jurist*, 21 (1961), 405–34.

Codex iuris canonici Pii X pontificis maximi iussu digestus, Benedicti papae XV auctoritate promulgatus. New York: P. J. Kenedy, 1918.

Congar, Yves. "L'Ecclésiologie de S. Bernard," in *Saint Bernard théologien: Actes du Congrès de Dijon, 15–19 septembre 1953*, pp. 136–90. Analecta Sacri Ordinis Cisterciensis, 9:3/4. Rome: apud Curiam Generalem Sacri Ordinis Cisterciensis, 1953.

Costello, John Michael. *Domicile and Quasi-Domicile.* Catholic University of

America, Canon Law Studies, 60. Washington: Catholic University of America Press, 1930.

Cram, Kurt Georg. *Iudicium belli: Zum Rechtscharakter des Krieges in deutschen Mittelalter*. Archiv für Kulturgeschichte, Beiheft 5. Münster: H. Böhlau, 1955.

Cramer, Valmar. "Albert der Grosse als Kreuzzugsprediger," *Das Heilige Land*, 77(1933), 17–28, 56–77, 102–16, 144–55.

———. "Humbert von Romans Traktat 'Ueber die Kreuzpredigt'," *Das Heilige Land*, 79(1935), 132–53; 80(1936), 11–23, 43–60, 77–98.

———. "Kreuzpredigt und Kreuzzugsgedanke," *Das Heilige Land*, 81(1937), 142–53; 82(1938), 15–36.

———. "Zur Geschichte und Charakteristik der Kreuzpredigt," *Das Heilige Land*, 79(1935), 85–104.

Daniel, Norman. *Islam and the West: The Making of an Image*. Edinburgh: Edinburgh University Press, 1962.

Denifle, Heinrich. *Die Entstehung der Universitäten des Mittelalters bis 1400*. Berlin: Wiedmann, 1885; r.p. Graz: Akademische Druck- und Verlagsanstalt, 1956.

D'Ercole, Giuseppe. "Foro interno e foro esterno nella penitenza delle origini cristiane," *Apollinaris*, 22(1959), 273–304.

Dictionary of Moral Theology, comp. Francesco Roberti, ed. Henry J. Yannone. Westminster, Md.: Newman Press, 1962.

Didier, Noël. "Henri de Suse en Angleterre (1236?–1244)," in *Studi in onore di Vincenzo Arangio-Ruiz nel XLV anno del suo insegnamento*, 2:333–51. 4 vols. Naples: Jovene, 1953.

———. "Henri de Suse, évêque de Sisteron (1244–1250)," *RHDF*, 4th ser., 31(1953), 244–70, 409–29.

———. "Henri de Suse, prieur d'Antibes, prévôt de Grasse (1235?–1245)," *Studia Gratiana*, 2(1953), 595–618.

Dietterle, Johannes. "Die Summae confessorum (sive de casibus conscientiae) von ihren Anfängen an bis zur Silvester Prierias (unter besonderer Berücksichtigung ihrer Bestimmungen über den Ablass)," *Zeitschrift für Kirchengeschichte*, 24(1903), 353–74.

Duggan, Charles. *Twelfth-Century Decretal Collections and Their Importance in English History*. London Historical Studies, 12. London: Athlone Press, 1963.

Emden, A. B. *Biographical Register of the University of Oxford to A.D. 1500*. 3 vols. Oxford: Clarendon Press, 1957–59.

Erdmann, Carl. *Die Entstehung des Kreuzzugsgedankens*. Forschungen zur Kirchen- und Geistesgeschichte, 6. Stuttgart: W. Kohlhammer, 1935; r.p. 1955.

———. "Zur Entstehung der Formelsammlung des Marinus von Eboli," *Quellen und Forschungen aus italienischen Archiven und Bibliotheken,* 21(1929–30), 176–208.

Ewald, P. "Die Papstbriefe der Brittischen Sammlung," *Neues Archiv,* 5(1879–80), 277–414, 501–96.

Fabricius, J. A. *Bibliotheca latina mediae et infimae aetatis.* 6 vols. in 3. Florence: Thomas Baracchi, 1858; r.p. Graz: Akademische Druck- und Verlagsanstalt, 1962.

Feine, Hans Erich. *Kirchliche Rechtsgeschichte,* I, *Die katholische Kirche.* 3d ed. Weimar: H. Böhlau, 1955.

Fernando Ortega, Juan. "La paz y la guerra en el pensamiento agustiniano," *Revista española de derecho canónico,* 20(1965), 5–35.

Firth, Francis. "The 'Poenitentiale' of Robert of Flamborough," *Traditio,* 16(1960), 541–56.

———. "More about Robert of Flamborough's Penitential," *Traditio,* 17(1961), 531–32.

Fontana, Agostino. *Amphitheatrum legale . . . seu bibliotheca legalis amplissima. . . .* 5 vols. in 4. Parma: J. ab Oleo et H. Rosati, 1687.

Fournier, Paul. "Les Conflits de juridiction entre l'église et le pouvoir séculier de 1180 à 1328," *Revue des questions historiques,* 27(1880), 432–64.

———. "Etudes critiques sur le Décret de Burchard de Worms," *RHDF,* 3d ser., 34(1910), 41–112, 213–21, 289–331, 564–84.

———, and Gabriel Le Bras. *Histoire des collections canoniques en occident depuis les fausses décrétales jusqu'au Décret de Gratien.* 2 vols. Paris: Sirey, 1931–32.

Fransen, Gerard. "La Date du Décret de Gratien," *Revue d'histoire ecclésiastique,* 51(1956), 521–31.

———. "Deux collections de questiones," *Traditio,* 21(1965), 492–510.

———. "Les 'Questiones' des canonistes: essai de depouillement et de classement," *Traditio,* 12(1956), 566–92; 13(1957), 481–501; 19(1963), 516–31; 20(1964), 495–502.

———. "Tribunaux ecclésiastiques et langue vulgaire d'après les *Questiones* des canonistes," *Ephemerides theologicae Lovanienses,* 40(1964), 391–412.

Franz, Adolph. *Die kirchlichen Benediktionen im Mittelalter.* 2 vols. Freiburg i/Br.: Herder, 1909; r.p. Graz: Akademische Druck- und Verlagsanstalt, 1960.

Fuller, Thomas. *The Historie of the Holy Warre.* 2d ed. Cambridge: Printed by R. Daniel for Thomas Buck, 1640.

Gansiniec, Ryszard, and Gérard Fransen. "Le premier abrégé du Décret de Gratien," *Revue d'histoire ecclésiastique,* 52(1957), 865–70.

García y García, Antonio. "El concilio IV de Letrán (1215) y sus comentarios," *Traditio,* 14(1958), 484–502.

————. *Laurentius Hispanus: Datos biográficos y estudio crítico de sus obras.* Cuadernos del Instituto Jurídico Español, 6. Madrid, Rome: Consejo Superior de Investigaciones Científicas, 1956.

————. "Valor y proyeccíon histórica de la obra jurídica de San Raimundo de Peñafort," *Revista Española de Derecho Canónico,* 18(1963), 233–51.

Garrisson, Francis. "A propos des pèlerins et de leur condition juridique," *Etudes d'histoire du droit canonique dediées à Gabriel Le Bras* (2 vols.; Paris: Sirey, 1965), 2:1165–89.

Gaudemet, Jean. *L'Eglise dans l'empire romain (IV°–V° siècles).* Histoire du droit et des institutions de l'église en occident, 3. Paris: Sirey, 1958.

Gay, Jules. *Le Pape Clément VI et les affaires d'Orient (1342–1352).* Paris: Société nouvelle de librairie et d'édition, 1904.

Génestal, R. *Le Privilegium fori en France du Décret de Gratien à la fin du XIV° siècle.* 2 vols. Paris: Ernest Leroux, 1921–24.

Gieysztor, Alexander. "The Genesis of the Crusades: The Encyclical of Sergius IV (1009–1012)," *Medievalia et Humanistica,* 5(1948), 3–32; 6(1949), 3–34.

Gillmann, Franz. "Hat Johannes Teutonikus zu den Konstitutionen des 4. Laterankonzils (1215) als solchen einen Apparat verfasst?" *Archiv für katholisches Kirchenrecht,* 97 (1937), 453–66.

————. "Johannes Galensis als Glossator, inbesondere der Compilatio III," *Archiv für katholisches Kirchenrecht,* 105(1925), 488–565.

Gilson, Etienne. *The Christian Philosophy of St. Thomas Aquinas,* trans. L. K. Shook. New York: Random House, 1956.

Girard, Paul Frédéric. *Manuel élémentaire de droit romain.* 8th ed., rev. by Félix Senn. Paris: Rousseau, 1929.

Gleiman, Lubomir. "Some Remarks on the Origin of the *Treuga Dei,*" *Etudes d'histoire littéraire et doctrinale,* 17(1962), 116–37.

Glorieux, P. *La Littérature quodlibétique de 1260 à 1320.* 2 vols. Paris: J. Vrin, 1933.

————. *Répertoire des maîtres en théologie de Paris au XIII° siècle.* 2 vols. Paris: J. Vrin, 1933.

Gnegel-Waitsches, Gisela. *Bischof Albert von Riga: Ein Bremer Domherr als Kirchenfürst im Osten (1199–1229).* Hamburg: August Friedrich Velmede, 1958.

Göller, Emil. *Die päpstliche Pönitentiarie von ihrem Ursprung bis zu ihrer Umgestaltung unter Pius V.* 4 vols. in 2. Bibliothek des Königliche preussische historischen Instituts in Rom, 3/4, 7/8. Rome: Loescher, 1907–11.

Góngora, Mario. *El estado en el derecho indiano, epoca de fundacion (1492–1570).* Santiago de Chile: Instituto de investigaciones historico-culturales, 1951.

Goñi Gaztambide, José. *Historia de la bula de la cruzada en España.* Victoriensia: Publicaciones del Seminario de Vitoria, 4. Vitoria: Editorial del Seminario, 1958.

Gossman, Francis Joseph. *Pope Urban II and Canon Law.* Catholic University of America, Canon Law Studies, 403. Washington: Catholic University of America Press, 1960.

Gottlob, Adolf. *Kreuzablass und Almosenablass: Eine Studie über die Frühzeit des Ablasswesens.* Kirchenrechtliche Abhandlungen, 30/31. Stuttgart: Ferdinand Enke, 1906; r.p. Amsterdam: P. Schippers, 1965.

————. *Die päpstlichen Kreuzzugssteuern des 13. Jahrhunderts: Ihre rechtliche Grundlage, politische Geschichte und technische Verwaltung.* Heiligenstadt: Franz Wilhelm Cordier, 1892.

Grabmann, Martin. *Die Geschichte der scholastischen Methode.* 2 vols. Freiburg i/Br.: Herder, 1909–11; r.p. Berlin: Akademie Verlag; Graz: Akademische Verlagsanstalt, 1957.

Grabois, A. "Le Privilège de croisade et la régence de Suger," *RHDF,* 4th ser., 42(1964), 458–65.

Hagedorn, Francis E. *General Legislation on Indulgences.* Catholic University of America, Canon Law Studies, 22. Washington: Catholic University of America Press, 1942.

Hammill, John Leo. *The Obligations of the Traveler According to Canon 14.* Catholic University of America, Canon Law Studies, 160. Washington: Catholic University of America Press, 1942.

Haskins, Charles Homer. *Norman Institutions.* Harvard Historical Studies, 24. Cambridge, Mass.: Harvard University Press, 1918.

Heers, J. "La Vente des indulgences pour la croisade à Gênes et en Lunigiana en 1456," *Miscellanea storica Ligure,* 3(1963), 69–101.

Hefele, Karl Joseph, and H. Leclercq. *Histoire des conciles d'après les documents originaux.* 11 vols. in 22. Paris: Letouzey et Ané, 1907–52.

Herde, Peter. *Audientia litterarum contradictarum: Untersuchungen über die päpstlichen Justizbriefe und die päpstliche Delegationsberichtsbarkeit vom 13. bis zum Beginn des 16. Jahrhunderts* [in press].

————. *Beiträge zum päpstlichen Kanzlei- und Urkundenwesen im 13. Jahrhundert.* Münchener historische Studien, Abt. geschichtliche Hifswissenschaften, Bd. 1. Kallmunz: Michael Lassleben, 1961.

————. "Christians and Saracens at the Time of the Crusades: Some Comments of Contemporary Medieval Canonists," *Studia Gratiana,* 12(1967), 361–76.

————. *Marinus von Eboli: 'Super revocatariis' und 'De confirmationibus.' Zwei Abhandlungen des Vizekanzlers Innocenz IV. über das päpstlichen Urkundenwesen.* Tübingen: Max Niemeyer, 1964; r.p. from *Quellen und*

Forschungen aus italienischen Archiven und Bibliotheken, 42/43(1964), 119–264.

————. "Papal Formularies for Letters of Justice (13th–16th Centuries)," in *Proceedings of the Second International Congress of Medieval Canon Law* (q.v.), pp. 321–45.

Hertling, Ludwig. "Die Professio der Kleriker und die Entstehung der drei Gelübde," *Zeitschrift für katholische Theologie,* 56(1932), 148–74.

Heyer, Friedrich. "Ueber Petrus Collivaccinus von Benevent," *ZRG, KA,* 30(1916), 395–405.

Hill, John Hugh, and Laurita L. Hill. "Contemporary Accounts and the Later Reputation of Adhémar, Bishop of Puy," *Medievalia et Humanistica,* 9(1955), 30–38.

Historical Manuscripts Commission. *Fifth Report.* 2 vols. in 1. London: HMSO, 1876.

————. *Sixth Report.* London: HMSO, 1877.

————. *Eighth Report.* 3 vols. in 1. London: HMSO, 1881.

————. *Reports: Various Collections.* Vol. 1. London: HMSO, 1901.

A History of the Crusades, ed. Kenneth M. Setton et al. Vols. 1 and 2. Philadelphia: University of Pennsylvania Press, 1955, 1962; rev. ed., Madison: University of Wisconsin Press, 1969.

Holtzmann, Walther. "Die Dekretalensammlungen des 12. Jahrhunderts," in *Festschrift zur Feier des zweihundertjährigen Bestehens der Akademie der Wissenschaften in Göttingen* (Göttingen: Springer, 1951), 2:83–145.

Hubrecht, G. "La 'juste guerre' dans le Décret de Gratien," *Studia Gratiana,* 3(1955), 161–77.

Hughes, Kathleen. "The Changing Theory and Practice of Irish Pilgrimage," *Journal of Ecclesiastical History,* 11(1960), 143–51.

Huygens, R. B. C. "Guillaume de Tyr étudiant: un chapitre (XIX, 12) de son 'Histoire' retrouvé," *Latomus,* 21(1962), 811–29.

Johnson, Edgar N. *The Secular Activities of the German Episcopate, 919–1024.* University of Nebraska Studies 30/31. Lincoln: University of Nebraska, 1932.

Joranson, Einar. "The Great German Pilgrimage of 1064–1065," in *The Crusades and Other Historical Essays, Presented to Dana C. Munro. . . ,* ed. Louis J. Paetow (New York: F. S. Crofts, 1928), pp. 3–43.

Kantorowicz, Ernst H. *The King's Two Bodies: A Study in Medieval Political Theology.* Princeton: Princeton University Press, 1957.

————. "*Pro patria mori* in Medieval Political Thought," *AHR,* 56 (1951), 472–92.

Kantorowicz, Hermann. *Studies in the Glossators of the Roman Law.* Cambridge: at the University Press, 1938.

Kaser, Max. *Das römische Privatrecht.* 2 vols. Handbuch der Altertumswissenschaft, Abt. 10, Teil 3, Bd. 2. Munich: C. H. Beck, 1955–59.

Kay, Richard. "Mansi and Rouen: A Critique of the Conciliar Collections," *Catholic Historical Review,* 52(1966), 155–85.

Kennedy, V. L. "The Content of Courson's *Summa," Mediaeval Studies,* 9(1947), 81–107.

———. "Robert Courson on Penance," *Mediaeval Studies,* 7(1945), 291–336.

Kibre, Pearl. *Scholarly Privileges in the Middle Ages: The Rights, Privileges, and Immunities of Scholars and Universities at Bologna, Padua, Paris, and Oxford.* Mediaeval Academy of America, Publications, No. 72. Cambridge, Mass.: Mediaeval Academy of America, 1962.

Kötting, Bernhard. *Peregrinatio religiosa: Wallfahrten in der Antike und das Pilgerwesen in der alten Kirche.* Forschungen zur Volkskunde, 33/35. Münster: Regensberg'sche Verlagsbuchhandlung, 1950.

Koch, Walter. *Die klerikalen Standesprivilegien nach Kirchen- und Staatsrecht unter besonderer Berücksichtigung der Verhältnisse in der Schweiz.* Freiburg i/Schweiz: Kanisiuswerk, 1949.

Kohler, Charles. *Mélanges pour servir à l'histoire de l'Orient Latin et des croisades.* 2 vols. Paris: Ernest Leroux, 1900–6.

Krey, August C. "William of Tyre," *Speculum,* 16(1941), 149–66.

Kurtscheid, Bertrand. "De studio iuris canonici in Ordine Fratrum Minorum saeculo XIII," *Antonianum,* 2(1927), 157–202.

Kuttner, Stephan. "Bernardus Compostellanus antiquus: A Study in the Glossators of the Canon Law," *Traditio,* 1(1943), 277–340.

———. "Damasus als Glossator," *ZRG, KA,* 23(1934), 380–90.

———. "Les Débuts de l'école canoniste française," *Studia et documenta historiae et iuris,* 4(1938), 193–204.

———. "Decretalistica," *ZRG, KA,* 26(1936), 436–70.

———. "The Father of the Science of Canon Law," *The Jurist,* 1(1941), 2–19.

———. "Graziano: l'uomo e l'opere," *Studia Gratiana,* 1(1953), 17–29.

———. *Harmony from Dissonance: An Interpretation of Medieval Canon Law.* Latrobe, Pa.: Archabbey Press, 1960.

———. "Joannes Andreae and His Novella on the Decretals of Gregory IX," *The Jurist,* 24(1964), 393–408.

———. "Johannes Teutonicus, das vierte Laterankonzil und die Compilatio Quarta," in *Miscellanea Giovanni Mercati,* 5: 608–34. 6 vols. Studi e Testi, 121–26. Vatican City: Bibliotheca Apostolica Vaticana, 1946.

———. *Kanonistische Schuldlehre von Gratian bis auf die Dekretalen Gregors IX.* Studi e Testi, 64. Vatican City: Bibliotheca Apostolica Vaticana, 1935; r.p. 1961.

———. "Notes on Manuscripts," *Traditio,* 17(1961), 537–42.

————. "Pierre de Roissy and Robert of Flamborough," *Traditio*, 2(1944), 492–99.

————. *Repertorium der Kanonistik (1140–1234): Prodromus corporis glossarum*, I. Studi e Testi, 71. Vatican City: Bibliotheca Apostolica Vaticana, 1937.

————. "Wer war der Dekretalist 'Abbas antiquus'?" *ZRG, KA*, 26(1937), 471–89.

————. "Wo war Vincentius Hispanus Bischof?" *Traditio*, 22(1966), 471–74.

————. "Zur Biographie des Sicardus von Cremona," *ZRG, KA*, 25(1936), 476–78.

————. "Zur Entstehungsgeschichte der Summa de casibus poenitentiae des hl. Raymond von Penyafort," *ZRG, KA*, 39(1953), 419–34.

————, and Antonio García y García, "A New Eyewitness Account of the Fourth Lateran Council," *Traditio*, 20(1964), 115–78.

————, and Eleanor Rathbone. "Anglo-Norman Canonists of the Twelfth Century: An Introductory Study," *Traditio*, 7(1949–51), 279–358.

Labande, Edmond-René. "Recherches sur les pélerins dans l'Europe des XIᵉ et XIIᵉ siècles," *Cahiers de civilisation médiévale*, 1(1958), 157–69, 339–47.

Ladner, Gerhard B. "The Concepts of 'Ecclesia' and 'Christianitas' and their Relation to the Idea of Papal 'Plenitudo Potestatis' from Gregory VII to Boniface VIII," *Miscellanea historiae pontificiae*, 18(1954), 49–77.

————. "Greatness in Mediaeval History," *Catholic Historical Review*, 50(1964), 1–26.

————. *The Idea of Reform: Its Impact on Christian Thought and Action in the Age of the Fathers*. Cambridge, Mass.: Harvard, 1959.

Lalanne, Ludovic. "Des pèlerinages en terre sainte avant les croisades," *Bibliothèque de l'Ecole des Chartes*, 8(1845–46), 1–31.

LaMonte, John L. "Some Problems in Crusading Historiography," *Speculum*, 15(1940), 57–75.

Landau, Peter. *Die Entstehung des kanonischen Infamiebegriffs von Gratian bis zur Glossa Ordinaria*. Forschungen zur kirchlichen Rechtsgeschichte und zum Kirchenrecht, Bd. 5. Cologne: H. Böhlau, 1966.

Landgraf, A. "Das Sacramentum in voto in der Fruhscholastik," in *Mélanges Mandonnet. Etudes d'histoire littéraire et doctrinale du moyen âge*, 2:97–143. 2 vols. Bibliothèque Thomiste, 14. Paris: J. Vrin, 1930.

Langlois, Charles-Victor. *Le Règne de Philippe III le Hardi*. Paris: Hachette, 1887.

Lea, Henry Charles. *A History of Auricular Confession and Indulgences in the Latin Church*. 3 vols. Philadelphia: Lea Brothers, 1896.

————. *A History of the Inquisition of the Middle Ages*. 3 vols. New York: S. A. Russell, 1956.

————. *Studies in Church History*. Philadelphia: Henry C. Lea's Son, 1883.

Le Bras, Gabriel. "Le Droit canon dans la littérature quodlibetique," *ZRG, KA,* 77(1960), 62–80.

————. "Théologie et droit romain dans l'oeuvre d'Henri de Suse," in *Etudes historiques à la mémoire de Noël Didier* (Paris: Editions Montchréstien, 1960), pp. 195–204.

————. "Le Triomphe de Gratien," *Studia Gratiana,* 1(1953), 3–14.

————, Charles Lefebvre, and Jacqueline Rambaud-Buhot. *L'Age classique, 1140–1378: Sources et théorie du droit*. Histoire du droit et des institutions de l'église en occident, 7. Paris: Sirey, 1965.

Leclercq, H. "Pèlerinages aux lieux saints," *Dictionnaire d'archéologie chrétienne et de liturgie,* 14:65–176.

Leclercq, Jean. "La Collection de lettres d'Yves de Chartres," *Revue bénédictine,* 56(1946), 108–25.

————. "Gratien, Pierre de Troyes, et la seconde croisade," *Studia Gratiana,* 2(1954), 585–93.

————. *Jean de Paris et l'ecclésiologie de XIIIe siècle*. L'Eglise et l'état au moyen âge, 5. Paris: J. Vrin, 1942.

————. "Mönchtum und Peregrinatio im Frühmittelalter," *Römische Quartalschrift,* 55(1960), 212–25.

Legendre, Pierre. "Miscellanea Britannica," *Traditio,* 15(1959), 491–97.

L'Epicier, Alexis Henri Marie. *Indulgences, Their Origin, Nature, and Development*. 3d English ed. London: Burns, Oates, and Washburn, 1928.

Leroquais, V. *Les Pontificaux Manuscrits des bibliothèques publiques de France*. 4 vols. Paris: Protat Frères, 1937.

Levy, Ernst. *Sponsio, fidepromissio, fideiussio. Eine Grundfragen zum römischen Bürgschaftsrechte*. Berlin: Franz Vahlen, 1907.

Lewis, Charles E. "Ricardus Anglicus: A 'Familiaris' of Archbishop Hubert Walter," *Traditio,* 22(1966), 469–71.

Lindner, Dominikus. *Die Lehre vom Privileg nach Gratian und den Glossatoren des Corpus iuris canonici*. Regensburg: Alfred Coppenrath, 1917.

Lot, Ferdinand, and Robert Fawtier. *Histoire des institutions françaises au moyen âge*. 3 vols. Paris: Presses Universitaires de France, 1957–62.

Lunt, William E. *Papal Revenues in the Middle Ages*. 2 vols. Records of Civilization, Sources and Studies, 19. New York: Columbia University Press, 1934.

McCall, John P. "Chaucer and John of Legnano," *Speculum,* 40(1965), 484–89.

Mackinney, Loren C. "The People and Public Opinion in the Eleventh-Century Peace Movement," *Speculum,* 5(1930), 181–206.

McNeill, John T. *A History of the Cure of Souls*. New York: Harper & Row, 1965.

Maitland, Frederick William. *Roman Canon Law in the Church of England.* London: Methuen, 1898.

Mandonnet, Pierre. "La Carrière scolaire de Saint Raymond de Peñafort," *Analecta sacri Ordinis Fratrum Praedicatorum,* 14(1920), 277–80.

Manitius, Max. *Geschichte der lateinischen Literatur des Mittelalters.* 3 vols. Handbuch der Altertumswissenschaft, 9. Abt., 2. Teil, Bd. 1–3. Munich: C. H. Beck, 1911–31.

Martin, F. Olivier. *Histoire de la coutume de la prévôté et vicomté de Paris.* 3 vols. in 2. Paris: Ernest Leroux, 1922–30.

Mayer, Hans Eberhard. *Bibliographie zur Geschichte der Kreuzzüge.* Hanover: Hahn, 1960.

———. *Geschichte der Kreuzzüge.* Urban Bücher, 86. Stuttgart: W. Kohlhammer, 1965.

———. "Zum Tode Wilhelms von Tyrus," *Archiv für Diplomatik, Schriftgeschichte, Siegel- und Wappenkunde,* 5/6 (1959–60), 182–201.

———. "Zur Beurteilung Adhémars von Le Puy," *Deutsches Archiv,* 16(1960), 547–52.

Mitchell, Rosamond J. *The Laurels and the Tiara: Pope Pius II, 1458–1464.* Garden City, N.Y.: Doubleday, 1963.

Mollat, G. "L'Oeuvre oratoire de Clément VI," *Archives d'histoire doctrinale et littéraire du moyen-âge,* 3(1928), 239–74.

Morey, Adrian. *Bartholomew of Exeter, Bishop and Canonist: A Study of the Twelfth Century, with the Text of Bartholomew's Penitential from the Cotton MS. Vitellius A. XII.* Cambridge: at the University Press, 1937.

Munro, Dana C. "The Speech of Pope Urban II at Clermont, 1095," *AHR,* 11(1906), 231–42.

Murray, Alexander. "Pope Gregory VII and His Letters," *Traditio,* 22(1966), 149–202.

Noonan, John T., Jr. *Contraception: A History of its Treatment by the Catholic Theologians and Canonists.* Cambridge, Mass.: Belknap Press, 1965.

———. *The Scholastic Analysis of Usury.* Cambridge, Mass.: Harvard University Press, 1957.

Nörr, Kurt. "Der Apparat des Laurentius zur Compilatio III," *Traditio,* 17(1961), 542–43.

———. "Die Summen 'De iure naturali' und 'De multiplici iuris diuisione'," *ZRG, KA,* 79(1962), 138–63.

Noth, Albrecht. *Heiliger Krieg und heiliger Kampf in Islam und Christentum: Beiträge zur Vorgeschichte und Geschichte der Kreuzzüge.* Bonner historische Forschungen, 28. Bonn: Ludwig Rohrscheid, 1966.

Nys, Ernst. *Le Droit de la guerre et les précurseurs de Grotius.* Brussels: C. Muquardt, Merzbach, et Falk, 1882.

Ochoa Sanz, Javier. *Vincentius Hispanus canonista boloñes del siglo XIII.*

Cuadernas del Instituto Jurídico Español, 13. Madrid, Rome: Consejo Superior de Investigaciones Científicas, 1960.

Ortolon, T. "Guerre." *Dictionnaire de théologie catholique,* 6:1899–1962.

Ottaviani, Alfredo. *Institutiones iuris publici ecclesiastici.* 4th ed., rev. by G. Damizia. 2 vols. Vatican City: Typis Polyglottis Vaticanis, 1958–60.

Oursel, Raymond. *Les Pèlerins du moyen âge: les hommes, les chemins, les sanctuaires.* Paris: Fayard, 1963.

Pacaut, Marcel. *Alexandre III: étude sur la conception du pouvoir pontifical dans sa pensée et dans son oeuvre.* L'Eglise et l'état au moyen âge, 11. Paris: J. Vrin, 1956.

Painter, Sidney. *William Marshall, Knight-Errant, Baron, and Regent of England.* Baltimore: Johns Hopkins Press, 1933.

Parry, J. H. *The Spanish Theory of Empire in the Sixteenth Century.* Cambridge: at the University Press, 1940.

Paulus, Nikolaus. *Geschichte des Ablasses im Mittelalter vom Ursprunge bis zur Mitte des 14. Jahrhunderts,* 3 vols. Paderborn: Ferdinand Schoningh, 1922–23.

Pissard, H. *La Guerre sainte en pays chrétien: essai sur l'origine et le développement des théories canoniques.* Paris: A. Picard, 1912.

Plöchl, Willibald M. *Geschichte des Kirchenrechts.* 3 vols. Vienna: Verlag Herold, 1955–59.

Poggiaspalla, Fermino. "La chiesa e la partecipazione dei chierici alla guerra nella legislazione conciliare fino alla Decretali di Gregorio IX," *Ephemerides iuris canonici,* 15(1959), 140–53.

———. "La condotta della guerra secondo una disposizione del III concilio Lateranense," *Ephemerides iuris canonici,* 12(1956), 371–86.

Poli, Antonio. *De litteris commendatitiis ad sacra facienda in jure canonico.* Rome: Pontificium Athenaeum Lateranense, 1956.

Porges, Walter. "The Clergy, the Poor, and the Non-Combatants on the First Crusade," *Speculum,* 21(1946), 1–21.

Post, Gaines. " 'Blessed Lady Spain'—Vincentius Hispanus and Spanish National Imperialism in the Thirteenth Century," *Speculum,* 29(1954), 198–209.

———. "The So-Called Laurentius Apparatus to the Decretals of Innocent III in Compilatio III," *The Jurist,* 2(1942), 5–31.

———. *Studies in Medieval Legal Thought: Public Law and the State, 1100–1322.* Princeton: Princeton University Press, 1964.

Proceedings of the Second International Congress of Medieval Canon Law, ed. S. Kuttner and J. J. Ryan. Monumenta iuris canonici, ser. C, vol. 1. Vatican City: S. Congregatio de seminariis et studiorum universitatibus, 1965.

Quantin, Pierre Michaud. "A propos des premières summae confessorum," *Recherches de théologie ancienne et médiévale,* 26(1959), 264–306.

Rambaud-Buhot, Jacqueline. *"Les Paleae* dans le Décret de Gratien," in *Proceedings of the Second International Congress of Medieval Canon Law* (q. v.), pp. 23–44.

Rashdall, Hastings. *The Universities of Europe in the Middle Ages.* 2d ed., rev. by F. M. Powicke and A. B. Emden. 3 vols. Oxford: Clarendon Press, 1936.

Regout, Robert. *La Doctrine de la guerre juste de Saint Augustin à nos jours d'après les théologiens et les canonistes catholiques.* Paris: A. Pedone, 1935.

Remy, Ferdinand. *Les Grandes Indulgences pontificales aux Pays-Bas à la fin du moyen âge (1300–1531).* Louvain: Uystpruyst, 1928.

Richard, Jean. "La Papauté et la direction de la première croisade," *Journal des Savants* (1960), 49–58.

———. "Sur un passage du 'Pèlerinage de Charlemagne': le Marché de Jérusalem," *Revue Belge de philologie et d'histoire,* 43(1965), 552–555.

Richardson, H. G., and G. O. Sayles. *The Governance of Mediaeval England from the Conquest to Magna Carta.* Edinburgh: at the University Press, 1963.

Rivera Damas, Arturo. *Pensamiento político de Hostiensis. Estudio jurídico-histórico sobre las relaciones entre el sacerdocio y el imperio en los escritos de Enrique de Susa.* Pont. Atheneum Salesianum, Facultas Iuris Canonici, Studia et textus historiae iuris canonici, vol. 3. Zurich: Pas, 1964.

Rivière, Jean. *"In partem sollicitudinis:* Evolution d'une formule pontificale," *Revue des sciences religieuses,* 5(1925), 210–31.

Rohricht, Reinhold. *Deutsche Pilgerreisen nach dem Heilige Lande.* 2d ed. Innsbruck: Wagner, 1900.

Rossi, Guido. "Contributi alla biografia del canonista Giovanni d'Andrea," *Rivista trimestrale di diritto e procedure civile,* 11(1957), 1451–1502.

Rousset, Paul. "Etienne de Blois, croisé, fuyard et martyr," *Genava,* new ser., 11(1963), 183–95.

———. *Les Origines et les caractères de la première croisade.* Neuchâtel: La Baconnière, 1945.

Runciman, Sir Steven. *A History of the Crusades.* 3 vols. Cambridge: at the University Press, 1951–54.

Russell, Jeffrey B. *Dissent and Reform in the Early Middle Ages.* Publications of the Center for Medieval and Renaissance Studies, No. 1. Berkeley: University of California Press, 1965.

Sarti, Mauro, and Mauro Fattorini. *De claris archigymnasii Bononiensis professoribus a saeculo XI usque ad saeculum XIV,* ed. C. Albicino and C. Malagola. 2 vols. Bologna: Merlani, 1888–96; r.p. Turin: Bottega d'Erasmo, 1962.

Savigny, Friedrich Karl von. *Geschichte des römischen Rechts im Mittelalter.* 2d ed. 7 vols. in 4. Heidelberg: J. C. B. Mohr, 1834–51.

Schillmann, Fritz. *Die Formularsammlung des Marinus von Eboli*. Bibliothek des preussischen historischen Instituts in Rom, 16. Rome: W. Regensberg, 1929.

Schmitz, Hermann Joseph. *Die Bussbücher und die Bussdisciplin der Kirche*. Mainz: Franz Kircheim, 1883.

Schmitz, Philibert. "Les Sermons et discours de Clément VI, O.S.B.," *Revue bénédictine,* 41(1929), 15–34.

Schorr, George F. *The Law of the Celebret*. Catholic University of America, Canon Law Studies, 332. Washington: Catholic University of America Press, 1952.

Schreiber, Georg, ed. *Wallfahrt und Volkstum in Geschichte und Leben*. Forschungen zur Volkskunde, 16/17. Dusseldorf: L. Schwann, 1934.

———. *Kurie und Kloster im 12. Jahrhundert: Studien zur Privilegierung, Verfassung und besonders zum Eigenkirchenwesen der vorfrarziskanischen Orden vornehmlich auf Grund der Papsturkunden von Paschalis II. bis auf Lucius III. (1099–1181).* 2 vols. Kirchenrechtliche Abhandlungen, 65–66. Stuttgart: Ferdinand Enke, 1910; r.p. Amsterdam: P. Schippers, 1965.

Schulte, Johann Friedrich von. *Die Geschichte der Quellen und Literatur des canonischen Rechts von Gratian bis auf die Gegenwart.* 3 vols. in 2. Stuttgart: Ferdinand Enke, 1875–80; r.p. Graz: Akademische Druck- und Verlagsanstalt, 1956.

Schwerin, Ursula. *Die Aufrufe der Päpste zur Befreiung des Heiligen Landes von den Anfängen bis zum Ausgang Innocenz IV: Ein Beitrag zur Geschichte der kurialischen Kreuzzugspropaganda und der päpstliche Epistolographie.* Historische Studien, 301. Berlin: Ebering, 1937.

Setton, Kenneth M. "Lutheranism and the Turkish Peril." *Balkan Studies,* 3(1962), 133–68.

Sivan, Emmanuel. "Le caractère sacré de Jérusalem dans l'Islam au XIIᵉ–XIIIᵉ siècles," *Studia Islamica,* 27(1967), 149–82.

Small, R. C. *Crusading Warfare (1097–1193)*. Cambridge Studies in Medieval Life and Thought, new ser., 3. Cambridge: at the University Press, 1956.

Sprandel, Rolf. *Ivo von Chartres und seine Stellung in der Kirchengeschichte*. Pariser historische Studien, 1. Stuttgart: Anton Hiersemann, 1962.

Stickler, Alfons M. "Alanus Anglicus als Verteidiger des monarchischen Papsttums," *Salesianum,* 21(1959), 346–406.

———. "Il decretista Laurentius Hispanus," *Studia Gratiana,* 9(1966), 463–549.

———. *Historia iuris canonici latini institutiones academicae,* 1, *Historia fontium.* Turin: Pontificio Ateneo Salesiano, 1950.

Stiernon, Daniel. "Rome et les églises orientales," *Euntes docete,* 15(1962), 319–85.

Stuart, Dorothy M. "The Banquet of Vows," *History Today*, 4(1954), 748–53.

Teetaert, A. "Summa de matrimonio Sancti Raymundi de Penyafort," *Jus pontificium*, 9(1929), 54–61, 218–34, 312–22.

———. "La 'Summa de poenitentia' de Saint Raymond de Penyafort," *Ephemerides theologicae Lovanienses*, 5(1928), 49–72.

Throop, Palmer A. *Criticism of the Crusade: A Study of Public Opinion and Crusade Propaganda*. Amsterdam: N. V. Swets & Zeitlinger, 1940.

Tierney, Brian. "Two Anglo-Norman Summae," *Traditio*, 15(1959), 483–91.

Toubert, Pierre. "Les Déviations de la croisade au milieu du XIII° siècle: Alexandre IV contre Manfred," *Le Moyen Age*, 69(1963), 391–99.

Turlan, Juliette. "L'Obligation 'ex voto'," *RHDF*, 4th ser., 33(1955), 502–36.

Ullmann, Walter. *The Growth of Papal Government in the Middle Ages*. 2d ed. London: Methuen, 1962.

———. "The *Paleae* in Cambridge Manuscripts of the *Decretum*," *Studia Gratiana*, 1(1953), 161–216.

———. *Medieval Papalism: The Political Theories of the Medieval Canonists*. London: Methuen, 1949.

Valls-Taberner, Fernando. *San Ramón de Peñafort. Obras selectas de Fernando Valls-Taberner*, vol. 1, pt. 2. Madrid: Consejo Superior de Investigaciones Científicas, 1953.

Vanderpol, Alfred. *La Doctrine scolastique du droit de guerre*. Paris: A. Pedone, 1919.

Van Espen, Zeger Bernhard. *Jus ecclesiasticum universum*. 4 vols. Louvain: n.p., 1753.

Van Hove, A. *De privilegiis; de dispensationibus*. Commentarium Lovaniense in Codicem Iuris Canonici, vol. 1, tom. 5. Malines: H. Dessain, 1939.

———. "La Notion du privilège," *Nouvelle revue théologique*, 49(1922), 5–18, 74–85.

———. *Prolegomena ad Codicem Iuris Canonici*, 2d ed. Commentarium Lovaniense ad Codicem Iuris Canonici, vol. 1, tom. 1. Malines: H. Dessain, 1945.

Vasiliev, A. A. *History of the Byzantine Empire, 324–1453*. 2d English ed. Madison: University of Wisconsin Press, 1952.

Vaughan, Richard. *Matthew Paris*. Cambridge: at the University Press, 1958.

Vazquez de Parga, Luis, José Maria Lacarra, and Juan Uría Ríu. *Las peregrinaciones a Santiago de Compostela*. 3 vols. Madrid: Consejo Superior de Investigaciones Científicas, Escuela de Estudios Medievales, 1948.

Vetulani, A. "Le Décret de Gratien et les premiers décrétistes à la lumière d'une source nouvelle," *Studia Gratiana*, 7(1959), 273–354.

———. "Gnieźnieński R kopis Formularza Marina de Ebulo," *Prawo Kanoniczne*, 4(1961), 211–22.

———. "Über die Distinktioneneinteilung und die *Paleae* im Dekret Gratians," *ZRG, KA,* 22(1933), 346–70.

Villey, Michel. *La Croisade: essai sur la formation d'une théorie juridique.* L'Eglise et l'état au moyen âge, 6. Paris: J. Vrin, 1942.

———. "L'Idée de la croisade chez les juristes du moyen âge," in *Relazioni del X Congresso Internazionale di Scienze Storice,* 3:565–94. 6 vols. Biblioteca storia Sansoni, new ser., 22–27. Florence: G. Sansoni, 1955. Vol. 3, 565–94.

Vinogradoff, Sir Paul. *Roman Law in Medieval Europe.* 2d ed. Oxford: at the University Press; Hildesheim: Georg Olms, 1961.

Vogel, Cyrille. "Composition légale et commutations dans le système de la pénitence tarifée," *Revue de droit canonique,* 8(1958), 289–318; 9(1959), 1–38, 341–59.

———. "Le Pèlerinage pénitentiel," *Revue des sciences religieuses de l'Université de Strasbourg,* 38(1964), 113–53.

Waas, Adolf. *Geschichte der Kreuzzüge.* 2 vols. Freiburg i/Br.: Herder, 1956.

Waddell, Helen J. *The Wandering Scholars.* Garden City, N.Y.: Doubleday, 1955.

Waley, Daniel. *The Papal State in the Thirteenth Century.* London: Macmillan, 1961.

Walz, A. "S. Raymundi de Penyafort auctoritas in re paenitentiali," *Angelicum,* 12(1935), 346–96.

Watt, John A. "The Theory of Papal Monarchy in the Thirteenth Century: The Contribution of the Canonists," *Traditio,* 20(1964), 179–317 (also published separately, New York: Fordham University Press, 1965).

———. "The Use of the Term 'Plenitudo Potestatis' by Hostiensis," in *Proceedings of the Second International Congress of Medieval Canon Law* (q.v.), pp. 161–87.

Wattenbach, Wilhelm. *Deutschlands Geschichtsquellen im Mittelalter: Vorzeit und Karolinger,* ed. Wilhelm Levison et al. 4 vols. Weimar: H. Böhlau, 1952–57.

Weigand, Rudolf. "Mitteilungen aus Handschriften," *Traditio,* 16(1960), 556–64.

———. "Neue Mitteilungen aus Handschriften," *Traditio,* 21(1965), 480–91.

Wernz, F. X. *Ius decretalium.* 6 vols. Rome: Typographia Polyglotta S.C. de Propaganda Fide; Prati: Giachetti, 1898–1912.

Willging, Joseph C. "Decree," *The Jurist,* 5(1945), 292–93.

Williams, Schafer. "Concilium Claromontanum, 1095: A New Text," *Studia Gratiana,* 13(1967). *Collectanea Stephan Kuttner* (spec. issue), 3:27–43.

Windass, G. S., and J. Newman. "The Early Christian Attitude to War," *Irish Theological Quarterly,* 29(1962), 235–47.

Wolff, Robert Lee. "Romania: The Latin Empire of Constantinople," *Speculum,* 23(1948), 1–34.

Woolf, C. N. S. *Bartolus of Sassoferrato: His Position in the History of Medieval Political Thought.* Cambridge: at the University Press, 1913.

Zavala, Silvio A. *Las instituciones jurídicas en la conquista de América.* Madrid: Centro de Estudios Históricos, 1935.

LIST OF MANUSCRIPTS

Arras
  Bibliothèque Municipale
    MS. 1064 (271)
Cambridge
  Christ's College
    MS. Dd.1.2
  Corpus Christi College
    MSS. 10
      38
      441
  Fitzwilliam Museum
    MS. McClean 137
  Gonville and Caius College
    MSS. 23/12
      28/17
      44/150
      71/38
      151/201
      283/676
  Pembroke College
    MSS. 72
      201
  St. John's College
    MS. 142 (F.5)
  Trinity College
    MSS. B.XI.10
      O.V.17
      O.X.2
  University Library
    MSS. Ii.6.18
      Kk.6.1
      Ll.2.10
Durham
  Cathedral Library
    MSS. C.II.1
      C.II.6
      C.III.4
      C.III.8

University Library
    MS. Cosin V.III.3
Innsbruck
  Universitätsbibliothek
    MSS. 90
      266
      339
      368
      590
Lincoln
  Cathedral Library
    MSS. 2
      38
      121
London
  British Museum
    MSS. Add. 18367
      Add. 18369
      Arundel 435
      Royal 9.E.VII
      Royal 10.A.III
      Royal 10.B.IV
      Royal 10.C.III
      Royal 11.A.II
      Royal 11.C.VII
      Royal 11.D.II
  Lambeth Palace
    MSS. 39
      49
      105
Munich
  Bayerische Staatsbibliothek
    MSS. Clm. 3879
      Clm. 5664
      Clm. 6352
      Clm. 7536
      Clm. 17562

Neustift-bei-Brixen
  Stiftsbibliothek
    MS. 4
Oxford
  Bodleian Library
    MSS. Laud. Misc. 646
        Tanner 8
Paris
  Bibliothèque Nationale
    MSS. lat. 3892
      lat. 3932
      nouvelles acquisitions latins
      1576

Sankt Florian
  Stiftsbibliothek
    MS. XI.605
Vatican City
  Bibliotheca Apostolica Vaticana
    MSS. Borgh. Lat. 261
      Pal. Lat. 658
      Reg. Lat. 1061
      Vat. Lat. 1378
      Vat. Lat. 2280
      Vat. Lat. 2663
      Vat. Lat. 3976
      Vat. Lat. 3994

INDEX OF LEGAL CITATIONS

Roman Law

Inst.
1.2.6, 35*n*
1.22 pr., 47*n*
1.25 pr., 21*n*
1.25.14, 140*n*
2.10.1, 83*n*
2.11, 140*n*
2.19.6, 140*n*
3.13 pr., 121*n*

Cod.
1.14.9, 12, 35*n*
1.17.1, 35*n*
3.38.11, 98*n*
4.18.3, 102*n*
5.1, 58*n*
5.17.7, 127*n*
6.25.4 pr., 88*n*
6.28.1, 102*n*
6.42, 80*n*
6.42.32.2, 80*n*
6.50.1.16, 78*n*
9.27.22 pr., 112*n*
10.40.2.7, 11*n*
50.60.3, 47*n*

Dig.
1.1.1.2, 141*n*
1.4.1, 35*n*
2.8.16, 63*n*
5.1.11, 98*n*
12.1.26, 140*n*
18.1.67 pr., 97*n*
23.1, 58*n*
24.2.6, 127*n*
26.1.1–44, 140*n*
30.65.1, 62*n*

32.69 pr.
33.7.12, 98*n*
33.7.18.2, 63*n*
35.1.99, 62*n*
44.7.3 pr., 121*n*
45.1.46.2, 78*n*
45.1.134, 58*n*
45.1.137.4, 63*n*
46.3.31, 79*n*
47.17, 98*n*
48.19.26 pr., 112*n*
49.16.1, 140*n*
49.17.1–20, 140*n*
50.1.20, 11*n*
50.12.1.1, 61*n*
50.12.2 pr., 34*n*, 98*n*, 99*n*, 107*n*, 122*n*
50.12.2.1, 43*n*
50.12.2.2, 34*n*, 78*n*
50.12.3 pr., 99*n*
50.12.3, 107*n*
50.16.203, 11*n*
50.16.239.2, 11*n*

Nov.
1.4 pr., 80*n*
5.8, 105*n*
40, 7*n*
51 pr., 100*n*
53 pr., 112*n*
69, 112
74.4, 103*n*
117.11, 127*n*

Auth.
5.4, 100*n*
Coll. 5 tit. 8 pr., 112*n*
6.1.4, 103*n*

Canon Law

GENERAL INDEX

118n; theology of, 45–46; of chastity, 46; of marriage, 46; to perform evil act, 47, 54; general, 47; special, 47; simple, 47, 51, 55, 71, 89, 103, 107, 118n; indispensable, 48; public, 49; of women, 49, 102–3, 108, 112; implicit, 49–50; manifest, 59–60; commutation of, 64, 68–69, 75, 76, 78–79, 81, 84, 88, 90–92, 94, 96, 103–4, 113, 127; conditional, 71, 103, 117, 121–22; irredeemable, 71; of married women, 71; of serfs, 71; redeemable, 71; married persons, 77, 78–79, 80, 88, 93, 96–97, 98–99, 110–11, 112, 113, 195; heritability of, 78, 80, 81, 87, 98; of continence, comp. with crusade vow, 81; of continence, dispensation from, 81, 105; omission of, treatment in *Comp. IV,* 82–83; voluntary, 89, 103; necessary, 89, 103; absolute, 90; pure, 90, 103; capacity to make, 100; harlots', 103; devotional, 104; militant, 104; theological *questiones* on, 110–11; commutation of, reforms proposed, 112–13; canonistic doctrines of, summarized, 113–14; creates obligation, 121–22; implication defined as a result of crusades, 192n

—, crusade: lacking in Spanish *reconquista,* 25n; similarity to pilgrimage vow, 30; in Urban II's speech at Clermont, 31–33; not treated by decretists, 65; specifically treated in decretal collections, 67; in *Comp. I,* 68–69; postponement authorized, 77; in *Comp. III,* 77–78; treatment of by Laurentius Hispanus, 80–81; not solemn, 86; development of, 113–14; differentiated from pilgrimage vows, 116–17; content of, 116–18; discharge of, proof of, 124–27; release from, 131–38; commutation of, 134–36; mentioned, 84–85, 96, 102–3, 118n

—, treatment of: by Ivo of Chartres, 36–37; in *Decretum Gratiani,* 39–45; by Peter Lombard, 45–46; by Paucapalea, 46; by Rolandus Bandinelli, 46–47; by Rufinus, 47–48; in *Summa Parisiensis,* 48–49; by Stephen of Tournai, 49–50; by Joannes Faventinus, 50–51; by Huguccio, 52–53; in *Glossa Palatina,* 57–59; by Laurentius

Hispanus, 57–59, 78; by Richardus Anglicus, 58–59; in Innsbruck glosses, 59–60; by decretists, summarized, 64–65; by Innocent III, 69–70; in *Comp. III,* 77–78; in *Comp. V,* 84; in *Notabilia "Potius utendum est,"* 85; Damasus Hungarus, 86–87; by Bernardus Compostellanus antiquus, 88; by Raymond of Peñafort, 88–94; in *Decretales Greg. IX,* 93; by Guilielmus Redonensis, 94; in *Summa "Quid sit symonia,"* 94–95; by Bartholomaeus Brixiensis, 97; by Innocent IV, 98–99; by Hostiensis, 99–107; by Monaldus, 107–8; by Guilielmus Durandus, 109–10; by St. Thomas Aquinas, 110–11; by Joannes Andreae, 111; by Bartolus of Sassoferrato, 111–12; by William Lyndwood, 112; by Pierre Grégoire, 113

—, obligations of. *See* Obligations, votive

Walter, Abp. of Rouen, 162
Walter de Lacy, 163
Walter of Avesnes, 134
War: authority to proclaim, 19–20; just, 19–20; goals of, 20; as spiritually meritorious, 21–28. *See also* Holy war
William, Count of Upper Burgundy, 26
William, son of Swift, 130
William Marshall, 132n
William of Pagula, 107n, 151n, 178n
William of Rennes. *See* Guilielmus Redonensis
William of Tyre, 125
Winchelsey, Abp. of Canterbury, 158
Women: participation in crusade, 32, 77; power of wife to make vows, 44. *See also* Marriage
Worcester, Synod of, II, 158
Worms, 133n
Würzburg, 69, 187
Wyberton (Lancs.), 130

York, archdeaconry of, 135n
Yorkshire, East Riding, archdeaconry of, 135n

Zemeke, Johann. *See* Joannes Teutonicus